Fodor's 89

Hawaii

Fodor's Travel Publications, Inc.
New York & London

ISBN 0-679-01656-2

Fodor's Hawaii

Editor: David Low
Area Editors: Jodi Belknap, Thelma Chang, Tom Horn, Lyle Nelson, Marty Wentzel
Maps: Pictograph
Drawings: Michael D. Conway
Cover Photograph: Rita Ariyoshi

Cover Design: Vignelli Associates

CONTENTS

Foreword   v
    Map of the Hawaiian Islands, vi–vii

Facts at Your Fingertips
    Planning Your Trip, 1; When to Go, 1; How to Get There, 2; Cruise
    Ships Serving Hawaii, 3; Package Tours to Hawaii, 4; What to Take, 5;
    Travel Documents, 5; Restrictions on Import and Export, 5; Tips for
    British Visitors, 5; What It Will Cost, 6; Hotels and Other Accommod-
    ations, 7; Dining Out, 8; Drinking Laws, 10; Local Time, Business
    Hours, and Holidays, 10; Sports, 10; Hints for Photographers, 15;
    Senior-Citizen Discounts, 16; Security, 16; Hints for Disabled Travel-
    ers, 16; Telephones and Emergency Numbers, 16; Island Speech, 17

PORTRAIT OF PARADISE: An Introduction to the Hawaiian Islands   21

HAWAII'S HISTORY: Kings and Queens, Missionaries and Whalers,
    Sugar and Tourism   37

HAWAII'S BEACHES: Sizes, Shapes, Moods, and Colors for
    Every Taste   47

OAHU: Hub of Island Life   55
    Exploring Honolulu, 57
        Map of Honolulu for Orientation, 58–59
        Map of Downtown Honolulu, 68–69
        Map of Honolulu Points of Interest, 74–75
    Exploring Oahu, 80
        Map of Oahu, 82–83
    Practical Information for Oahu, 95
        Map of Waikiki Hotels, 96–97

HAWAII: Nature's Primeval Showplace   153
    Exploring Hawaii, 154
        Map of Hawaii, 155
    Practical Information for Hawaii, 167

MAUI: Roses, Romance, and Rainbows   186
    Exploring Maui, 187
        Map of Maui, 188
    Practical Information for Maui, 198

MOLOKAI: Friendly, Easy-Going, and Traditional   217
    Exploring Molokai, 219
        Map of Molokai, 220
    Practical Information for Molokai, 226

CONTENTS

LANAI: The Warm and Rustic Pineapple Isle   230
   Exploring Lanai, 232
    Map of Lanai, 233
   Practical Information for Lanai, 236

KAUAI: Where Dreams Come True   238
   Exploring Kauai, 242
    Map of Kauai, 243
   Practical Information for Kauai, 259

INDEX   273

FOREWORD

Offering a perfect climate, dazzling scenery, a friendly population, as well as all 20th-century amenities and a full range of vacation-style choices, the Hawaiian Islands are one of the world's most popular vacation spots. Located at the crossroads of the Pacific, Hawaii, though very much a U.S. state, continues to hold the allure of a "foreign place," particularly to American visitors.

Of the 20 islands in the Hawaiian archipelago, only seven are inhabited. *Fodor's Hawaii* is designed to help you choose which island, or combination of islands, would best suit your travel ideal—as well as your time and budget requirements—from the urban and resort appeal of Oahu to the more tranquil vacation options among the Neighbor Islands—Hawaii, Maui, Molokai, Lanai, and Kauai. We have tried to put together the widest range of activities for each island and within that range to offer you selections which are worthwhile, safe and of value. The descriptions we provide are just enough for you to make intelligent choices from among our selections.

While every care has been taken to assure the accuracy of the information in this guide, the passage of time will always bring change, and consequently the publisher cannot accept responsibility for errors that may occur.

All prices and opening times quoted here are based on information available to us at press time. Hours and admission fees may change, however, and the prudent traveler will avoid inconvenience by calling ahead.

Fodor's wants to hear about your travel experiences, both pleasant and unpleasant. When a hotel or restaurant fails to live up to its billing, let us know and we will investigate the complaint and revise our entries where the facts warrant it.

Send your letters to the editors of Fodor's Travel Publications, 201 E. 50th Street, New York, NY 10022, or 30–32 Bedford Square, London WC1B 3SG, England.

PACIFIC OCEAN

HAWAII

0   miles   50

0   km   50

✈ Airport   🚢 Seaport

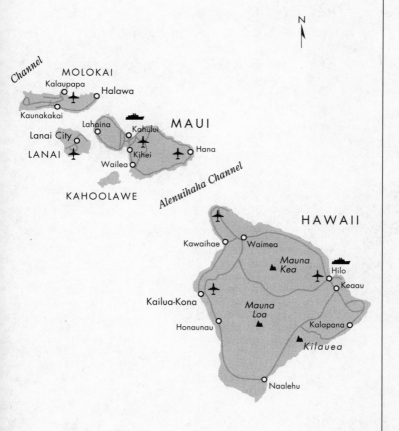

N

Channel

MOLOKAI

Kalaupapa   Halawa

Kaunakakai

MAUI

Lahaina   Kahului

Lanai City   Hana

LANAI   Kihei

Wailea

KAHOOLAWE

Alenuihaha Channel

HAWAII

Kawaihae   Waimea

Mauna Kea

Hilo

Keaau

Kailua-Kona

Mauna Loa

Honaunau   Kalapana

Kilauea

Naalehu

FACTS AT YOUR FINGERTIPS

PLANNING YOUR TRIP. The easiest way to take that first step toward a Hawaii holiday is to make a date with a travel agent. It will cost you nothing since the travel agent gets a commission from the supplier of services at the other end. The travel agent can advise you on major attractions and least expensive packages if you have budget concerns. Often the travel agency has personnel who have done Hawaii. Hawaii is a very popular place to visit even if Honolulu recently passed Anchorage as America's most expensive city in terms of living costs.

The best way to be prepared to talk over your needs and desires with a travel agent is to read this book first and list the places and things to do that most interest you. Of course, many travelers have a flair for independent planning and want to do things themselves. That means they can call for reservations with an airline and a hotel after looking over the listings later in this guide. Once you're on the ground in Hawaii you can easily arrange your own bus tours and outings as almost every hotel has an activities desk in the lobby with up-to-date information.

Fountainhead of all island information is the *Hawaii Visitors Bureau (HVB)*. Main office is 2270 Kalakaua Avenue, Honolulu 96815. It is on the eighth floor, telephone 923–1811. Branch offices are in Hilo and Kailua-Kona, Hawaii; Wailuku, Maui, and Lihue, Kauai. The bureau also maintains offices on the Mainland at 441 Lexington Avenue, Room 1407, New York, NY 10017; at 3440 Wilshire Boulevard, Los Angeles, CA 90010; at 180 N. Michigan Ave., Suite 1031, Chicago, IL 60601, and at 209 Post Street, San Francisco, CA 94108; Meetings and Conventions Office at 1511 K St. NW, Suite 415, Washington, DC 20005; 4915 Cedar Crescent, Delta, B.C. Canada, V4M 1J9; and overseas at 630 Shin Kokusai Building, 4–1, 3-chome, Maruno-uchi, Chiyoda-ku, Tokyo, Japan 100.

Between the friendly travel agent and your own keen wits, enthusiasms, and ideas you are halfway there. Planning and anticipation are half the fun. Remember, many people who have done Hawaii start planning a return trip to pick up the missing pieces even as they tighten their seatbelts for the takeoff for home.

WHEN TO GO. Hawaii's climate is nearly perfect all year round. There's not much difference between a day in June and one in January. And if there's a normal trade wind of fresh air to ventilate the Islands, there isn't any difference at all. Generally, it may seem a bit more humid in the summer months. But perfect weather, sunny and lovely, is the norm. Summer is not as uncomfortably hot and muggy as most of the continental 48 (Hawaiians call this the Mainland), and the winter months are a match for the Caribbean. The mean temperature fluctuates from 71 degrees in winter to 78 in summer. September is the hottest month, but there are no "seasons." Average annual rainfall for Honolulu is 25 inches, and November through March are the wettest months.

There is practically no "season" for hotel rooms any more. The trend is full hotels all year, with a higher winter rate between Christmas and April. Whether you decide to visit Hawaii in spring, summer, autumn, or winter, reservations are obligatory and should be made at least three months in advance, preferably four or five, especially for medium-priced accommodations in Honolulu.

Since every day in Hawaii is a nice day, you can plan on a day of swimming or golf almost without fear of a washout. Even on a rare wet day, the tour buses keep moving because the rain or mist is warm and usually does not last long.

Hawaiians love festivals and pageants. These are most often a celebration of ethnic character tied to Hawaii's various peoples, such as the Chinese or Japanese. A calendar of dates, Hawaii Special Events, can be obtained at Hawaii Visitors Bureau offices. In Waikiki it's at 2270 Kalakaua Ave., eighth floor. The *Honolulu Star-Bulletin* runs a daily doings "Pulse of Paradise" and free weekly visitors' magazines can be found in racks along Kalakaua Avenue, *This Week, Spotlight Hawaii, Waikiki Beach Press,* etc.

Detailed lists of special events can be found in the Practical Information Section for each island. A preview of some annual highlights: In *January* the Narcissus Festival will introduce you to Chinese delights. The State Legislature is either a laugh or deadly serious, depending upon your views of the body politic. *February* is a good time for PGA golf and the opera. In *March* the Cherry Blossom will offer Japanese delights. Kuhio Day is special to Hawaii's ethnic Hawaiians. Wesak Day in *April* will introduce you to Buddhism. May Day means flower leis in Hawaii, and Memorial Day means more flowers. Kamehameha Day, *June 11,* is a big deal with pageantry and a parade. Japanese Bon Dances in *July* are unique, as is *August's* Hula Festival. In *September* Aloha Week is where it's at. This is almost the best time to soak up Hawaii's spirits. Get into the fun in the streets, the stages, dancing, the parade, and multiple show events.

The orchid show in *October* is pretty special, while during *November* college and high school football has a lock on the locals. *December's* Honolulu Marathon is a major attraction with foreign runners coming from around the world, 2,000 from Japan alone.

HOW TO GET THERE. From the Mainland: By air. Jets have put Hawaii only 4½ hours from the West Coast. The Honolulu Airport terminal has been completely renovated to handle the volume of traffic created by wide-body jets. The biggest innovation in air travel to Hawaii in recent years is the non-stop service from cities in the East, Midwest, and Southwest.

There are all kinds of air fares. Your travel agent can punch up the latest on the computer. Things change by the minute and new package deals involving booking well in advance have changed the picture in the years since deregulation.

American carriers serving Hawaii include *United, Northwest, American, Continental, Delta, TWA, Hawaiian Airlines,* and *Pan American World Airways.* Most flights by these carriers originate in Los Angeles or San Francisco. Others originate from West Coast cities like Seattle and San Diego. Flights also come from Chicago, New York, Dallas, Anchorage, and other major cities. Some bypass Honolulu and go directly to Hilo, Kailua-Kona, or Kahului, Maui.

The other airlines which touch down at Honolulu have no U.S. traffic rights, but can bring passengers from foreign cities to Honolulu. These include *Qantas Airways, Canadian Pacific Air, Japan Air Lines, Philippine*

Air Lines, Air New Zealand, China Air Lines, Korean Air Lines, Singapore Airlines, Air Tungaru, Air Niugini, All Nippon Airways, and *Wardair Canada.*

Interisland Travel. Hawaiian residents fly from island to island as casually as most people commute by interurban train. There are two airlines that leave Honolulu with the regularity of a bus on a major street, *Hawaiian Air* and *Aloha Airlines.* They tie together the state from Lihue, on Kauai to the northwest, to Hilo on Hawaii to the southeast. Most flights are in jets which make the flight time to Hilo 41 minutes and only 18 minutes to Molokai, the closest island to Honolulu. These trips are so short that you don't have time for eating, but the stewardesses are quick with pineapple juice and a running commentary on what there is to see.

One of the nicest features of traveling by air in the Islands is that you'll invariably enjoy smooth, sunny flying: almost all flights are conducted in near-perfect weather. That's the bonus of traveling in the trade-wind belt.

In addition to the three airlines above, there are several "small plane carriers": *Princeville* and *Air Molokai* among others. There are also small charter air operators on all the islands. Their scheduled flights are fewer, but slightly cheaper than those listed above; in addition they have tours and charters, sightseeing and golf packages.

For those arriving at Honolulu International Airport and starting out with another airplane ride to a Neighbor Island, Lockheed provides a free wikiwiki shuttle that will take you and your carry-ons to the nearby interisland terminal.

CRUISE SHIPS SERVING HAWAII. Recently there has been a remarkable increase in the popularity of leisurely cruise ship vacation travel. Passengers who take a foreign cruise ship from a foreign port may disembark in Hawaii. However, passengers who embark on a foreign ship for a cruise to Hawaii from a U.S. port must return with that ship to the original U.S. port of embarkation, because Customs regulations prohibit point-to-point travel on foreign ships between U.S. ports.

In the early 1980s the SS *Independence* and SS *Constitution* began interisland cruises. No U.S. flag passenger ships had been in commission since the *Mariposa* and the *Monterey* until then.

Nothing compares with the thrill of approaching the Islands by water, especially for a first-time visitor, with its anticipation and dockside pageantry. Cruise schedules are generally planned a year or more in advance, so this year is a good time to begin thinking about *next* winter.

If time is unimportant to you, think about ships: a cruise is unforgettable. Lines often fly customers to a port to pick up the ship.

Aloha Pacific Cruises, 510 S. King St., Suite 201, Alexandria, VA 22314 (703–684–6263), is planning to return a refurbished SS *Monterey* to interisland seven-day cruise service in August 1988. Air-sea packages with American Airlines and pre- and post-sail hotel programs with Hilton Hawaiian Village range from $1,195 to $2,295.

American Hawaii Cruises, 550 Kearny St., San Francisco, CA 94108 (800–227–3666). The *Constitution* and *Independence* offer three, four, and seven-day runs through the Islands at 9 P.M. every Saturday from Aloha Tower in Honolulu.

Everything first class at prices ranging from under $1,000 per person and up, with many seasonal packages, featuring assorted extras, available.

The ships circle Molokai, take a look at Lanai and Kahoolawe, and then dock four times, in Hilo, Kailua-Kona, Kahului, and Nawiliwili. Each stop allows from one afternoon of sightseeing (at Kailua-Kona) up to two days (at Kauai). Both ships make occasional West Coast-Hawaii trips. *The Constitution* makes a three-week Christmas cruise, Honolulu to San Francisco to Los Angeles and back.

The ships have swimming pools, a golf driving range, tennis, areas for jogging and skeet, a gym, movie house, and nightclub. It's the new, old way to go.

Cunard/N.A.C. Line, Holland American Line, and **Royal Viking** have cruise ships passing through Honolulu once or twice a year.

Sea Link Hawaii, Inc., 505 Front St., Suite 230, Lahaina, HI 96761 (533–6899, Oahu), offers daily roundtrip ferry service interisland aboard a high-speed 118-foot touring yacht, the 150-passenger *Maui Princess.* Adult fares range from $21 one-way Maui to Molohai, to $42 one-way Maui to Oahu.

Bringing Your Car. The cost of shipping a car from Oakland by freighter is at least $500. We advise leaving your own car at home and renting one.

PACKAGE TOURS TO HAWAII. Travel agents have brochures full of all-expense packages that will take the guesswork right out of your inexperienced hands. All you have to do is be at the check-in or check-out counters to be shepherded about, always with someone else to worry about getting you around. For people unfamiliar with travel outside continental America, or for those jaded veterans who may be tired after years of international travel ad libs and hassles (perhaps never with reservations for anything, anywhere), the complete package is the answer.

Cartan, Tauck, Maupintour are among the many tours your travel agent will mention. *Island Holidays, American Express, Classic Hawaii, Roberts Hawaii, Pleasant Hawaiian Holidays,* and others in Honolulu offer ground packages of any length of stay on any island, or combinations of islands, at any price range (from the penthouse to the ground floor).

There are endless tie-ins between specific airlines and certain large hotel chains with facilities on each island. Hawaii's own airlines offer hotel packages with a U-drive thrown into the fly/drive deal. Condominiums are now commonly part of many good low-cost deals.

Any of these packages from Mainland cities include bus transfers from airport to hotel destination, bag handling, guides, meals, or perhaps an orchid on your pillow after a lei from a pretty girl at the airport. About your only out-of-pocket cost might be a candy bar, newspaper, or bottle of firewater.

There's one more way to see all the Islands in one hectic day while sticking with one Waikiki hotel for the duration of your stay. That's the all-day, dawn-to-dusk swing by air around the state. It's quick and exciting and better than never leaving Waikiki Beach. A number of one-day tours, available from *Hawaiian Air, See All Hawaii Tours, Panorama Air Tours, Akamai Tours, Scenic Air Tours Hawaii, Polynesian Express,* among others, include meals on different islands and several bus (or boat) rides to popular sites. The pick-up and drop-off points are at your hotel. The flights are in small aircraft with good viewing, two pilots, no flight attendants, and narrow aisles. Often, only about a dozen people will be on these trips. Limousines or vans await your arrival at each stop.

WHAT TO TAKE. Smart travelers to Hawaii travel light because they find everything they need right in the Islands. If you are going by air, since Hawaii is a domestic destination, the following rules apply: 1) you may check two pieces of luggage free and carry a third aboard the flight providing it fits under your seat; 2) each one may weigh up to 70 pounds; 3) the largest may have an overall dimension (height, length, and width added together) of 62 inches; 4) the next one may be up to 55 inches; 5) the smallest one may be up to 45 inches; 6) if the smallest one is no more than 9 inches on one side it may be carried on and put under the seat ahead of you. Rate for extra pieces is $25 if you have more than three bags. Apparel is summer informality, wash and wear sports shirts, light dresses, jeans, T-shirts, aloha shirts, and muumuus (best purchased in Honolulu). What you pack will depend on what you plan to do, but for women we suggest: a comfortable pair of slacks; a short-sleeved dress or skirt-and-blouse combination; shorts and tops; a sweater, light jacket, or stole for evenings and air-conditioned places; a cocktail dress for going out; bathing suit; dress shoes, walking shoes, and sandals. And for men: a slacks and sport jacket outfit and tie; knit or drip-dry shirts; casual slacks; shorts; swimming trunks; a light jacket or sweater; dress shoes, walking shoes, sandals, and sneakers if you like.

Don't forget hats; the sun burns more than you realize, and the tradewinds can be strong. You will never need woolens or furs at sea level in Hawaii, though you should bring a sweater or a light coat for the Volcano and other heights especially in the winter months. Casual and informal attire are the rule in Hawaii, and use of formal dress is rare. Bring a pair of comfortable walking shoes for sightseeing. Pack the minimum. When in doubt, leave it out!

TRAVEL DOCUMENTS. Persons who are not citizens of the USA require a passport and visa. Canadians need something to prove place of birth, such as a passport or birth certificate.

RESTRICTIONS ON IMPORT AND EXPORT. Plants and plant products are subject to control by the Department of Agriculture both on entering and leaving Hawaii. Pineapples and coconuts pass freely; avocados, bananas, litchis, and papayas must be treated. All other fruits are banned. Flowers pass except for gardenia, rose, jade vine, and mauna loa. Seeds, except in leis and jewelry, are banned. Also banned are insects, snails, coffee, cotton, cacti, sugar cane, all berries, and soils. Leave dogs and other pets at home. A strict 120-day quarantine is imposed to keep out rabies. For full details write to the Animal Quarantine Station, Department of Agriculture, State of Hawaii, 99–770 Moanalua Road, Aiea, HI 96701.

TIPS FOR BRITISH VISITORS. Tourist Information Services. Contact the Hawaii Visitors' Center, 15 Albemarle St., London W1X 4QI (tel. 01–492–1143).

Passports. You will need a valid passport and a U.S. Visa (which can only be put in a passport of the ten-year kind). You can obtain the visa either through your travel agent or directly from the *United States Embassy,* Visa and Immigration Department, 5 Upper Grosvenor St., London

W1 (tel. 01–499–3443). Note that visas can only be applied for by post; the Embassy no longer accepts visa applications made in person.

No vaccinations are required for entry into the U.S.

Customs. If you are 21 or over, you can take into the U.S.: 200 cigarettes or 50 cigars, or 3 lbs. of tobacco; 1 U.S. quart of alcohol; duty-free gifts to a value of $100. Be careful not to try to take in meat or meat products, seeds, plants, fruits, etc. And avoid narcotics like the plague. Returning from Hawaii you may bring home (1) 200 cigarettes or 100 cigarillos or 50 cigars or 250 grams of tobacco; (2) two liters of table wine and, in addition, (a) one liter of alcohol over 22% by volume (most spirits) (b) two liters of alcohol under 22% by volume (fortified or sparkling wine), or (c) two more liters of table wine; (3) 50 grams of perfume and ¼ liter of toilet water; and (4) other goods up to a value of £32.

Insurance. We recommend that you insure yourself to cover health and motoring mishaps, with *Europ Assistance,* 252 High St., Croydon CRO 1NF (tel. 01–680 1234). Their excellent service is all the more valuable when you consider the possible costs of health care in the U.S. It is also wise to take out insurance to cover loss of luggage (though check that this isn't already covered in any existing homeowner's policies you may have), as well as trip cancellation insurance. The Association of British Insurers, Aldermary House, Queen St., London EC4N 1TT (tel. 01–248–4477) will give comprehensive advice on all aspects of vacation insurance.

Air Fares. We suggest that you explore the current scene for budget flight possibilities. Unfortunately there is no longer standby service on any of the major airlines; but do check their APEX and other fares which may be a considerable saving over the full price. Quite frankly, only business travelers who don't have to watch the price of their tickets fly full-price these days—and find themselves sitting right beside an APEX passenger! You may be lucky and find a reasonably priced flight to Honolulu in the small ads of some newspapers and magazines. In early 1988 seasonal roundtrip prices ranged from £543 to £714 and included seven days' car hire.

Tour Operators. The following offer multi-center tours of the Hawaiian Islands:

Albany Travel (Manchester) Ltd., 190 Deansgate, Manchester M3 3WD (tel. 061–833–0202).

Amathus Holidays, 51 Tottenham Court Rd., London W1P 0HS (tel. 01–580–7597).

Columbus World Wide Travel, 85 London Wall, London EC2 (tel. 01–638–0411).

Cutlers Gardens, 10 Devonshire Sq., London EC2M 4YP (tel. 01–929–4251).

Speedbird Holidays, Alta House, 152 King St., London W6 0Q4 (tel. 01–741–8041).

WHAT IT WILL COST. Most things in Hawaii are expensive, yet people of moderate means are investigating the state as a vacation playground. The family on a tight budget has to be careful. Air fares to Hawaii have fluctuated wildly in recent years. While the average hotel room in the state has been pegged at around $57 a day for a double, you can pay much more than this, or considerably less, especially if two couples traveling together split costs. (See "Hotels and Other Accommodations" below.)

A person or couple who decides on a lot of swimming or beach sunning, walking, riding the city's bus system, or taking in the many free events— such as the Kodak Hula Show or the Honolulu Academy of Arts—will find that doing Hawaii needn't break the bank at Monte Carlo.

In Honolulu, a couple can eat pretty well for $15 each if they are careful with menu listings. A meal can be even less than that at a fast food outlet or at the type of small chop suey houses outside Waikiki that are frequented by the locals.

The city bus in Honolulu is 60¢, U-drives are reasonable, and the driving is not too difficult. Not many visitors use taxis, often the only way to get around elsewhere. Taxis are not allowed to cruise.

For $50 a day a couple can survive and enjoy themselves, although they would be boasting if they told friends later that they stayed at the "Ritz." But $100 a day for a couple is closer to what it really takes to have fun and not hold back much. At $250 a day your friends will think you're trying to do an imitation of King Kalakaua, "the Merrie Monarch."

Food, hotels, and tours on the Neighbor Islands cost almost the same as they do in Honolulu. The problem is that the interisland air fares needed to get from island to island run up expenses, and air travel is the only way to get out of Waikiki. The perfect Hawaii vacation is one in which you avoid putting all your eggs in the Waikiki basket. To understand the Islands, to get a feel for the Hawaii experience in harmonious living, it is important not only to drive or bus through the outbacks of Oahu, far from Waikiki, but preferably to see parts of at least one other island (three others is better yet). The truth is that Waikiki is not Honolulu, which is not Oahu, which is not the state of Hawaii.

HOTELS AND OTHER ACCOMMODATIONS. Of the over 65,000 **hotel rooms** in the state, the majority are located in Waikiki, and most others are in clusters at Neighbor Island destination resorts, such as Kaanapali, Maui. Penthouses or suites in the top floors of the finest hotels run $100 to $1,000 a day. But very attractive rooms in nice, complete hotels (air-conditioning, color cable TV, restaurants, shops, ice machines, and so forth) can be had from about $40 to $75 a day. Smaller, older hotels, with a simpler living style, are available (usually walking distance from the water rather than right on the water) for less than $30, even as low as $20. Some people call these "a place to sleep."

The Neighbor Island clusters of hotels tend to be luxurious, isolated from the main flow of life in Hawaii, and often adjacent to magnificent, expensive golf courses.

Motels are rare in Hawaii; Waikiki has none. Lihue, Kauai, and Waimea in the Big Island's ranch country have motels. Otherwise in Hawaii you don't find a row or two levels of attached rooms, each with a parking stall outside and a restaurant around the corner from the office. People don't drive all day to reach Hawaii.

The **bed and breakfast** concept, so popular in other parts of the world, has been slow getting off the ground in Hawaii. The first in this business was *Bed and Breakfast Hawaii,* operating out of Box 449, Kapaa, Kauai, HI 96746 (822–7771). Examples include $35 for a one-bedroom apartment up St. Louis Heights on Oahu. A required membership fee is $5 and for another $6 you get a Hawaii directory. Neighbor Island examples include a studio cottage with a view on Molokai for $45, a home at Kapaa for

$25 single, $30 double, a Maine Coast-type house at Waimea, Big Island, for $25 and $35.

Bed and Breakfast Pacific Hawaii, at 19 Kei Nani Pl., Kailua, on Oahu (262–6026), has some 200 hosts spread around the state. A third operator, *Bed and Breakfast Honolulu* (595–6170), has statewide connections. *Bed & Breakfast Connections Maui Style,* Box 886, Kihei, Maui, HI 96753 (879–7865), is a Maui-based company.

There are only two **youth hostels,** one in Waikiki and the other a block from the University of Hawaii. The only place resembling a "tourist home" in the nostalgic sense is a block from this second hostel, yet it is very expensive.

There are **cabins** for roughing it as well as state and county parks for camping. (For reservations and permit information see individual island chapters.)

Condominiums, usually very large, entered the picture in the 1970s. Most operate like hotels but without the trappings. Some are just big buildings with tiny lobbies. Some are half-breeds, half hotels and the rest a block of apartments for longer term residency. Some are time-share operations.

Most people arrive at Honolulu Airport with hotel reservations already in hand. Others don't mind checking out the scene first; you can get a place for a night by using a hotel's wall telephone near the airport baggage claim area. Such pioneering is not dead; just rare.

Very few hotels in Hawaii operate on the American Plan (three meals). Those that do are isolated, tropical retreats.

Hotels throughout this guide fall into five categories: *Super Deluxe, Deluxe, Expensive, Moderate, Inexpensive.* The price ranges for each category will be listed in the Practical Information for each island.

DINING OUT. In Hawaii the accent is on international food. Chop suey houses are everywhere, particularly in downtown Honolulu or in smaller commercial districts of the city, such as Kalihi, Kaimuki, or McCully. At the larger hotels the menu is going to lean to American and Continental cuisine. Japanese restaurants are popular. Many of the newer ones are the tiny yakiniku, sushi-type rooms straight out of Tokyo that demonstrate the steady impact of the rise in visitors from Japan in the last decade.

Abundant seafood places are normal for islands in mid-ocean. The fish-of-the-day are those purchased at the docks in the morning by restaurant agents for your evening meal. Tastes differ but most people enjoy the large-sized ocean filets, particularly mahimahi.

Fast food franchises are everywhere. What young America eats is also habit-forming in Hawaii.

Oddly, many visitors never sample Hawaiian food, the pig and poi fare, unless they sign up for a commercial luau.

Restaurants listed for each island will be listed by price range—*Deluxe, Expensive, Moderate, Inexpensive,* in each island chapter. There is a 4% state tax on all restaurant checks.

Hawaiian Cuisine. The cuisine of contemporary Hawaii is basically American, spiced with the adopted dishes of the many nations which have amalgamated in Hawaii. Residents of Hawaii have cosmopolitan tastes in food, and they eat well.

The classic Hawaiian feast is the *luau,* whose central dish is a whole-pig *puaa kalua*), steamed for hours in an *imu,* or underground oven. When you go to a *luau,* you will usually be invited to watch the pig being placed into the oven, an event which is often accompanied by much blowing on conch shells.

The pig, which has been skinned, eviscerated, scrubbed, and even shaved, is rubbed inside and out with rock salt and soy sauce. Then it is placed on chicken wire, and all cavities of the animal are filled with red hot stones from the *imu* fire. Tongs are usually used for this operation, but some Hawaiians toss the stone around by hand in a manner that makes a Hindu fakir's walking on fire look like a wading party. When the pig is stuffed with hot stones, its front and back legs are tied together and it is wrapped in the chicken wire. The embers are raked in the *imu,* and the pit is lined with fresh corn husks or banana leaves. The pig is lowered into the *imu* along with sweet potatoes, plantains (cooking bananas), and sometimes *laulaus* (pork, butterfish, and tender, spinach-like taro shoots, all neatly wrapped in *ti* leaves and steamed). When everything is in, more corn husks or banana leaves are piled on top of the pig thickly enough to keep the steam from escaping. The *imu* is then covered with wet burlap, and the pig is tucked in for a long nap. Earth is shoveled over the top of the *imu* so that no steam can escape. This final blanket of earth is then dampened, and the first part of the ceremony is over.

You can now go swimming, surfing, or sightseeing for about 4 hours while dinner is steaming in the *imu.* But be on hand when the pig comes out, steamed to a marvelous succulence, the meat falling off the bones. The great problem at a *luau* is to get this steamed pork served before it gets cold. You eat the *kalua* pig with your fingers in the traditional Hawaiian manner. And with it, you eat the traditional Hawaiian starch, *poi.*

Poi is a thick purplish-brown paste made from pounded taro root. It has an adhesive quality, which makes it easy to eat with one or two fingers, scooping it thus from bowl to the mouth. It's an acquired taste; most tourists don't like it at first. But it is a perfect foil for the pig and other *luau* dishes. Hawaiians love it, of course; and the poi mills of Hawaii can hardly keep up with the local demand. It is loaded with vitamin B, incidentally, and prescribed by Island doctors for babies, delicate stomachs, ulcers, and nervous disorders.

Other side dishes at the *luau* are *opihi,* a salty black mollusk, rather like a small clam; *lomi lomi salmon* (literally, rubbed salmon), which has been massaged with a marinade of chopped onions and tomatoes; and *chicken Luau,* a gastronomic delight consisting of tender morsels of chicken cooked with taro tops and coconut cream. Your plate should also be garnished with *limu* (dried seaweed), *paakai,* Hawaiian rock salt, and chopped roasted *kukui* nuts. The last is delicious, but should be eaten with great moderation; it is the classic Hawaiian purgative. *Pipikaula,* or Hawaiian jerked beef, is also served as a side dish.

The best way to experience the *luau* is to wangle an invitation to a private one, or a public one given as a benefit. If all else fails, try a commercial sitting, but the style of these *luaus* borders on a Detroit assembly line. Call the *Royal Hawaiian Hotel, Hilton Hawaiian Village, Sheraton-Waikiki,* or *Paradise Park* for times and places and plan to spend about $34, unless it's the Chuck Machado luau at the *Outrigger Hotel* (836–0249), which comes to $24.50. Or, to get away from Waikiki, there's a Paradise Cove luau on the Leeward Coast, $39.50 including the bus ride (945–3539).

By all means sample the local seafood while you are in the islands; *moi* (mullet), *ulua,* mahimahi, (dolphin), *opakapaka* (pink snapper), turtle, and lobster, as well as the *ahi,* or fresh yellowfin tuna. Charcoal-broiled mahimahi is in itself worth a trip to Hawaii. And don't forget the Island avocados, stuffed with Pacific crab, and the wonderful fruit salads with fresh mango, papaya, and pineapple. Order taro cakes when you see them, try the banana muffins and bread, and the Hawaiian breakfast specialties of macadamia nut, banana, or coconut pancakes with syrup. In the dessert line, you should try macadamia and coconut ice cream and all the papaya, passion fruit, and guava sherbets. To top it off, the rich black brew of the Islands' own Kona coffee.

DRINKING LAWS. The minimum drinking age in Hawaii is now 21. Beer, wine, and liquor are served at most restaurants in Hawaii. The exceptions are a few small neighborhood places without a license where they don't mind you bringing in a six-pack or bottle of wine. Young people are required to show a driver's license, school identification, or something else which shows a mug and birthdate. Package sales are made in retail liquor stores whose hours usually are 6 A.M. to midnight. Liquor is also sold in large chain groceries, small markets, and drugstores. Cabarets serve liquor between 10 P.M. and 4 A.M., but the average bar, especially the many Korean bars, close at 2 A.M. or earlier if business is flat. Some hotels are licensed to have their bars remain open till 4 A.M. if entertainment is offered.

LOCAL TIME, BUSINESS HOURS, AND HOLIDAYS. There is no daylight savings time in Hawaii because there are sufficient hours of sunshine in the winter months. Remember, Honolulu would be south of Key West and Havana. Thus Hawaii is five hours behind New York in the winter, six hours in the summer. On July 4, when it is noon in New York and 9 A.M. in San Francisco, it is 6 A.M. in Hawaii. Put another way, the West Coast is two hours ahead of Honolulu in December, three hours in July. Put a third way, think of every day ending in Hawaii.

Many big retailers, like Sears, open between 9 and 10 A.M. depending upon which shopping mall, and close at 6 P.M. Monday and Tuesday, 9 P.M. Wednesday through Friday and at 5:30 or 6 P.M. on Saturday. Many smaller businesses open at 7:30 or 8 A.M. Many shut down Saturday noon. Others, even in shopping malls, operate on Sunday between 11 A.M. and 4 P.M. Banks usually open at 8:30 or 9 A.M., and close at 3 except for a 6 P.M. closing on Friday.

Hawaii has the same major holidays as other states. The additional ones: Kuhio Day, March 26, and Kamehameha Day, June 11. Because these two days are not federal holidays, military bases and post offices are open as usual, but everything else is shut down.

SPORTS. For details on outfitters, facilities, see the Practical Information section for each island.

The azure blue that surrounds the Islands is the setting for fun times all year long. The water is always warm and the weather is almost always good, providing every opportunity for swimming, surfing, sailing, canoeing, and wonderful fishing, ranging from surfcasting and deep-sea trolling to skindiving for the greatest variety of fish you've ever come across. Water conditions are not always perfect—high winds or winter storms in the North Pacific can create too much whitewater for safe sailing or surfing if the break is above eight feet. World-class professional surfers can handle surf of 20 feet, but that's too breathtaking for the average visitor, especially one from America's heartland.

Year-round good weather, featuring balmy trade winds, help make Hawaii a sports paradise for people of all ages. Golf, tennis, and fitness pursuits, such as jogging and biking, are natural interests in the Island State. You'll have plenty of opportunity for horseback riding and hiking on the snake-free, poison-ivy-free trails which wind through all the islands. Some hiking is a little risky because of heavy marijuana cultivation in areas usually guarded by aggressive males.

In addition to the typical Hawaiian water sports, there is hunting for birds and game including deer, wild goat, sheep, and boar. You can even slide down a muddy mountainside on a ti leaf if you like, or over a lava tube waterfall. And, surprising as it may be, Honolulu has an ice rink for those visitors who want to keep winter skills honed in a perpetual summer environment and Mauna Kea, a mountain on the Island of Hawaii, has winter skiing.

But the action starts at the water's edge. **Swimming** and wading are free and safe on most beaches. Oahu has dozens of ideal beaches; Waikiki is not the best, just the most crowded and publicized. Girl watchers tend to prefer Waikiki, but the water and scenery can be extraordinary elsewhere, such as Kailua, Kahana Bay, or Laie.

The steady, endless curl of foamy combers can be near perfect at Bellows Beach on Oahu for **bodysurfing,** an easily learned skill that requires timing at the takeoff point and keeping the body rigid like a board for the best results. After wading, swimming, and bodysurfing, however, the water costs money.

Surfing is the most Hawaiian of sports and the youngest set can find joy in rentable boogie boards to skim at the water's edge. (The Polynesians paddled out on surfboards to meet Captain Cook, and they haven't gotten tired of it yet.) Waikiki will probably be your center of training. If you're a good swimmer and a natural athlete, you may be able to master the board by imitating the experts you'll see riding them in. The boards do take some mastering. They're about 10 feet long and weigh about 35 pounds. Light and fast, they are easy as pie to paddle, but hard to balance when you first stand up on them. You'll get a lot of sympathetic *aloha* from the beach boys as you try to catch the first small waves and rise to a standing position on the board. They'll usually give you a couple of pointers. But if it doesn't "come easy" to you, as the Islanders say, you can arrange for professional lessons. Your beach-boy teacher will show you how to time the waves, when to start paddling, how to control your direction by leaning to left and right, how to rise as you catch the wave, how to stand, and how to maneuver the moving board by exerting pressure with your feet. If you have a good sense of balance, chances are you will catch on quick. Once you have mastered the art of surfboarding, you will be an addict. Though surfboards require no greater skills than skiing or learning to balance a bicycle, it's the height and size of the waves that for many visitors often rule out plans for surfing or windsurfing (using a board with a colorful sail). Oahu's North Shore beaches in winter months often are treacherous. In general, surfing is for the hardy.

On the other hand, **outrigger canoe rides** require no special skill and are a community effort. Beachboys show paddlers what to do. Water equipment shops are everywhere in Waikiki and Honolulu. Other concessionaires deal with paddleboats, kayaks, jet skis, water skis, and parasails, the latter being for the extremely adventurous who thrill at the prospect of hanging solo 50 feet above the waves.

Oahu is just right for **sailing and boating.** There are yacht clubs and slips for boat owners and rental services. One can drive into valleys of residential tracts in Honolulu far from the water and see large powerboats, for fishing or pleasure or both, sitting on trailers in driveways. Water is assumed to be consistent with the Hawaiian lifestyle.

For the average visitor most boat activity centers on deep water fishing, catamaran rides, excursions to destinations, or eat/drink/dance cruises off shore, though these are hardly sports. Sailing lessons and rentals, however, are available, although outboard racing is limited due to few calm surfaces.

Deep-sea fishing, always within sight of the mountainous islands, has been a part of marine recreation for generations. However, this sport poses two problems: 1) it's an expensive day; and 2) you don't get to keep the fish. But that fact in itself makes it a sport, some would say.

The southwest coast of Maui, the Kona coast of Hawaii, the Na Pali cliffs of Kauai, and the Waianae coast of Oahu are among the best in the archipelago for game fishing. Fish in these parts are called by their Hawaiian names: *ahi* is yellowfin tuna; *mahimahi* is dolphin; *au* is marlin; *ulua* is Jack Crevalle; *aku* is skipjack. The *Hawaii Big Game Fish Club* has a deep-sea fishing tournament at the end of May and awards trophies.

The annual Hawaiian International Billfish Tournament held every summer at Kailua-Kona is today recognized as the world's foremost marlin fishing tournament. Similar to the Olympic Games, the billfish tournament attracts teams representing many foreign nations each summer. In addition, many teams from the United States come to the famous fishing areas to compete for world championship honors. If you don't want to go out in a boat for the big ones, stick your rod in the sand with your line out over the reef as the kamaainas do.

Freshwater fishing in Hawaii consists entirely of introduced species, except for several species of endemic gobies or *o'opu.* Because of the mountainous, volcanic terrain, there are no natural lakes, and few rivers. The state maintains five public fishing areas. On Kauai there is a short trout season at Kokee in summer; and bass, catfish, and carp are available at Wailua reservoir. On Hawaii there are bass and catfish in the Kohala and Waiakea reservoirs. Fishing for small and large mouth bass, bluegills, catfish, carp, and snakeheads is available at the Wahaiwa reservoir on Oahu and places on the other islands. One catfish at Wahaiwa ran 48½ pounds. Seasons differ depending upon the species of fish. Kauai is the only island with freshwater rivers and streams.

The abundance of colorful reef fish and fighting game fish in the clear waters of Hawaii makes the islands one of the world centers for **skindiving.** Among the edible and colorful reef fish are *aholehole* (bass), *aweoweo* (big eye), *kumu* (goat fish), *menpachi* (squirrel fish), *manini* (convict fish), because of its black vertical stripes), and *uhu* (parrot fish). Favorite game fish in deeper water beyond the reef are *Kahala* (amberjack) and *ulua,* one of the most delicious of Island fish. Sharks are, fortunately, rare in Hawaiian waters, but turtle and squid are abundant.

Best diving areas are Oahu and Waikiki, Black Point, and Hanauma Bay (for beginners); Haleiwa, Makapuu, and Laie. The last is considered one of the best red fish and lobster grounds in all Hawaii. Hanauma Bay is now a preserve, and spearfishing is prohibited. The Neighbor Islands are relatively untouched. As a result the fish are plentiful and unwary, a combination made for the skindiver. The southern coast of Kauai, the Kona coast of Hawaii, the northern coast of Molokai, and the waters between West Maui and Lanai are bountiful.

Hunting is limited to boar and game birds, and guides are almost a must. Deer and goats are fair game on other Islands. The big game includes sheep, goats, Axis or Indian Spotted deer, and wild boar. The last, found in all islands except Lanai, weigh up to 300 pounds, have razor-sharp tusks that can do a lot of damage, and are wily and ferocious. Over 7,500 are killed annually, but since they breed at the same rate, the boar population remains static. The feral sheep are found mostly on the high slopes of Mauna Kea on the Big Island. About 300 of them are killed annually, and more than one Hawaii visitor has gone home with a magnificent ram's head for his collection. The handsome Axis deer, with bucks often weighing as much as 200 pounds, are found on Molokai and Lanai, where they can be taken on a 1-buck-per-person limit during a limited public hunting season and on a fee basis on private lands (no season).

Nimrods can also hunt the Mouflon (European) Big Horn Sheep on Lanai and the black tail deer on Kauai during limited seasons in October.

There are 15 game birds on the open hunting list: Chinese ring-necked pheasants, Japanese blue pheasants, California Valley quail, Japanese quail, Gambel's quail, bamboo partridge, Chukar partridge, Chinese lace-necked doves, barred doves, wild turkey, mourning dove, and black, gray, Erckel's francolin, and Kalij pheasant. The game bird season in Hawaii is unusual, permitting hunting on weekends and holidays from the first Saturday in November through the third Sunday in January.

There are no fewer than 19 public hunting areas in Hawaii, covering 1,020,000 acres, or about 75 acres per hunter. A list of public hunting grounds and hunting regulations may be obtained from the State Department of Land and Natural Resources, 1151 Punchbowl, Honolulu. It has offices at Hilo, Hawaii; Wailuku; Maui; Kauai; Lanai City, Lanai; and Kaunakakai, Molokai. The division also sets the length of hunting seasons and specifies bag limits. Only rifles using cartridges that supply a muzzle energy of at least 1,200 foot pounds are permitted. Bow hunting supplies one of the special diversions for Hawaiian nimrods. There is an indefinite archery season for sheep at Pohakuloa on the Big Island. A license costs $15.

Golf and tennis, often twins at resort developments, are popular and natural for Hawaii as participant sports. The 28 golf courses on land-tight Oahu offer dramatic ocean and mountain views. Getting a starting time can be as difficult as making a birdie. There are operators in Waikiki who move golfers in vans to semi-public courses. Golfing in Hawaii differs from many other locales. Putts often break toward the ocean. Fairways are often built over hard, volcanic surfaces and Lava grass that can grab an iron. Roughs are often devilishly thick and the sand in traps is often coarse, coral based, not fine. Many municipal tennis courts are both free and on the go all night. The better synthetic surfaces are at hotel resorts and charge a fee. The Moanalua Golf Course dates back to 1898. In recent years Jack Nicklaus and all the world's best have played TV tournament golf in Hawaii, and the state has produced several national champions. Stars of the tennis world also have played exhibitions or appeared in tournament matches often promoted at Neighbor Island hotels.

Like swimming, it costs little or nothing to walk, hike, jog, bike, or skateboard Honolulu's streets and sidewalks. Walking may not qualify as a sport but 10,000 entries make the annual Honolulu Marathon quite a sporting event that attracts runners from everywhere. Hiking dates back to prehistoric Hawaii and its peoples' many mountain trails; later the missionaries had to use their feet to investigate their new, unfamiliar environment. Some walked great distances and circled islands. Nowadays road races include all-night relays around Oahu and the 37-mile Run to the Sun from sea level to the top of 10,000-foot Haleakala. Today organized hiking clubs, with know-how, welcome visitors to join with them in negotiating ridge lines and mountain tops for spectacular views. (Check with the Hawaiian Trail & Mountain Club or the Sierra Club.) Fitness centers are a new rage, though participants in the ancient arts, such as tai chi and karate, are not new. Weightlifting has been popular in Honolulu for years; Olympic great Tommy Kono lives in Honolulu.

Other sports that have a dedicated following in Hawaii include ice skating, bowling, horseback riding (but no racing), an occasional auto, stockcar, drag or motorcycle race, handball, racquetball, and variations off walls (but no jai alai), skiing (on Mauna Kea only), lawn bowling, archery, pistol shooting, gliding, hang gliding, kite flying, frisbee throwing, softball, rugby, soccer, volleyball, shuffleboard, even cockfighting and chess. Cockfighting is illegal but popular with locals. Some of the sports just listed require a fee to participate.

Oahu has only three stables that rent horses, many bowling lanes, only one ice rink. Motorcycle racing, hang gliding, and frisbee throwing tend to attract the young; lawn bowling and chess excite the elderly.

Looking backward, Oahu had horse racing early in the century before it was outlawed. One major automobile race at Mokuleia more than 25 years ago failed to endure on the sports calendar. Police have tried to eliminate cockfights, without success.

The big three of **spectator sports**—football, baseball, and basketball—have fascinated Hawaii fans and visitors for more than 50 years. There's also something of an international flavor seen in attending golf, tennis, boxing, sumo wrestling, and polo matches. Admission is charged also for "rasslin," auto racing, some swimming meets, college volleyball, weightlifting (sometimes it is tied to a beauty pageant), and there are regularly scheduled rodeos at Waikoloa on the Island of Hawaii.

No tickets are needed to view the Honolulu Marathon, the Molokai canoe race, the Transpac Yacht Race, or any of the major international surfing championships.

Aloha Stadium in Honolulu, the only stadium in the country that can switch from football to baseball configuration with the push of a button, seats 50,000 and is home to University of Hawaii football, the prep leagues and three bowls, the Hula, Aloha, and Pro. It's also home for a Triple A minor league baseball team affiliated with the Pittsburgh Pirates. Boxing and basketball are seen at Neal Blaisdell Center, which seats about 7,000. World championship fights have been held in Honolulu because the city has had a reputation as a good fight town since the 1930s. Highlight of the basketball season is the Rainbow Classic, which features Top 10 college teams.

University of Hawaii has been playing intercollegiate football since 1920 with early opponents arriving after a six-day trip by ship. Hall of Famer Cap Anson and his Chicago White Stockings and a major league all-star baseball team came to Hawaii in 1888 only to be prevented from playing because of the monarchy's blue laws (doubtless a missionary influence). Babe Ruth, Jimmie Foxx, and others followed and did play, starting in 1933, en route to Japan.

Both football and golf from Hawaii have received national TV exposure. The Hawaiian Open at Waialae is the major golfing event. Sixty years ago international swimming meets, usually involving Duke Kahanamoku and Johnny Weissmuller, drew great interest but the format has been dead for decades. Today interest centers more on commercialized surfing, the marathon, Ironman, and shorter running events, which are also televised.

For years locals and outside promotional interests have dreamed of and discussed a professional football or major league baseball franchise for Honolulu. The geographical isolation of Hawaii and a population below major league standards places such hopes on hold.

HINTS FOR PHOTOGRAPHERS. The scenic splendors of the islands, the number of festivals, the multitude of interesting racial types, and the generally sunny weather may combine to make Hawaii the most photographed place in America. *Kodak Hawaii* does the biggest business ever, and there are numerous camera shops which provide 1-day processing service on Kodachrome film and everything you need for still photography and motion pictures. Among the best-stocked are *Colvin's* at 2053 Kalakaua Avenue and at the Beachcomber, *Central Camera Inc.* at 1105 Bishop Street, *Anderson's Camera House* at 1349 Kapiolani Blvd., and *Francis Camera Shop* in the Ala Moana Shopping Center. Best black and white print shop is *PhotoPlant,* 1221 Kapiolani Blvd., Suite 506. For rapid color service check *Technicolor, Inc.* at 760 Halekuwila Street or the *Eastman Kodak Company* at 1122 Mapunapuna. For special problems check with *Light, Inc.,* 627 South St., Suite 102 (526–0693).

Here are some tips:

If the sun is shining and your camera is loaded with any of the following: Kodacolor II, Kodachrome 64 or Ektachrome X, you can shoot normally at 1/125 at f/11, or, for variations, with Kodachrome 25 at 1/125 at f/8, or 1/250 at f/5.6. If using Kodachrome 40 movie film (type A) try between f/11 and f/16. This is for the average scene in Hawaii: the Napali Cliffs of Kauai in the morning, the Kamehameha Statue in Honolulu, Devastation Trail at the volcano, or the Iao Needle on Maui, if it isn't raining. Now, with the film advanced and the shutter cocked, you will be ready to take any average subject or scene in a range of about 12 feet to infinity. Keep in mind, however, that in order to secure the best results with color film, it is suggested that you keep the sun behind you and on the subject, *especially when taking pictures of people.* Watch out for shadow areas as these tend to block up on color film. Where the subject matter is a little darker, such as the Fern Grotto on Kauai, the lens opening should be increased to f/5.6 or f/4 with the still film listed above or between f/5.6 and f/8 with the movie film.

Darker subjects, a *lei* stand in early morning, under a banyan tree with no sunlight, open up to f/4 and for movies to f/4 to f/5.6.

For brights scenes, such as Waikiki under a July sun, try Kodacolor II and similar film at 1/125 at f/16, and your movie camera should be set between f/16 and f/22.

When indoors, such as Kawaiahao Church, use a flash. But for a night athletic event, f/2.8 at 1/60th will work if the film is ASA 160, or try the new Kodacolor 400 with ASA 400, ideal for low-light photography.

Load your camera in dim light and don't leave rolls or cartridges around a long time before developing.

Those using Instamatic cameras don't have to worry about shutter speeds, but keep the sun behind you. With many better cameras the built-in light meter should set you up. Read directions on Fujicolor and other Japanese films because speeds can differ. Fuji films are marked "R" for slides, "N" for prints.

SENIOR-CITIZEN DISCOUNTS. The elderly get a break here and there. Discounts for seniors means 65 years in most cases, but not always.

Expect discounts at restaurants, sporting events, theaters, for U-drive rentals, at city golf courses, some markets, for prescription drugs, eye glasses, hearing instruments, and interisland flights. Honolulu County has no ID card system but Kauai and Hawaii Counties do.

SECURITY. Let's face it, America is inflicted with the stain of street crime, and Hawaii is part of America. Use common sense. Don't leave your purse or camera sitting around in hotel lobbies, or on a bench along Waikiki's crowded streets, or in your unlocked U-drive while you are admiring a beach. Bad guys lie in wait.

Show caution in your hotel home. Toughs sometimes slip past hotel security, prey on elevator riders late at night, break into rooms. Use your head around Honolulu, as you would in any major city, if around some of the town's sleazier bars late at night. Don't walk in dark public parks.

As we've said, if camping, be careful to check first with parks officials who will have recommendations on what spots to avoid. There are a few beautiful beach areas that can be bad news. Locals know and can tell you.

The joy of hiking, as much as camping, has felt the impact in recent decades of a new phenomenon, the big bucks business of growing illegal marijuana in isolated, forested, or agricultural areas. The innocuous, unwary hiker, intoxicated by the sun and idyllic scenery, might suddenly be looking down a gunbarrel. These things are not normal, but they happen.

HINTS FOR DISABLED TRAVELERS. Some of the larger, expensive hotels have ramps, rooms, 29-inch bath doors, shower grabbers, parking stalls, and low telephones for people in wheelchairs. Most major points of interest and street corners in Honolulu have ramps, as do most shopping centers and showrooms.

Two operators on Oahu of note: Handi-vans for the handicapped, 524–4626, get a pass at 650 S. King St., 24-hour advance notice; and Handi-Cabs of the Pacific will take you anywhere, 524–3866, free wheelchairs, $3 pickup, 80 cents per mile.

Grant Wheelchair and Repair, 636 Queen St., 842–2215, Honolulu, can fix any problem. Avis rents hand control vehicles. Several organizations in Honolulu provide companion support.

TELEPHONES AND EMERGENCY NUMBERS. The area code for the entire state is 808. A call to the West Coast is 65¢ the first minute, New York 70¢, and less for additional minutes.

911 will get you the *police* or *fire* department, an *ambulance* or the *suicide center.*

In Honolulu, you can get a *doctor* at 524–2575 anytime, day or night. If you need a *dentist,* call 536–2135. The *Waikiki Drug Clinic* is at

922–4787; *Coast Guard Rescue,* 536–4336. To learn if the surf is up, call 836–1952.

Finally, the *time* is announced at 983–3211, the *weather* forecast at 836–0121.

If you've been clipped by a business on an item or service, call either the *State Office of Consumer Protection,* 548–2540, or the Better Business Bureau, 942–2355.

ISLAND SPEECH. Since Hawaiian place names and expressions play such an important part in enriching the local scene, your own pleasure in a visit to Hawaii will be enhanced by knowing a little Hawaiian. Here are just a few easy rules to help you get the hang of it.

Every syllable and every word in Hawaiian ends with a vowel. With the exception of vowel combinations which tend to become diphthongized, such as *au* (ow), *ai* (eye) and *ei* (ay), each vowel should be pronounced separately. *Aa,* mentioned above, for example is pronounced ah-ah. Although some Hawaiian words have only vowels, most have consonants, and the consonant always begins a syllable. Example: Ka-me-ha-me-ha. The phonetics of Japanese are very similar. There are no double consonants; in Hawaiian you can always count on a vowel to step in and stop that sort of nonsense.

The accent of most Hawaiian words falls on the penultimate (next-to-the-last) syllable. Consistent with this rule, the first syllable of a two-syllable word is accented: KO-na, KA-ne, PA-li. An exception occurs here when the second syllable has become diphthongized; ha-PAI, ma-KAI, which are fundamentally ha-PA-i and ma-KA-i.

Here's a simple table to help you in pronouncing Hawaiian vowels:

Pronounce A as in above
Pronounce E as in weigh
Pronounce I as in marine
Pronounce O as in no
Pronounce U as in true.

Give the seven consonants their English equivalents. W is the only exception here. When it introduces the last syllable of a word, it is sometimes pronounced as a v. The famous Polynesian drink, *awa,* is thus pronounced "ava"; Ewa plantation is called "Eva."

Here's a small glossary of the Hawaiian words which are in common use in general conversation in the islands. You will hear these words and expressions everywhere in Hawaii, and you will see them printed in many places, including the pages of this guide.

aa—rough, crumbling lava as distinguished from *pahoehoe,* which is smooth.

ae—yes.

akamai—smart, clever, possessing *savoir-faire.*

ala—a road or a path.

alii—a Hawaiian chief, a member of the chiefly class; also plural.

aloha—love, affection, kindness. Also a salutation meaning both greetings and farewell.

aole—no.

auwai—a stream.

auwe—alas, woe is me!

ehu—a red-haired Hawaiian.

ewa—in the direction of Ewa plantation, west of Honolulu.

hala—the pandanus tree, whose leaves *(lauhala)* are used to make baskets and plaited mats.

hale—a house.

hana—to work.

haole—originally a stranger or foreigner. Since the first foreigners were white, *haole* now means a white man.

hapa—a part, sometimes a half.

hapa haole—part *haole,* a person of mixed racial background, part of which is white.

hauoli—to rejoice. *Hauoli Makahiki Hou* equals Happy New Year.

heiau—an ancient Hawaiian temple.

holo—to run.

holoholo—to run from one place to another, to visit.

holoku—a long Hawaiian dress, somewhat fitted, with a scoop neck and a train. Influenced by European fashion, it was worn at court.

holomuu—a recent cross between a *holoku* and a *muumuu,* less fitted than the former but less voluminous than the latter, and having no train.

honi—to kiss, a kiss. A phrase which some tourists may find useful, quoted from a popular *hula,* is *Honi Kaua wikiwiki:* Kiss me quick!

hoomalimali—flattery, a deceptive "line," bunk, baloney, hooey.

huhu—angry.

hui—a group, club, or assembly. There are church *huis* and social *huis.*

hukilau—a communal fishing party in which everyone helps to drive the fish into a huge net, pull it in, and divide the catch.

hula—the national dance of Hawaii.

imu—the underground ovens in which pigs are roasted for *luaus.*

ipo—sweetheart.

ka—the definite article.

kahuna—a priest, doctor, or other trained person of old Hawaii, endowed with special professional skills which often included the gift of prophecy or other supernatural powers.

kai—the sea, salt water.

kalo—the taro plant from whose root *poi* is made.

kalua—to bake underground. A *kalua* pig is a pig that has been roasted thus, the pièce de résistance of a Hawaiian feast.

kamaaina—literally, a child of the soil, it refers to people who were born in the Islands or have lived here for a long time.

kanaka—originally a man or humanity in general, it is now used to denote a male Hawaiian or part-Hawaiian.

kane—a man, a husband. If you see this word on a door, it's the men's room.

kapa—also called *tapa,* a cloth made of beaten bark and usually dyed and stamped with a primitive geometric design.

kapakahi—crooked, cockeyed, uneven. You've got your hat on *kapakahi.*

kapu—keep out, prohibited. This is the Hawaiian version of the more widely-known Tongan word *tabu* (taboo).

kaukau—food, to eat. Its derivation is Chinese. It is widely used in the Islands, and any Island kid will come running when he hears it.

keiki—a child; *keikikane* is a boy child, *keikiwahine* a girl.

kokua—help.

kona—the south, also the south or leeward side of the islands whence come the *kona* wind and *kona* rain.

kuleana—a homestead or small plot of ground on which a family has been installed for some generations without necessarily owning it. By extension, *kuleana* is used to denote any area or department in which one has a special interest or prerogative. You'll hear it used this way: If you want to hire a surfboard, see Moki; that's his *kuleana.* And conversely: I can't help you with that; that's not my *kuleana.*

lamalama—to fish with a torch.

lanai—a porch, a covered pavilion, an outdoor living room. Almost every house in Hawaii has one.

lani—heaven, the sky.

lauhala—the leaf of the *hala* or pandanus tree, widely used in Hawaiian handcrafts.

laulau—literally, a bundle. In everyday usage, *laulaus* are morsels of pork and butterfish, wrapped along with young taro shoots in *ti* leaves, then steamed, a favorite Hawaiian dish.

lei—a garland of flowers.

lomilomi—to rub or massage, also a massage. *Lomilomi* salmon is salmon which has been rubbed with onions and herbs.

luau—a Hawaiian feast, also the leaf of the taro plant used in preparing such a feast.

luna—a plantation overseer or foreman.

mahalo—thank you.

makai—toward the sea.

malihini—a newcomer to the Islands.

mana—the spiritual power which the Hawaiians believed to inhabit all things and creatures.

manawahi—free, gratis.

mauka—toward the mountains.

mauna—mountain.

mele—a Hawaiian song or chant, often of epic proportions.

menehune—a Hawaiian pixie. The *menehunes* were a legendary race of little people who accomplished prodigies of work, like building fishponds and temples in the course of a single night.

moana—the ocean.

muumuu—the voluminous dress in which the missionaries enveloped Hawaiian women. Now made up in bright printed cottons and silks, it is an indispensable garment in an Island woman's wardrobe.

nani—beautiful.

niu—coconut.

nui—big.

okolehao—a liqueur distilled from the *ti* root.

pake—a Chinese. Give this *pake* boy some rice.

palapala—book, printing.

pali—a cliff, precipice.

panini—cactus.

paniolo—a Hawaiian cowboy.

pau—finished, done.

pilikia—trouble. The Hawaiian word is much more widely used here than its English equivalent.

poi—the paste made from pounded taro root, staple of the Hawaiian diet.

puka—a hole.

pupu—Hawaiian hors d'oeuvre.

pupule—crazy, like the celebrated Princess Pupule. This word has replaced its English equivalent in Island usage.

wahine—a female, a woman, a wife, and a sign on the ladies' room door.

wai—fresh water as opposed to salt water, which is *kai.*

wikiwiki—to hurry, hurry up.

Pidgin English is the unofficial language of Hawaii. It is heard everywhere: on ranches, in warehouses, on beaches, and in the hallowed halls (though not in the classrooms) of the University of Hawaii. It's still English and not much tougher to follow than Brooklynese—it just takes a little getting used to.

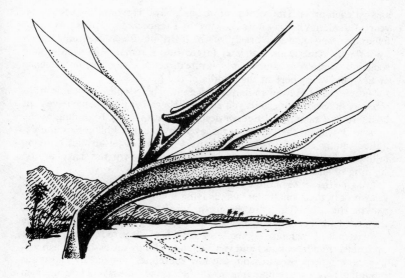

PORTRAIT OF PARADISE

An Introduction to the Hawaiian Islands

By
TOM and KAREN HORTON

Tom and Karen Horton are former residents of Hawaii and coauthors of The Dolphin Guide to Hawaii *and* The Dolphin Guide to Los Angeles. *Tom Horton is also coauthor of* The Dolphin Guide to San Francisco, *author of* SuperSpan: The Golden Gate Bridge, *and a frequent contributor to* Spirit of Aloha, *Aloha Airlines's inflight magazine.*

For a thousand years and more, people the world over have traveled great distances to discover the Hawaiian Islands and then, often as not, they have come ashore quite unprepared for the full magnitude and flowering mystique of such a treasure, left like a teardrop in the vast emptiness of the Pacific Ocean. It is one of the most isolated places on earth, and not even jet airplanes and satellite communications can remove the sense of detachment from the rest of the world that has kept these enchanted islands conspicuously, compellingly different.

Hawaii is a fully enfranchised part of America, so unlike the rest of America that it can satisfy the exotica of travel abroad without leaving the United States. Its heritage comes from the South Pacific islands of Polynesia, yet it is distinct from those distant islands, having developed a culture and a personality uniquely its own. After centuries of feudal-like existence, a rigid system of ruling chiefs and commoners on islands divided

21

against each other, Hawaii was united as a royal kingdom for nearly 100 years. But along the way it was coveted by France and by Russia and once fell under the flag, ever so briefly, of Great Britain. It was eventually taken by force by Americans, but later forged into a remarkable multi-ethnic society by those who came from opposite directions, creating a confluence of East and West here in the middle of the Pacific.

Nature made Hawaii radiantly different. The people who came from so many different homelands and adopted Hawaii as their home have kept it different, a rainbow of human design. From the very beginning to the present day, from the voyage of discovery by the first Polynesian double-hulled sailing canoes to the 20th-century stream of jet airlines bringing millions to the Islands, Hawaii has never ceased to stir the senses at first sighting of such an actual portrait of paradise.

Imagine the sense of disbelief among the seafaring Polynesians who had known only their small, flat islands lying low in the placid South Pacific waters. Here, 2,000 miles to the north, across an open sea devoid of land, they suddenly came upon islands unlike any they had seen before. These were islands of such unimaginable size! Walls of sheer rock thrust straight up from a thunderous surf and vanished into cloudy mists. Long, lush valleys carved their way in from the low shorelines, flanked by enormous mountains with water plunging down their spines like rivers flowing from the sky. The tallest of these mountains on the largest of these islands presented the strangest sight of all—its peak was as white as the meat of the coconut! But all else appeared green and fertile, rich with the promise of great bounty from the land and from the generally peaceful seas that washed up on sandy shores. Islands appeared one after the other in a gently curving line until eight had been counted.

Imagine, a millennium later, the delighted shock felt by one of the world's greatest ocean navigators, Captain James Cook, when he sailed north from Tahiti to reach the North American continent. The discovery of islands this far into the North Pacific was totally unexpected, as was the presence of the island inhabitants. The famed English explorer was the first Westerner to express astonishment at the very existence of islands in a solitary realm of the Pacific where they seemed out of natural position, and to wonder at the courage and skill required of the Polynesians who discovered and settled these islands of such overwhelming beauty.

Fortunately, you do not have to imagine the sensation of discovering Hawaii. After such a long period of splendid isolation, these became islands open to the world. And a special sense of discovery still prevails for anyone approaching Hawaii's golden shores and evergreen mountains for the first time. Although Hawaii's remoteness is now measured in hours rather than days spent crossing thousands of miles of ocean, the Islands' deepest charms have in fact become more elusive as Hawaii has become more accessible. But the true charms remain, an invitation to a unique experience for all who earnestly seek them.

You should not allow the ease with which great distances are now conquered to obscure a respect for just how far you have traveled when you reach Hawaii. Five hours of comfortable flying time from the West Coast of America can too easily diminish an appreciation for the isolation of the Hawaiian Islands. The Marquesas, believed to be the possible origin of the Polynesians who discovered Hawaii, is 2,400 miles to the south. California is 2,390 miles to the east. Traveling west from Hawaii, you would have to cross 3,850 miles of open ocean to reach Japan; 4,900 miles to China; 5,280 miles to the Philippines.

The birth of Hawaii at such a geologically unlikely place was also a belated and an extremely violent one. The Islands are almost wholly volcanic, each one thrust upward from the depths of the ocean by titanic eruptions of volcanic peaks built along a line across the ocean floor. A powerful and prolonged building force at work, quiet eruptions on the sea floor built up turtle-backed mountains called shield volcanoes that eventually broke the ocean surface in explosions of steam. As eruptions continued above sea level, the top of volcanoes eventually sank inward to form huge craters, or calderas. Meanwhile, other forces worked at sculpting the islands. Waves chiseled high sea cliffs and streams cut deep valleys, gradually carving the rounded shield volcanoes into jagged mountain ranges, such as the Koolau Range on Oahu. Sea level rose and fell, corals and algae built fringing reefs around the islands, streams cut valleys into the reefs, valleys were flooded to create such shore cuts as Pearl Harbor, and lava flows continued to build smaller volcanic cones such as Diamond Head.

Volcanic explosions were followed by tidal waves of immeasurable size. Savage torrents of rain swept across the emerging land masses, which were no sooner formed than their fragile foundations were violently shaken by successions of earthquakes. The forces of nature unleashed upon these newborn islands must have looked and sounded like the end of the world rather than the creation of one. But the finished product was heavenly to behold, possessed of a beauty not to be found in any other set of islands in any of the world's oceans.

Although the building process occurred over millions of years, the creation of Hawaii still came nearly 300 million years *after* most of the earth's land masses were securely in place. These are youthful islands in the geological life of the earth. On the youngest of the islands, the island of Hawaii, the natural forces that first began the job so long ago are still at work as volcanoes regularly erupt and send new lava spilling over flows left there centuries before.

It was those millions of years of fiery construction, pushing the volcanoes higher and higher above the ocean surface, that made the Hawaiian Islands such a rare fusion of softness and might. The inviting, gentle beauty of smooth sandy beaches will in many places give way swiftly to high, impregnable walls of sea cliffs. Fragrant tropical beauty may be the lace border around a stoic, broad-shouldered interior dominated by mountains that rise as high above the ocean floor as any on earth. Most visitors anticipate the beauty of Hawaii that awaits them. But many are stunned to discover the awesome dimensions to which that beauty extends across this seemingly small chain of islands.

There is another quality to Hawaii that cannot be measured in mountain heights or the sunny allure of beaches fringed by palm trees. There are other places in other oceans—even in this same ocean—with sunny weather and white sand beaches, places where mountains rise even higher, the land is greater in size and diversity and the history more dramatic. But nowhere else is there a place so small as Hawaii with such a world of differences among its people and their cultures blending so naturally with an exotic environment. The life of Hawaii, as it is lived today and as it was lived hundreds of years before, is as important to any meaningful understanding of these islands as the beauty of the land itself.

Look for the differences that shape life in Hawaii and you will understand why these remain islands to be discovered, and to be treasured.

A Consistently Hospitable Climate

Basic to Hawaii's appeal as a vacation destination is, of course, its equable climate. Although the Islands are well within the tropics, giving them a satisfying uniformity of warm, sunny weather throughout the year, they do not suffer the higher humidity common to many of the world's tropical zones. For this, Hawaii can thank the trade winds, the northeasterly winds that blow across the islands with blessed consistency. They were first called trade winds because of the trading ships that relied on them to speed their passage across the Pacific. Hawaii relies on the trade winds to moderate what might otherwise be uncomfortably hot, humid weather. That, in fact, is exactly the kind of weather that can occur whenever the trade winds stop. (Such still, humid conditions are known in Hawaii as Kona weather, despite protests at such labeling from residents of the Kona Coast on the island of Hawaii.)

This natural harmony of sunshine and trade winds during most of the year allows Hawaii to accurately present itself as an all-seasons vacation destination for sun followers. Unlike many glamorous sunshine resort areas that have balmy weather in winter months but are unbearably hot and humid during the summer, Hawaii's temperatures vary only slightly through the year. As the *Atlas of Hawaii* defines it, "The outstanding features of Hawaii's climate include mild and equable temperatures the year round, moderate humidities, persistence of northeasterly trade winds, remarkable differences in rainfall within short distances, and infrequency of severe storms."

This does not mean a complete absence of seasonal variations and trends, however subtle they might appear to the visitor accustomed to the traditional contrasts of the four seasons. There are essentially only two seasons in Hawaii, summer and winter. Summer is marked from about May to November, when the weather is generally the warmest, the trade winds the most persistent and rainfall the lowest. Winter, such as it is by Hawaii standards, begins sometime in November and lasts until April. During these months the weather is slightly cooler and rainfall greater.

But the variations between the two seasons are minimal enough to give the Islands a relatively accurate image as enjoying endless summers. The range of temperatures varies little, from lows of 73 to 74 degrees in late February and March to highs in the 80s from August to October. Temperatures as high as 90 degrees are rare, except, it must be noted, on Oahu. A mercury reading that high was once unheard of, but it is now all too common to see 90- and 91-degree days in August or September on Oahu. Island meteorologists have explained that Hawaii's most densely populated and developed island has, in fact, gotten hotter because of all the concrete and asphalt, especially in the heavily urbanized central part of Oahu. Trade winds blowing across Honolulu, Waikiki, and the rest of the island now encounter a preponderance of concrete and asphalt that heats the air and makes summers hotter than they were 20 years ago.

Hottest months on all islands are generally August and September; the coolest are February and March, which are also among the wettest months. The heaviest rains can come anytime from October to April, but there are amazing contrasts in the amount falling on different parts of the state and on different parts of the same island. Some higher elevations may average more than 400 inches of rain a year, totals that rival the heaviest rainfall on earth, while the average in some leeward lowlands may be no more than 10 inches or less. Waikiki owes some of its success as Hawaii's first beach resort area—Hawaiian royalty were the first to recognize its attractions—to its low average annual rainfall of about 27 inches, making it one of the driest parts of the island. Similarly, the most popular Neighbor Island resort areas such as Kaanapali and Wailea on Maui, the Kona and Kohala Coasts on the island of Hawaii, and Poipu on Kauai, benefit from modest annual rainfall.

But, be forewarned: areas with the lowest annual rainfall can be suddenly drenched by the heaviest downpours. Downtown Honolulu, for instance, averages only about 24 inches of rain a year, but has been pommeled with 17 inches in a single day. Sudden storms can cover a lowland area with three inches of rain in one hour. Hawaii's records of more than 11 inches an hour and nearly 40 inches in 24 hours compete for the dubious honor of being some of the world's heaviest downpours.

But the vast majority of resort hotels and condominiums hug the sunny coastlines where rainfall is far below that recorded on the slopes of Hawaii's mountains. And there is one other advantage to being in Hawaii if you love sunshine: the great clarity of the islands' smog-free atmosphere permits nearly three-fourths of the incident solar energy to penetrate all the way to sea level on a clear day. So you not only see more of the sun in Hawaii, you actually have more of its warming energy reaching you while you recline on a sandy beach, perhaps giving thanks for the trade winds blowing across the beach as you slowly turn a golden brown.

Close Islands Set Apart

It is one of the first clichés you will hear in Hawaii, but it has to be included in any introduction to the Islands: each island is different, with a distinctive personality all its own. This is a truth that has held up despite the enormous changes experienced on all the Islands as tourism has advanced beyond its Waikiki beginnings to cover nearly the entire state.

As the jet age has drawn Hawaii closer to the average traveler from the United States, so has it made the principal islands in the chain seem more tightly linked together. Until the late 1970s, almost all the jet airliners bringing visitors to Hawaii landed only on the island of Oahu. From there, visitors either remained to vacation exclusively in Waikiki, or transferred to interisland jets and smaller commuter aircraft that took them to the outer islands of Maui, Molokai, Lanai, the Big Island of Hawaii, and Kauai. All of that has changed dramatically. Several major U.S. carriers now fly direct to Maui, Kauai, and the Big Island. And the islands beyond Oahu long ago ceased to be known as the "Outer Islands," opting instead for the appelation of Neighbor Islands to better define their increasing accessibility and popularity among tourists who in years past rarely ventured beyond Waikiki. By 1983, some 21 percent of Hawaii's 4 million tourists were bypassing Waikiki entirely and heading directly to a Neighbor Island.

Fortunately, this spread of tourism to the Neighbor Islands has not come at the expense of their individual identities. Tourism has certainly altered the appearance of the Neighbor Islands in specific locales, but each island retains its own personality, made up of differences in everything from size and scenery to weather, beaches, people, culture, history, and resort development—or the lack of it. There are also appreciable differences to be found and enjoyed within each island. Striking contrasts in the nature of the land and the lifestyles of the people can be found on opposite sides of the same island, no more than an hour or two apart on a modern highway. It is this diversity that makes island-hopping so popular among first-time visitors. Those who vacation regularly in Hawaii, however, tend to choose a favorite island—more specifically, a favorite part of a particular island—and return there year after year.

The Hawaiian Islands form an archipelago which actually extends far beyond the eight main islands, reaching across 1,523 miles of the Pacific Ocean to take in 132 islands, reefs, and shoals scattered southeast to northwest across the Tropic of Cancer. But the Hawaii that is best known to the world is confined to eight islands grouped closely together: Hawaii, Maui, Oahu, Kauai, Molokai, Lanai, Niihau, and Kahoolawe (in order of size). These islands account for more than 99 percent of the total land area of 6,425 square miles in the State of Hawaii. Six square miles of land area that is also part of the state is located across hundreds of miles of open sea, from the tiny Northwestern Hawaiian Islands to Kure Atoll in the north and Nihoa in the south. The 50th state is not the smallest. Rhode Island, Connecticut, and Delaware are smaller. The island of Hawaii, commonly referred to as the Big Island, is three times as large as Rhode Island (and nearly twice the size of all the other Hawaiian Islands combined).

Tourism is presently concentrated on four islands: Oahu, Maui, Kauai, and the Big Island of Hawaii. Molokai, largely undeveloped with only one major resort area, is trying to attract more development and more tourists, but to date less than 20,000 of more than 5 million annual visitors choose to spend any time on Molokai. Up until recently, Lanai, the tiny island devoted to growing pineapple, has had just one rustic 10-room lodge to accommodate overnight visitors. But the company that owns the island of Lanai, Castle & Cooke, is building two tourist resorts, scheduled to open in 1989. Niihau, a small, privately owned island, is operated as a cattle ranch and populated almost entirely by Hawaiians. It was closed to the public until 1987, when it instituted helicopter tours from Kauai. The only inaccessible isle is Kahoolawe, a tiny, barren island off the southwest coast of Maui that has long been used by the Navy as a target for bombing exercises and in the last decade has become an emotional issue among Hawaiian activists who have tried to stop the bombing and reclaim the island.

The eight main islands form a gentle curve from northeast to southwest, with Niihau and Kauai at the northwest end and the Big Island of Hawaii occupying the southeast position. The other five islands are more closely grouped in between. From certain vantage points some of the islands seem no more than a ferryboat ride away, an intriguing prospect if the channels between the islands were not so rough and subject to choppy waters. It is only 23 miles from the east tip of Oahu across the white-capped Kaiwi Channel to the western shores of Molokai, where guests of the resort at that end of Molokai can make out the profile of Diamond Head across the channel. Maui is most fortunate of all islands in its scenic location among other things. Along the beaches of West Maui, sunbathers can contemplate serene views of Molokai and Lanai; day trips to these islands on catamarans and sailing yachts are popular Maui excursions.

In the view of many visitors—including those who have yet to actually visit—Hawaii can be divided into two parts: Waikiki and the Neighbor Islands. According to this view, Waikiki represents a conglomeration of high-rises, unchecked commercialism and big-city-style congestion. The Neighbor Islands, on the other hand, represent the natural beauty of Hawaii's open spaces. This is an understandable view, one that is not without some basis in fact, but it is far from an accurate portrait of Hawaii. Without question, the one-square-mile area that is Waikiki contains as high a concentration of tourism as any one place on earth. But venture beyond Waikiki to the Windward Coast and the rural North Shore and you will discover Oahu to be one of the most beautiful islands in the chain, with gorgeous, uncrowded beaches, a backdrop of modest-sized but stately mountains, and central plains covered by fields of pineapple. West Maui, conversely, is a Neighbor Island scene that has become so popular and has grown so fast, that its unending lineup of high-rise hotels and condominiums now gives that side of Maui its own version of Waikiki congestion.

In truth, each island has unique attributes, as well as drawbacks. Travelers who relish the glamor and nonstop action of Waikiki are excited, not dismayed, by the bright lights of 40-story hotel towers, wall-to-wall dining, entertainment and shopping, and in the middle of it all, a long, curving beach filled with beautiful and maybe-not-so-beautiful people from every corner of the globe. Waikiki partisans may bluntly dismiss the Neighbor Islands as boring. But for those who find Oahu's fast pace and intense concentration of humanity and tall buildings too much like life in Mainland cities they sought to escape, the Neighbor Islands are the salvation of Hawaii. These visitors rejoice in the calm and beauty of Kauai, the open spaces and soaring heights of the Big Island, or the easygoing luxury and versatility of Maui's seaside resorts.

There are eight islands to be seen in Hawaii, seven that can be visited, but there is a world of differences to be discovered on each of them.

The Luxury Islands

Resort living in Hawaii has evolved into the best of two worlds—elegance and bare feet. The newest selection of hotels and condominiums, especially on the Neighbor Islands, offers new levels of luxuriousness, even while adhering to the currently fashionable tendency toward low-to-medium density developments and away from the high-rise concrete monoliths of the not-so-distant past. But at the same time that island hotels have become more elaborate in design, they have turned more playful in spirit. In many of them, the only time you are actually surrounded by four plain walls is when you're in your room, and even here you are treated to balmy views of ocean and beach and mountains, or, at the very least, the manicured garden landscaping and ornate statuary of the hotel grounds. In today's island hotels you often have an ocean view while you're registering at the front desk. Before you even have a chance to tour the natural wonders of Hawaii, you pass meandering streams, waterfalls, fish ponds, banyan and palm trees, flowering gardens, exotic birds, millions of dollars in Pacific-Asian art and statuary—all on the way to your room. The hotel "coffee shop" is likely to be an open-air veranda looking across expansive lawns and gardens that lead down to a sunny beach fringed by rolling surf.

But a hotel or condominium with ocean views is no longer sufficient satisfaction for the modern generation of physical fitness enthusiasts who pursue active vacations. Hawaii hotels have responded with an emphasis on outdoor activities, handing out jogging maps along with the customary brochures directing guests to restaurants, bars, and shops. Fleets of seagoing craft of varied size and challenge—Hobie Cats, windsurfing boards, kayaks, pedal boats, catamarans, fishing charters—await the guest who prefers to do more than just swim in the warm Pacific waters. Hotels keep their own giant catamarans parked near the beach, ready to take guests on a romantic sunset cruise or a day sail to a secluded cove for snorkeling and scuba diving among the brilliant underwater reefs that encircle the Islands. There are saunas and weight-lifting rooms, aerobic dance classes beside and *in* the hotel pools, horseback trail rides along the beaches or into the nearby mountains, hiking trails through the resort's own preserves of nature and Hawaiian history, and guided excursions to the many attractions near the resorts or a short distance away.

It's a wonderful dilemma for the energized visitor. There's more to see and do on each island than ever before, but the new resorts also pride themselves on being complete self-contained vacation destinations. This means you can spend time at the beach, go sailing or snorkeling, play golf and tennis, dine in fine restaurants, shop for international gift items, enjoy the best of island entertainment—without ever stepping beyond the resort property. Ah, but when you do venture beyond the grounds of your hotel or condominium, this is when the real adventure of Hawaii begins.

The Active Islands

You may first notice it riding to your hotel or condo from the airport: people jogging along the highways, on city sidewalks, through the parks and across every conceivable type of terrain, from beaches to busy thoroughfares. There seems to be an endless stream of men, women, and children jogging up, down, and around Diamond Head at nearly all hours of day and night. And why not? Every day is a perfect day for running in Hawaii, where even the rain that might fall on you is warm. There are probably more joggers per capita in the islands than anywhere in the world. And when they aren't out jogging, the resident islanders are likely to be spending their non-working hours on the golf courses and tennis courts or in the water swimming, surfing, sailing, and fishing—doing anything that can best be done outdoors in the sunshine. Add the new generation of travelers who also prefer an active lifestyle even while on vacation, and you have an updated vision of active islands to offset the traditional travel-poster view of reclining bodies on golden beaches.

Warm weather, clean air and an active lifestyle not only means a better life for those fortunate enough to live in Hawaii, but it brings a longer life. Hawaii has the highest life expectancy of any state, 78.02 years. Many of the visitors are also looking to enhance their health with a week or more of sunshine, surf, and outdoor activity. Gone are the days when the average tourist divided vacation time between a Waikiki hotel room, Waikiki Beach, and the closest bars and restaurants. And while many still see the Islands by tour bus or rented cars, thousands of others prefer to move across and around, to the top and to the bottom, of every island in every way possible. New ways are made available to them every year.

Visitors ride horses or hike into the lunar-like crater of Maui's dormant volcano, 10,000-foot-high Haleakala, or coast down it on cruiser bikes that take off above the cloud line and don't stop until they reach sea level after 38 miles of winding, scenic roadway. They sail across the channel from Lahaina to Lanai and Molokai, where they feast on fresh pineapple and barbecued ribs Hawaiian-style, on the beach, after snorkeling in waters so clear you could see for a mile—if there weren't a million fish of a thousand colors blocking your view. Visitors ride Zodiac rubber boats on bouncing waves past the steep sea cliffs of the awesome Na Pali Coast of Kauai; kayak down the Wailua River and hike into Kauai's mysterious Kalalau Valley. They fish for giant marlin off the Kona Coast and for freshwater trout in the high mountain streams of Kauai. They ride across the Maui skies like human kites in the daredevil sport called parasailing, or they survey the Islands from the saddle while riding across the emerald-green ranchlands of Kauai's North Shore, into the Big Island's windswept Kohala Mountains, and along the grassy plateaus above the sea on the unspoiled Hana Coast of Maui.

Hawaii enjoys showing its visitors how to do something they've never done before, something done with easy pleasure in the Islands. Throughout all islands there are ideal conditions to learn to snorkel, scuba, sail, surf, and windsurf. There are three good reasons why Hawaii is one of the best places in the world to learn water sports: warm water, clear water, and calm water. Added to the hospitable conditions of the natural elements is the convivial expertise of trained instructors. Because so many people of all ages are venturing into the ocean for the first time during a Hawaii vacation, cruise operators place a high priority on expert instruction, careful supervision, and ocean safety. Instructors will show you how to use the equipment and tell you important facts about the ocean. This they usually manage to do while making you laugh, relax, and comfortably enjoy yourself while at the same time learning valuable lessons about the dangers, as well as the pleasures, of Hawaii's ocean waters.

There are instructors and guides eager to introduce you to just about every outdoor activity available on every island: surfing, hang-gliding, plane gliding on Oahu; sailing, parasailing, downhill mountain bicycling on Maui; marlin fishing, parasailing, wild game hunting and snow-skiing on the Big Island of Hawaii; kayaking, canoeing, Zodiaking, bass and trout fishing on Kauai; bird and game hunting on Molokai; snorkeling, scuba-diving, water-skiing, windsurfing, deepwater fishing, horseback riding, hiking, golf, and tennis on all the Islands. And of course you may prefer to actively enjoy the Islands on your own, at your own pace and preference. Either way, an introduction to the active side of Hawaii will lead you to the best of Hawaii.

The Surprising Interior

You might naturally assume that if you're looking for cool mountain majesty instead of warm, sunny beaches, Hawaii would be out of the picture. You would be wrong. Hawaii has some of the highest mountains in the United States, soaring spires of perpetual greenery—sometimes covered on top with deep snow—that can hold their own with the peaks of Colorado's Rocky Mountains or California's Sierra Nevada range. Hawaii's highest summits, Mauna Kea (13,796 feet) and Mauna Loa (13,677 feet) are in the same alpine league as Colorado's Pikes Peak (14,108 feet) and California's Mt. Whitney (14,495 feet). In scientific terms, Mauna Kea and Mauna Loa, both located on the Big Island of Hawaii, qualify as the highest mountains on earth. Their earth base extends far below the ocean surface and, from that point to the top, the two peaks reach vertical heights of nearly 30,000 feet, a few hundred feet higher than Mt. Everest.

No other state has a physical landscape so dominated by volcanic landforms. The result is not only impressive in terms of elevation, but also in sheer beauty. The convulsive volcanic activity and constant erosional action of the sea carved the Islands into massive natural sculptures of towering peaks, deep valleys, steep canyons, and high fluted sea cliffs. Hawaii's mountains, for all their massive size, are partially hollow. They are giant shield volcanoes constructed of innumerable thin lava flows with large craters formed at the summits by collapse of the mountaintops. Maui's Haleakala, for instance, collapsed into a crater that is half-a-mile deep and seven miles across.

But these unusual works of nature's art serve as more than brawny backdrops for the sea-level tropical scenery. While protected from commercial development, Hawaii's higher altitudes are, in today's computer terminology, user-friendly. And the islands are conveniently compact so that you can easily enjoy the beach and mountains in the same day. In addition to day trips to the top of an island, there are overnight options. While there is a refreshing absence of slick hotels or condominiums, you can find a cozy room in rustic mountain lodges and public cabins. There are also public campsites to accommodate outdoorsmen and small, organized tours specializing in outdoor exploration. Alternative lodging ranges from the historic Volcano House that rests on the rim of smoldering Kilauea Crater on the Big Island and Kokee Lodge's comfortable cabins with fireplaces at the cool, 3,600-foot level of Kauai, to spartan cabins on the floor of Maui's Haleakala crater. Day use of Hawaii's mountain slopes can be anything from horseback riding and bicycling to snow-skiing atop Mauna Kea and a famous mule ride down a Molokai cliff high above the sea. There are also spectacular "flight-seeing" helicopter tours on every island that allow you to look down on the island heights.

The uninformed who assume that most of Hawaii has now been paved over by commercial tourism are simply unaware of the vast amount of undeveloped land, much of it inaccessible to all but the hardiest of hikers. Only approximately 4 percent of Hawaii's land is in urban use. Of some 4 million acres of island land, 1.9 million are protected as conservation land; another 1.9 million are zoned for agriculture; less than 200,000 acres are zoned for urban use.

The silent, unspoiled beauty of interior Hawaii still impresses visitors, as it did Mark Twain. He spent much of his four months in the Islands on horseback, exploring what he described as "the stately mountains bordering the dream-haunted Manoa Valley . . . the blossomy gorge called the Iao Valley . . . the healing solitudes of Haleakala . . . the mightiest active volcano on the earth's surface [Kilauea]."

Cultural and Artistic Islands

Hawaii's cultural life is enriched with more homegrown ethnic diversity than can be found in any state in the United States. Hawaiian music and dance is performed before large audiences by both the older and the newer generation of islanders who have become vitalized by a renaissance in Hawaiian culture, while more recent arrivals continually present new forms of artistic expression inspired by Hawaii's many-faceted charms.

The culture of Hawaii, rooted in the heritage of a thousand years of Hawaiian life and legend, has also come to mean the cultures of Japan, China, Korea, Portugal, Philippines, Samoa, Tahiti, Europe, and the United States. In addition to a faithful preservation of ancient Hawaiian traditions, cultural and religious traditions from distant homelands are perpetuated throughout the Islands. Evidence of this can be seen in Japanese and Chinese temples, as well as colorful festivals celebrating the history of many different nations. The hula is recognized around the world as the poetic dance of the Hawaiian Islands, but Japanese bon dancing—dancing to drums to honor ancestral souls—is as popular in Hawaii today as it was among the homesick plantation workers a hundred years ago. All during the summer there are Japanese O-Bon celebrations at the Japanese Buddhist temples. And the cultural calendar in Honolulu may include not only the annual Hawaii Opera Theatre season, but also appearances by the Peking Opera. The Honolulu Symphony, founded in 1901, presents a full season of concerts, special events, guest artists, and an annual appearance by the San Francisco Ballet. There may also be visits by the Tokyo Ballet, the Pearl of the Orient Dance Company from the Philippines, and perhaps the Onoe Kikunobu Dance Company of Japan. Kabuki theater is regularly performed in Honolulu along with musicals and dramas by three resident theater companies. The annual Hawaii International Film Festival features films from Asia, the Pacific and the United States.

Authentic Hawaiian culture commands a strong, visible presence on all islands, both in contemporary events and in glimpses of a culture reaching back centuries before Captain Cook's arrival. From the constant enjoyment of Hawaiian song and dance to royal palaces, museums, ancient religious shrines, and well-preserved or authentically restored historical sites, the Islands are a treasury of Hawaiian culture. In fact, the Hawaiian culture is felt more strongly today than it has been for many years, thanks to what is hailed in the Islands as the Hawaiian renaissance. It began in the early 1970s with a renewed interest in all facets of Hawaiian life, expressed most prominently by a revival of the traditional hula and by the enthusiasm of a modern generation of island musicians for authentic Hawaiian folk music. It has also involved a greater interest in the Hawaiian past and a renewed emphasis on the Hawaiian identity, which too often was lost in a modern society where tourism is the dominant industry. But the visitor also benefits from this cultural renaissance. There are festivals and special events taking place throughout the year on all islands, providing visitors with an opportunity to enjoy authentic island activities such as hula and musical festivals, arts and crafts fairs, lei-making festivals, outrigger canoe races, even Hawaiian-style rodeos in the uplands of Maui, Kauai, and the Big Island.

The kind of Hawaiian music tourists once expected—the hapa-haole songs written by Hollywood-inspired composers to evoke a sultry musical image of a hula girl, moonlit beach, and steel guitar—was not really the music of the Islands. Genuine Hawaiian folk music is now played for both tourists and locals throughout the Islands, as well as contemporary music performed by island groups reflecting the modern rock influence. There is probably more live music of all kinds performed in Hawaii than in any place of comparable size in the world. The hula has had a rebirth along with authentic Hawaiian music. Hula *halaus* (schools) have proliferated. The Merrie Monarch Festival in Hilo, honoring the memory of King Kalakaua as the one who revived the hula after the missionaries outlawed it as a dance "designed to promote lasciviousness," has become the premier Hawaiian event of the year. More than 500 dancers and chanters from dozens of *halaus* throughout Hawaii compete in a week-long festival of ancient hula that is sold out months in advance and has come to be recognized as the most exciting dance competition in the Pacific.

Visual arts are exactly that in Hawaii—highly visible. There may be more art on public display in Honolulu than in any city of comparable size in America. It covers the walls and graces the courtyards of every public building, fills the lobbies of banks and office buildings, shows up in the parks, and exhibits itself every weekend at the most unlikely outdoor art gallery—the Honolulu Zoo Art Fence, where island artists display their paintings along the back fence of the zoo. Hawaii was the first state to pass a law, in 1967, setting aside 1 percent of all construction appropriations for new state buildings to be spent on art for display in public buildings and public spaces. Thirty-five other states now have similar laws.

Honolulu magazine visual arts critic Frank Tillman has observed, "I have never been in a place where the arts are so public and which, in their great variety, touch so many people. This has completely to do with the tendency to synthesize what is Eastern and what is Western, and with the different people here of varying background, and with the dissolving of the conventional distinction between the fine arts and useful arts. Hawaii has evolved as a state that turns its arts toward the community while exploring new forms of artistic involvement. The arts here bring us together."

New forms include marine art, celebrating the Islands' spectacular variety of underwater life. The massive but graceful humpback whale, the leaping dolphins, the mysterious manta rays, and the brilliantly colored reef fish are depicted in oil paintings, acrylics, watercolors, photographs, and sculptures of bronze, stone, wood, and ceramic. The annual Maui Marine Art Expo is the largest of its kind in the world, featuring the best known marine artists in America, and helping to establish Maui as the nation's leader in marine art.

Hawaiian-Pacific-Asian art is on display throughout the islands, from such prestigious centers as the Honolulu Academy of Arts, to multi-million-dollar collections of art and statuary displayed in lavish resort hotels, to glossy commercial galleries and small, storefront galleries tucked away in old plantation towns and sleepy villages far from the glitter of commercial resorts.

America's Most Multiethnic Society

The approximately 1 million residents of America's 50th state represent the nation's most multi-ethnic society. According to 1980 Hawaii State Department of Health surveys, the largest ethnic group in Hawaii is Caucasian, accounting for 26.3 percent of the resident, non-military population. A close second in number, at 23.5 percent, are Japanese. Following in order of percentage of the population are: part Hawaiian, 17.9 percent; Filipino, 11.2 percent; mixed ethnic races other than part Hawaiian, 9.4 percent; Chinese, 5.1 percent; Korean, 1.3 percent; Black, 1.3 percent; Samoan, 1.2 percent; unmixed Hawaiian, 1.0 percent; Puerto Rican, 0.7 percent; others, or unknown, 1.2 percent.

But statistics do not convey the true picture of Hawaii's people. This remarkable confluence of East and West is best demonstrated in the everyday life of the Islands, in which the multitude of ethnic backgrounds manifests itself in everything from language and religion to fashions and food. Nowhere else in America are lifestyles so consciously influenced and so visibly modified by the interaction of so many different ethnic groups. Life in the Hawaiian Islands, even after 30 years of statehood and the phenomenal growth as a modern society catering to the world's travelers, remains unique: a Hawaiian-American-Asian-Polynesian rainbow of life constructed from a world of differences adapted to one special place. It becomes, in the end, the island way of life.

And there are still people coming from great distances with dreams of becoming part of that way of life. Some still come, as the first trading ships came, believing Hawaii to be a golden place to pursue profit. Others come believing it to be the perfect place to simply be lazy. Many of these, the ones who come in search of profits or pure leisure, are the ones who eventually go back to where they came from, having discovered the appreciable difference between visiting what appears to be a paradise and the reality of living there.

The cost of paradise comes high. An unexceptional home may cost $200,000; a medium-quality condominium may be well above $100,000. Control of the land, or at the very least the ability to afford to live on the land, remains Hawaii's most emotional, volatile, and divisive issue. The ownership of land, from the ancient days of ruling Hawaiian *alii* (royalty) to the 19th-century takeover by American merchants and sugar plantation lords, has historically remained in the hands of a very few. On Oahu, for instance, some 18 landholders still own approximately 40 percent of the island's privately held land. (Considerable amounts of prime land are also owned by the military.) Leasehold property has thus become a strange fact of life for the average Hawaii homeowner, especially on the island of Oahu, where 80 percent of the state's population resides. It is more common than not to own an ordinary $200,000 home, or even a $1 million showplace, and not own the land upon which the home sits. Instead, a homeowner is given a long-term lease, maybe 55 years, and pays annual lease rent to the estate that owns the land, estates that trace their prosperity back to the mid-19th-century era of missionaries and enterprising Yankee merchants. Mainland arrivals find this leasehold system bewildering, but soon learn to live with it as an unavoidable facet of island ways.

In 1984, however, the U.S. Supreme Court upheld the constitutionality of a 1967 Hawaii land-reform law requiring the breakup of large private land holdings and their redistribution to small homeowners. Lawyers for leasehold tenants forecast that the Supreme Court ruling will bring significant changes for Hawaii's middle-class homeowners. But to accommodate Oahu's growing population of some 800,000, there is extreme pressure for expansion of urban land use. During the last 20 years, when Hawaii's population increased 50 percent, less than 2 percent of agricultural land was changed to urban, and most of that was on the less populated Neighbor Islands.

Salaries have never kept pace with the cost of living in Hawaii, which is always near the top in any national survey. The fact that so many goods must be imported from the Mainland or other sources adds to the cost of Island life. Not surprisingly, Hawaii has historically had the highest number of working wives per capita of any state. Even their husbands may work more than one job in order to supplement the family income. But there are trade-offs: waking up every morning to sunshine and blue skies, birds singing, and trade winds carrying the fragrance of blossoms perpetually in bloom. And come *pau hana* (through work), or the weekend, the resident islander can casually visit the kind of beach for which tourists spend thousands of dollars to spend a few sunburned days in its presence.

A Feast of Islands

Food is important everywhere, but it's important enough in Hawaii to be regarded as part of the unusual social fabric of the islands. Island food is as much a cultural ingredient as a means of sustenance. Whether it is two people sitting down to "talk story," or a backyard luau, food commands center stage, right along with the song and dance. As in all aspects of the Island way of life, food reflects the diversity of the population. Japanese sashimi and sushi, Chinese manapua and dim sum, Korean kimchee and kal bi, and all the Hawaiian favorites—poi, kalua pig, laulau, lomi lomi salmon—are as commonplace as steak and potatoes, cheeseburgers and hot dogs, which you will also find in adequate supply.

For the average tourist, there was a time not terribly long ago when island food meant a restaurant meal of frozen mahimahi and perhaps a slice of mile-high coconut cream pie. But Hawaii's restaurants have become more international, more sophisticated, and, at the same time, more responsive to what the land and sea around them can provide for their tables. European chefs brought in by the big hotels fall in love with 12 months of sunshine and put down tasty roots, some of them eventually moving out of the hotel dining rooms to open their own intimate French and Continental restaurants. The European influence upgrades the quality of food in the hotels as well as enriching the restaurant choices throughout the Islands.

But European chefs and tastes do not dominate any more than American preferences override the island taste for a mixed ethnic menu. Like everything else, European and American ingredients and cooking skills are blended as part of the flavoring of the unique East–West stewpot. European-trained chefs adopt Asian methods and apply them to fresh island fish, vegetables and fruits. There is a variety of fresh island foods in Hawaii's restaurants today, whether the menu is French, Chinese, Japanese, Korean, Thai, Vietnamese, Moroccan, Greek, Italian, or fancified American bar-and-grill. You name it, Hawaii has it—but with ocean views and trade winds rustling the linen.

Hawaii's best restaurants, in and out of the hotels, no longer rely strictly on the standard wholesalers to stock their kitchens. They go straight to the source, to the fishing boats that deliver daily catches and to the farmers of Kahuku, Waianae, Upcountry Maui, the Big Island, and Kauai, who grow the best onions, lettuce, watercress, papayas, or mangoes, or raise Maui rabbits and Maui catfish. No longer are island diners impressed by something on the menu that has been "flown in fresh from the Mainland." They prefer the taste of something trucked in from Kula, Kohala, or Kahuku.

Good food in beautiful restaurants with glorious views is the end result. But for the full story of food in Hawaii, look beyond the restaurants. Look to the roadside stands selling fresh fruits; the beat-up vans near the beaches selling plate lunches, manapua and shaved ice; the country stores selling cone sushi, Portuguese sweet bread, and crack seed. For a view of the full picture of island food, look to an island original such as the market, across from the Yat Tung Chow Noodle Factory, in the Chinatown section of old Honolulu. This market is the last permanent open-air market in Hawaii, dating back to 1904, a place where three generations of families have been selling the best food that can be grown in these islands, or taken from the sea, to people who still prefer a people market to a supermarket. Here you will see sidewalk displays of opakapaka, mahimahi, ono, and onaga; marinated crispy ducks hanging by their feet; a whole pig displayed at Foo Ying Chee's Sing Hing Meat Market; great quantities of the island staple at Chong Choy Chow Poi Shop; layers of fresh sashimi at Take Gibo's Stall; mounds of fresh island fruits and vegetables at Young Yung Stall.

Foods such as these come from all over the Islands, and it is important to know what came from where. Kahuku watermelon means it's the sweetest melon grown. Real Maui onions, the ones responsible for all the fame, are grown only in Kula, high on the slopes of Mount Haleakala, and not down in the flatlands of Kihei (or on Molokai, a part of Maui County, where they grow a lot of onions and sell them as *Maui* onions). People in Hawaii eat about twice as much fish per capita as people in any state in the United States, and probably rank equally high in consumption of fresh island fruit such as papaya, bananas, mangoes, and, of course, pineapple.

Food is an export crop in Hawaii, but this is of minor significance compared with its importance to Island life. Island food is so unique, islanders coined their own pidgin-English phrase to describe the goodness of it: "Broke your mouth!"

Aloha: The True Meaning

No one word symbolizes Hawaii and its people more than the word *aloha*. The definitive Hawaiian–English dictionary by Mary Kawena Pukui and Samuel H. Elbert lists its multiple meanings: "*Aloha:* love, affection, compassion, mercy, pity, kindness, charity; greeting, regards; sweetheart, loved one; beloved, loving; to love, show kindness, mercy, pity, charity, affection; to remember with affection; to greet, hail. Greetings! Hello! Good-bye! Farewell! Alas!"

Alas, indeed. *Aloha* is one of the most important words in the Hawaiian language *and* one of the most misunderstood. Hawaiian scholar and author George Sanford Kanahele, who has written a book examining the evolution of traditional Hawaiian values before and after the arrival of Captain Cook, explains that aloha does not mean a selfless love and a tradition of giving without expecting anything in return. It was, to the Hawaiians, a word that conveyed a reciprocal agreement, the sense of giving and receiving something in return.

The correct word for Hawaii's traditional welcome to the traveler is not aloha, but *hookipa,* the Hawaiian word for hospitality. Hospitality was one of the most important Hawaiian values, placing a high sense of esteem on welcoming and entertaining with warmth and spontaneity a guest or visitor, even a total stranger. In traditional Hawaiian society the person who failed to offer hookipa was put up as an object of public scorn. The Hawaiian offered hookipa, or hospitality, to enhance his own sense of honor and prestige.

These values, later translated by non-Hawaiians and promulgated by tourism promoters as the meaning of aloha, have survived as one of the fundamental beliefs of the Hawaiian way of life. But the true interpretation

of aloha is not what Hawaii has to give, but what it has to share. There
needs to be reciprocity: those who come to share in the joys of the Islands
should reciprocate by respecting the history and culture of the Islands.
Do that and you will take home a true feeling of aloha for the Hawaiian
Islands.

HAWAII'S HISTORY

Kings and Queens, Missionaries and Whalers,

Sugar and Tourism

By
TOM and KAREN HORTON

For unknown millions of years these were islands without human habitation, islands alone in a vast sea with an untold period of waiting in silence. The first to discover this solitary paradise were the people of Polynesia, an oceanic realm of the South Pacific given its name by Europeans who used the Greek words meaning "many islands." There were indeed many islands to be found in the immensity of the Pacific Ocean south of the equator, some of them inhabited by the seafaring Polynesians as early as 1100 B.C. Many more islands in the southern and eastern expanses of the Pacific were settled within a few centuries of the time of Christ. Among the last to be reached, about the time of A.D. 500, was the small chain of islands far removed from the rest, seeming out of place in the distant North Pacific.

Nearly a thousand years before the voyage of Columbus, the Polynesians left their islands in the South Pacific (probably the Marquesas or Tahiti) with destination unknown, setting a course across an uncharted sea in search of a new home. They had watched with wonder the migration of a small, gold-speckled bird, the Pacific golden plover, known to the people of Polynesia as the bird of the north. The eggs of the bird of the north, it was said, must be buried on land not far across the water, though certainly farther than anyone had ever gone before. They would thus follow the flight of the bird of the north and, if Tangaroa, god of the sea, and Tane, Tu, and Rongo, gods of nature, favored their voyage, they would find a new home. They launched double-hulled sailing canoes carved with stone tools from trees, lashed together with braided coconut fiber, with joints filled with caulking made of breadfruit sap and coconut fiber, and sails made of plaited pandanus leaves. They took provisions for the voyage—trusting the voyage would end before the provisions—and seeds and plants for the new land. They navigated by the stars of the northern sky and prayed to Laamaomao, god of the winds. In this way they crossed 2,000 miles of open sea several centuries before the first Vikings left Europe's shores. After many days they came at last to land. Rising before them were islands of a size and splendor beyond anything they had ever seen before. They gave to them the name of one of the largest of the islands they had left—*Havaiki.*

And for a thousand years, no one else came.

The next epic voyage of discovery originated in the far distant world of another ocean. It was launched from the shores of England in the summer of 1776, precisely eight days after the rebelling American colonies had issued their Declaration of Independence from England. Captain James Cook, commander of the HMS *Resolution* and the consort vessel HMS *Discovery,* had already established his reputation as England's greatest explorer of the world's uncharted oceans. Cook had discovered dozens of South Pacific islands on two earlier voyages. On this, his third venture into the Pacific realm, he was looking beyond tiny islands to a greater discovery, the legendary Northwest Passage that navigators believed to be a seaway link between the Pacific and the Atlantic. His explorations would take Cook, for the first time, north of the equator into unfamiliar seas of the North Pacific. He sailed from England, around the southern tip of Africa, to New Zealand, and on to Tahiti. Then, reaching an uncharted atoll north of Tahiti on December 24, 1777, Cook dropped anchor for several days and named it Christmas Island. When he left, he set a course for the top of the North American continent and did not expect to see land again until he had crossed some 3,000 miles of ocean.

But just 16 days later, at dawn on January 18, 1778, all hands on the reeling decks of the *Resolution* and the *Discovery* gazed in astonishment at a high island hovering into view as a deep blue hump of land on the northeast horizon. Then another island, looking smaller from a distance but rising even higher out of the water, was soon sighted to the north. Cook had chanced upon the islands of Oahu and Kauai. It was Kauai where he landed, making the first contact between the Western World and the Hawaiian Islands. The great navigator was filled with wonder at the presence of such islands this far north, and amazed as well by their inhabitants.

"At this time we were in some doubt whether or not the land before us was inhabited," Cook wrote in his journal. "This doubt was soon cleared up, by seeing some canoes coming off from the shore towards the ships. I immediately brought to to give them time to come up, there were three and four men in each and we were agreeably surprised to find them of the same nation as the people of Otahiete [Tahiti] and the other islands we had lately visited." It was with great admiration of the Polynesian sailing skills that Cook wrote, "How shall we account for this nation spreading itself so far over this vast ocean?"

The Hawaiians had lived in splendid isolation for a thousand years. Now, with the coming of Western man, it seemed that history was determined to accelerate its pace in exposing these once hidden masterpieces of nature to the rest of the world. British explorers were soon followed by British traders, then American and French and Russian. Whalers came from Nantucket and New Bedford. Missionaries came from New England. Traders and merchants and farmers came from throughout the United States and from Europe. The islands were planted in sugar cane, which had grown wild before the plantations, and workers were brought from China, Japan, Puerto Rico, Korea, the Philippines, Portugal, Germany, and Norway, to work in the cane fields. Not everyone stayed, but many did. From throughout the United States, more people continued to come, and more stayed. Hawaii had been a divided chain of islands ruled by opposing chiefs at the time of Cook's arrival, but within 17 years it was united as one kingdom under the iron rule of King Kamehameha, who used Western guns and ships to conquer the Islands in bloody invasions that pitted armies of thousands of Hawaiians against each other. Nearly a hundred years later, American businessmen used the force of arms to overthrow the Hawaiian monarchy, replacing it briefly with a republic, then annexing it to the United States as a territory. Ultimately, at the dawning of the jet age, Hawaii became America's 50th state in 1959. Hawaii had gone from a virtual Stone Age to a modern, 20th-century society in less than 200 years.

A Strong Presence of History

Despite this rush of history across the Hawaiian Islands following the arrival of Cook, evidence of the past has not been completely lost among the proliferation of high-rises and the explosive growth of tourism. On each island—yes, even on crowded Oahu in the shadow of Waikiki's concrete and glass towers—there is an abundance of visible history, tracing an island evolution from the days of ancient Hawaii to the monarchy period, from the 19th-century era of missionaries and whalers to the long reign of "King Cane" that planted the roots of Hawaii's multi-ethnic society in the Islands' sugar cane fields. And of course the pivotal role of Hawaii in America's military and war history is still very much in evidence.

Unlike colder climates, where history is contained in houses, churches, and government buildings, Hawaii's distant past is often found on the land itself. *Aina,* or land, is a sacred word in the Hawaiian language, a spiritual feeling more than a possessive one. The words first proclaimed by King Kamehameha III in 1843, *"Ua mau ke ea o ka aina i ka pono,"* later became the official motto of the 50th state: "The life of the land is preserved in righteousness." State and federal laws have made archaeology a priority ahead of almost any development, requiring archaeological site investigations before any new construction can begin. This not only results in protecting what is known to exist, but often leads to new archaeological discoveries. A stronger sense of preservation has also brought new examples of coexistence between Hawaii's past and present. Luxury resorts built on the South Kohala Coast of the Big Island of Hawaii in the 1980s have been careful to maintain the historical integrity of the land. Hotels, condominiums, and golf courses have come into place without disturbing important archaeological sites. For instance, the ancient King's Trail, a narrow footpath through the coastal lava fields linking the Kohala and Kona Coasts, is now more prominently in view because it parallels the seaside golf courses of the Mauna Lani and Waikoloa resorts. Also protected and restored within the grounds of these two Big Island resorts are ancient Hawaiian burial caves, royal fish ponds, and petroglyph fields. Such sites have not only been saved from the bulldozer, but they are now well marked by informational signs to educate resort guests about the Hawaiian way of life that thrived here for hundreds of years.

Any visitor with a serious interest in Hawaiian history should spend as much time as possible on the Big Island of Hawaii, which surpasses all others in its wealth of historical sites. There is simply a stronger feeling of Hawaii as it was in the days before Cook on this island. It is, after all, the island that gave birth to the conquering warrior King Kamehameha. You can view both his birthplace and the seaside retreat where he spent his last days. Kamehameha's birthplace is a remote, windswept, haunting site on the lonely northwestern shores of the Big Island. From this silent place in history you can look across the churning waters to the eastern coastline of Maui, just 26 miles away, and imagine the ocean covered by the ships and war canoes of Kamehameha's mighty armies as they launched the invasion of Maui that began the first successful conquest of all the islands. Close by Kamehameha's birthplace is Mookini Heiau, one of the island's many *heiaus,* the sacred places of worship that Hawaiians built by erecting massive walls of lava rock. Mookini Heiau is believed to be more than 1,500 years old and, according to Hawaiian legend, its 30-foot-high walls were built in a single night by 18,000 men carrying stones from a valley 14 miles away.

Kamehameha, born in the 1750s, was brought to Mookini Heiau for secretive birth rites before he was rushed away and hidden in Waipio Valley to protect him from certain death. Island chiefs had been warned by their *kahuna* (priests) that the child was destined to be "a slayer of chiefs." The *kahuna* were correct. At Puukohola Heiau National Historic Site, you can view the last major Hawaiian temple built, and one of the largest in the Islands. It was erected in 1791 at the command of Kamehameha to honor his war god. For an appropriate dedication Kamehameha invited his principal rival on the island, Chief Keoua, and had him slain immediately upon his arrival, then offered him as a sacrifice upon the new *heiau.*

A more peaceful view of the time of King Kamehameha is to be seen in the Kona Coast village of Kailua. This is where Kamehameha returned from Honolulu in 1812, accompanied by several favorites from among his 21 wives, to quietly live out the last seven years of his life. *Kamakahonu,* "The Turtle Eye," was Kamehameha's home, where he also rebuilt Ahuena Heiau and rededicated it to Lono, god of agriculture and prosperity. The shoreline site, now part of the grounds of Hotel King Kamehameha, was reconstructed under supervision of the Bishop Museum to show visitors how the living complex would have looked when Kamehameha lived there.

The Big Island's inventory of historic sites also includes Puuhonua o Honaunau, "Place of Refuge at Honaunau," a sacred sanctuary originally built about 1550 as a place of escape for Hawaiians who had broken the sacred laws, or *kapu,* and now authentically rebuilt as a national historical park; Lapakahi State Historical Park, a reconstructed Hawaiian fishing village depicting how the Hawaiians lived, worked, and played on this site more than 600 years ago; and Kealakekua Bay and the Captain Cook Monument, marking the spot where the great navigator was slain in a tragic confrontation between Hawaiians and the English seamen.

The Royal Kingdom of Hawaii

Hawaii is the only state in America that was once a royal kingdom, so the history of Hawaii's kings and queens naturally holds great fascination for visitors. The days of the monarchy are most prominently recalled on the island of Oahu, where most of the royal drama occurred, after a short interlude in Lahaina, during the early 19th century. Grand showplace of Hawaiian royalty is Iolani Palace, the elaborately restored, four-story Italian Renaissance palace that Hawaii's last reigning king, David Kalakaua, built in 1882 after he had made his first trip to America, viewed the White House, and returned home feeling himself underhoused.

It was in Iolani Palace that Hawaii's only reigning queen and last reigning monarch, Queen Liliuokalani, was imprisoned for nearly eight months by the American businessmen who had forcibly removed her from the throne in 1893 and negotiated annexation of the Hawaiian Islands by the United States five years later. It marked the end of a royal dynasty begun by Kamehameha I that lasted 98 years. Following the death of Kamehameha I, the story of Hawaiian royalty became one overshadowed by personal tragedy and a continuing loss of real power. Many of the ruling kings died at an early age, without heirs, and none of them were ever able to summon the leadership skills of Kamehameha I. Indeed, one of the reasons Queen Liliuokalani was deposed was that she exhibited a strong will and a determination to regain power for the throne, thus posing a threat to the vested interests of American businessmen who by then were in firm control of the island economy and its politics.

Not far from downtown Honolulu, in the misty folds of Nuuanu Valley, is another of Oahu's royal treasures, Queen Emma's Summer Palace, home of the wife of King Alexander Liholiho (Kamehameha IV). It is a royal residence with a history of the misfortune that plagued Hawaii's kings and queens. Queen Emma was the Hawaiian-Caucasian granddaughter of John Young, the English seaman who was a trusted adviser to Kamehameha I during the king's successful invasions of Maui and Oahu. Queen Emma at the age of 27 suffered the death of her infant son Prince Albert and her husband the king within 15 months of each other. She then tried in vain to succeed her husband to the throne. In a vote by the Hawaii Legislature, Queen Emma lost to David Kalakaua by a vote of 39 to 6. Thereupon the queen's loyal supporters rioted, stoning the legislature and killing one member by throwing him from a second-story window of Iolani Palace.

Also located in Nuuanu Valley is the Royal Mausoleum, planned by King Kamehameha IV and Queen Emma following the death of little Prince Albert in 1862. Tragically, the king died before construction began. Six of Hawaii's eight monarchs are buried in the Royal Mausoleum: Kings Liholiho (Kamehameha II), Kauikeaouli (Kamehameha III), Alexander Liholiho (Kamehameha IV), Lot (Kamehameha V), David Kalakaua, and Queen Liliuokalani. King William Lunalilo is buried in a tomb outside the entrance to Kawaiahao Church, in deference to his expressed desire to remain closer to his people. The remains of King Kamehameha I, after his death at Kailua-Kona in 1819, were taken by high chiefs to a secret burial cave and have never been found. Hawaiians have a saying: "The morning star alone knows where Kamehameha's bones are guarded."

Missionaries and Whalers

The year 1820 was a pivotal one in the history of the Hawaiian Islands. King Kamehameha I had died the previous year and immediately afterward came the death of the *kapu* system that had dictated the order of Hawaiian society since the first Polynesians had found a new home on these distant islands. *Kapus* were forbidden acts, laws that primarily set the ruling *alii* above the commoners. As pagan as it might seem in retrospect, involving as it did human sacrifice and punishment by death for breaking the *kapu* (such as the forbidden act of women eating with the men), it was the accepted governing system of the Hawaiians and they had followed it for untold generations. After Kamehameha I, the *kapu* system crumbled under the weight of Western influences.

It was during this transitional period that the brig *Thaddeus,* 168 days out of Boston, arrived in 1820 with the first company of the American Board of Commissioners for Foreign Missions. The missionaries dispersed their meager numbers among the main islands of Hawaii, Maui, Kauai, and Oahu. At first they lived in grass shacks, but in 1821 the first permanent mission station was erected in Honolulu. It was a white frame house that had been prefabricated in New England and brought around the Horn with the first missionaries. That pioneer building, now known as the Mission Houses Museum, still stands on its original site, not far from Iolani Palace and the State Capitol. Other exhibits of early missionary history are preserved throughout the islands, at such 19th-century missionary homes as the Bailey House in Wailuku, Maui, and the Waioli Mission House in Hanalei, Kauai, and in many beautiful old stone churches on all of the Islands.

Some of the best preservation and restoration of missionary history, as well as many other facets of 19th-century Hawaii history, is found in the colorful little seaside village of Lahaina on the west shores of Maui. Lahaina has become one of the most popular tourist meccas in Hawaii, crowded with bars, restaurants, shops, and elbow-to-elbow tourists, but it has also kept its past highly visible. The Lahaina Restoration Foundation, one of the most progressive historical organizations in Hawaii, has restored an impressive number of historic sites to their original condition.

Lahaina's history is especially dynamic because it played such an important role in the early days of two groups of voyagers who landed in Lahaina with entirely opposite ideas—the missionaries and the whalers. The first whaling ships began appearing in 1819. A year later the missionaries came. And for the next 40 years, until the decline of the Pacific whaling industry, the missionaries and the whaling crews were locked in moral battle to determine who would prevail in Lahaina. The missionaries had come to deliver the Hawaiians from their "heathen" ways by converting them to Christianity. The whaling crews, after long months at sea, came to Lahaina for revelry, landing with an enormous appetite for grog and women. Attempts by the missionaries to ban the sale of liquor and prohibit Hawaiian women from boarding the whaling ships—laws that came into effect for a period—sometimes resulted in violence. Ships fired on the town and angry sailors rioted in the streets of Lahaina.

The history of this fascinating era is well preserved in the center of Lahaina. Here you can tour the Baldwin House, a restored 1835 missionary home. Adjacent to it is the Masters' Reading Room, a coral building erected in 1834 as a gentlemanly retreat for whaling captains and masters who often aided the missionaries in their struggle to prevent the ship's crews from debauching Lahaina. Also near the Lahaina Harbor are the ruins of the Brick Palace occupied briefly by King Kamehameha I, and the site of the 1854 Lahaina Fort; the Lahaina Courthouse, built in 1859, is still in use. Moored at the harbor is the Carthaginian II, rebuilt as a four-rigged bark to depict an 1850s whaling ship.

The Sugar Isles

The most dynamic and lasting change to be made to the land and the people of Hawaii came from the cultivation of a crop that had long grown wild in the islands—sugar cane. American merchants in Honolulu financed the planting of the first commercial sugar plantation on Kauai in 1835. Plantations followed on Oahu, Maui, and the Big Island of Hawaii. By the late 1800s, sugar had become "king" in Hawaii. At the end of the 19th century it was virtually Hawaii's only export. By 1910 there were 52 sugar plantations covering 214,000 acres and employing 43,917 workers. By 1920 sugar in Hawaii was worth $119.5 million. King Cane would rule the Islands' economy well into the 20th century, consolidating in turn the power of the famous "Big Five" companies—American Factors (now Amfac), C. Brewer, Alexander & Baldwin, Castle & Cooke, and Theo H. Davies—that controlled the sugar and therefore controlled the Islands economically and politically until after World War II.

It was also because of sugar that Hawaii became the ethnic melting pot of the Pacific. When it first became clear that great profits could be made growing sugar cane in Hawaii, it was also plain that new sources of labor had to be found. The native population had declined drastically as diseases brought to the Islands by foreigners decimated the Hawaiians, whose numbers fell from an estimated 300,000 in 1778 to 71,000 by 1853. For a solution, sugar planters looked to the East. Chinese contract laborers were first brought to Hawaii to work in the cane fields in 1852. Twenty-five years later, alarmed at the number of Chinese (half the plantation work force and a quarter of the total population), the plantation owners sought to offset the Chinese presence by bringing in workers from Portugal. Then, in the 1880s, thousands of Japanese began arriving in Hawaii as contract laborers. They in turn were followed, in lesser numbers, by Koreans and Filipinos. Many of the workers came to Hawaii with the intention of saving the money they earned cutting cane and returning to their homelands at the end of the labor contracts. Some did return, but many more remained and made Hawaii their home. It was the making of one of the most unusual multi-ethnic societies in the world as the Asian ways of life gradually blended with the Hawaiian and American influences in shaping a modern Hawaii unlike any other state in the United States.

Sugar has long since lost its economic dominance over the islands, dropping to second place behind military defense spending by the 1940s and falling even lower on the scale of importance as tourism became the number one Hawaii industry in the 1960s. The death of the sugar industry in Hawaii has been forecast for some time, but "King Cane" still clings to life. You can view the tall green fields of cane waving in the winds on the flatlands and hillsides of Maui, Kauai, and the Big Island. The best exhibit of 19th-century plantation life is the Grove Farm Homestead on Kauai, a sugar plantation dating back to 1864. Grove Farm has been well preserved as an example of the days when each of the island's several plantations were self-contained communities. Visitors to Grove Farm are shown through a camp house, guest cottage, and main plantation home, all looking much as they did when the economy of the Hawaiian Islands was almost wholly dependent on such plantations.

The history of the many ethnic groups that first came to Hawaii to work in the cane fields is visible wherever you go in the islands: beautiful religious shrines such as the Byodo-In Temple on the Windward Side of Oahu and the Lahaina Jodo Mission on Maui; a completely restored Chinese fraternal hall and altar room, the Wo Hing Temple in Lahaina; the old Chinatown section of Honolulu, where many of the Chinese moved after leaving the cane fields of the Neighbor Islands and where the residential and commercial scene is now an exotic mixture of Chinese, Filipinos, Japanese, Koreans, Caucasians, Hawaiians, and Samoans. On the islands of Maui, Kauai, and the Big Island you will also find plantation ghost towns, ramshackle old communities with boarded-up wooden storefronts that once did a prosperous business when the towns were filled with plantation workers. Some of these forgotten plantation towns have found new life as young artisans and entrepreneurs move in, refurbish the turn-of-the-century buildings and open colorful boutiques, art galleries, restaurants, and shops.

Hawaii's Military Role

Hawaii's strategic importance as a naval base in the Pacific was predestined as early as 1840 when the first U.S. geodetic survey of the Hawaiian Islands singled out Pearl Harbor, lying not far west of downtown Honolulu, as having enormous potential for harboring America's largest war ships. Control of Pearl Harbor by the U.S. government was a major negotiating point in granting duty-free access to the American sugar market for Hawaii's planters. King David Kalakaua and the Hawaiian population tried in vain to oppose any military takeover of the harbor. But in 1887 Kalakaua reluctantly agreed to a reciprocity treaty that gave Hawaii sugar planters valuable trade protections and gave the United States exclusive use of Pearl Harbor as a naval station. Dredging of the channel and construction of the drydock began in 1908—one year after Fort Shafter, headquarters for the Army, had become the first permanent military post in the islands—and Pearl Harbor was formally dedicated by the U.S. Navy in 1919. It was 22 years later, in the dawn hours of December 7, 1941, that Pearl Harbor was thrust upon the consciousness of the entire American public by the attack on the U.S. Pacific Fleet by Japanese planes and the loss of more than 2,500 lives. Tours of Pearl Harbor and the *USS Arizona* Memorial draw some 1.5 million visitors every year.

The military presence in the Islands, however, ranges well beyond Pearl Harbor. Schofield Barracks, made famous by the movie and the book, *From Here to Eternity* (a World War II novel written by James Jones, who was a young soldier at Schofield) remains an important army training post. The central Oahu land occupied by Schofield Barracks was first assigned to the U.S. Army after the annexation of Hawaii in 1898. Nearly a million soldiers trained at Schofield during World War II. Other large military bases on Oahu include Hickam and Wheeler Air Force Bases, Ft. Shafter Army Base, and Kaneohe Marine Corps Air Station. There are more than

50,000 military personnel in Hawaii and more than 60,000 military dependents, almost all of them on the island of Oahu. Military spending, close to $2 billion annually, is second only to tourism as a source of income in Hawaii.

The Final Step—Our 50th State

Although the design to make the Hawaiian Islands a state was clearly stated in the years following the overthrow of the monarchy and annexation to the United States as a territory, Hawaii's struggle for statehood was one of the longest, and among the most acrimonious, in American history. It took Hawaii longer than any other U.S. territory except New Mexico to become a state. Racism was the central cause for delaying statehood as conservative elements of Congress resisted for years the idea of Hawaii as a state because of the Islands' heavily non-Caucasian population. The Japanese surprise attack on Pearl Harbor served to harden the opposition in Congress and among the American public at large. Even when racial barriers began to recede, there were new fears implanted in official minds: Hawaii's labor movement of the 1950s was charged with being Communist controlled. Eventually, however, nothing could deny the demand for statehood, and Congress finally passed the bill admitting Hawaii into the union on March 12, 1959. When word reached Honolulu the mayor began ringing the bell at Honolulu Hale (City Hall) and the Royal Hawaiian Band played "Hawaii Ponoi." Car horns honked, church bells chimed, and ships' whistles blew. People danced in the streets far into the night, and the sky turned red from a giant bonfire on Sand Island. The flames were visible from hillside homes throughout Honolulu, where the tallest building on the island at the time was the 10-story Aloha Tower that had been built in 1921 to guide steamships into Honolulu Harbor.

Into the Jet Age

The year 1959 was to mark yet another turning point in the history of Hawaii. In the same year as statehood was granted, the first Boeing 707 jet airplanes arrived. They streaked across the Pacific from the West Coast of California to Honolulu in an astonishing five hours, nearly two hours faster than the previous speed record. No one could have foreseen at the time what incredible changes these jets would bring to the new state of Hawaii.

During that first year of statehood, 243,216 tourists visited Hawaii. The stream of tourist traffic, and the accompanying rise of hotels and condominiums, grew at a frenzied pace until tourism was soon the dominant industry in Hawaii, the most important source of income on nearly all the Islands. Today, the annual number of tourists has climbed above the 5 million level.

It all began, of course, on Waikiki Beach. The first tourist hotel, the Moana, was built there in 1901. It still stands, now operated as a Sheraton hotel, dwarfed by the high-rises that have grown up around it. In the previous century, Hawaiian royalty had kept homes on Waikiki Beach, followed in turn by prosperous businessmen who used Waikiki cottages to escape the noise and congestion of Honolulu. While the Moana was the pioneer on Waikiki Beach, the era of major tourism for Hawaii actually began in 1927, when the Matson Navigation Company built the majestic Royal Hawaiian Hotel. Until World War II, sailing to Hawaii on one of the Matson luxury liners and spending long, languid vacations on Waikiki Beach, pampered in the splendor of the Royal Hawaiian Hotel, was one of the world's most glamorous forms of travel. It also helped to make Waikiki Beach one of the best known beaches in the world. The Royal Hawaiian Hotel has also survived as a reminder of the early days of island tourism, when "Boat Day" was always the cause for a festive celebration of song and dance and flower leis in a distinctive island greeting for the arrival of each ship.

Now, of course, thousands of tourists arrive daily in Waikiki and throughout the Hawaiian Islands, flying there almost as routinely as they might make any other ordinary vacation trip. *Almost,* but not quite, because Hawaii is not an ordinary place and a trip to these islands could only become routine to someone who has suffered a complete loss of sensitivity to the natural beauty of land and sea so richly endowed upon islands where so many people have come from so many different, distant places to live the special magic that is Hawaii.

HAWAII'S BEACHES

Sizes, Shapes, Moods, and Colors for Every Taste

By
TOM and KAREN HORTON

The beaches of Hawaii come in a wonderful array of sizes, shapes, and even colors. They are the ribbons—usually white or golden brown, but sometimes black and also green—tied around the island packages of pleasures. Many of the coastlines are knitted together by one long, wide, sandy beach after another. Some of the beaches wait right outside your hotel or condominium. Others are set off by matching green strips of grassy public parks. And many are hidden from easy public view or access, sunning silently behind thickets of kiawe trees, between high rocky points, and in secluded coves. There are beaches to suit every taste: beaches filled with people and activity; quiet beaches affording almost complete privacy; beaches that are ideal for swimming, surfing, windsurfing, bodysurfing, snorkeling, surf fishing, and Hobie Cat sailing; or beaches that are best for simply taking the sun, strolling barefoot in the sand and surf, or sharing a romantic sunset.

Like everything else in Hawaii, the beaches can be enjoyed 12 months of the year. January or June, you can usually count on sunny days, and you can always rely on the Pacific waters to be warm and clear.

There are, however, vast differences in the safety conditions of the surf off different beaches at different times of the year. The rule for approaching Hawaii beaches is simple but critical: exercise extreme caution any time you leave the beach and enter the water. The beauty of the beaches and the seemingly gentle advance of the ocean surf can be deceiving, lulling visitors into dangerous assumptions. Beneath the gently rolling waves may lurk a powerful rip current or a sudden drop into deep water. Shorebreaks, places where waves break close to shore or directly on it, can make swimming extremely hazardous. Backwash, when the water from a spent wave returns seaward, can also spell trouble if the backwash moves at a fast speed over a sudden dropoff from the shoreline. Rip currents, the result of pressure building up from successive incoming waves, are an unseen danger that causes most of the drownings and near-drownings at island beaches.

Some beaches also change character from summer to winter, although on the surface they may appear to be equally inviting on a warm, sunny day. But the winter months, roughly from September to April, bring high surf and strong rip currents that make swimming inadvisable. This is particularly true of any beach that is not protected by coral reefs from the open ocean, allowing the powerful surf to come directly into the beach. Such beaches are always potentially more dangerous for average swimmers, but the danger rises considerably during high winter surf.

Naturally, the beaches fronting the major resort developments are generally the safest beaches for average swimmers and bodysurfers. Public beach parks are also good choices. Remote beaches with few if any people on them may appear to be a wonderful alternative to a crowded resort beach, but there are often dangerous surf conditions present. You should never venture into the water alone at a deserted beach. And if you find yourself at a beach with other people and notice that no one is swimming, there's probably a good reason, such as a dangerous undertow or strong rip currents. When in doubt about the safety of the ocean at a beach where there are no lifeguards, the second-best approach is to ask an island resident if it's safe to swim—but the best approach is to find another beach with a lifeguard and some assurance of safety.

To avoid having your vacation turn into a painful nightmare, you should also exercise caution and take protective measures against the sun. Don't take the Hawaiian sun at face value. The sun is hotter in Hawaii because the Islands are close to the equator, meaning you can burn more quickly than you would at a beach back home. And if you try to acquire a golden Hawaiian tan too fast, you may end up red as a broiled lobster instead. The intensity of the island sun during midday, especially during the summer months, can mean sunburn for anyone who exposes their pale skin to the sun for two or three hours. Ration your sun exposure carefully, increasing it gradually, and don't stint on sun screen lotions.

Overall, however, you will find the beaches of Hawaii easy to find, generally safe, wonderfully relaxing, and impossible to ignore. Whether your preference is for swimming, sunning, something more adventurous, or just sight-seeing, each island has a variety of beaches from which to choose.

Oahu Beaches

Waikiki Beach has long been one of the most famous beaches in the world—and most of the time it looks as if a good portion of the world is represented there, elbow-to-elbow on beach towels covering nearly every square inch of sand. In truth, Waikiki Beach is not one but a series of beaches along a curving shoreline some two miles long, from the shadow of Diamond Head directly across from Kapiolani Park to the Hilton Hawaiian Village complex that is the last of the lineup of high-rise hotels fronting the beach. Each section of the beach has its own name and its own personality as well. It begins with Sans Souci Beach, in front of the New Otani Kaimana Beach Hotel (opposite Kapiolani Park), where Robert Louis Stevenson left this memorable endorsement after spending several weeks at the Sans Souci Hotel in 1893: "If anyone desire such old-fashioned things as lovely scenery, quiet, pure air, clear sea water, good food, and heavenly sunsets hung out before his eyes over the Pacific and the distant hills of Waianae, I recommend him cordially to the 'Sans Souci.' "

All of those qualities, except the quiet, still attract millions to Waikiki Beach. The portion at the eastern end, known as Queen's Surf Beach Park, is a less crowded alternative to the stretch of Waikiki Beach directly in front of the high-rise hotels, and therefore more popular among resident islanders. Beginning with Kuhio Beach Park and Waikiki Beach Center, almost opposite the Hyatt Regency Waikiki, and extending to Royal-Moana Beach (in front of the Moana and Royal Hawaiian Hotels) to Gray's Beach (in front of the Halekulani Hotel), the beach is usually filled with tanning bodies. But this is also where you find the greatest concentration of Waikiki Beach activities, from surfing lessons and outrigger canoe rides to the best surfside beach bars maintained by the Moana and the Royal Hawaiian Hotels. Fort DeRussy Beach, with the greenery of Fort DeRussy Beach Park behind it, is the widest part of Waikiki Beach and another popular choice for residents who try to avoid the crowded areas in front of the hotels; but a rocky, coral bottom makes swimming here less enjoyable (although quite safe). Kahanamoku Beach, named for Hawaii's Olympic swimming champion, legendary surfer, and beloved hero, the late Duke Kahanamoku, fronts the Hilton Hawaiian Village and is one of the most spacious and best parts of Waikiki Beach.

Ala Moana Beach Park, a couple of blocks beyond the western end of Waikiki Beach, is a beautiful beach with the bonus of 76-acre Ala Moana Park. This is the most popular beach among Honolulu residents, an ideal place for good swimming year round, with safe beach and surf conditions for children. Most weekends Ala Moana Beach Park is filled with local families who spend the day picnicking, but it's rarely crowded during the week.

The Windward Coast of Oahu offers a spectacular choice of beaches, but some of them are too hazardous for average swimmers. Sandy Beach Park and Makapuu Beach are the island's most famous bodysurfing beaches, but the high surf and treacherous rip currents make these beaches more a spectator sport for the average visitor (lifeguards make more rescues here than anywhere on the island). Two large, gorgeous beaches farther along the Windward Coast where bodysurfing and swimming can be done safely most of the time are Waimanalo Beach Park and Bellows Field Beach Park. Waimanalo Beach is not usually crowded; Bellows Field Beach, a part of the military reservation that's open to the public on weekends and holidays, is one of the most popular weekend outings for island residents.

Two fine beaches on the Windward Side of Oahu, used mostly by residents of the bedroom community of Kailua and overlooked by most tourists, are Lanikai Beach and Kailua Beach Park. Both are large beaches with safe swimming throughout the year and plenty of elbow room; Kailua Beach has also become the center of windsurfing activity on Oahu.

A jewel of a relatively hidden beach on the Windward Coast, almost an hour's drive from Waikiki, is Malaekahana Beach Park. The crescent-shaped beach is nearly a mile long, secluded from the highway by iron-wood trees and sand dunes. Honolulu families once kept private beach homes at Malaekahana, but it has been expanded into a public park with excellent picnic and camping facilities.

On the North Shore are some of the most famous surfing beaches in the world, due to some of the highest surfing waves on earth. Sunset Beach Park, Ehukai Beach Park, Pupukea Beach Park, Waimea Bay Beach Park, and Haleiwa Beach Park are a surfer's paradise, especially during the winter months when the waves are rolling in at heights of up to 20 feet. Obviously, since only the most experienced surfers dare challenge these waves, the average tourist sticks to the shore—and even here you must be careful during winter months or you could be carried off the beach by a sudden wave of awesome size and power. Some of these beaches are safe for swimming during the summer months, but essentially the water is off limits to all but the brave and the foolhardy from about October through April. (An exception is Haleiwa Beach, with safe swimming all year.)

Maui Beaches

Maui is arguably the island with the best beaches in Hawaii, although Oahu and Kauai partisans will be quick to argue the point. The three major Maui resorts—Kaanapali Beach Resort, Wailea Resort, and Kapalua Resort—all benefit from excellent beach frontage. The coastal strips of condominiums along West Maui in the Kahana–Napili area and in Kihei on the southwest side of Maui also have easy access to beaches. In fact, you are rarely very far from a good beach unless you head Upcountry Maui.

Kaanapali Beach is two miles long with safe swimming and all the attendant beach activities found on the doorstep of resort hotels. All of Kaanapali Beach Resort's hotels and some of the condominiums are located right on the beach, meaning it's relatively crowded (but nothing like Waikiki Beach). There's also excellent snorkeling off Kaanapali Beach, most notably at Black Rock in front of the Sheraton Maui Hotel.

Kapalua Resort's only hotel, the Kapalua Bay Hotel, is a short stroll across manicured lawns to beautiful Kapalua Beach (still known by many locals as Fleming Beach), where there's good swimming, snorkeling, scuba-diving, and windsurfing. The resort condominiums, however, are less conveniently located for easy beach access. About a mile past Kapalua Resort is one of the finest secluded beaches on West Maui, D. T. Fleming Beach Park, a lovely place for a quiet picnic and a few quiet hours under the sun on a long, wide beach protected by low sand dunes and high Kakaluapuna Point. Swimming, however, can be hazardous during high surf.

All along the shores of West Maui, extending to either side of Lahaina for several miles, there are nice beach parks with complete picnic facilities and safe swimming: Lahaina Beach, Launiupoko State Wayside Park, Kulanaokalai Beach, and Wahikuli State Wayside Park. Rarely are they crowded. Kahana Beach is a narrow, often rocky beach flanked by an endless string of condominiums; it is not among Maui's finest beaches in any regard. Immediately north of Kahana Beach, however, Napili Bay shelters a lovely little beach that has long made this a favorite location for Maui condominium vacations.

Wailea Resort, on the southwest shores, is blessed by one of the finest stretch of beaches of any resort in Hawaii. Wailea Beach, which actually consists of five beaches along the curving shoreline, begins in front of the Inter-Continental Maui and Stouffer's Wailea Beach Hotels, winds past the resort condominiums, and extends another couple of miles until it links up with the Kihei area beaches. Kihei may have some of the most unattractive strips of concrete condominiums to be found anywhere in Hawaii, but it also has an unbroken string of good beaches, from Maipoina Oe Lau Beach Park beside Maalaea Bay to Kalama Beach Park and Kamaole Beach Parks (numbered Kamaole I, II, and III). Beyond Wailea Resort there are yet more impressive beaches: Polo Beach, secluded behind low sand dunes with good swimming and snorkeling; and Puu Olai Beach, also known as Makena Beach.

Beaches along the northeast and east side of Maui, where there are no major resort developments, are fewer in number and quality, but some of them appeal to the adventurous who prefer to scout out beaches that are off the tourist track. You will find uncrowded beaches where you can sun, swim, surf, snorkel, scuba, and beachcomb in almost complete privacy. Beaches on the northeast and east side include Waihee Beach Park, Spreckelsville Beach, H.A. Baldwin Park (most popular beach park on this side of Maui), Lower Paia Park (a center of windsurfing), and Hana Beach Park, the safest swimming beach on East Maui.

Big Island Beaches

The first drawback you will hear about the Big Island of Hawaii is that it has no beaches. This is not true. It is true, however, that the Big Island has considerably fewer white sand beaches than the other islands. The reason for this is that the Big Island is the youngest of all the islands, one that in fact is still growing as its volcanoes (the only active volcanoes in the state) continue to erupt and create new pieces of land from lava flowing to the edges of the island. Beaches are larger and more artistically formed on the older islands (Kauai, Oahu, Maui), where nature has had more time to apply the handiwork of the elements. The largest beaches on any island will be found on coasts exposed to North Pacific swells.

On the west coastline of the Big Island, where the majority of the resort hotels and condominiums are located, good beaches are few and far between. But you can still log your beach time on accommodating sand if you choose the right resort or if you are willing to drive a few miles beyond your hotel or condominium. Unquestionably the most perfect hotel beach on the island, perhaps in all of Hawaii, is the one at the Mauna Kea Beach Hotel on the South Kohala Coast. This postcard-perfect vision of a tropical beach, half-moon-shaped around a calm swimming bay with sandy bottom, is a major reason why Laurance Rockefeller selected this site, considered relatively remote at the time, to build one of the world's most beautiful resort hotels in 1965. A few miles south of the Mauna Kea, on the same sunny Kohala Coastline (one of the lowest rainfall coasts in Hawaii), are two newer luxury resorts with good beach frontage, the Mauna Lani Resort and Waikoloa Resort. Although the beaches are not of the same pristine quality as Mauna Kea's, Mauna Lani and Waikoloa do offer large sandy beaches, calm inshore waters for swimming and snorkeling, and a variety of other beach activities. The spectacular Hyatt Regency Waikoloa, a $360-million resort scheduled to open in September of 1988, will also have ample beach frontage. At the northern end of the Kona Coast, the unique South Seas-style Kona Village Resort has a small beach that is not impressive compared to a perfect white sand beach, but it's adequate for sunbathing and swimming.

Hotels and condominiums in the Kona Coast village of Kailua, and all along Alii Drive to Keauhou Bay, have wonderful ocean views and magnificent sunsets, but essentially no beaches. There might be a meager strip of sand in some locations to provide an alternative to the hotel or condo swimming pool, but don't expect to find a quality beach. The best Kailua-Kona has to offer are a couple of small beaches on Alii Drive, the salt-and-pepper-sand beach at Kahaluu Beach Park, and Magic Sands Beach, which is also known as "Disappearing White Sands Beach" because it tends to come and go with the tides.

There is one great non-resort beach on the west coast of the Big Island: Hapuna Beach, about 24 miles north of Keahole Airport, which can compare favorably to a white sand beach on any island. Hapuna Beach is a half-mile long and offers good swimming, snorkeling, and scuba-diving much of the time, although swimming can be hazardous during high winter surf. Hapuna Beach, however, is not expected to remain a nonresort beach much longer. Mauna Kea Properties has begun planning for its South Kohala Resort, which will feature a new luxury hotel overlooking the beach. Two miles north of Mauna Kea Beach Hotel, Spencer Beach Park is a sheltered cove with good swimming and picnic facilities, but the beach is not very good.

The Big Island's most famous beaches are favored more by photographers than beach-goers. These are the black sand beaches at Waipio Bay on the northeast coast and at Kaimu on the southeast coast in the Puna District, as well as an unusual green sand beach at Ka Lae in the Kau District.

Kauai Beaches

As the oldest island in the chain, Kauai has sound scientific support for its claim to have the most beautiful beaches in Hawaii. There are magnificent white sand beaches all around the island, although some of the most gorgeous beaches along the Na Pali Coast on the North Shore are inaccessible except by boat or helicopter. However many are willing to pay the expense of hiring a helicopter to drop them at a secluded beach by themselves. But you will have no trouble finding a beautiful beach on Kauai that's walking distance from your hotel or condominium or, at the worst, a short drive in a rent-a-car.

The South Shore of Kauai is the best for beach lovers, not because the beaches there are necessarily superior to others, but because there is generally more sunshine. The most popular area is Poipu Beach, where hotels such as the Waiohai, the Poipu Beach Hotel, and the Sheraton Kauai are blessed by a string of Poipu beaches that offer some of the island's best swimming, snorkeling, and bodysurfing—plus the island's most reliable sunny weather. For an unusual excursion, try Salt Pond Beach Park, a short drive from Poipu; it has safe swimming, a shady park for picnicking, ancient salt ponds, and interesting tide pools.

Hotels and condominiums along the east shores of Kauai also have excellent beach frontage, but the beaches here are often windy and the swimming conditions less than ideal because of strong surf and potentially dangerous rip currents during winter months. The choices include Hana-maulu Beach, just north of Lihue; Lydgate Beach Park, just south of the Wailua River and a popular beach park for the east shore; Anahola Bay Beach Park, a few miles north of Kapaa, one of the largest beaches on this side of the island with parts of it generally safe for swimming. In Lihue, the Westin Kauai Hotel overlooks a fine sandy beach, Kalapaki Beach, with balmy views across Kalapaki Bay.

As you move around the island to the North Shore, you will encounter some of Kauai's most scenic beaches. But in winter months on the North Shore you also encounter high surf, and therefore these are not good times to be in the water. Even then, however, the beaches are marvelous for sunning, strolling, beachcombing, and photography. Many are safe for swimming in summer months, some may even be okay during calm winter days, but most of these North Shore beaches do not have lifeguards, so extreme caution should be the rule at all times. Two of the best white sand beaches, both relatively secluded and never crowded, are Kalihi Wai Bay Beach and Anini Beach. The huge Princeville Resort, covering the grassy plateau above Hanalei Bay, has superb ocean views from its many condominiums, but none of them can offer direct beach frontage. The Sheraton Princeville, however, is built as a series of terraced buildings cascading down the face of Puupoa Point, so that guests not only have sensational views of the ocean and Hanalei Bay, but can follow terraced steps down to a sandy beach. In nearby Hanalei Town, the long, curving beach looking out on half-moon-shaped Hanalei Bay is one of the most pleasant beaches on the island. Two miles past Hanalei Town is Kauai's most celebrated beach, Lumahai Beach, where much of the movie *South Pacific* was filmed. Just before the end of the road at Haena Point, Haena Beach Park has lovely white sand beaches, picnic facilities, and good swimming during summer months. At the end of the North Shore road, Kee Beach is another perfect jewel of a beach, with good swimming and snorkeling in summer.

Some of Kauai's best beaches are relatively unknown to tourists. These are the several miles of Kekaha Beaches on the western shore, where there are no resort hotels or condominiums. If you want beaches with plenty of elbow room, these are worth the drive.

Molokai Beaches

Like most everything else about Molokai, there is a quiet sense of undisturbed beauty along the island's beaches. Since there is only one resort development on Molokai and few tourists, there is essentially no such thing as a crowded beach on the island.

The Kaluakoi Hotel and Golf Club and the two luxury condominium complexes at the Kaluakoi Resort on the west end of the island overlook long, wide, white sand beaches. From here the sunset views are sensational, and once the sky darkens you can see the lights of Oahu twinkling 23 miles away, across the Kaiwi Channel. The down side to all this is that the wind blows fairly regularly and quite strongly at this west end of Molokai, and the swimming off the beaches is not always safe because they are unprotected by any coral reefs, resulting in dangerous currents and frequently high surf. You will no doubt marvel at the beauty of Papohaku Beach, just south of Sheraton Molokai, the largest white sand beach in Hawaii. It is more than two miles long and 100 yards wide; during World War II, U.S. Marines practiced beach landings here before shipping out to invade Japanese-held islands in the Pacific.

The small hotels and condominiums found along the south shore of Molokai, in or near the island's only town, Kaunakakai, face the ocean, but do not have quality beaches.

Driving around the east end of Molokai, you'll pass a number of small, scenic beaches, as well as beautiful bays with melodic names: Honouli Wai, "Bay of the Dark Blue Water," and Honouli Maloo, "Dry Dark Bay." At the end of the road you come to Halawa Valley, one of the most scenic spots in Hawaii. There is a long, curving beach at the head of Halawa Valley, with picnic facilities and safe swimming on calm days, but there are hazardous rip currents during the frequent high surf. It is certainly one of the most peaceful, scenic places for a picnic anywhere on the island.

Lanai Beaches

The tiny island of Lanai, used almost exclusively for growing pineapple and presently limited in tourist accommodations to one small lodge, has some fine beaches that are actually used a lot by visitors from Maui. Catamarans and sailing yachts make daily crossings from Lahaina to Lanai, where the day's activities include swimming and snorkeling and picnicking at Lanai's pristine beaches.

The two most popular beaches are Hulopoe Beach and Manele Beach, with good swimming, bodysurfing, snorkeling, and scuba-diving. These are located at the lovely twin bays of Hulopoe Bay and Manele Bay, on the south shoreline, and this is where Castle & Cooke, the parent company of Dole, plans to develop Lanai's first tourist resort. Another popular beach for exploring is Shipwreck Beach, on the northeast shoreline, where there is ample evidence of the ships that struck the offshore reef and gave this beach its name.

OAHU

Hub of Island Life

By
LYLE E. NELSON

Lyle E. Nelson, a long-time resident of Hawaii and an extensive traveler, recently retired from the staff of the Honolulu Star-Bulletin *after 31 years.*

One of the most beautiful islands in the world, Oahu, which means "the gathering place," has been host to more than 4 million visitors per year in recent years.

Third largest in area of the Hawaiian Islands after Hawaii and Maui, Oahu's 617 square miles already surpass the British Isles and Japan in density of population. Honolulu, the capital city, is largely responsible for this state of affairs. Its population, over 900,000 strong, increases daily with new citizens arriving by jet in such alarming proportions that political leaders ponder ways to set up barricades without doing an injustice to democracy's inherent right of movement. Having already spread to the city limits and carved big residential sections from mountains and valleys, the population expanded in a vertical direction, beginning in the 1960s. This rash of skyscraper development continues unabated in the 1980s, though slowed by economic constrictions through the mid-1970s. The new look extends from one end of the city to the other, from Waialae to Pearl Harbor, with heavy concentrations of tall buildings in Waikiki, downtown, Punchbowl-Makiki, and the Salt Lake district near Pearl Harbor.

55

But these excrescences are almost lost against the noble background of the Koolau Mountains. When you're motoring around the island, through sugar and pineapple fields and picturesque plantation towns, through rural communities past virgin valleys, and along a coast of desolate grandeur, chances are that you won't be thinking of population explosions. Nor is the landscape defaced; there are no billboards on Oahu, nor on any other Hawaiian Island, thanks to a group of local ladies whose militancy, masked behind the disarming gentility of their collective name, The Outdoor Circle, has forced more than one merchant to renounce the studied ugliness of outdoor advertising.

Despite a recent rush to the suburbs, portions of Oahu thus remain more or less as they were when Captain Cook first saw them more than 200 years ago. The mountains, though pierced by an occasional tunnel and ribboned by roads, have not changed in aspect for centuries. There are two ranges: the Koolau, running from southeast to northwest, and the Waianae, in the western part of the island. Flat-topped Kaala, rising to 4,030 feet in the latter chain, is Oahu's highest peak. Between the two ranges are the fertile Leilehua and Schofield plains, where they grow pineapples, sugar, soldiers, and vast housing tracts reminiscent of suburban America anywhere.

Economically speaking, the military is big business on Oahu. Sugar and pineapple, over the years, have become less economically important. Tourists meanwhile flock to Oahu.

Oahu has the only royal palace on American soil; schools which were functioning when California was illiterate; the only major university within a radius of 2,000 miles; 1,300 miles of improved roads; "the purest water in the world"; cable, radio-telephone, and satellite connection with all parts of the globe; 100 percent electrification of homes; a fire boat in addition to the usual complement of engines; the most cosmopolitan police force on earth; 27 newspapers (published in English, Japanese, Chinese, Filipino, and Korean) from dailies to monthlies; about 200 churches accommodating most of the major religions of the world plus a few you never heard of; two sugar plantations; a pineapple cannery which is the largest fruit-packing plant in the world; the world's most famous beach; and what many regard as America's most exotic city.

Long before most of the brave accomplishments just cited, this town at the crossroads of the Pacific had a reputation. Weary sailors on the highroads of the sea told each other—perhaps in answer to a mad query: Hast seen the White Whale?—of a fair haven in the midst of the vast ocean, a land of languorous, brown-skinned women, soft climate, welcome, and heartsease. When ships put in at Honolulu, it was hard to get the crew back on board.

It still is, even though history has turned that fair haven into a world center, a naval bastion, the bustling boomtown capital of America's fiftieth state.

Much Island development on a king-size scale had its genesis with the arrival in the Islands of the late Henry J. Kaiser. The famed industrial giant came only for a vacation in 1954 but, like many before him and since, he stayed. On arrival, he found the best hotel rooms booked solid for a year in advance. Disgusted, he bought a home in Kahala and decided to look into the hotel shortage.

One year later, he had purchased a slum area on the sea just *ewa* of Fort DeRussy and opened the first palm-thatched cottages of his *Hawaiian*

Village Hotel. After many a hassle with *kamaainas* and public officials, he got a green light from Congress to reclaim submerged lands off his property and created not only a new beach, but that poster adjunct of a South Sea resort: a tropical lagoon. He consented to use the moon already established above the premises, but decided to plant half a moon on his property. Using Kaiser aluminum, naturally, 23 of Kaiser's men took 23 hours to put up a moonlike geodesic dome designed by Buckminster Fuller. Today, more than 1,200 people can sit down in it, under a chandelier like something out of the old Roxy theater, and enjoy the Don Ho Show.

"The equivalent of more Waikikis will be required and assuredly will be built to keep pace with the jet age," he said before he died in 1967. Kaiser sold the village to the Hilton chain for a tidy profit, and he also developed a massive village of houses in and around an old mullet pond in the Koko Head area on 6,000 acres leased from Bishop Estate.

Do not be alarmed at what happened to Honolulu. The billion-dollar building boom continues. But this growth was inevitable in the face of a burgeoning U.S. population and heightened interest in Hawaii as a tourist magnet. Waikiki perhaps has suffered the most from this growth. The land is valuable and scarce. This means high-rise buildings, some ugly, some not. In the 1930s Waikiki was filled with small single-family bungalows lower than the palms. A recent survey showed that now 1.8 percent of all housing is independent houses; the rest consists of hotels, apartments, townhouses, duplexes, or condos. Whether to build skyscrapers or restrict their height pained planners and politicians for years. Obviously the developers usually won, but not always. The high-rise building joined the television antenna and freeway to pull Polynesia into the American way of despoliation in the name of progress. The freeways and suburban tracts have caused traffic jams that rival Los Angeles in intensity, and make the question of a fixed-guideway mass transit system a major political argument that pits perplexed planners against ecologists in sustained conflicts. Heavy traffic is caused by the highest car-to-road-capacity ratio in the country. A few years ago, North Dakota had about the same number of registered vehicles as Hawaii. But Hawaii puts them on 3,900 miles of road, whereas North Dakota has 106,530 miles of highway.

Yet this burgeoning city, sprawled out for fifteen miles between the dazzling green backdrop of the Koolau mountains and the blue Pacific, still keeps its ancient charm. The state legislature still opens in an atmosphere of flowers, music, and *aloha.* There is nothing perfunctory, nothing synthetic about the *hulas,* the music, and the smiles which greet the *malihini.* The tradition of Hawaiian hospitality remains intact. The spirit of this capital, open-hearted, uncritical, affectionate, is too firmly established to be crushed by domes and monoliths. Honolulu is still a fair haven. And it's still a hard place to leave.

Exploring Honolulu

Headquarters for your Honolulu sightseeing is probably a poolside chair or a mat on Waikiki Beach, and you may be tempted to do all your sightseeing from here in a supine position. There is much to be said for this method. It will leave an indelible impression of three things Hawaii is famous for: sun, surf, and beautiful women. If you have the strength, roll

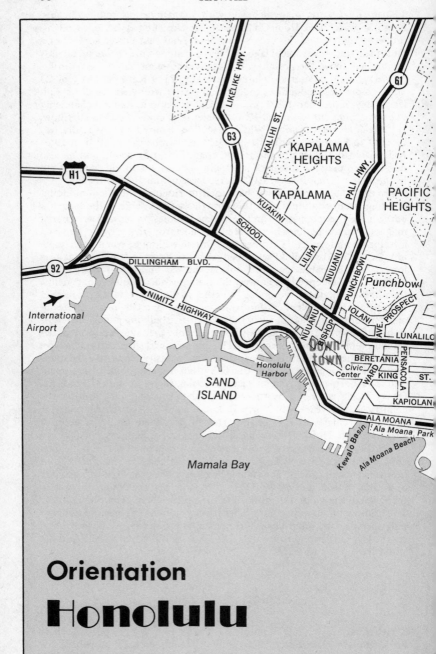

Orientation

Honolulu

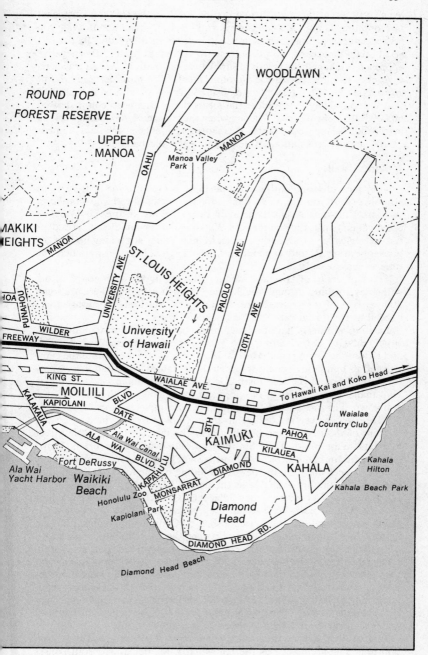

over and look at the map. It may tempt you to *holoholo* (go someplace) in Honolulu. If not, you can always roll back and read about what you missed later, regaling your friends with what you didn't do. "We didn't go to Iolani Palace; we didn't see the Pali." In some quarters, this negative approach is taken as the height of sophistication. With Hawaiian travelers, it reaches its climax with the announcement, "We most certainly didn't go to Waikiki." One reason some visitors give Waikiki a wide margin is that tourists always outnumber the locals there. One head count showed 50,000 tourists in Waikiki on a day when there were 18,700 locals working in the hotels and restaurants. Permanent residents in Waikiki number 14,000, mostly in small apartments and a few old bungalows.

Manoa Valley

Your map of Honolulu reveals that there is much to see or to miss, as you choose. If you are at Waikiki, directly north, ahead and *mauka* of you, are Kalakaua Avenue, the main drag of Waikiki; the Ala Wai, the canal which marks the boundary of Waikiki: a lower-middle-class residential section called Moiliili; then green Manoa Valley stretching up into the pocket between Round Top and St. Louis Heights. Many visitors take the time to look over Manoa.

The University of Hawaii campus is the highlight of Manoa. Visitors will enjoy strolling through the 300-acre Manoa campus. There are some 500 varieties of trees and shrubs, including the celebrated "sausage tree" as well as the "dead rat" and "cannonball" trees.

Leading architects have designed many of the buildings, including Ossipoff, Edward Durell Stone, Leo Woo, John Carl Warneke, I. M. Pei, and Skidmore, Owings and Merrill. Many works of art decorate the campus and its buildings. The most famous is the mural by the late Jean Charlot in the lobby of the administration building, Bachman Hall. It depicts Hawaiians in two stages of development from loincloth to academic cap and gown. The most interesting sculpture on campus is probably Alexander Liberman's fiery red-orange abstract, *Gate of Hope,* which is located in front of the engineering building near the intersection of Dole Street and East-West Road. Tony Smith, who once worked for Frank Lloyd Wright, did the black steel "The Fourth Sign," referring to the astrological sign of Cancer, fronting the new art building on the mall. (Handouts for self-guided tours are available at the office of University Relations.)

Located on a 21-acre campus adjacent to the University of Hawaii at Dole Street and East–West Road, the unique East–West Center is a national educational institution established by Congress in 1960 to promote better relations and understanding between the United States and nations of Asia and the Pacific through cooperative study, training and research. Each year the Center has some 2,500 participants who come from more than 40 nations and territories to exchange experiences and ideas on problems of mutual concern to East and West in conferences, workshops, seminars, and research projects. Some 33,000 persons have participated in Center programs to date. The proper name for E–WC is Center for Cultural and Technical Interchange Between East and West, Inc.

Just strolling among the grounds and magnificent buildings is in itself uplifting. The architect was the renowned I. M. Pei. Burns Hall houses the five institutes and administrative offices. Jefferson Hall, the centerpiece, is the starting point for free guided tours at 1:30 P.M. Wednesday and Thursday, telephone 944–7283. Jefferson's interiors feature panelling of teakwood from Thailand and murals by two internationally renowned artists—Charlot of Hawaii and Affandi of Indonesia. A serene and symbolic Japanese garden, donated by major Japanese business interests, lies behind Jefferson. A willow tree from the Imperial Palace grounds in Japan is a gift from the Emperor. You can have a cafeteria-style lunch here overlooking the gardens. The food reflects many of the cultures represented at the Center. Next to Jefferson is a charming little Thai pavilion. The newest addition is the Center for Korean Studies modeled after the 14th century Kyongbok Palace in Seoul.

Punahou School, one of the oldest prep schools in America, is located at Wilder Avenue and Punahou Street at the entrance to Manoa. One reason for visiting Punahou School presents itself between July and October at night, when the night-blooming cereus is in flower on the stone wall which bounds the campus on the *ewa* (Punahou Street) side. Called *Panini-o-Kapunahou* (the Punahou cactus) by Hawaiians, these flowers are a Mexican cactus brought by a sailor from Acapulco and given to one of the early missionary teachers at Punahou Academy. The teacher planted them here, and they still bloom to the delight of all who behold them. Come about 8 P.M. (darkness falls early in the tropics) to watch the beautiful white petals unfold, exposing a sunburst of yellow stamens. The spectacle is especially memorable on moonlit nights.

Behind the University of Hawaii is Mid-Pacific Institute, at 2445 Kaala Street off University Avenue. There are two color attractions on the green campus of this private prep school. One is provided by that immigrant from tropical Asia, the rainbow shower tree *(Cassia hybrida)*. This particular specimen runs a gamut from pale lemon yellow to rosy apricot from June until the end of August. The second attraction is the 90-foot mural on the façade of the auditorium by the noted Island artist Juliette Mae Fraser. The late Miss Fraser put the rainbow shower tree into the shade, and her production blooms the whole year round. Kawaiahao Hall, the big stone edifice, is the oldest multi-story building in the valley. Built in 1908, it was renovated and converted to a Fine Arts Center in 1982. (The institute is open from 8 A.M. to 3:30 P.M.)

Deep in Manoa Valley at 3016 Oahu Avenue, is the Waioli Tea Room (with restaurant, gift shop, and snack bar) owned and operated by The Salvation Army and featuring fresh-baked pastries made daily on the premises. Lunch is served in a setting of tropical foliage viewed from an open lanai dining room or the more formal windowed Kauai Room. Chief attraction on the grounds is Robert Louis Stevenson's Grass House, transplanted here from Waikiki in the 1920s. Whether the famous author actually wrote in this house is a moot point. In any event, it's a charming version of the little grass shack. Also visit the Waioli Chapel and view the unusual stained glass windows by local artist Erica Karawina. To see the chapel you may have to slip in between weddings involving young couples from Japan who arrive by limousine in a steady procession all day long. Waioli is open from 8 A.M. to 3:30 P.M. daily except Sunday and some holidays, but reservations are suggested (988–2131).

To the right of Manoa Valley are St. Louis Heights, Palolo Valley, and Wilhelmina Rise, topped by Maunalani Heights and the newer housing developments on the hill ridge stretching toward Hawaii Kai. Seen at night from the Ala Wai, these elevated neighborhoods look like beautiful diamond clips sparkling against the velvet blackness of the valleys.

At the base of Wilhelmina Rise is a residential area called Kaimuki. It is almost like a separate town, with stores and banks along its main street, Waialae Avenue. Going west, or *ewa*, Waialae Avenue eventually becomes King Street, the main street of downtown Honolulu. At this end of Waialae, on the *mauka* side, you can see the red-tiled roofs of the St. Louis High School and Chaminade College campuses. The Lunalilo Freeway, better known as the H1, slices through Kaimuki and skirts the University toward Pearl Harbor. And then if you go in the other direction from Kaimuki (eastward toward Koko Head) on Waialae Avenue, it passes under the freeway with Kahala Mall on the right and becomes Kalanianaole Highway. If you can pronounce that name trippingly on the tongue, you are already half-Hawaiian.

Kalanianaole Highway passes a number of small *makai* estates, the *mauka* residential suburbs, such as affluent Waialae-Iki, reaching up the hills to the clouds and back into the valleys of Aina Haina, Niu, Kuliouou, and Hawaii-Kai, and leads you to the scenic glories of Koko Head, the Blow Hole, and Makapuu. Here you leave Honolulu and are on your way around the island.

Back to Waikiki

Come back to Waikiki and the map. That noble and familiar crater on your right is Diamond Head. Just behind it, between Kaimuki and Waikiki, is Kapahulu, a slightly bent route that links Waikiki with St. Louis Heights. This mini-district has mostly fast food and other restaurants. Kapahulu also has an answer to San Francisco's Ghirardelli Square, Kilohana Square, a complex of fascinating shops. There are two exclusive little enclaves on the *mauka* and *ewa* slopes of Diamond Head: Diamond Head Circle and Noela Drive. Here you can see some of Honolulu's most attractive architect-designed homes, surrounded by delightful landscaped gardens.

Kapiolani Park, large, flat and shady, flanks Diamond Head on the *ewa* side and is the site of the Honolulu Zoo, which has been greatly improved in recent years. Kapiolani Park is also a major gathering place for Honolulu's vast army of joggers: Honolulu may have the largest percentage of joggers in the United States, or even the world. Kalakaua Avenue and a shoreline string of new high-rise apartment buildings and hotels border the park. The ironwood-lined avenue runs between the park and the buildings along the coast and becomes Diamond Head Road at the southern base of Diamond Head. From here you will have splendid views of the sea. Beyond Diamond Head a small tongue of lava juts out into the Pacific. This is Black Point, studded with homes which have been built to capitalize on lovely views, both *mauka* and *makai*. In atmosphere, this section is not unlike Carmel, California or Cape Ann, Marblehead, and other substantial settlements on the rugged coast of New England.

Luxurious Estates

Beyond Black Point you are in Kahala, an exclusive residential area owned and leased in individual lots by the Bishop Estate. There are some luxurious miniature estates on the *makai* side of Kahala Avenue, some comfortable suburban-looking houses and gardens on the *mauka* side. Aukai Street, which parallels Kahala Avenue one block inland, is Junior Executive Row, as are the broad streets of Waialae-Kahala farther inland.

Kahala Avenue ends at the Waialae Country Club and the fabulous Kahala Hilton Hotel, built in 1963, where a left turn will take you along Kealaolu Avenue to Kalanianaole Highway.

At this point, you will want to look over the $10 million Kahala Mall, a shopping center with a "cool, carpeted, covered" image. It's all inside. You walk over rugs, under chandeliers, and around plants in air-conditioned comfort to shop at 51 stores in a unique 20 acre "one-stop" concept complex. The Kahala Mall will complete the eastern end of Honolulu.

But this is where you came in. Have another sip and turn your attention to the left side of the map, the *ewa* part of the town. The inverted bow-like silhouette of Round Top dominates Manoa Valley on the right and will provide you with sweeping views of the city from the Waianae Range to Diamond Head. Just *ewa* of Round Top you will see Makiki Heights. Here, secluded in wonderful gardens, are the most beautiful homes in all Hawaii, perhaps in the world. Architecturally influenced by the Orient, they are at once luxurious and simple, a reflection of the wealth and good taste of their owners, many of whom are descendants of New England missionaries for whom ostentation was virtually a sin. Many Makiki residents have traveled extensively in the Orient and throughout the world and have brought back bronzes, paintings, ceramics, and sculpture of museum quality. In their homes these objects are not imprisoned behind glass but remain a casual part of daily life. Entertaining in these homes is one of the fine arts. Usually informal and seemingly effortless, it recalls the gracious living of a departed era. There is nothing quite like it in the rest of America or in Europe. If a house and garden tour of the Makiki Heights area is on the agenda when you are in Honolulu, don't miss this glimpse of *kamaaina* Hawaii. The Outdoor Circle has a three-house tour for groups, by appointment. There are no individual tours.

Last Resting Place

Ewa of Makiki is Puowaina, or the Punchbowl, in whose green, grassy crater are 27,000 graves of American war heroes of all races who gave their lives in World War II, Korea, and Vietnam. Below Punchbowl is downtown Honolulu, teeming with the life of waterfront, market place, and city hall.

Both lower Makiki and the slopes of Punchbowl are slowly undergoing a transformation from an area of quiet homes to a land of high-rise apartment living and increasing congestion. But back of Punchbowl, in Pauoa Valley, sits something old. The *Honolulu Sake Brewery and Ice Co. Ltd.,* the only one in the United States, predates Prohibition, and today spends nearly half its production time on making shoyu sauce.

Nuuanu Avenue, which becomes Pali Highway midway up the valley, leads from the waterfront past the *ewa* flank of Punchbowl into historic Nuuanu Valley, past the Royal Mausoleum, old Island estates, and spanking new subdivisions, through the cool, eucalyptus-scented uplands to the Nuuanu Pali and one of the world's most spectacular views. On your way up to this view, stop at the Royal Mausoleum to the right on Nuuanu Avenue above Judd Street. Begun in 1865, the Mausoleum was still unfinished when Kamehameha IV was buried here the same year. In 1867, the royal occupants of the crypt at Iolani Palace were removed and entombed here. Only two members of the Kamehameha dynasty lie elsewhere. They are

Kamehameha the Great, whose burial place, kept secret in accordance with an ancient tradition of the *alii*, is still unknown, and King Lunalilo, who is buried on the grounds of Kawaiahao Church. King Kalakaua and his queen, Kapiolani, are also interred here. Their tomb is marked with a marble plaque in front of which a realistic portrait bust of the Merry Monarch stares at the curious visitor. The royal chapel on the premises is Gothic in inspiration, has stained-glass windows and walls paneled in native *koa* and *ohia* wood. It was consecrated in 1909 at the request of Prince Kuhio, Hawaiian delegate to Congress. Tall and stately royal palm trees punctuate the grounds of the Royal Mausoleum, like *kahilis* guarding the mortal remains of Hawaii's kings and queens. Also buried on the grounds is Charles Reed Bishop, who gave the bulk of his wealth to Kamehameha Schools on his death. Bishop arrived in Honolulu in 1846, founded Bishop Bank, married Bernice Pauahi, the princess, and was foreign minister to King Lunalilo. Today, Bishop Estate is the largest of the private lands in the state. Just behind the mausoleum and bordered by a wrought-iron fence is the grave of English sailor John Young, a companion of Kamehameha I prior to the arrival of the missionaries. Young died in 1835 at 93 after 46 years in the Islands. The Royal Mausoleum is open Monday & Friday from 8 A.M. to 4:30 P.M.

But back to the climb to Nuuanu Pali itself. This towering cliff, guarding the 1,200-foot-high pass and its road from Honolulu to Windward Oahu, is one of the scenic masterpieces of the Islands—in fact, of the world. You approach the Pali by way of Nuuanu Avenue. From a picturesquely cluttered downtown street of small Chinatown shops, it widens into a residential boulevard and thence into a super-highway. Portions of the old road remain usable and traverse more widely varied landscape than that observable from the new highway. You will pass new subdivisions, foreign consulates, many churches and cemeteries, and *kamaaina* estates whose homes stand at the end of avenues of royal palms or hidden by the thick foliage of tropical gardens.

The air becomes cooler as you pass Dowsett Highlands. The way to the top from Dowsett is quicker, but a more beautiful, wooded route is to take the old Nuuanu Valley road off to the right, just before the steep hill and at the end of the homes. This road is tree-lined, winding through Morgan's Corner and past a reservoir. It comes out on the Pali Highway farther up. Before long, you are riding through a splendid forest of aromatic eucalyptus trees. The sheer green walls of the Koolau Mountains rise on either side, often laced with silver cascades whose water, blown upward by the wind, creates the peculiar phenomenon known as the Upside-Down Falls. As you approach the Pali Pass, the scenery takes on the aspects of a virgin rain forest, with vine-draped trees crowding together, thick as a jungle. Before you enter the tunnels that take you through the mountain to the windward side of the island, a turn-off to the right from the super-highway takes you to the precipice, a lookout point carved from the wall of a cliff, and the glorious view of Windward Oahu bursts upon your vision, a sweeping panorama of razor-edged viridian mountains, earth which is ochre, orange, and dark red, fields of the tenderest green, and the distant sea, turquoise, violet, and amethyst over the shallows, deepening to cobalt and ultramarine where it joins a sky of such pure and vivid blue as to make cerulean seem greenish by comparison.

Historically, the Pali was the setting for the climax of Kamehameha the Great's invasion of Oahu in 1795. Having landed at Waikiki and Waialae, his warriors crossed the plain to Nuuanu Valley, where the defenders decided to make a stand. Despite valiant resistance on the part of the latter, the forces of Kamehameha moved irresistibly up the valley, driving the others before them. Some escaped over the mountain ridges which hem in the valley. The rest who were not killed or captured in the retreat were forced over the Pali precipice and met death on the jagged rocks 1,000 feet below. The chief, Kalanikupule, escaped this fate only to meet a worse one. His army annihilated, he wandered in misery through the Koolau Mountains for several months before being captured and sacrificed to Kukailimoku, Kamehameha's war god. A thousand skeletons lay bleaching in the sun at the base of the Pali, and Kamehameha was the master of Oahu.

Note: the Pali lookout is often whipped by winds, strong enough, in the old days and on the old road that clings to the cliff on the right, to have ripped the top from more than one convertible. A great diversion of tourists is to flip pennies end over end from the brink of the cliff and have them come back to you or fly over your head. But hold onto your hat, your children, and the protecting concrete wall. What you see directly below you from the lookout is the Pali Golf Course and across the road the buildings of tiny Hawaii Loa College.

Ewa of Nuuanu Valley are Alewa Heights, the Kapalama-section locale of the Bishop Museum and Palama Settlement, and Kamehameha Heights, dominated by the Kamehameha Schools for boys and girls of Hawaiian or part-Hawaiian ancestry. Few schools anywhere can boast such equipment and such an endowment: they are the chief beneficiaries of the vast revenues of the Bishop Estate.

Hickam Air Force Base and its neighbor, Honolulu International Airport, can easily be seen from Kapalama Heights. This military base is the home of the Air Force's 15th Air Base Wing and scene of considerable MAC (Military Airlift Command) activity as large C-5 and C-141 transports fly back and forth across the Pacific with stops at Hickam.

Base operations was the scene of the arrival and departure of most of the major figures in the Vietnam drama and tragedy in the 1960s, including Presidents Johnson and Nixon and many Asian leaders. Not far from base operations on the aircraft parking asphalt is a plaque marking the spot where the first astronauts to leave earth and circle the moon (the *Apollo 8* crew) returned to earth and stepped out of a Navy plane that had flown them to Hawaii from an aircraft carrier. Hickam is also the home of several Hawaii Air National Guard units, including the 199th Tactical Fighter Squadron, which provides round-the-clock air defense for Hawaii. One building at Hickam still carries the bomb fragment scars of December 7, 1941 that were not plastered over.

Also located on the Kalihi side of town is the pineapple cannery whose distinctive pineapple tower is seen to the left on the ride on Nimitz Highway from the airport to Waikiki. The cannery, a division of Castle and Cooke Foods, formerly the Dole Company, advertises itself as the biggest fruit packing company in the world. No one to date has disputed this claim. The pineapple cannery, occupying 56 acres of Hawaii's industrial Iwilei section, produces 50 percent of Hawaii's total. It can process 3 million "pines" in 24 hours, enough to keep you in upside-down cakes for the rest of your life. That 195-foot-tall pineapple you see atop the cannery is actually a water tank.

The cannery tour that the company has offered for the past 60 years took on a new aspect in 1988. At a cost of $3.3 million, a spacious portion of the cannery was transformed into Dole Cannery Square, where visitors now learn about one of Hawaii's key historic industries in two 60-seat theaters. A pavilion features cafe seating for sampling modern Dole products like sorbet; there's a series of specialty shops as well. The tour, which includes transportation from Waikiki, costs $5. Call 531–8855 for further information.

Ewa of Kapalama is a section known by few tourists: Kalihi, a working-class area of box-like wooden houses and small garden plots. This is one terminus of Mass Transit Lines, whose modern yellow buses can reach all the points indicated in this brief orientation. You can take a bus to Kalihi-Kai, deep into Kalihi Valley, or continue beyond Kalihi on the No. 1 bus to Umi Street, where you transfer to the No. 13 bus headed for Tripler. Get off at Ala Mahamoe and walk a short distance to lovely Moanalua Gardens, a 26-acre section of the Damon Estate, where you can wander through a tropical landscape of flowers, trees, and ponds.

Behind the gardens, *mauka,* stretches Moanalua Valley itself. If you're feeling ambitious and like to hike, try Moanalua Valley, on the other side of the ridge where Tripler Hospital lies but part of the same ancient land division, or *ahupua'a.* The trail into the Valley begins 1½ miles above Moanalua Road (Red Hill bus stops at intersection), above Moanalua Golf Course (the oldest course west of the Rockies). The valley has been impacted by cattle and foreign plant introductions, but 210 of the 317 plant species found here were growing in these Islands before Captain Cook; 155 are found nowhere else in the world. An old carriage road crosses seven bridges built by Italian stone masons at the turn of this century to the spot where Kamehameha named a baby following the Battle of Nu'uanu and won the allegiance of the Oahu people. There's a "Garden of Eden" legend which centers here, too. Group tours can be arranged by calling the Moanalua Gardens Foundation, which takes its name from the fact that Moanalua Gardens have been extended into the two Moanalua valleys by the property owners. Guided walks are conducted on the third Tuesday of each month, reservations required. They start at 10 A.M. at the end of Ala Aolani Street and take about 4½ hours (telephone 839–5334).

Walking in Waikiki

Most Honolulans, unless they are the hiking type, walk only from house to car, from car to office, shop or beach, and from shop to shop, providing the shops are close together. Some of the population, particularly the senior citizens, *holoholo* on the bus. Still, there is no law against walking. As has been noted, pedestrians in Honolulu have a sort of favored status. But walking sounds too purposeful. Strolling would be a more appropriate word for the pace which the tropics compel, and there are a number of places in Honolulu where you can stroll and enjoy the crowded shopping malls, such as the new one near the Royal Hawaiian Hotel and the International Market Place across the street. The rest of the passing show on Kalakaua Avenue may at times gets pretty scruffy, particularly in the blocks between Lewers and the Waikiki Gateway Hotel on the *mauka* side. The clothing is often a laugh, and almost anything suffices as a costume. There are natives and those who are going that way in *muumuus, aloha* shirts and shorts, crazy shirts, occasional sarongs, and occasional plastic suits for reducing. The shops offer their wares, with and without benefit of windows, and the whole atmosphere of this perpetual vacation-land can be summed up by the Hawaiian word, *Hoomanawanui*. English translation: let's take it easy. But don't get stepped on. Sometimes nearly 50,000 visitors are in Waikiki, many trying to stroll Kalakaua at once. Still, it's a colorful mob scene. Two warnings: gyp joints and some of the sleazy pornographic shops once confined to the downtown area have invaded Waikiki and are to be avoided, and so are the young Hare Krishnas who panhandle aggressively on Kalakaua Avenue. Waikiki's crime figures have dropped, and legal moves may discourage hustling street venders and prostitutes, who have moved to Kuhio Avenue. Mini-parks and street alignments leading to more pedestrian promenades may make the beach area more attractive.

Two popular attractions within walking distance of almost any Waikiki hotel is the nightly (6:15 P.M.) heel-clicking "changing" of the Royal Guards in the Bishop Court at King's Village on Kaiulani Avenue next door to the Hyatt Regency Hotel. The other is the Kodak Hula Show in Kapiolani Park from 10 to 11:15 A.M. Tuesday through Saturday, January to September, Tuesday through Thursday the other months. Gates open at 8:30 A.M. for this free show. Visitors bring cameras and sit in bleachers.

If big yachts or simple sailboats ignite your desire to escape from it all and sail away, take a stroll along the slips of the nearby Ala Wai Yacht Basin. This picturesque yacht harbor at the end of the Ala Wai is site of both the Waikiki and Hawaii Yacht Clubs, and a very exciting place when the trans-Pacific racers are coming in. An excellent way to see the yachts is to ride the glass elevator in the Westin Ilikai Hotel.

At the other end of Waikiki is Diamond Head, Hawaii's most celebrated landmark, most often seen in noble profile from the angle of Waikiki Beach. Many visitors are surprised to learn that it is, in fact, an extinct volcanic crater, and fail to recognize it when approaching it from the east. Once the home of the fire goddess Pele, before she "settled" permanently if fitfully in Kilauea Crater, the headland used to be called *Leahi*, "place of fire," by the Hawaiians. It got its present name in the early 1800s, when some British sailors, doubtless several sheets to the wind, picked up the mica-like volcanic crystals known as "Pele's tears" and announced the discovery of diamonds. The top of Diamond Head is Leahi Point, 760 feet above the sea. You can see the interior of the crater from Wilhelmina Rise or Maunalani Heights. You can drive into it through a tunnel off Diamond Head Road, and you can even hike to the top for a striking view of Waiki-ki.

Also nestled into the slope off Poni Moi Road is La Pietra, a replica of a Florentine-style villa, built by industrialist Water F. Dillingham in 1922. It is now a high school for girls, and also on the Hawaii Register of Historic Places. The pink home was once the focal point of Honolulu society.

On Diamond Head Road is the Diamond Head Lighthouse and the home of the rear admiral in command of the 14th Coast Guard District. The first lighthouse was built here in 1899 and rebuilt in 1917. The 19th Lighthouse District superintendent lived next door until the merger of the service with the Coast Guard in 1939. Admirals took over the home in 1946.

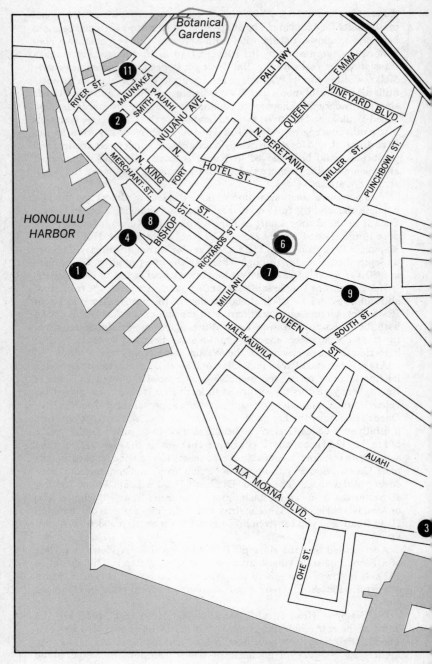

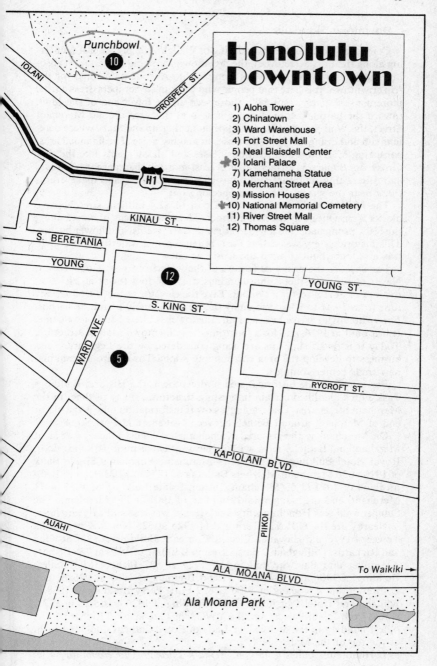

Punchbowl
10

Honolulu Downtown

1) Aloha Tower
2) Chinatown
3) Ward Warehouse
4) Fort Street Mall
5) Neal Blaisdell Center
6) Iolani Palace
7) Kamehameha Statue
8) Merchant Street Area
9) Mission Houses
10) National Memorial Cemetery
11) River Street Mall
12) Thomas Square

IOLANI

PROSPECT ST.

H1

KINAU ST.

S. BERETANIA

YOUNG

12

YOUNG ST.

S. KING ST.

WARD AVE.

5

RYCROFT ST.

KAPIOLANI BLVD.

AUAHI

PIIKOI

ALA MOANA BLVD.

To Waikiki →

Ala Moana Park

Downtown Honolulu

Compared to the aimless wandering of Waikiki, the purposeful sauntering along the Fort Street Mall, the downtown shopping center, is an absolute bustle. Catch the No. 2 bus along Kuhio Avenue in Waikiki for the trip downtown. It is here that people who work in skyscrapers dress a trifle more conservatively, especially those seen at the lower end of the Mall, toward the harbor. More elegance is seen in this area around Merchant Street, the Wall Street of Honolulu, than farther up the Mall, where derelicts sun and evangelists join the buses in making noise. The financial area, consisting of savings and loan businesses and glassy giants like the new Grosvenor Square, is attractive, or at least more so than perhaps 30 years ago. Interesting sculpture and mini-parks dot the area, and make everything near the waterfront worth checking out.

The Mall, completed in 1969 at a cost of $2.4 million, stretches five blocks from Queen to Beretania Street. There are dozens of stores along the brick promenade and a wide variety of trees, palms, and flower bushes. This historic artery was called Fort, because at the waterfront end there was a redoubt built to keep the Russians out.

For decades the principal feature of the waterfront was Aloha Tower. Never mind its aesthetic shortcomings; this 184-foot tower at Pier 9 at the foot of Fort Street is a symbol. Take the elevator to the 10th floor any time from 8 A.M. to 9 P.M. and enjoy the view of Honolulu and the harbor. For visitors who arrive by sea or air, the tower is like a hand of welcome. It was built in 1926, and for a long time was downtown's tallest structure. Today it is dwarfed. Plans are being considered by the Legislature and business to develop the area surrounding Aloha Tower into a spanking-new trade center complex.

For a look at the historical side of downtown, the Historic Buildings Task Force identified certain interesting structures, many of them in the Merchant Street area. Undergoing a slow transformation now is the oldest end of Merchant around Bethel, between Nuuanu and Fort Streets.

On Merchant is the restored Kamehameha V Post Office of 1871 at Merchant and Bethel Streets, with its pleasant Davis mini-park next door; Royal Hotel Building of 1890 at 14 Merchant; Yokohama Specie Bank of 1910 at 36 Merchant; Melchers Building of 1854 at 51 Merchant; Bishop Bank of 1877 at 63 Merchant; Bishop Estate Building of 1896 at 71 Merchant; and the Stangenwald Building of 1901 at 119 Merchant. The Stangenwald was Honolulu's first high-rise; it was restored 81 years later.

Nearby are the O.R.&L. Terminal of 1925 at 325 North King; Aloha Tower of 1926 and Hawaiian Electric Company Building of 1927 at King and Richards; Dillingham Transportation Building of 1929 at 735 Bishop; Alexander and Baldwin Building of 1929 at 822 Bishop; McCandless Building of 1906 at 925 Bethel; Friend Building of 1887 at 926 Bethel; C. Brewer and Company of 1930 at 827 Fort; Perry Building of 1888 at Nuuanu and Hotel; Territorial Office Building of 1926 (restored in 1975) across from Iolani Palace; and the YWCA of 1926 at 1040 Richards. The oldest building in the area is Our Lady of Peace Cathedral at 1184 Fort, at the top of the Mall, 1843.

If Honolulu's oldies grab you, *A Walk Through Old Honolulu* by O. A. Bushnell is on sale at bookstores. Many of these national historic buildings are being utilized now by young entrepreneurs for shops, restaurants, or bars with exotic names. The Historic Hawaii Foundation is in the process of putting up informational markers of the type seen in many other states. A mural by Juliette May Fraser and others that shows what downtown looked like in 1876 can be seen in the Bishop Building at 1136 Union Mall.

The new look downtown includes the glass Grosvenor Center at Alakea and Queen; Century Square at Bishop and Beretania; the impressive new 28-story Bishop Square between King and Hotel; Kauikeaouli Hale, the new district court building at Hotel and Alakea; 1001 Bishop and Executive Centre at Bishop and Hotel; the Central Pacific Plaza at King and Alakea; Honolulu Tower on Beretania near Kukui Plaza; and Watkins Center on King near Bethel.

Chinatown

There's plenty of local color along the Fort Street Mall, although since the late 1970s derelicts have posed a problem. If you really want to explore the less "touristed" side of Honolulu, stroll along Hotel, Pauahi, Smith, and Maunakea Streets and you'll see a honky-tonk neighborhood frequented by sailors and specializing in tattoo parlors, dubious massage establishments, gypsy fortune tellers, and kindred institutions where the accent is apt to be on the *gyp*. There's some hot nightlife in these parts, but according to local bourgeois opinion, Smith and Maunakea Streets are sordid and dangerous.

The area between Nuuanu Avenue and River Street is not so disreputable as this might imply. There's actually more crime in Waikiki. Respectable Chinese merchants, and newer businessmen from Vietnam and other Southeast Asia areas have their stores and restaurants here. There are herb shops, Oriental dry goods shops, and those fascinating Chinese food shops where even the most catholic of gourmets may find his comeuppance in that greatest of delicacies, an egg which is a century old and which looks and smells every single year of it. Don't hesitate to sample the little Chinese restaurants in this neighborhood.

One block *ewa* of Maunakea Street is River Street, which flanks the Nuuanu Stream as it winds its way into Honolulu Harbor. Once the scene of legalized houses of prostitution alleged to have been leased to various Mamie Stovers by respectable *kamaaina* landowners, River Street now has blossomed with the completion of the River Street Mall, a promenade walk along the stream. Some $10 million was spent by four Chinese benevolent societies to develop this old area into the Cultural Plaza.

Many merchants speak foreign languages, adding color to the Plaza as they offer everything from acupuncture, turquoise, and rare pottery to Oriental silks and screens. You can bargain for Hawaii's finest jade, much the same as if you were in Hong Kong, and there is even a Buddhist monk who sells books.

The Cultural Plaza and other changes made by the bulldozer, including the removal of slums on the *mauka* side of Beretania, have brought new high-rise apartments and some low-cost housing. Still left standing, at 1315 River Street, is an interesting structure, its Oriental flavor accentuated by a red and gold Chinese temple, Taoist shrine for the numerous descendants of the Lum clan in China.

And on the *mauka* side of Vineyard there are other urban renewal buildings that replaced in the 1960s the tenements that once scarred the heart of the city. The three giant high-rise apartment buildings surrounded by handsome gardens are called Queen Emma Gardens and were the first in a series of renewal projects that will eventually remake the face of Old Honolulu.

There are other changes in Chinatown. The old mom-and-pop family shops, the heart of the tradition, are fading from the scene; the children and grandchildren have intermarried and fled. Into the heart of the area have moved aged Filipinos from the plantations, new Filipino immigrants, and some Vietnamese trying to start fresh. Also new are renovated buildings, new paint, new ideas, spiffy offices hidden behind old brick, and a half dozen new art shops. Chinatown can be fascinating by day when the stores are open, though there is a ghetto poverty aspect to it, but after sunset things get a bit seedy.

At the harbor end, where River Street meets Nimitz Highway, is Pier 15 and the wholesale fish market. From here a few steps *ewa* will take you across Nuuanu Stream to College Walk, and another few steps in the *mauka* direction will land you in Aala Park.

Aala Park stands alone in the open, though it still hosts resting, tired citizens of the downtown area, the real people who live in the heart of the city far from the fleshpots of Waikiki. Chances are you won't find another tourist here, or anywhere *ewa* of the Nuuanu Stream.

Ala Moana

For a different kind of promenade, go to the Ala Moana Center, and stroll up and down the mall. This esplanade and the complex of shops which surrounds it constitute one of the handsomest shopping centers in the world. There are 155 stores, including the only Sears, Roebuck we ever heard of that sells orchids and warns its customers not to board the escalators barefoot. Ceramic fountains, murals, mosaics, palm trees, and other aspects of landscape architecture have been skillfully combined in this ensemble. The contrast with the shops of River Street could hardly be greater, but it is just such contrasts that give Honolulu its flavor.

Not far away are the *Ward Warehouse* and *Ward Centre* with dozens of interesting shops located across the street from Kewalo Basin. A short walk away is *Farmers Market* and *Parkview GEM,* a discount store. (For more on shopping, see *Practical Information for Oahu.*)

Kewalo Basin is at the *ewa* end of Ala Moana Park. This is home base for Hawaii's commercial fishing fleet of sampans which come in around 5:30 A.M. to unload the catch that ends up on plates of visitors in Honolulu's finest restaurants, including two good seafood spots right on these docks, John Dominis and Fisherman's Wharf, and others across the street in the Ward Warehouse and Ward Centre.

Another logical spot for combining the pleasures of strolling and sightseeing is the civic center of Honolulu, whose nucleus is Iolani Palace. The palace is located in a park bounded on the *makai* side by King Street, on the *mauka* side by Hotel Street. Richards Street flanks the palace grounds on the *ewa* edge, and Likelike Street forms the Waikiki boundary. (Call 538–1471 for information.) Within a two-block radius of this downtown oasis are historic Kawaiahao Church, the state Capitol; Iolani Barracks, the governor's residence; Washington Place; the Library of Hawaii; Honolulu Hale (City Hall); and the early mission houses. The Capitol is worth a look.

Described as "the most interesting and unusual of capitols," it replaces *Iolani Palace,* which was too small for the expanding business of annual legislative sessions. The new building is a rectangular structure with a 90-foot square opening in the roof which allows the soft, warm rains to fall on the main floor five floors below. On either side are the two volcano-shaped (cone-shaped) sunken chambers of the legislature. Reaching up from the main floor are 40 giant cement ribs and columns. Most art of interest in the building is in the Governor's or Lieutenant Governor's offices on the top floor. The public is invited to enter these offices to look at the art work, all done by Island artists. Outside, on the Beretania Street side of the building, stands Marisol's "Father Damien," a replica of which is in Statuary Hall of Congress. At the other entrance is a new statue of Queen Lilioukalani by Marianna Pineda. The queen, who was put under house arrest at Iolani Palace in the counterrevolution of 1895, looks sad, but regal. The mosaic on the rotunda floor by Tadashi Sato is titled "Aquarius" and is especially interesting when viewed from the upper floors. The open concept of the building was architect John Carl Warnecke's idea for capturing both the spirit of freedom and utilizing Hawaii's marvelous climate. The $25 million building was finished in 1969. Pews in the galleries are of koa wood, some 25 feet above the oratory. But there is more wind outside the Senate and House chambers than inside, say critics of the architect. The legislature convenes in regular session each year at 10 A.M. on the third Wednesday in January, in the Capitol. (If you have any questions, telephone the Lieutenant Governor's office, 548–2544.) Across the street from the Damien statue and next to the Governor's residence is the eternal flame, a reminder of those Island men who have lost their lives in recent wars.

Moved coral stone by stone in 1965 to make room for the Capitol, Iolani Barracks is a touch of medievalism in Hawaii. This stone building with its crenelated turrets and cross-shaped *meurtrières* was built in 1871 during the reign of King Lunalilo. It took 4,000 coral blocks cut from reefs and another 2,350 from the Old Printing House and housed the Royal Household Guards, King Kalakaua's army of 65 men. Iolani Barracks, also called Halekoa, or soldiers' house, has been preserved as a historical monument, and they moved everything but the old dungeon, which may disappoint the kids. The barracks was the scene of a six-day mutiny in 1873 when the soldiers became upset with the strict rule of their Austrian captain. The guards were disbanded in 1893. The next occupants were the National Guard, the U.S. Quartermasters Corps (1898–1917), veterans organizations, and the school system office (1931–1934). Across the grass is the coronation pavilion, where the Royal Hawaiian Band, founded in 1837, plays every Friday at 12:15 P.M. except on holidays.

Across Beretania Street from the Capitol is Washington Place, the residence of the Governor of Hawaii which can be seen only from the exterior. The house was built in 1846 by New England Sea Captain John Dominis for his daughter-in-law, who became Queen Liliuokalani, last monarch of the Hawaiian Kingdom. The deposed queen lived there until her death in 1917, at which time the house was bought by the Territory of Hawaii to be the executive mansion. Sometimes called the Little White House of the Pacific, this spacious and charming white house was named in honor of George Washington. The grounds feature the rare pili nut tree.

Kitty corner from the Capitol, at 1301 Punchbowl Street, is the Queen's Medical Center; founded by Queen Emma who, together with her king,

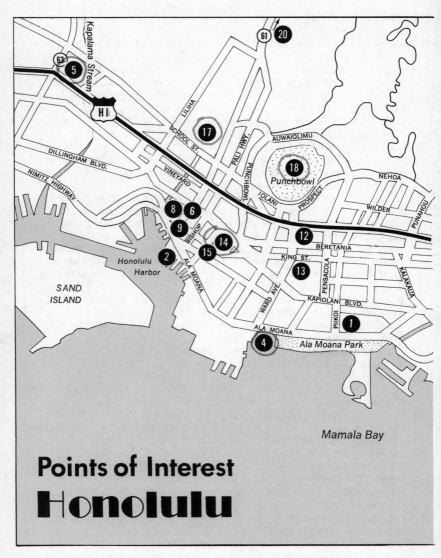

Points of Interest
Honolulu

1) Ala Moana Center
2) Aloha Tower
3) Aquarium
4) Kewalo Basin *(LAG)*
5) Bishop Museum
6) Chinatown

7) Zoo
8) Cultural Plaza
9) Downtown
10) East West Center
11) Fort De Russy
12) Honolulu Academy of Arts

THERE IS A NEW MARITIME MUSEUM BY ALOHA TOWER (#2)

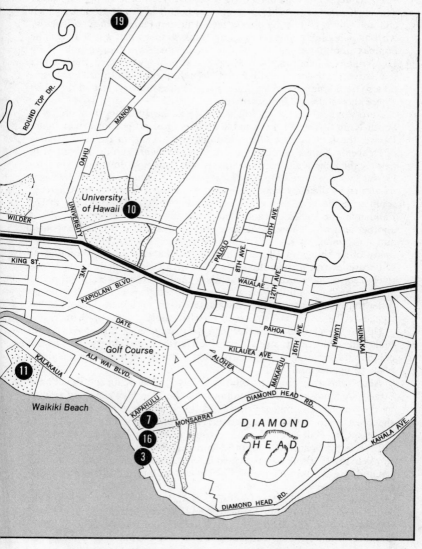

13) Neal Blaisdell Center
14) Iolani Palace
15) Kamehameha Statue
16) Kapiolani Park
17) Liliuokalani Gardens
18) National Memorial Cemetery

19) Paradise Park
20) Queen Emma Museum

THOUGHT THIS WAS FOSTER GARDENS (SEE P. 128)

Kamehameha IV, organized a drive to give Hawaii a modern hospital. The chief interest for visitors in perfect health is in the grounds, which contain, along with other lovely trees, the unusual *Bombax ellipticum,* with its pale pink pompons and huge pink stamens half a foot long. The bombax trees bloom annually from January to May. Planted in 1866 by Dr. William Hillebrand, the Queen's first attending physician, the bombax is a native of Mexico, but Hillebrand brought these from India. The hospital also has a small art gallery, the Queen Emma Gallery, just off the lobby where shows change frequently.

Across the street facing Iolani Palace is the Judiciary Building, 417 South King Street. Of more noble architectural proportions than Iolani Palace, the Judiciary Building, also known as Aliiolani Hale, or "House of Heavenly Kings," is chiefly noted today for what stands in front of it, namely the King Kamehameha Statue. A landmark of downtown Honolulu, this gilded bronze statue is a focal point of Hawaii's civic center. Commissioned by the Hawaiian legislature, the statue was cast by an American sculptor living in Florence. The ship bringing it to Hawaii sank in the Falklands; the legislature collected the insurance ($10,000) and ordered another one, which now stands here. The original statue was later salvaged and now stands in Kamehameha's birthplace, Kohala, Hawaii. Like so many other things in Hawaii, the statue, whatever its shortcomings as sculpture, evokes a romantic association with events which, though relatively recent, have an almost legendary quality. There were royal palms around the statue until 1967, when some joker gave a bogus tree-cutting order to tree trimmers before officials were even out of bed. The order was signed "Albert Camus," a French novelist already dead by then.

Up the street from Kamehameha's outstretched arms, at 478 South King Street, is a quiet, lovely place, the Hawaii State Library. This restful colonnaded building is a model of what a library should be, a delightful place to browse and read.

Across the street from the Library is City Hall, at King and Punchbowl Streets. A handsome civic building with the blue Hawaiian sky framed by the walls of an immense courtyard. Each month, a new art show fills the open patio, and evening concerts feature everything from jazz to Strauss. City Hall has a Hawaiian name, *Honolulu Hale* and reflects the interest in the Spanish Rudolph Valentino style that swept Southern California in the 1920s. It was dedicated in 1929. Between it and a new municipal building is Isamu Noguchi's black metal sculpture, "Sky Gate," a conversation piece.

Down Punchbowl Street from City Hall, toward the waterfront, is the Kuhio Federal Building. Dedicated in 1977 by Rosalynn Carter and daughter Amy, the Prince Jonah Kuhio Kalanianaole Federal Office Building is non-symmetrical, it is nine stories in one place, four in another. Interesting art includes a moving metal sculpture by George Rickey and one that doesn't move by Peter Voulkos. The building is the location of monthly art shows hosted by the Arts Council of Hawaii. Prince Kuhio Day, March 26, is also a major event at the Federal Building, much of it musical. The Old Federal Building at King and Richards Streets may be worth a visit. Modern Spanish Colonial Revival in style, it served federal agencies between 1922 and 1977.

The Kuhio Federal Building sits on the diamond head edge of Honolulu Harbor. For more than a century, the most pageantry and excitement engendered in Honolulu occurred on "Boat Day." For one thing, the old sailing ships used to bring the news, the VIPs, the eager neophytes who one day would run things, and the rascals and worthless.

Until the invention of the jet, "Boat Day" could mean up to six trans-Pacific luxury liners tied up at the same time. Or at least it meant the regularity of the good old *Lurline* arrival and the *lei* sellers. And the Royal Hawaiian Band would strike up *Aloha Oe* if leave-taking was at hand, as blond damsels, loaded with *leis,* would cry in the arms of bronze Hawaiian boys, the idyll all but over.

Today there are a few liners still making calls, but mostly it is cruise traffic, and townsfolk hardly get involved.

Very close to the Civic Center is Neal Blaisdell Center (NBC) and Punchbowl, the famed National cemetery that looks down upon the inner, oldest features of the city. At Blaisdell there's sure to be something going on to attract you to this cluster of public gathering places located about midway between Waikiki and downtown Honolulu. Perhaps a touring Broadway show, a boxing match, ballet, or concert, a Japanese circus, an ice show, art show, or sports car exhibit. If none of it appeals to you, or in the unlikely circumstance that nothing is going on at the moment, a stroll through the grounds will expose you to one of the finest examples of contemporary civic architecture in the country.

The $11 million complex covers 22 palm-studded acres laced with ornamental pools. There are three main buildings. The Arena at the Kapiolani entrance is a vast white mushroom, crowned at the center with a small orange pillbox. It seats up to 8,500 in air-conditioned and upholstered luxury.

The Exhibition Pavilion in the middle of the complex includes an all-purpose assembly hall (meetings, banquets, or high school proms), eight soundproof conference rooms, and more than an acre of exhibit space—covered, but partially open to light and trade-wind ventilation.

Facing Thomas Square is a magnificent Theater–Concert Hall. Shallow arches enclose the loggia surrounding the entrance; chandeliers from Belgium and more than 50 pieces of bronze and copper sculpture by Bumpei Akaji ornament the red-carpeted foyer. The balconied hall accommodates nearly 2,200 in Continental seating—no aisles, but ample access to your seat between rows. Lights, sound, and other stage facilities are among the finest. The theater is the home of the Honolulu Symphony Orchestra, whose season is September through mid-April, 12 concerts, three performances of each, plus three operas in February.

The National Memorial Cemetery of the Pacific rests atop Punchbowl Crater at the top of Puowaina Drive, a vast field of 27,000 graves of dead World War II, Korea, and Vietnam soldiers. (Closed to vehicles in May 1986, it was reopened to foot traffic only in early 1988.) "Puowaina" the Hawaiians called this crater, and it could not have been more prophetically named: Hill of Sacrifice. The cemetery is an especially moving place on Memorial Day, when Hawaii's families of all races come to put flowers on the graves of their sons, and on Easter Sunday morning, when thousands flock to the Hill of Sacrifice for a special service at dawn. Besides servicemen, the cemetery contains dependents, former Governor of Hawaii John A. Burns, World War II journalist Ernie Pyle, and 24 Medal of Honor recipients. The panorama of Honolulu and Oahu from the rim of the crater provides a striking contrast to the silent necropolis inside it. For those wanting a crash history course on the Pacific war (1942–45) and information on where the people buried here fought, there are walls of mosaic maps located at the top of the memorial's steps, which provide a graphic understanding of the campaigns. Allow more than an hour to read it all. The dominant figure at the top of the stairs is Columbia standing triumphant on the bow of a ship. The Courts of the Missing that flank the stairway include the names on marble of many men whose remains were not recovered, due to explosions, sinkings, air crashes, and similar deaths. In 1978, two additional courts were dedicated for those Missing In Action in Vietnam.

Honolulu's Oriental Churches

In addition to these attractions, Honolulu's many churches and temples deserve special attention, not only because they reflect the multi-cultural complexity of the city (recent statistics showed that Hawaii is 34.2 percent Protestant, 31.1 percent Catholic, 11.8 percent Buddhist, 2.5 percent Mormon, and 0.3 percent Jewish), but also because many of them are of more than passing architectural interest. For the average visitor, the Chinese, Japanese, and Korean temples and churches will be most appealing because most foreign to his own aesthetic and religious experience. Some temple tours are available. These are an educational experience. Hawaii's Buddhist priests are teachers at heart; don't hesitate to ask them questions about their religion. All of the places of worship described below welcome visitors.

A good introduction to Buddhism is provided by a visit to the Soto-Zen Mission Temple at 1708 Nuuanu Avenue. Its bizarre architecture, inspired by the Gaya Temple in India, is rich with Buddhist symbolism, the octagonal towers representing stages in Buddha's Way of Life. This temple is also typical of Honolulu's fusion of racial and national styles; although the exterior of Soto Mission is that of a Hindu temple, the interior could hardly be more Japanese in decor and design. The fundamentals of Buddhism are explained at 9:30 every Monday morning in English.

A few blocks away, at 1727 Pali Highway, is the Honpa Hongwanji Temple. One of the largest Buddhist temples in the state, it is the equivalent of a cathedral, with 35 smaller temples of the Jodo Shin sect of Buddhism under its jurisdiction throughout Hawaii.

A little farther up the valley on the right is an orange pagoda, a replica of the Sanju Pagoda in Nara, best seen from the lookout on Pali Highway. The pagoda is part of a Buddhist cemetery that lies next to Nuuanu Mortuary's cemetery. Nearby, at 22 Craigside Place, is the Kinkaku-ji, or Golden Pavilion of Kyoto, in a green reflecting pool.

Shingon Temple, on Sheridan Street, is affiliated with a 1,150-year-old sect in Koyasen, Japan. The bronze lanterns in front are as eyecatching as the interiors.

Possibly worth a visit is a replica of the 900-year-old Byodo-in Temple near Kyoto, Japan, built in a cemetery in Ahuimanu Valley near Kaneohe, 47–200 Kahekili Highway, (239–8811). Open 9 A.M. to 5 P.M.

Shintoism, more exclusively Japanese than Buddhism, came to Hawaii as early as 1898. The Shinto religion has long been associated with marriage ceremonies and other happy fêtes, in contrast with Buddhism, to which the Japanese traditionally turn for consolation and support in times of sorrow. Shintoism has also gone hand in glove with the most extreme forms of Japanese nationalism, and hence was suspect in Hawaii during the war. Devout families in Hawaii are apt to have both Buddhist and

Shintoist shrines in their houses, but the Hawaiian-born children of these families take an increasingly dim view of ceremonies which they no longer understand and of whose efficacy they are skeptical. Yet Shinto persists in Hawaii, adding the silhouette of its curved and pointed roofs and its painted *torii* gates to the Island scene. The Izumo Taisha Kyo Mission at 215 North Kukui Street is the oldest Shinto shrine still standing in Honolulu. It dates from 1906. In a different area, you will find another, the Ishizuchi, at 2020 South King Street.

Interesting new churches in Honolulu include the Church of World Messianity at 3510 Nuuanu Pali Drive. Japanese architect Robert T. Katsuyoshi has the 14 pillars, representing the teachings of the religion, supporting a boomerang roof that seems in flight. At 888 North King Street is the Tensho-Kotai-Jingu-Kyo Hawaii Hall, built in 1976, for followers of Ogamisama, the Dancing Goddess. And a female minister built and operates a new temple in Manoa Valley, The Koganji Temple at 2869 Oahu Avenue.

Many Island Orientals have adopted the Christian religion, and this has frequently resulted in the happy marriage of Western doctrine with Eastern architecture. The most notable example of this in Honolulu, and one which you should not miss, is the Makiki Japanese Christian Church at 829 Pensacola Street. Built in 1932, when a bit of Victorian fantasy was still permitted, the church, architecturally speaking, is a Japanese castle resplendent with swooping rooflines, cupolas, balconies, and ornamental cornices. The golden dolphins atop its tower seem far less incongruous than the cross, which is relegated, as though by aesthetic instinct, to a subsidiary position at the apex of each gable. The lines of this church are beautiful, clean, and sharp against the Hawaiian sky, and the dazzling white of painted wood is tempered by the judicious use of a black and tan trim which punctuates the composition. No American city can offer you an experience quite like this. To admire this building from the exterior is to be transported momentarily to the shogunal castle at Nagoya. But step inside and you are in the Congregational precincts of puritan New England.

There are a number of other Christian churches whose architecture has been strongly influenced by the Orient. The First Chinese Church of Christ at 1054 South King Street is a notably charming example, with its pagoda-like bell tower, its tile roof, its upswept eaves, and its ceramic pediment combining to provide a vision of Cathay in the heart of Honolulu. More severe but equally colorful is the striking Church of the Crossroads at 1212 University Avenue. Designed by architect Claude Stiehl, this church has stood here as symbol of interracial harmony and an inspiration to architects since 1935. Note the covered portico, the bold exterior use of Chinese red, and inside the church, the carved chancel rail by Marguerite Blasingame.

Of political as well as architectural interest is the Korean Christian Church at 1832 Liliha Street. This was founded in 1918 by Syngman Rhee during his first long exile, when the Japanese were in control of his native land. Rhee, long the President of South Korea, returned to Hawaii in his old age when he was forced out of Seoul by the army, and here he died in 1965. Rites were held in this church, whose façade is reminiscent of the Great South Gate of Seoul.

The most recent combination of Occidental doctrine and Oriental form is to be found at St. Luke's Mission Church at 45 North Judd Street. The architecture, except for the cross which rises from the gable, is thoroughly Chinese, recalling the days when eaves swept upward to bounce evil spirits from the roof. The religion practiced here is Protestant Episcopal. The congregation is predominantly Korean, but everyone is welcome. A typically Hawaiian situation.

A few hundred yards *mauka* of St. Luke's is an interesting Chinese church. This one, pure Buddhist, is at 42 Kawananakoa Place. It is a remodeled house in a garden with a superb monkey pod tree. Its original owners would never recognize it now, all red lacquer and gold, lavishly decorated, an almost theatrical version of a Buddhist temple.

Exploring Oahu

To "see all the beauty" of Oahu involves three separate tours, and these in turn involve a certain amount of duplication. This is not exactly a hardship on an island whose tropical splendors may be equaled, but have not to our knowledge been surpassed. We have made each of the tours at least a dozen times during a long residence in the Islands, and can affirm that custom does not stale their infinite variety. The three roundtrips from Honolulu may be labeled the Grand Island Circuit (which some tour companies call the Circle Island Tour), the Eastern Tip Circuit (the Little Circle Island Tour), and the Waianae Tour.

The Grand Island Circuit

This tour is the most ambitious. Allow between seven and nine hours to do it Hawaiian style, with plenty of time for swimming, picnicking, and sightseeing at leisure. This circuit includes all that is most characteristic of Oahu with the exception of the Nuuanu Pali, which can be seen in a 15-minute drive from downtown Honolulu and whose charms have already been suggested above. If you don't mind rushing, you can drive the circuit in about two hours without stopping to take a breath.

The Grand Circuit begins in Waikiki, follows Kalakaua Avenue, Diamond Head Road, and Kalanianaole Highway (Route 72) toward Koko Head and Koko Crater. Just before you reach these two Kokos, you want a look at two others, the Koko Marina Waterfront Village Shopping Center, at the entrance to the Kaiser-Aetna Hawaii Kai housing development, and Koko Isle, man-made in the middle of one of the marinas. The village is ten miles from Waikiki. Seven restaurants in the attractive complex include a lobster house and steak house. And there are many shops, clothing stores, variety stores, and snack shops.

Hawaii Kai's growth was a major development of the 1970s. Now sitting in front of the green mountains in its several valleys is a row of high-rise condominiums, most built in 1974. Not far away is Esplanade on Lunalilo Home Road, most interesting architectural feature of the valley and similar to the apartment clusters one might expect to see in Sweden, Mexico City, Montreal, or Israel.

But let us continue on toward Koko Head, Koko Crater, and the Blow Hole. Koko Head is 645 feet high and looks like the back of a stranded whale; Koko Crater is 1,200 feet high and looks like a volcanic cinder cone, which is just what it is. Both are more than 10,000 years old, relics of Oahu's last volcanic top-blowing. On your right you'll see the road to lovely Hanauma Bay, a crater with one side washed away by a pounding sea. And you'll twist around ancient flows to a lookout spot where the islands of Lanai and Molokai can be seen on a clear day, and whales, too, during the January–March mating season. Next is the Blow Hole, an over-rated lava formation that often gushes a geyser if there is good wave action. Past Blow Hole is Sandy Beach with its heavy surf, the place where Harry Huffaker, the swimming dentist, came ashore after a fantastic nonstop swim from Molokai inside a sharkproof cage.

The two Hawaii Kai Golf Courses are on the left before reaching the extreme eastern tip of the island at Makapuu Lighthouse. At this point, from Makapuu Point you swing northwest, still on Route 72, pass Sea Life Park to your left, and continue along the rugged windward coastline of Oahu. On your right is Kaupo Beach Park, whose cove-subdued waves are about one tenth the height of the monsters at Makapuu. About a mile offshore is Manana Island, not Spanish for tomorrow but Hawaiian for rabbit. You'll never hear it called Manana; that's for the maps. But there are hares running around on Rabbit Island, which is not strictly for the birds, though terns and shearwaters love the place both for nesting and as a fishing base. This area is also the location of a wide 700-foot-long pier and small boat harbor operated by Makai Range, Inc. to provide a berthing, launching, and support area for undersea operations in offshore waters.

There is something spectacular about the celebrated *palis* of the Koolau Range, looming up on your left as you approach Waimanalo. They are sheer walls of green and brown rock, rising abruptly from the narrow coastal plain, and fluted from summit to base as though by the hand of some cosmic sculptor. This striking effect is the result of cycles of water erosion during which streams cut into the relatively soft lava rock which had coated the hard core of the range. These majestic *palis,* whose carved primordial mess reminds some tourists of herds of charging elephants, form the background for Waimanalo, a former plantation village now growing into another suburb. Travelers passing through this busy town are sometimes startled by the many colorful hang-gliders that dot the skies above the *palis.* Leaping off those cliffs became somewhat popular with the young in the 1970s. Just off the highway is a new pine grove village home for several Waimanalo venders who used to line the highway. Called Hui Mea O Hana Hawaii, they sell arts and handicrafts, like shell necklaces they've made themselves and not shipped in from Hong Kong.

Beyond Waimanalo you will see, rising on your left, the twin summits of Olomana Peak, 1,643 feet high, dividing Waimanalo Valley from Maunawili. By turning right shortly after passing the Olomana Golf Course you can wander through Keolu Hills, an urban sprawl created out of open fields after some developer flicked his magic wand. Or, if you stay on the divided highway, you will be faced with a choice of route. You can turn left on Route 61, at the Castle Hospital junction, which will lead to Kaneohe if you turn right at the Castle Junction traffic light or send you to Honolulu if you go straight up the hill via the pali tunnels. A right at the Castle Hospital junction on 61 will take you to Kailua and then you can return to Kaneohe either via the new highway (630)—the Mokapu Saddle Road, which begins at Kalaheo High School and leads to the shore road (Kaneohe Bay Drive) that hugs Kaneohe Bay. By going through Kailua and turning right you can see the fine beach at Kailua and the attrac-

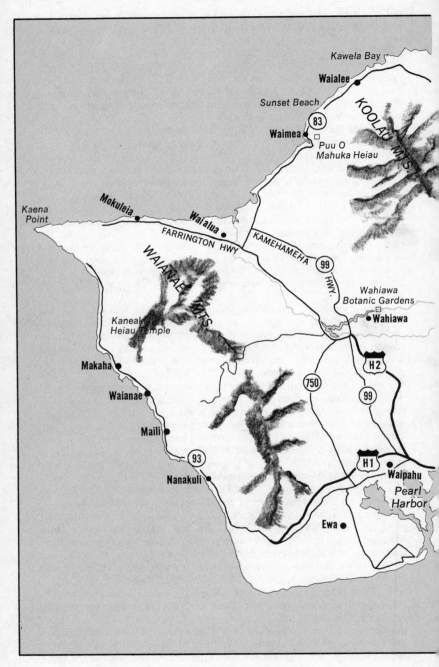

Kawela Bay

Waialee

Sunset Beach

KOOLAU WEST

83

Waimea

Puu O
Mahuka Heiau

Kaena
Point

Mokuleia

Waialua

FARRINGTON HWY

KAMEHAMEHA

WAIANAE MTS

99

HWY

Wahiawa
Botanic Gardens

Wahiawa

Kaneak
Heiau Temple

Makaha

H2

750

99

Waianae

Maili

H1

Waipahu

93

Pearl
Harbor

Nanakuli

Ewa

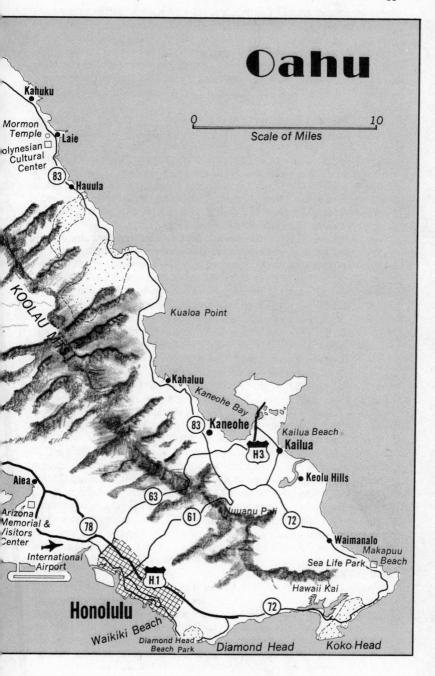

Oahu

0   10
Scale of Miles

Kahuku

Mormon
Temple
olynesian   Laie
Cultural
Center
83   Hauula

KOOLAU MTS.

Kualoa Point

Kahaluu

Kaneohe Bay

83   Kaneohe

Kailua Beach

H3   Kailua

Aiea

Arizona
Memorial &
Visitors
Center

Keolu Hills

63

61   Nuuanu Pali   72

International
Airport

Waimanalo

Makapuu
Beach

Sea Life Park

H1

Hawaii Kai

Honolulu

72

Waikiki Beach

Diamond Head
Beach Park   Diamond Head   Koko Head

tive residential district of Lanikai. The town of Kailua itself is a phenomenon. Thirty-five years ago there was a small village here. Today it's a thriving community of commuters who tunnel through the *pali* to work in Honolulu and come back to enjoy the relaxing atmosphere of the windward side. The supermarkets, banks, and department stores of Honolulu have set up attractive branches here, and Kailua gets more populous every day. In 1980 it had reached 35,873 and neighboring Kaneohe was up to 29,500.

Take a few minutes to drive along the dead-end road to Lanikai and its sparkling, palm-fringed beach. Offshore are the tiny Mokulua Islands. One of them, Moku Manu, is a haven for terns and man-of-war birds, which obligingly perform the important commercial function of leading fishermen to the schools of fish. Kailua Bay has plenty of these, and you'll see many a surfcaster trying his luck on the beach. A famous Hawaiian fish story insists that Ulanui, one of Kamehameha's runners, snatched a fish from these waters and ran with it so fast to Waikiki that it was still flopping when he set it down before the king.

The swimming at both Kalama and Kailua beaches is wonderful. The water, turquoise blue, is clearer than it is at Waikiki, and the waves are good for bodysurfing, at least the kind we like—they never reach the horrendous proportions of those at Makapuu. Kailua Beach Park has a dual personality: white sand at the edge of the sea, grass and a canal-fed pond slightly inland. All this plus the palm trees, the offshore islands, and the backdrop of cloud-capped Koolau Mountains combine to form an ideal tropic landscape. The temptation is to linger, but the rest of Oahu calls.

From Kailua you will drive across the base of Mokapu Peninsula, which is occupied by the Kaneohe Marine Corps Air Station, and thence south briefly through Kokokahi to join Kamehameha Highway (Route 83) and continue the Grand Circuit. Or you can take the freeway shortcut from Mokapu Drive to Kaneohe. Or detour to the new Hoomaluhia Regional Park in Kaneohe, the largest city park. Take Kionaole Road or Luluku Road, both off Kamehameha Highway. Open 9 A.M. to 3 P.M. There are easy two-hour guided hikes daily all week at 10 A.M. and 1 P.M., with time-outs for resting. A mile and a half beyond Kaneohe you will come to Heeia. The Heeia pier is headquarters for exploring the underwater coral gardens and other attractions of Kaneohe Bay. Honolulu Sailing Company, Box 1500, Kaneohe, HI 96744 (235–8264), offers snorkeling tours of Kaneohe Bay, for four or more adults. The tours provide an opportunity to see fantastic coral formations in the depths of the bay and some weird, long orange worms that populate it. A diver brings up things to look over. Not far away is Coconut Island, site of the University of Hawaii's Marine Biology Laboratory. There is a superb *mauka* view across Kaneohe Bay, from the glass-bottom boat.

Windward Expeditions, 789 Kailua Rd., Kailua, HI 96734 (263–3899) offers tours of Kailua Bay and Mokapu Point in an open six- to eight-passenger Zodiac. The three-hour, $60 per person trips take passengers close to eight small islets and bird sanctuaries off the windward coast, and past famous beachfront homes, including the one where the television show "Magnum, P.I." is shot. A guide provides a fascinating narrative about the history and legends of the region. If the seas are not too high, the tour highlight is a ride deep within a sea cave on one of the islands.

Kahaluu to Kahana Bay

Three miles beyond Heeia you will come to Kahaluu, which was Libby-ville when Libby, McNeill and Libby had a pineapple cannery here to process the pines from their Kaneohe plantation. When a blight attacked the crop, and the company, for economic reasons, moved to Wahiawa, the Hawaiians insisted it was all due to divine intervention. The old gods were furious at the desecration of ancient temples in the area. In any event, Libbyville is no more, and things are moving in Kahaluu, turning a once rustic area into something else, mostly houses and townhouses in the interior valleys. A new inland highway at the foot of Wilson Tunnel hooks up with the coast just north of Kahaluu Point. Back in this valley, Kahaluu is waking from a long slumber. There are new homes, roads, an interesting cemetery, the Valley of the Temples, and a replica of a 900-year-old Uji, Japan, Buddhist temple. In this area you will see both taro, from which *poi* is pounded, and bananas, but production of both have dipped in recent years.

Not far along the road, you reach the former Waiahole Poi Factory and then Kualoa Point, right down at the end of Kaneohe Bay, where you will see the little island called Chinaman's Hat which rises 206 feet above the water. It looks more like a *poi* pounder to us. Its official name is Mokolii, and it punctuates a magnificent landscape-seascape as you look southeastward down the whole sweep of Kaneohe Bay and the Koolau Mountains. Kualoa has been developed into beach parks both for overnight camping and lazy Sunday afternoon use, despite a tendency to be breezy. Because of its great importance in the life of native Hawaiian people, this regional park is listed in the National Register of Historical Places. It is undoubtedly one of the most beautiful picnic and camping areas on Oahu. Across the road from the park is Kualoa Ranch, where you can rent horses, Tuesday through Sunday.

An HVB warrior marks the stone ruins of Oahu's first sugar mill, erected in 1864, as you motor north to Kaaawa and the Crouching Lion, an old fishing shrine which dominates Kaaawa Beach from the top of a cliff, below a restaurant with the same name.

From Kaaawa the road swings left to follow the contours of lovely Kahana Bay. The valley on your left, watered by Kahana Stream, is a tropical idyll of banana, breadfruit, and mango trees. The beach in the cove is reached through a thick *kamani* grove and is fringed by ironwoods and pandanus trees, which look as though they were walking on their stilt-like roots. A vast State Park, which ultimately will encompass most of Kahana Valley from its apex to the bayfront, is under development.

Sacred Falls

If you're in an athletic mood, however, you may wish to push on five miles to Hauula and Sacred Falls. Watch for the sign which will indicate a rough dirt road turning left into the cane fields. You follow this road southwest for a mile and a half, park your car, take a deep breath, and start hiking up the trail. Do not be misled by robust types who refer to this as an easy walk. It is a tough two-mile hike up a rough mountain ravine, not recommended for the halt, the feeble, cardiac cases, or women in high-heeled shoes. In short, it's a hot little walk; take our word for it. The reward? The Sacred Falls plunge 87 feet from the cliff into the gorge, forming a mountain pool perhaps deep enough for a dip. The ravine is only 50 feet wide here. The Koolau *palis* loom 2,500 feet above you. This place can be enchanting, or the *palis* frightening. But best you skip this one if you are pressed for time.

Next major stop on your Grand Island Circuit is Laie, just three miles north of Hauula. The atmosphere may remind you of a Polynesian version of Salt Lake City. The Mormons were active as missionaries here, and the population of Laie is made up largely of Mormons from around the Pacific region.

Mormon Temple

You may want to walk around the beautiful grounds of the Mormon Temple at Laie, but non-practicing Mormons have not been permitted to enter the temple since the edifice was rededicated in 1978 after a $1-million remodeling. It is the first Mormon temple built outside the continental United States. It was the largest west of Utah from 1919, when it was built under the direction of Samuel Woolley, to the late 1950s, when the Los Angeles temple took total floor space honors. A square white building whose simple lines suggest the massive horizontal silhouette of Egyptian temples, the Mormon Temple has been likened to the Taj Mahal, to which it bears no resemblance whatsoever. It does stand, like the Taj, before a reflecting pool in the midst of formal gardens, but there the likeness ceases. The temple grounds are open to visitors every day from 9 A.M. to 9 P.M., and a guide is on hand to take you through the terraced gardens and tell you about the religion of the Latter-Day Saints and the history of the Laie Colony. The brief lecture and a free movie are educational experiences. Outside of Salt Lake City, the Hawaii LDS visitors center has the most visitors of any Mormon historical site in the world.

Another attraction in Laie is Brigham Young University–Hawaii, located on your left just before entering the town. Opened in 1955, it now has over 1,600 students about 90 percent of whom are Mormon. The school was built by Mormons while on their church mission. All students vow not to use drugs, tobacco, alcohol, coffee or tea, or wear beards or miniskirts.

At the campus entrance foyer, one sees a 33-foot mosaic depicting a flag-raising ceremony at Laie in 1921. Made of glazed tesserae, the sections were flown from Rome. The murals on either side were done by Edward T. Grigware of Cody, Wyoming. There is also a Museum of Natural History, featuring 3,000 bird specimens, 2,500 mammals, 2,500 fish and 1,000 amphibians and reptiles. Hours vary, but tours can be arranged by telephoning 293–3816. After leaving Laie you proceed north past Malaekahana State Park with its fine beach and picnic facilities.

At Kahuku you are at the halfway point of the Grand Circuit. It is only 44 miles from this former sugar plantation town back to Honolulu.

As you leave Kahuku you will notice on your right an abandoned sugar mill, which was open for public tours for several years. Also to your right you'll see experimental windmills, which officials hope will cut energy costs, and experimental aquaculture farms.

The highway reaches the sea again near Kawela Bay. Many Honolulu families have built unpretentious vacation places on this remote sandy beach with its lovely ironwood trees, through which the trade winds sing at night. Just this side of Kawela, Del Webb built the swanky resort retreat the Turtle Bay Hotel and a golf course. The elegance of this retreat is quite a contrast to life along Sunset Beach, where Oahu's flower children live simple lives. The sea booms against the rocky coast as you drive southwest to Waimea. Here's where young athletes ride the big breakers, especially at the Banzai Pipeline. Pipeline, Sunset-Ehukai and Waimea, all in this area, are considered to be among the five most dangerous beaches on Oahu. The other two are Sandy Beach and Makaha. En route, an HVB warrior indicates the George Washington Stone, a rocky silhouette on the cliff above Paumalu Beach. Despite the obvious resemblance, the Hawaiians will have none of this. It isn't George, they say, but Prince Kahikilani of Kauai, lover of a supernatural bird girl. He left her in order to surfride the long combers of Paumalu Beach. She gave him a red *lehua lei* and he promised he would never kiss another woman. Moments later, another woman appeared on the beach, hung an *ilima lei* on the prince and received the traditional kiss in response. Two of the bird girl's spies immediately flew off to report this peccadillo, whereupon the bird girl flew after her lover, tore the *ilima lei* from his neck, hung another *lehua lei* on him, and flew off. Prince Kahikilani, in hot pursuit, was turned to stone halfway up the cliff of Paumalu. Above these cliffs are the Comsat discs that relay telephone calls and TV to the Far East and Mainland via satellites 22,500 miles out in space.

Waimea Valley, a canyon extending for two miles into the mountains, is steeped in Hawaiian lore. There was a school here for the training of *kahunas. Heiaus* stood like sentinels in the mountains; the ruins of Oahu's largest, Puu-o-Mahuka, can be seen on a ridge north of Waimea Bay. It was here in 1780 that a temple priest predicted the conquest of Hawaii by the *haoles.* The canyon, watered by Kamananui and Kaiwikoele Streams, was the scene of a disastrous flood in 1894, forcing a large Hawaiian community to abandon this historic valley. Historical events notwithstanding, Waimea Bay is known internationally as the location of some of the biggest surfing waves in the world. During winter months waves can reach heights of 20 to 30 feet. Some 1,800 acres of the area are part of Waimea Falls Park (admission $8.50), with a restaurant, Hawaiian games site where you can try sports like spear-throwing, an arboretum, and other facilities surrounding 45-foot Waimea Falls and the natural pool below it. You can spend the day 35 miles away from Honolulu in this park or across from the world famous surfing beach at Waimea.

If you've had enough of these valleys, picnic, or relax on the rolling sand dunes of Waimea Bay. But stay out of the ocean at this point; be content to admire it as it hurls itself against the unprotected beach. You'll have ample opportunity to swim at Haleiwa, a few miles farther south. Just before reaching this little seaside town you'll come to a dairy farm on the *mauka* side of the road which is worth visiting if you have small children and need a break for them—farm animals to ogle. Then on to picturesque Haleiwa.

Efforts are underway to preserve Haleiwa's sleepy qualities. The town is fast becoming a classic example of plantation living 50 or 70 years ago. Many handicraft and art shops run by young Mainland *malihinis* now dot the town, most in good taste.

Sugar and Pineapples

From Haleiwa you can visit Waialua Plantation, noted for its progressive labor-management relations, management having led the way in forming Hawaii's first plantation community association. You can also continue from here to Mokuleia and, by dirt road, to the western tip of the island at Kaena Point. But this is a detour more logically combined with the Waianae Circuit described below. There is still much to see on the Grand Circuit from Kamehameha Highway, which now cuts inland below Waialua and climbs steadily for 1,000 feet through cane fields to Leilehua Plateau if you are on Kaukonahua Road. On your right as you climb is Kaala, whose flat top, 4,030 feet above sea level, is the highest point on Oahu. As you approach the tableland of Leilehua, the green of sugar cane gives way to the darker green of spiked leaves deployed row upon row for miles around like an army in formation against the dark red powdery earth. This is pineapple country, and you've never seen a finer agricultural sight in your life. The greater part of Leilehua Plateau is devoted to the cultivation of these fruits, each one reposing in a kind of heraldic green-gold splendor on its nest. Clear to the mountains it goes, this stunning pattern of red, green, and gold, like a superb rug of formal design carpeting the volcanic crust of the island. While the fields are a thing of beauty, the 40 percent dip in production in the last few years worries the industry. There used to be a fine for snatching pines. We confess to minor depredations, but plead our former military status and a variation of the attractive nuisance clause. Petty theft is no longer justified, however. If you are driving on Kamehameha Highway, an alternate route to Wahiawa, there is a fine pine pavilion where you can eat your fill of ripe pineapple for a fee much smaller than a fine. Don't miss the chance. No pineapple, canned or "fresh," has ever tasted like this Hawaiian version straight from the stalk. The addition of sugar is unthinkable. If anything, you'll want a dash of salt to counteract the high acidity. One word of advice: be moderate. These pineapples are so luscious that you may end up with something you haven't had since you ate too many green apples as a child.

Wahiawa

As you approach Wahiawa, you will see a gap in the Waianaes on your right. This is Kolekole Pass, through which Japanese planes zoomed down on sleeping Schofield Barracks one memorable Sunday morning.

Wahiawa, straddling the highway between the two forks of the Kaukonahua Stream, has the look of a growing urban community. It is a busy community of some 16,653 people, its population augmented by frequent incursions from the surrounding plantation towns and nearby Schofield Barracks. It is the nucleus of several housing developments constructed for plantation workers by Dole Company. Wahiawa is also the depot for pineapple shipments by truck to the Honolulu canneries 14 miles away. A growing community, catering to service families from Schofield and Wheeler Air Force Base, Wahiawa has some wonderful overgrown general stores, one of which has burgeoned into a fascinating Island department store. At the end of California Avenue there is the Wahiawa Botanical Garden, an oasis of tropical trees and shrubs.

Those interested in military things might find it worthwhile to go inside Schofield Barracks and visit the Tropic Lightning Historical Center. In a remote corner of the Schofield Barracks base is a quiet, tree-shaded post cemetery. What makes it different is that it contains the graves of seven soldiers executed for murder or mutiny and four Italian prisoners of war who somehow were brought to Hawaii from the deserts of North Africa in World War II.

The Sacred Birthstones

A place of special interest for anthropologists and students of Polynesian history is Kukaniloko near Wahiawa, in a pineapple field on the Waialua side of Kaukonahua Gulch. This half-acre plot is the historic Place of the Sacred Birthstones, where Hawaiian women of royal blood came to have their children. The stones, protruding three feet above the ground, are vestiges of a maternity center whose origins are lost in the mists of time before recorded history. It is known, however, that Kukaniloko was used up to the reign of Kamehameha the Great. The birthstone, called Kukaniloko, was the primitive equivalent of a delivery table, designed to support the woman in labor. The stones which surrounded the central stone were for the *alii,* the high chiefs and chieftesses of Oahu, who assisted at the birth like medical students in a contemporary operating room.

The Wahiawa Hongwanji Temple at 1067 California Avenue may be worth a visit. The altar Buddha is carved from Japanese cypress and decorated with gold leaf. The urn room, always open, is a triumph of simplicity.

Schofield Barracks is best seen from Wilikina Drive, which skirts Wahiawa. Schofield is headquarters for the 25th Infantry Division, which has been here since 1954, except for its Vietnam campaigns. It is one of the most attractive army posts in America. It was catapulted into world prominence on December 7, 1941 and has never been the same since that morning and subsequent developments, which have included *From Here to Eternity* and the organization of Sergeant O'Reilly's Wolfhounds. Schofield's nearest neighbor is Wheeler Air Force Base, home for dozens of Army helicopters, combat veterans of Vietnam. Wheeler is not open for visiting, though the place has historic interest—it is the Le Bourget of the Pacific, the place where Maitland and Hegenberger in their Army Fokker made the first flight from California to Hawaii (1927). Seven years later Australian Sir Charles Kingsford-Smith took off from Wheeler on the first flight by anyone from Hawaii to California.

From Schofield on into Honolulu there are alternate routes. If in a hurry take the new H-2 freeway that cuts across the gulches and ravines, and over the longest bridge on the island, the shortest route back to town or remain on Kamehameha Highway, Route 99, skirting Wheeler, through Waipio, through the middle of Mililani Town and then descend through the cane fields of Oahu Sugar Company, crossing the huge red gash in the earth known as Kipapa Gulch. From either road you'll have a panoramic view of Pearl Harbor from the road and glimpses of Diamond Head in the distance. Now you come to a maze of concrete superhighways. Go right on H-1 and you whip over the tops of cane fields and housing areas toward Makaha. Turn left on H-1 and you speed past the new Pacific Palisades residential community, where 8,000 live, and around Aiea on the mountain side and back into the city—unless you hit the rush hour, in which case you can sit bumper-to-bumper and listen to your car radio. You can elect to stay on Kamehameha Highway, which leads into Pearl City, runs near Pearl Harbor, and leads back to Honolulu by way of the airport.

Two Roads to Honolulu

Between Pearl City and Aiea, on the *mauka* side of old Kamehameha Highway, you will see what is left of the rural country this once was—neat watercress beds like a touch of old Japan and just a step from Pearl Harbor.

Now this stretch changes by the week with overpasses, shopping centers, a bread factory, houses, apartments, businesses, junkyards, and a never-ending stream of automobiles. Aiea itself is changing. Once a sleepy plantation town and site of a sugar refinery, now it has the new Pearlridge Shopping Center. Farther up the red hills are several new housing developments. The Pearlridge is a showpiece in itself, with more gaudy colors in its air-conditioned interiors than the Kahala Mall at the opposite end of the city. The ruins of Keaiwa Heiau are in the Ewa Forest Reserve above Aiea Heights. This *heiau,* devoted to medicine, was set in a garden of herbs, plants, and trees, all of which had medicinal properties known and used by the Hawaiians, who had an almost perfect health record before the white man presented them with syphilis, measles, and other "civilized" diseases with which their pharmacopoeia couldn't cope. If you have the time, drive to the top of Aiea Heights and visit this area. It's cool and aromatic and has lovely views south over Pearl Harbor, west toward the Waianaes, and east to Honolulu. One of the better hiking trails in the Koolau Mountains has its origin in the park.

From Aiea, there are three ways of returning to Honolulu. One is Kamehameha Highway (Route 99), which dips immediately south, continues to skirt Pearl Harbor, passes near Foster Village, where residents sport one of the highest average incomes in the state, and continues under the new H-1 ramp that passes the airport and becomes Nimitz Highway (Route 92) as it passes through an industrial and warehousing area, before crossing Keehi Lagoon. H-1, as it skirts Aiea, turns right at Aloha Stadium and becomes the ramp at the airport. It then connects back with the older portion of H-1 at Middle Street.

The third route, Moanalua Road (Route 78), is faster and a little more interesting, since there are still reminders of rural Oahu along this route, *mauka* views of mountains and valleys and the delights of Moanalua Gardens. At the same time, you will also have a glimpse of vast Tripler Army Hospital, whose 1,500 beds were prepared in anticipation of a possible invasion of Japan, and you will drive past Fort Shafter, a bonton post, headquarters for the United States Army's Western Command. Nerve center of all army activities in World War II, it is girded by a wall built at that time by unregenerate Italian prisoners of war. On one of these is inscribed in perfect Tuscan the legend: Built for the Enemy. So much for the vestiges of history. Fort Shafter looks now, as it did then, more like a country club than an army post, another indication that Hawaii has a way of imposing its beauty in the most unlikely places. Shafter, in fact, is becoming more notable as a green oasis with every passing year, since Honolulu's housing developments are reaching around it like an urban octopus. Shafter, when conceived in 1906, was out of town. No more. For a different look backward, go to the Kaewai Elementary School library in Kalihi and see a mural by David Asherman showing the royal family at a picnic in 1859 at the site of today's school.

The Eastern Tip Circuit

If your time is very limited, you can have a concentrated sample of Oahu's beauty in a two-to-three-hour swing from Honolulu around the eastern end of the island. For rugged coastal scenery, this would be hard to beat, but it is not characteristic, for sugar and pineapple are not visible at this end of the island except in supermarkets. The tour can be taken either by way of Waikiki and Diamond Head, returning by way of the Pali and Nuuanu Valley, or vice versa. Since we have already explored this area in the former direction, let's go by way of the *pali*. We recommend this approach in any event; it avoids the return *pali* climb, which is still less than a pleasure, despite the celebrated *pukas* designed to make it easier.

The view from the *pali* has already been described. If you haven't seen it yet, it is an excellent idea to begin the eastern circuit from this point, even though the rest of the tour may be an anticlimax by comparison. The descent from *pali* pass to windward Oahu provides a series of breathtaking vistas. In the old days, on the Windward Oahu Bus, it also produced a series of minor cardiac crises as the bus rattled around the hairpin turns, now nearly slamming into the mountain wall, now teetering on the edge of eternity with all the passengers literally gasping at the view.

At Castle Junction you should bear right on the road that leads through lush Maunawili Valley to Kailua. From here on around, you will be seeing the initial attractions of the grand circuit but in reverse order. The stunning close-ups of the fluted Koolau *palis* will be on your right, at their most impressive if you see them in that special sharp relief provided by the morning sunlight. This is not to deprecate the subtle advantages of seeing them later—*à contre-jour,* but do not take the drive in this direction too late in the afternoon or you may be bothered, after Koko Head, by the glare of the descending sun.

Stop at Makapuu Point to look back at the inspiring view of the windward coast: Waimanalo Bay with Rabbit Island offshore, the ship *Essex* looking beached at Sea Life Park, and the noble mass of Mokapu guarding the northern reaches of Kailua Bay.

The drive from Makapuu along the eastern ridge of the island to Koko Head is one of the scenic wonders of the world. Below you on your left the lava headlands meet the Pacific, so blue at this point as to suggest the purple depths which Homer called wine-dark. On your right the dazzling blue Hawaiian sky meets a volcanic landscape and the locale of an occasional scene from the "Hawaii 5-O" television series.

This unforgettable impression is brief. The Garden of Eden has already been created at Hanauma Bay. Beyond Lunalilo Home Road, which leads to this valley, lie hundreds of homes of Hawaii Kai, grouped geometrically around the marina once known as Kuapa Fishpond, formerly the most flourishing on Oahu. As you start to cross this ancient royal pond, modern Honolulu comes to meet you, as Hawaii Kai has transformed this area into something new and strange. Will this destroy the beauty of Oahu? The answer is implicit at Aina Haina, Waialae-Kahala, and other flowering subdivisions which once tore up the earth between here and Diamond Head. The houses are barely visible for the trees. Never underestimate the recuperative power of the tropics, except where zoning allows high rises. They made their appearance at Hawaii Kai in the 1970s.

The Waianae Tour

The special character of the arid west coast of Oahu is perhaps best indicated by the fact that few tours are scheduled for this area. In other words, you won't find many tourists on the Waianae circuit, just Hawaiians. This, of course, is part of the place's charm. Once totally rustic, in recent years there have been changes, including the industrial complex near Barbers Point, with refineries, and the resort, condominium, and golf courses in Makaha Valley.

The Waianae Mountains, older and higher than the Koolaus, dominate this region, and if the Navy ever relinquishes its hold on Lualualei then Kolekole Pass may become passable for the view from the top. The spectacular road which winds through the pass has been under military jurisdiction for years. The military keeps the road closed because of the Navy's Lualualei Ammunition Depot and its many magazines on the leeward side of the mountains. The spectacular Navy communications towers in Lualualei are taller than the Empire State Building.

You can get an inkling of what Kolekole Pass is like by driving up to it. This should be done from the Schofield Barracks side. Access to Naval Magazine Lualualei is restricted to persons bearing valid U.S. Department of Defense military ID cards. You obtain permission beforehand by writing: Commanding Officer, Naval Magazine, Lualualei, Oahu, HI 96792 to make the crossing toward the ocean. But, for the view only, drive through cool, thickly forested uplands to the pass, from which you have superb views westward toward the sea and eastward over the Leilehua Plateau to the Koolau Range. So far and no farther. You come to a gate, which is not only closed but guarded. Ask the soldier at the gatehouse if it's all right to take the side road to Kolekole Stone. This is just a formality; he always says yes. The stone, shaped like a huge calabash with deeply fluted sides, is more than eight feet tall. It has been sitting here considerably longer than the United States Army, and according to Hawaiians *it* is the real guardian of the pass. It is no ordinary rock, but Kolekole, a kind of early Hawaiian patron saint of travelers, a kindly demi-goddess, standing here through the ages and receiving floral offerings, including her favorite strands of perfumed *maile* leaves, from all who come through the pass.

Apart from this tantalizing glimpse of the interior, the motorized tourist's acquaintance with the Waianaes will be mostly restricted to the coast. You begin the Waianae tour from Honolulu by taking the H-1 Freeway around Pearl Harbor and Pearl City, or you get on the slower Nimitz Highway. Kamehameha Highway through Pearl City, a city of 42,535 that grew 55 percent in 10 years and through cane fields toward Waianae. If you wish to catch the flavor of the old sugar mill days during which the community was founded, you can visit the Plantation Village and Cultural Garden Park at Waipahu. The park, when completed, will be a living park with botanical gardens and old plantation homes that can be visited. Arakawa's is special for shopping, a traditional and typical general store.

The Western Coast

As you pass through the cane fields, Waipahu, Pearl Harbor, and everything to Diamond Head are spread out on your left. On your right are the southern fringes of the Waianae Mountains descending to the coastal plain. They are little more than toy mountains here. Puu Palailai, opposite the turnoff to Barbers Point Naval Air Station, is less than 500 feet high. That new housing development on your right is Makakilo, a city of 7,714. To the left are the refineries and warehouses of expanding Campbell Industrial Park. These refineries underscore the state's dependence upon foreign oil, much of it Indonesian, for 98 percent of its fuel. The beach site of the former home of Alice Kamokila Campbell may be developed into an $800-million creation called West Beach. There will be homes, hotels, a marina, and golf courses. And farther along, the coast, quiet for generations, is showing the growth that can be seen everywhere in Hawaii. The population of the leeward coast doubled, to about 31,000 in the 1963–73 decade.

You reach the sea at Kahe Point. From here you have your first extended view up the western coast, an arid stretch of black rock and white sand whose desolate beauty is punctuated by *kiawe* trees, leaning with the wind toward the sea and providing a lattice of welcome shade on the beaches. The coast is spacious and bare, rather than lush. No reef protects it from offshore currents.

Nanakuli, 26 miles from Honolulu, is a Hawaiian homesteading area, a corner of "authentic" Hawaii. Three miles north of Nanakuli is a spot with the most mellifluous name we have ever heard: Lualualei-Maile. It seems almost incongruous that this should be the setting for a Naval Ammunition Depot. It's just two miles from Lualualei to Waianae, with its fine sand beach and tiny fishing port protected by a breakwater.

Surfers' Paradise

Makaha has an excellent beach for swimming, sunning, or picnicking in the latticed shade of feathery *kiawe* trees. It is also a surfers' paradise, with combers that tower 20 to 40 feet. During the Makaha surfing meets in the winter months, the local boys are joined by experts from California and faraway Australia.

A craze of the early 1970s that captured the interest of many Mainlanders is the collecting of puka shells, those little white gems with the hole (puka) in the middle. The best hunting grounds are along this coast, especially Makaha and Kaena Point and the North Shore at Sunset Beach. One warning: don't leave valuables in your car when shell hunting or surfing. Police have been harassed by reports of rip-offs and an assortment of more serious crimes on the Leeward Coast.

At Makua, 40 miles from Honolulu and just before the end of Farrington Highway, you can explore Kaneana Cave. Formed of lava rock and coral, it was once the alleged home of Kaneana, a deity who had the disconcerting habit of changing his outer form from human being to shark without warning.

Not far beyond the cave, Farrington Highway turns to coral fill and gravel that is usually impassable. Until recent years the beach at this corner of Oahu was virginal in its simplicity and beauty. People just weren't around. Then squatters created a shantytown on the beach and recent times have seen confrontations between state bulldozers (the state wants a park) and the squatters, who want an undisturbed, simple life-style. Even Hurricane Iwa on November 23, 1982, failed to blow them away. Work is done on landslides across the old railroad bed periodically, but figure on walking the last two miles to reach Kaena Point, Oahu's seldom-visited western tip.

Kaena Point

Just as you think you've come to an idyllic place that is really out of this world, you'll be reminded of how much the world is with you everywhere by a sign which indicates the proximity of a satellite tracking station: No Visitors. You'll have to be content with a glimpse of the equipment, like something from science fiction, from outside a wire fence.

An automatic lighthouse stands at the tip of Kaena Point, a desolate spot with a lonely beauty of its own. The road improves on the Mokuleia Coast side of the point, but remains unpaved for another four miles.

At Mokuleia you will again enjoy the pleasures of an asphalt road and, from the beach, a magnificent panorama of the northern coast of Oahu. From Mokuleia you dip south on Kaukonahua Road, skirting the southern edge of Waialua and thence ascending a beautiful stretch of road through ironwood trees, past the University of Hawaii Experimental Station on the right, the Kaukonahua Stream on the left, to Wahiawa in the heart of the Leilehua Plateau. From here it's a 19-mile drive on a familiar road back to Honolulu. After this, you've done absolutely everything there is to do.

PRACTICAL INFORMATION FOR OAHU

HOW TO GET THERE. Air travel is the way almost everyone gets to Oahu. Boat travel, the only way before Pan American World Airways's first passenger load aboard the China Clipper arrived in 1936, is now a memory. Jets land at Honolulu International Airport every few minutes every day. The flight from West Coast cities, primarily San Francisco and Los Angeles, takes 4½ hours, give or take 15 minutes depending upon the status of the jet stream.

United Air Lines has dominated service since 1946, especially after purchasing Pan Am's Pacific routes in 1985. Others servicing Oahu for many years: *Northwest Airlines, Western Airlines, American Airlines, Trans World Airlines,* and *Continental Airlines.* New competitors are: *Delta* and *Hawaiian Air* with flights to five West Coast cities, Anchorage, Alaska, Samoa, and Tonga. *Pan American World Airways* also reinstated service in 1987.

For which foreign carriers stop in Honolulu see *Facts at Your Fingertips.*

If you plan a Neighbor Island visit after Oahu, there are frequent, regular flights.

ACCOMMODATIONS. There are more than 100 hotels or hotel apartments in Waikiki with 38,600 rooms, more than half of all rooms in the state. In 1986 they averaged $68.30 per room; the off-the-beach average was $44.05.

Many hotels on Oahu are truly luxurious and beautiful. The outstanding resort developments, however, are found on the Neighbor Islands. Waikiki has a number of inexpensive, pedestrian hostelries, and some bordering on the threadbare or with questionable clients.

All accommodations listed have private baths, and prices quoted are for European Plan (food not included). There is no room tax in Hawaii. Something new is that many are adding a few dollars onto their rates for the Christmas-to-Easter winter period. Hotel price categories based on double occupancy are: $105 and up, *Super Deluxe;* $60–$105, *Deluxe;* $40–$60, *Expensive;* $25–$40, *Moderate;* below $30, *Inexpensive.*

Note: Almost all the deluxe hotels have rooms available for less than $60.

Large Hotels in Waikiki

Super Deluxe

Halekulani. 2199 Kalia Rd., Honolulu, HI 96815 (923–2311). Once a popular low-key set of 37 bungalows, this has been rebuilt into a superb collection of 5 buildings from 2 to 16 stories. The main building was retained, as was the famed House Without a Key. The 456 rooms include beachfronts, off-beach, small suites, garden rooms, and a Royal Suite. There are 22 rooms equipped for wheelchairs. The old parking lot is a garden; the new parking lot is across the street. The emphasis is on quiet and elegance. Each room has 3 telephones. Owned by Mitsui Real Estate of Japan. *LaMer* is a top French restaurant; *Orchids* is the new name for the old dining room that was left intact.

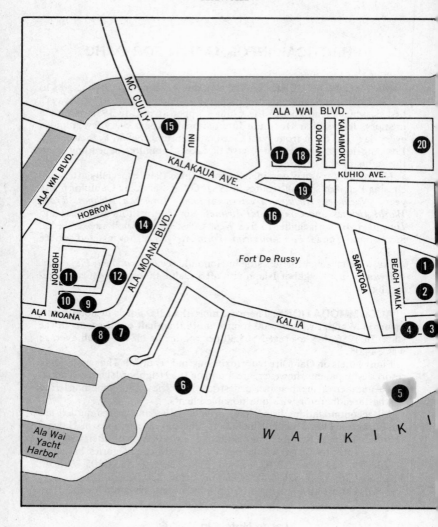

Waikiki Hotels

Ambassador Hotel **17**
Aston Waikiki Tower **3**
Best Western Waikiki Plaza **16**
Coral Reef Hotel **27**
Discovery Bay **10**
Halekulani Hotel **54**
Hawaii Dynasty **12**
Hawaiian Monarch Hotel **15**
Hawaiian Regent **43**
Hilton Hawaiian Village **6**
Holiday Inn-Waikiki Beach **42**
Holiday Isle **56**

Hyatt Regency Waikiki **46**
Ilikai Hotel **8**
Inn on the Park **14**
Island Colony **25**
Kuhio Village Hotel **33**
Maile Court **18**
Miramar **29**
Marine Surf Waikiki **24**
Outrigger Coral Seas Hotel **1**
Outrigger East **30**
Outrigger Edgewater Hotel **4**

Outrigger Malia **23**
Outrigger Prince Kuhio **35**
Outrigger Reef **5**
Outrigger Reef Towers **55**
Outrigger Surf **26**
Outrigger Waikiki **49**
Outrigger West **28**
Pacific Beach Hotel **44**
Park Shore **41**
Princess Kaiulani Hotel **47**

Waikiki

ALA WAI CANAL

ALA WAI BLVD.

ALOHA

NOHONANI

NAHUA

WALINA

KANEKAPOLEI

ROYAL HAWAIIAN

LEWERS

SEASIDE

KUHIO AVE.

TUSITALA

KUHIO AVE.

OHUA

King's
Village

KAIULANI

UNIU

LILIUOKALANI

PAOAKALANI

International
Market Place

KALAKAUA AVE.

KOA

Royal Hawaiian
Shopping Center

HELUMOA

B E A C H

Aquarium

Kapiolani
Park

Prince Kuhio
Beach Park

Quality Inn Waikiki **38**
Queen Kapiolani **39**
Royal Hawaiian Hotel **50**
Sheraton Moana Surfrider **48**
Sheraton Waikiki **53**
Waikiki Banyan **36**
Waikiki Beachcomber **51**
Waikiki Circle Hotel **45**

Waikiki Gateway Hotel **19**
Waikiki Grand Hotel **40**
Waikiki Hobron **11**
Waikiki Marina **9**
Waikiki Parc **52**
Waikiki Resort **34**
Waikiki Sand Villa **31**
Waikiki Surf **21**

Waikiki Surf East **22**
Waikiki Surf West **20**
Waikiki Sunset **37**
Waikiki Townhouse **32**
Waikiki Village **2**
Waikikian **7**

Kahala Hilton. 5000 Kahala Ave., Honolulu, HI 96816 (734–2211). It is about 10 minutes by car from Waikiki—a pleasant drive around Diamond Head and through one of Honolulu's most beautiful residential areas. A shuttle bus service costs $1.75 one-way and puts guests in touch with the main stem as they desire. Except for an occasional shopping foray, most prefer to remain close to the comfort and luxury of the hotel. Kahala Hilton rises in gleaming splendor on the shore of Kahala Beach.

Extensive landscaping is very much a part of the architecture, with multicolored bougainvillea cascading from the *lanais* (balconies). High ceilings, dramatic chandeliers, and tasteful furnishings give the public rooms a feeling of graceful living. Shutters and other Polynesian accents contribute to the informality. The hotel boasts not only its own beach and swimming pool but a lagoon stocked with rainbow-hued reef fish and dolphins. The Lagoon Terrace rooms are cottage-style, built around the lagoon where the pet porpoises play.

Orchids placed on guests' pillows each evening add a romantic touch. In fact there's a clinic on flowers each Friday at 11:30 A.M. There is a nurse on duty; a physician on call; also a sauna and expert masseuse. Of the hotel's 370 luxurious rooms, 56 are suites, and many rooms have private *lanais.* There is no charge for children who occupy a room with their parents. Reservations can be made at any Hilton hotel. The Kahala Hilton is a frequent winner of the AAA Five Diamond Award.

Deluxe

Colony Surf. 2895 Kalakaua Ave., Honolulu, HI 97815 (923–5751). 171 condominium units and penthouse suites (and 50 hotel rooms) on the beach at Diamond Head with complete kitchen, laundry, maid and garage service start at $100. Some of the apartments are privately owned; it is also the home of *Michel's Restaurant,* which offers excellent French cuisine and vivid marine sunsets and is also open for breakfast and lunch. Swank *Outrigger Canoe Club* is right next door. No children under 12 permitted. A new addition is the *Colony East.* These 50 units face the park and Diamond Head. Air-conditioned and with kitchenettes. Located on the grounds is *Bobby McGee's Conglomeration* nightclub.

Discovery Bay. 1778 Ala Moana Blvd., Honolulu, HI 96815 (944–8555). A 43-story condo with 666 rooms, 150 of which are hotel units. Five-day minimum. Three restaurants, *Bon Appetit, Renoun Milano,* and *McDonald's,* shops, pool, cocktail lounge.

Hawaiian Regent. 2552 Kalakaua Ave., Honolulu, HI 96815 (922–6611). An elegant, architectural-award-winning luxury hotel overlooking the beach at Waikiki.The 1,350 luxury rooms feature two double beds, refrigerators, color TVs, and private *lanais.* There are shops, tennis, two swimming pools, three ballrooms, and 11 meeting areas that can accommodate up to 900. Its four restaurants include the multi-award-winning *Third Floor,* which many consider the finest in town. Also *The Summery* for informal family dining; the *Cafe Regent* for light meals and ice cream specialties; *Tiffany* for a cosy meal in comfort. The *Garden Court Lounge* offers music for listening and dancing in the open atmosphere of a tropical courtyard. The *Library* has won awards for its interior design as a piano bar. The *Lobby Bar* offers some of Hawaii's finest music. Located on the land which was once the home of Queen Liliuokalani, the *Hawaiian Regent* aims to retain the spirit of regal Hawaiian hospitality.

Hilton Hawaiian Village. 2005 Kalia Rd., Honolulu, HI 96815 (949–4321). This is the fabulous 22-acre complex built by the late Henry

J. Kaiser in 1955. Hilton bought and enlarged it until the *Village* now has 2,525 air-conditioned rooms. A $100-million refurbishment has made it even more elegant.

There are four swimming pools, a lagoon, Duke Kahanamoku Beach, and the only private dock in Waikiki, mooring for the 72-foot *Hilton Rainbow I* catamaran. Convention and conference facilities include the Mid-Pacific Conference Center that can seat 3,500 persons, and assorted smaller rooms and *lanai*. The 10 restaurants and 13 lounges include the *Golden Dragon* Chinese restaurant, *Beach Bar* and several cocktail lounges including the *Garden Bar, Beach Bar, Hau Tree Bar, Tapa Bar,* and *Golden Dragon Bar.*

The exotic *Rainbow Bazaar Shopping Center* has many of the 100 shops in this self-contained resort complex. Its restaurants include Shasteen's, J's Pancake House, Pizza Place, Hatsuhana snack bar, *Village Ice Cream Parlour,* and *Benihana of Japan*. Other features are a Thai temple and a Japanese pagoda.

The 31-story *Hilton Rainbow Tower,* designed for this complex by Island architect Edwin L. Bauer, has the world's tallest murals, brilliant arching rainbows, at either end. The 1968 addition has 800 rooms, and the landscaping is delightful.

The 1,056-room *Tapa Tower,* opened in 1982, has 35 floors, a dining room, bar, and cafe. This $100 million addition makes the village second only to the Las Vegas Hilton in the number of rooms.

Holiday Inn-Waikiki Beach. 2570 Kalakaua Ave., Honolulu, HI 96815 (922–2511). Across the street from Kuhio Beach, this new one is a deluxe beachfront hotel of 25 stories with 637 air-conditioned rooms. There are two restaurants, the *Captain's Table,* a gourmet offering with a good view of Waikiki after dark, and *The Sandwich Island Coffee House,* a family-type place. *The Captain's Lounge* has nightly entertainment. A poolside bar complements two other cocktail lounges. Convention facilities can handle 200. Write Holiday Inn—Waikiki Beach, 2570 Kalakaua Ave. Honolulu, HI 96815.

Hyatt Regency. 2424 Kalakaua Ave., Honolulu, HI 96815 (922–9292). A giant luxury hotel, one of the newest, located across the street from the oldest, the *Moana*. Chris Hemmeter, creator of *King's Village* next door, built this 1,234-room palace, making it one of the big four in Honolulu hotels. The *Hyatt Regency* has everything the modern hotel can offer: air conditioning, television, pools, restaurants, shops, and meeting rooms. The lobby is up, the central waterfall comes down, and the Edward Brownlee sculpture that hangs suspended is a conversation opener. This central area is called the Great Hall, and besides the Brownlee you can see both 40-floor towers that mark this $100 million creation. The top 36 rooms have been turned into the Regency Club, with special elevator keys, a Continental breakfast, and a complimentary limousine thrown in. Dining or drinking rooms are *Bagwells,* the *Colony, Spats, Terrace Grille, Trappers, Harry's Bar,* and the *Elegant Dive.*

The Ilikai. 1777 Ala Moana Blvd., Honolulu, HI 96815 (949–3811). Stands at the gateway to Waikiki, a sort of standout high rise where many such structures choke the area. It glistens in the sun as it rises 30 stories to the sky above the Ala Wai Yacht Harbor. There are 800 spacious hotel rooms, each with a private *lanai* with view, radio and television, bath, and many with kitchenettes or bars. Minimum rate for a single in the newest part of the hotel facing Hobron Lane is $99. Mountain and ocean views higher, as are suites. The restaurants at the Ilikai complex defy comparison for continuously excellent cuisine in Honolulu. Thirty stories in the sky, via an outside glass elevator, is the *Champeaux,* for Sunday brunch only, dining in glass-enclosed luxury. Others are *Maiko's* Japanese restaurant, the *Centre Court, Pier 7,* the *Power Station, Annabelle's* for the disco set, and *Angles* for drinks. Nearby in the Ilikai Marine is the *El Crab Catcher* seafood restaurant. Recreation is unlimited at the Ilikai. There are 2 freshwater swimming pools, a sunway to the sandy beach, and 7 tennis courts. The hotel was sold to a Japanese company in 1987 and is under new management.

Outrigger Prince Kuhio. 2500 Kuhio Ave., Honolulu, HI 96815 (922–0811). This 620-room luxury hotel features air-conditioned rooms with ocean or mountain views, the elegant *Protea* restaurant, and a lovely tropical garden with waterfall. In 1985 the hotel introduced a Kuhio Club, a hotel within a hotel, with exclusive features. A block from Kuhio Beach and Kapiolani Park.

Outrigger Waikiki. 2335 Kalakaua Ave., Honolulu, HI 96815 (923–0711). On the site of old *Outrigger Canoe Club.* Near the *Moana Hotel* on the beach and across the street from the *International Market Place.* A high rise, each room has a *lanai* looking down on the sand. Restaurants include *Perry Boys' Smorgy, Blue Dolphin, Rigger, Chuck's Steak House, Brass Rail,* and *Molokai* room, cocktail lounges, a pool, shops, a meeting place, and 530 rooms.

Pacific Beach. 2490 Kalakaua Ave., Honolulu, HI 96815 (922–1233). A resort complex of 850 rooms overlooking Waikiki Beach and within walking distance of shopping areas and Kapiolani Park. Rooms offer views of the ocean, Diamond Head, and mountains, each with private *lanai,* color TV, air-conditioning, and refrigerator or full kitchen facilities.

A 280,000-gallon indoor oceanarium presents a unique treat for patrons of the hotel's restaurants, cocktail lounges, and disco, located at various levels, each with its own panoramic view of this collection of tropical sea life. The hotel has 2 tennis courts, a swimming pool, Jacuzzi, and a shuffleboard and game area. For meetings, conventions, and banquets there are 10 rooms capable of accommodating groups from 50 to 2,000.

Princess Kaiulani. 120 Kaiulani Ave., Honolulu, HI 96815 (922–5811). Addition of the new Diamond Head and 29-story Tower Wings brings accommodations in this big modern Sheraton-operated hotel to 1,156 rooms. In the center of Waikiki, at 120 Kaiulani Ave., the hotel is set back from the street in a tropical garden which features a large swimming pool. Rooms on lower floors overlook this. From the upper reaches of the hotel, there are *makai* views of the sea and wonderful views of the Koolau Mountains on the *mauka* side. Many rooms have small private balconies but views are rapidly being blocked. With its handsome modern lobby, *Colonnade Cafe, Kahili Bar,* and attractive shops, the *Princess Kaiulani,* built by architect Gardner Dailey in 1954, set the pace for hotels on the *mauka* side of Kalakaua. The new building has a Japanese restaurant called *Momoyama* and a Chinese restaurant, *Lotus Moon.* Suites are high above Waikiki with sweeping views.

Royal Hawaiian. 2259 Kalakaua Ave., Honolulu, HI 96815 (923–7311). One of the most famous hotels in the world, this pink stucco caravansary, once surrounded by lush tropical gardens, has an idyllic setting right on the beach overlooking Diamond Head. It has been through a number of changes in recent decades, and after Matson Navigation sold it, part of the gardens were used for additions and changes to the beach hotel scene. Sheraton built the 31-story *Sheraton-Waikiki,* one of the 10 largest hotel buildings in the world, right next door. On the other side of the property a 16-story wing was added to the old queen. It has 192 rooms, and although it came 42 years after the main building, and is a high rise, it retains the great arches and pillars of the "Pink Palace." All deluxe rooms face the ocean, and there is a pool. All Sheraton hotels in Waikiki are owned by Japanese financier Kenji Osano and operated by Sheraton.

Despite the monoliths that have leaped into the skies on both sides of the *Royal,* it retains its preeminence as a beach landmark, an oasis of yesterday amid the concrete that characterizes Waikiki today. It celebrated its first 50 years with a party in 1977.

Sheraton Moana Surfrider. 2365 Kalakua Ave., Honolulu, HI 96815 (922–3111). A $48-million-dollar historic refurbishment program and upgrade has returned this world-famous property, originally built in 1901, to a period of nostalgic elegance complemented by the best in modern resort amenities. The 390 rooms of the original Moana and adjacent 430-room Surfrider now have been incorporated into one hotel. The U shape of the old Moana main building is still the focal point of the complex, embracing a lovely banyan-shaded patio facing the Pacific, with the addition of a tasteful formal entrance arcade and a grand ballroom. The spaciousness and old-fashioned charm of a former age have been retained in high-ceilinged rooms and attentive service to guests. The charm includes a second floor of oak, a third of mahogany, and a fourth of maple. On either side of the Moana are the modern wings of the former Surfrider portions of the hotel. On the *ewa* (east side) the 21-story wing built by Kenji Osano contains smaller rooms than those in the Moana wing.

Sheraton-Waikiki. 2255 Kalakaua Ave., Honolulu, HI 96815 (922–4422). Now the biggest skyscraper on the beach and one of the 10 largest hotels in the world. This king of the Sheraton empire is 31 stories high, has 1,852 rooms, and is next door to the *Royal Hawaiian* which it overshadows mightily. Large variety of accommodations, all with private *lanais,* air conditioning, and color TV. This $50 million structure has three swimming pools, assorted bars, and five restaurants—*Hanohano, Ciao, Kon Tiki, Ocean Terrace,* and *Kau Kau* snack shop. The convention room seats 3,600; the elevator can lift two elephants. Also handy is a laundromat on the fourth floor. A glass elevator takes you to the *Hanohano* restaurant on top for a breathtaking look. A $50-million facelift has been completed.

Waikikian. 1811 Ala Moana Blvd., Honolulu, HI 96815.(949–5331). Located on a man-made lagoon on Waikiki Beach. There are 135 low-rise *lanai* rooms arranged in a setting of lush tropical gardens as Polynesian architecture and atmosphere are combined. Cocktails on your *lanai* at twilight from the *Papeete Bar* and poolside dining at the *Tahitian Lanai* add to the Island mood. Each evening the Waikikian Serenaders stroll outside the rooms. Located *ewa* of the *Hilton Hawaiian Village,* the entrance lobby features a "hyperbolic paraboloid" roof.

Waikiki Banyan. 201 Ohua Ave., Honolulu, HI 96815 (922–0555). 876 condominium units. There's tennis and a pool. Reservations: Wardair Hawaii.

Waikiki Beachcomber. For reservations write Amfac Resorts Hawaii, 2255 Kuhio Ave., Honolulu, HI 96815 (922–4646). 498 air-conditioned rooms in the heart of Waikiki at 2300 Kalakaua Avenue. A joint venture of Amfac, a major Honolulu company, and United Air Lines. The 26-story hotel is operated by Amfac Resorts Hawaii. *Liberty House,* an outstanding retail operation, occupies the ground floor. Swimming pool, shops, and 400-seat entertainment room. In addition to *Don the Beachcomber* and *Veranda Room* restaurants and a disco, there is the *Surfboard Lounge.*

Waikiki Sunset. 229 Paokolani Ave., Honolulu, HI 96815 (922–0511). There are 435 air-conditioned one- and two-bedroom suites with kitchen in this condominium apartment at 229 Paoakalani, only a block from the beach at the Diamond Head end of Waikiki. The recreation deck includes a pool, paddle tennis, basketball, shuffleboard and sauna. This new building has 38 floors.

Expensive

Aston Waikiki Tower. 200 Lewers St., Honolulu, HI 96815 (922–6424). Has 440 rooms a short distance from the beach. There are restaurants, shops, a pool, and cocktail lounges.

Best Western Waikiki Plaza. 2045 Kalakaua Ave., Honolulu, HI 96815 (955–6363). The former Holiday Inn Makai. 17-story hotel on the site of the famed old *Palm Tree* bar. Close to Fort DeRussy, this hotel has 250 rooms, air-conditioning, pool. The *Makai Sugar Company Restaurant* and cocktail lounge. For reservations write Ironwood Resorts, 677 Ala Moana, Suite 400, Honolulu, HI 96813.

Coral Reef. 2299 Kuhio Ave., Honolulu, HI 96815 (922–1262). 209 air-conditioned rooms in a new building behind the International Market Place. *Black Angus* restaurant, cocktail lounge, and shops. Slightly lower rates limited to garden wing which is across the street from the main building.

Holiday Isle. 270 Lewers St., Honolulu, HI 96815 (923–0777). 284 units at 270 Lewers, only a stroll from the beach and the shops on Kalakaua Avenue. Swimming pool. Atmospheric cocktail lounge is *Hunter's.* The restaurant is *Coconut Willie's.* A pleasant Hawaiian holiday hotel.

Inn on the Park. 1920 Ala Moana, Honolulu, HI 96815 (946–8355). A pool, shops, restaurant, and cocktail lounge. It has a view of Fort De-Russy and is a short walk from the beach. There are 130 rooms.

Island Colony. 445 Seaside Ave., Honolulu, HI 96815 (923–2345). An apartment hotel owned by Hasegawa Komuten (U.S.A.), has 740 units, 3 blocks from the beach. Opened recently, the hotel is close to the Ala Wai Canal. Pool, sauna, and Jacuzzi.

Kuhio Village. 2463 Kuhio Ave., Honolulu, HI 96815 (926–0641). Has 100 rooms less than 2 blocks from the beach. Has a restaurant and cocktail lounge.

Maile Court. 2058 Kuhio Ave., Honolulu, HI 96815 (947–2828). A new Colony hotel, 44-story addition to Waikiki. 508 rooms, pool, restaurant, meeting room, cocktail lounge. Budget U-drive tie-in.

Marine Surf Waikiki. 364 Seaside Ave., Honolulu, HI 96815 (923–0277). Has expanded from a small apartment hotel to a 25-story big one with 130 deluxe air-conditioned rooms. Studios have kitchenettes, and *lanais.* There is a swimming pool and *Matteo's Italian* restaurant. Color TV in each room.

Miramar at Waikiki. 2345 Kuhio Ave., Honolulu, HI 96815 (922–2077). Has 370 rooms, a pool on the fifth floor, and 2 restaurants, the *Old Vic* and *Parrot House,* and 2 lounges, the *Poolside Warrior Bar* and the *Old Vic Bar & Pub.* Recent $2 million renovation.

New Otani Kaimana Beach. 2863 Kalakaua Ave., Honolulu, HI 96815 (923–1555). A short stroll away from the bustling center of Waikiki. Only an avenue of stately ironwoods separates the hotel from the open, green expanse of Kapiolani Park. Its location is *Sans Souci,* less than a century ago the beach playground of Hawaiian royalty. Robert Louis Stevenson, it is said, whiled away many idle hours here in the shade of the broad *hau.* The historic *hau* tree now shades a romantic beachfront restaurant—one of the last in Waikiki. The atmosphere here is a mix of relaxing old Hawaii and traditional Japan. The magnificent *Grand Banquet Hall* is an authentic reproduction of the ancient formal assembly hall of *Nijojo* of Kyoto. The 138 guest rooms are comfortable, with contemporary furnishings. Recently 36 rooms were converted into 18 ocean suites and penthouses; an additional multimillion-dollar program that will enlarge the hotel's rooms is in progress. In the main dining room the menu is strictly American, but there's the *Miyako* Japanese restaurant featuring Genghis Khan-style cooking, where you prepare your own vegetables and meat.

Outrigger East. 150 Kaiulani Ave., Honolulu, HI 96815 (922–5353). 442 rooms, the *Jolly Roger* and *Chuck's Cellar* restaurants, bars, pool, shops, air-conditioning.

Outrigger Malia. 2211 Kuhio Ave., Honolulu, HI 96815 (923–7621). 328 rooms in a new 17-story tower including 52 in a renovated structure that used to be the *Aina Luana Hotel,* between Royal Hawaiian Ave. and Lewers in the heart of Waikiki. A Kelley hotel. Coffee shop, cocktail lounge, and tennis court on the roof.

Outrigger Reef. 2169 Kalia Rd., Honolulu, HI 96815 (923–3111). This Kelley hotel has 250 feet of frontage on an excellent beach. There are four restaurants in this one, underground parking, and a swimming pool. The suites with *lanais* overlooking the sea are very handsome, and there's a terrific penthouse. The 16-story, 883-room hotel has two sections. Doubles, roof garden suites, and penthouse accommodations.

Outrigger Surf. 2280 Kuhio Ave., Honolulu, HI 96815 (922–5777). 250 air-conditioned units, *Rudy's* restaurant, lounge, pool.

Outrigger West. 2330 Kuhio Ave., Honolulu, HI 96815 (922–5022). 660 rooms in the heart of Waikiki. The *Red Lion Spaghetti House,* meeting room, pool, bars, air-conditioning.

The Park Shore. 2586 Kalakaua Ave., Honolulu, HI 96815 (923–0411). At the corner of Kalakaua and Kapahulu Avenues, across from Kuhio Beach and the Zoo. The view is excellent, the location choice. *Denny's* restaurant, pool, 227 units.

Queen Kapiolani. 150 Kapahulu Ave., Honolulu, HI 96815 (922–1941). A Hawaiian Pacific Resorts development with 315 air-conditioned rooms in Polynesian motif in an 18-story $5 million high rise. It is across from the Zoo, a short walk from Kuhio Beach. High arch columns facing the street give the hotel distinction. The *Peacock Room* for dining features oil paintings of Hawaii's royalty and famous, with a sun deck and swimming pool outside. Rooms have a "gaslight era" decor, and a convention hall seats 700.

Waikiki Parc. 2233 Helumoa Rd., Honolulu, HI 96815 (921–7272). 298 rooms, 2 restaurants including one serving Japanese cuisine with one of Waikiki's few authentic sushi bars, in a new tower built behind the Halekulani by its proprietors from Japan.

Waikiki Resort. 2460 Koa Ave., Honolulu, HI 96815 (922–4911). 300 rooms on the corner of Lilioukalani. The *Fall's* restaurant and *Camellia,* a Korean restaurant, coffee shop, pool, shops, and all air-conditioned. It has a room–car feature.

Waikiki Village. 240 Lewers St., Honolulu, HI 96815 (923–3881). Half a block from the beach and in the center of things in Waikiki. 438 rooms, swimming pool, several restaurants and lounges, the *Red Lion, Pieces of Eight, Perry Boys' Smorgy,* and *Village Tavern.*

Moderate

Hawaii Dynasty. 1830 Ala Moana Blvd., Honolulu, HI 96815 (955–1111). 200 air-conditioned rooms. There is also a cocktail lounge, pool, restaurant, and gift shop.

Hawaiian Monarch. 444 Niu St., Honolulu, HI 96815 (949–3911). 44 stories, 278 rooms, another 120 as lease condos. Near the Ala Wai canal. Has *Cast 'N Kettle* and *Serena* restaurants, a cocktail lounge, pool, shops, and a meeting room. Now a Hotel Corp. of the Pacific operation.

Outrigger Reef Towers. 227 Lewers St., Honolulu, HI 96815 (923–3111). Built after the *Reef,* this 474-room building is operated in conjunction with the *Reef.* There is a swimming pool and three places to eat: *Al Harrington Show,* the *Islander,* and *Chuck's Cellar.*

Outrigger Waikiki Hobron. 343 Hobron Ln., Honolulu, HI 96815 (942–7777). A new 43-floor condominium/hotel. It has 576 rooms, studios, and deluxe rooms with coffee makers and refrigerators.

Quality Inn Waikiki. 175 Paoakalani Ave., Honolulu, HI 96815 (922–4671; 922–3861). 451 air-conditioned units, the *Mala* restaurant, cocktail lounge, pool, and shops. Rates in the Pali wing slightly higher than those in the Diamond Head wing.

Waikiki Gateway. 2070 Kalakaua Ave., Honolulu, HI 96815 (955–3741). 200 rooms, all air-conditioned, restaurant, pool, cocktail lounge. The 16-floor building has an interesting trapezoid shape. *Nick's Fishmarket* is in the building.

Waikiki Grand. 134 Kapahulu Ave., Honolulu, HI 96815 (923–1511). About a block from Kuhio Beach, overlooking the Zoo and Kapiolani Park. There are 128 rooms.

Waikiki Marina. 1956 Ala Moana Blvd., Honolulu, HI 96815 (955–0714). Near *Westin Ilikai.* 323 units with kitchenettes, restaurant, cocktail lounge, meeting room, pool, air-conditioning.

Waikiki Sand Villa. 2375 Ala Wai Blvd., Honolulu, HI 96815 (922–4744). Two blocks from the beach facing the mountains and canal. There are 223 rooms all air-conditioned, with television, restaurant (the *Noodle Shop*), cocktail lounge, pool. Children under 8 free.

Waikiki Townhouse. 2421 Tusitala, Honolulu, HI 96815 (923–4541). Built in 1979, has 32 stories and is closer to the canal than the beach. Kitchens, air-conditioning, color TV in 109 apartments.

Inexpensive

Ambassador. 2040 Kuhio Ave., Honolulu, HI 96815 (941–7777). 19-story structure on the site of the demolished *Waikiki Lau Yee Chai* restaurant, the Chinese chop suey showcase in Waikiki from 1923 to 1966. There are 315 rooms and a swimming pool. *Café Ambassador* and *Embassy Bar.*

Outrigger Coral Seas. 250 Lewers St., Honolulu, HI 96815 (923–3881). 110 units in an 8-story building. Restaurant. Some rooms have 2 double beds for 4 persons.

Outrigger Edgewater. 2168 Kalia Rd., Honolulu, HI 96815 (922–6424). One of many hotels built by Island architect Roy Kelley. Not on the water's edge, but just across the street from the *Reef,* and just a step from a good swimming beach at the Diamond Head end of Fort DeRussy.

There are 184 rooms in the 7-story main building. European Plan prevails, but there's a *Trattoria,* an Italian specialty restaurant, in the building. Some apartments with kitchens.

Waikiki Circle. 2464 Kalakaua Ave., Honolulu, HI 96815 (923–1571). It is a 14-story cylinder and, while it stands erect, it vaguely resembles the famous structure at Pisa. Near the Diamond Head end of Waikiki, the hotel is across the street from Kuhio Beach and within easy walking distance of Kapiolani Park in one direction and the shopping centers in the other. All 101 rooms have balconies, and the hotel's circular design permits a wide-range view from each.

Waikiki Surf. 2200 Kuhio Ave., Honolulu, HI 96815 (923–7671). Has 291 rooms, a swimming pool, shops, restaurant.

Waikiki Surf East. 422 Royal Hawaiian Ave., Honolulu, HI 96815 (923–7671). A Kelley hotel, with 103 rooms. Studios and family apartments, and a pool.

Waikiki Surf West. 412 Lewers St., Honolulu, HI 96815 (923–7671). 110 modern studio and 1-bedroom units with kitchenettes and private *lanais.* Swimming pool, a cocktail lounge. A very attractive 1971 addition by Roy Kelley.

Smaller Hotels in Waikiki

(Including apartment hotels and condominiums)
Expensive

The Breakers. 250 Beach Walk, Honolulu, HI 96815 (923–3181). A pacesetter for small hotels, designed by Island architect Edwin L. Bauer A.I.A., completed in 1954. Both Polynesian and Oriental influence are apparent in the attractive buildings grouped around a tropical garden and freshwater swimming pool. The architect has made excellent use of such details as *shoji* doors, adjustable louvers, Hawaiian shakes roof, and private *lanais,* achieving an arresting combination of dignity and informality. This very inviting hotel is now owned by Kyoto interests. All 66 units are equipped with electric kitchenettes for light cooking. Some garden suites.

Diamond Head Beach Hotel. 2947 Kalakaua Ave., Honolulu, HI 96815 (922–1928). Recently renovated. 61 units in a 14-story building. A Colony hotel. Budget U-drive tie-in.

Hawaiiana. 260 Beach Walk, Honolulu, HI 96815 (923–3811). 95 studio rooms, all with kitchenettes, done in the Hawaiian manner in a delightful tropical setting with two swimming pools, patio. Free coffee and juice mornings. Other touches include *leis* for ladies and children on departure and entertainment Wednesdays and Saturdays. The beach is very close. An all-Hawaiian staff. The hotel is air-conditioned.

Imperial Hawaii Hotel. 205 Lewers St., Honolulu, HI 96815 (923–1827). Has 40 rentals—out of 290 units—close to the beach. Restaurants, cocktail lounge, pool, shops. First Hotel Hawaii also has 40 units in this complex. Telephone 926–2781.

Pacific Monarch. 142 Ulunui Ave., Honolulu, HI 96815 (923–9805). 216 units in the heart of Waikiki, 200 yards from beach. A pool and cocktail lounge. A Colony Hotel. At same location is **Silver's Pacific Monarch,** a condominium with 98 hotel units starting at $36.

Waikiki Lanais. 2452 Tusitala St., Honolulu, HI 96815 (923–0994). A condo with 160 units, 65 of which are hotel rooms. Three-day minimum, pool. Children under 12 free. Reservations: Hawaii Island Resorts, Inc., Box 212, Honolulu, HI 96810.

Waikiki Shore Apartments. 2161 Kalia Rd., Honolulu, HI 96815 (926–4733). 100 units. Studios, single or double, two-bedroom apartments available. This one bumps against the *Reef.* Three-day minimum, no children under 12.

Westbury. 1700 Ala Moana, Honolulu, HI 96815 (942–7722). A new 40-story condominium overlooks the Ala Wai Yacht Basin. The 142 units with kitchens start at $65 double, also tennis, pool, whirlpool, two saunas.

Moderate

Aloha Surf. 444 Kanekapolei, Honolulu, HI 96815 (923–0222). 15-floor structure cornering Ala Wai Blvd. had a recent $1 million renovation. One view of Diamond Head, the other toward Pearl Harbor. The 196 rooms are air-conditioned. Swimming pool and restaurant. This hotel is owned by a Tokyo investment house and has Japan suites with *tatami* mats and *futons.*

Hawaiian King. 417 Nohonani, Waikiki, Honolulu, HI 96815 (922–3894). 52 attractive suites, each including private bath, bedroom, *lanai,* sitting room, and kitchen. Air-conditioned, swimming pool. In center of Waikiki not far from beaches. Write to the manager.

Kai Aloha. 235 Saratoga Rd., Honolulu, HI 96815 (923–6723). One-bedroom suites and *lanai* studios in a modern building just 2 minutes from the beach. All-electric kitchens, sundeck, self-service laundry, private phones. The 18 units are air-conditioned.

Pacific Palms. 441 Lewers St., Honolulu, HI 96815 (923–2502). 38 rooms three blocks from the beach. No telephones. All with kitchens.

Royal Islander. 2164 Kalia Rd., Honolulu, HI 96815 (922–1961). 100 rooms and 12 stories. Has a restaurant, lounge, and *lanais* for each room. Has a floor for non-smokers.

Royal Kuhio. 2240 Kuhio, Honolulu, HI 96815 (923–2502). 49 one-bedroom apartments across from *Marine Surf,* with air-conditioning, a pool, barbecue pits, and paddle tennis. One-bedroom apartments here start at $43. Children under 12 free, using a pullout bed. No telephones. Write Paradise Management Corp., Suite C-207, Kukui Plaza, 50 S. Beretania Street, Honolulu, HI 96813.

Sherry Waikiki. 334 Lewers St., Honolulu, HI 96815 (922–2771). Has 100 rooms with a swimming pool. Three can get a small studio between $44–$74.

White Sands Waikiki Resort. 431 Nohonani St., Honolulu, HI 96815 (923–7336). Has 78 units with kitchens. Children under 14 free. Pool.

Inexpensive

Continental Surf. 2426 Kuhio Ave., Honolulu, HI 96815 (922–2755). 140 studio rooms.

Driftwood. 1696 Moana Blvd., Honolulu, HI 96815 (949–0061). Has 72 studio-*lanai* apartments. Two blocks from the beach and Ala Moana Shopping Center. Rooms with kitchenettes and telephones. Pool. Maid service.

Hale Pua Nui. 228 Beach Walk, Honolulu, HI 96815 (923–9693). "House of the Big Flower" with 22 studio-type units for up to 3 persons. All-electric kitchens, private phones. One block from Waikiki Beach. Children must be 12 or older. Two-day minimum.

Ilima. 445 Nohonani St., Honolulu, HI 96815 (923–1877). 98 units, all with kitchens. This 16-story building is near the Ala Wai canal with a sun roof on the 10th floor.

Niihau Apartment Hotel. 247 Beach Walk, Honolulu, HI 96815 (922–1607). 30 units. Seven-day minimum, 1- and 2-bedroom apartments are air-conditioned, all with phones.

Reef Lanais. 225 Saratoga Rd., Honolulu, HI 96815 (923–3881). Another Roy Kelley creation, 110 air-conditioned rooms. Restaurant, cocktail lounge, pool.

Royal Grove. 151 Uluniu Ave., Honolulu, HI 96815 (923–7691). Has 110 rooms and apartments, and there are a pool and patio. This pink building is a short walk from the beach. It's the *Royal Grove* because kings once sat under the palms there.

Waikiki Holiday. 450 Lewers St., Honolulu, HI 96815 (924–3615). Recently refurbished, 76 units in a high-rise. *Shalimar* restaurant, a pool and short walk to beach. Write Great American Management Group, 1900 Waikiki Trade Center, Honolulu, HI 96815.

Waikiki Prince. 2431 Prince Edward St., Honolulu, HI 96815 (922–1544). 24 units. This 1970 hotel is air-conditioned. No telephones.

Waikiki Surfside. 2452 Kalakaua, Honolulu, HI 96815 (923–0266). 80 units across the street from Kuhio Beach.

Rock-bottom

Ala Wai Terrace. 1575 Ala Wai Blvd., Honolulu, HI 96815 (949–7384). An apartment-hotel with 239 rooms, a 7-day minimum and no telephones. The $16 minimum for a studio is now the lowest rate in Waikiki. The same studio taken for 30 days drops that rate to $13 a day.

Holiday Surf Apartment Hotel. 2303 Ala Wai Blvd., Honolulu, HI 96815 (923–8488). 34 units on the canal, single studios and doubles, all with kitchenettes. Family bedrooms for 4. Rooms are $4 less in the annex.

Malihini. 217 Saratoga Rd., Honolulu, HI 96815 (923–9644). Less than a block from the beach and an easy walk to anything in the heart of Waikiki. 30 studios with kitchenettes, tile tub showers, and maid service. No telephones.

Waikiki Terrace. 339 Royal Hawaiian Ave., Honolulu, HI 96815 (923–3253). All one-bedroom apartments with private *lanais*. Sun deck for guests. A good, well-run apartment hotel with 24 rooms in center of Waikiki district. Two-month minimum Apr.–Nov.

In a special category is the **Hale Koa** at Fort DeRussy 2055 Kalia Rd., Honolulu, HI 96815 (955–0555), for military or retirees and their dependents. It has 416 rooms on the beach near the Hilton Hawaiian Village, restaurants, shops, meeting rooms, cocktail lounges, and an outdoor luau with stage. Call toll-free (800–367–6027) for reservations.

Outside Waikiki

Deluxe

Ala Moana Americana. 410 Atkinson Dr., Honolulu, HI 96814 (955–4811). This is a $36.6 million, 40-story skyscraper, that offers 1,194 rooms and a convention ballroom that seats 650. Four restaurants, three cocktail lounges, and pool. The restaurant on top, *Plantation Coffee Shop* is open 24 hours. *Nicholas Nickolas,* is the highest in Honolulu. *Okazuya* specializes in Japanese cuisine. The *Royal Garden* and *Mango 'n Miso* cater to visitors. There's also the *Hawaiian Hut,* combining a Polynesian revue with dining and dancing before it turns into a discotheque in the early morning hours.

Expensive

Pacific Grand. 747 Amana St., Honolulu, HI 96814 (955–1531). Condo with 360 units, 75 hotel rooms. Three blocks from Ala Moana beach. Restaurant, cocktail lounge, and pool.

Pagoda. 1525 Rycroft St., Honolulu, HI 96814 (941–6611). A 12-story hotel near Waikiki and Ala Moana Shopping Center with a unique "floating" restaurant and Japanese gardens. 340 rooms. International Ballroom that seats 500. Pool. Carp feeding 8 A.M., noon, and 6 P.M.

Inexpensive

Nakamura. 1140 South King St., Honolulu, HI 96814 (537–1951). Sort of midway between downtown and Waikiki. 40 units.

Town Inn. 250 N. Beretania St., Honolulu, HI 96814 (536–2377). Across a stream from the Chinese Cultural Plaza and downtown business. 26 rooms.

Oahu Hotels Outside Honolulu

Deluxe

Hawaiian Princess. 84–1021 Lahilahi St., Honolulu, HI 96792 (696–6400). Was completed in 1980 at Makaha Beach. The 127-unit condominium has 40 hotel units. The 16-story building has a swimming pool and jacuzzi. No telephone.

Sheraton Makaha Resort and Country Club. Write Box 896, Waianae, HI 96792 (695–9511). This was the first major resort development on Oahu outside Waikiki. The $33 million project was the dream of Chinn Ho, a Honolulu millionaire. But the development in Makaha Valley, 45 minutes from Waikiki, came upon hard times and closed in 1975. It has since reopened, and Sheraton took over management in 1982. Has 196 units. There are two 18-hole golf courses. The complex is about a mile from the beach. Also tennis, shops, a pool.

Turtle Bay Hilton and Country Club. Write Box 187, Kahuku, HI 96731 (293–8811). This major luxury resort was built as far away from Waikiki as possible. The 487-room, $20 million layout on the North Shore, 3.5 miles west of Kahuku, has got it all. Built on the water, the entrance is through the renovated championship golf course. The complex includes restaurants, bars, pools, tennis courts, shops, meeting facility. The lobby was redesigned to deter wind. Horseback riding on the beach. Hawaii Pacific Helicopters offers service to Turtle Bay, 836–1566. There is a shuttle from the airport for $15. Also on the property are 85 **Kuilima Vacation Condominiums,** 3-day minimum (293–2494).

Expensive

Pat's at Punaluu. 53–567 Kamehameha Hwy., Hauula, HI 96717 (293–8111). A condo of 136 units with 30 hotel units on the beach on the Windward Coast. The only such facility between Kailua and Kuilima. Restaurant, cocktail lounge, and pool. Two-day minimum.

Moderate

Makaha Shores. Write Hawaii Hatfield Realty, 85–833 Farrington Hwy., Suite 201, Waianae, HI 96792 (696–7121). At famed Makaha Beach, where the big breakers roll in, 88 apartments in 6-story building with fine ocean and mountain views. Kitchens, *lanais,* pool. No telephones; children under 12 free. Close to the Makaha golf courses. Seven-day minimum starting at $200 per week.

Mokuleia Beach Colony. 65–615 Farrington Hwy., Waianae, HI 96792 (637–9311). 30 units in cottages with kitchens on the North Shore beach. Isolated. Pool, tennis court. Minimum 7 days.

Not listed in the groupings on preceding pages are a number of small hotels, especially in Waikiki. Two condominiums in Waikiki worth mentioning are: **Foster Towers,** 2500 Kalakaua, with 145 rooms (923–6813); and **Tradewinds Plaza,** 2572 Lemon Rd., with 80 units (922–4555).

Near the airport are the 306-room **Holiday Inn—Honolulu Airport** (836–0661), part of the national chain; the 416-room **Pacific Marina Inn** (836–1131), the 270-room **Best Western Plaza Hotel** (836–3636) at the Airport, the former Ramada Inn, now run by Ironwood Resorts. All are on or just off Nimitz Highway.

For those visiting servicemen at Pearl Harbor or Hickam Air Force Base it might be convenient to stay at one of these airport motels. Another idea is to try the hotels and apartments in the Aiea area, such as the 35-room **Hawaiian Horizon Hotel** (488–4900) and 36-room **Juliana Towers Hotel Apartment** (488–5128).

There is also the **Laniloa Lodge Hotel** in Laie with a restaurant but no cocktail lounge. 44 units next to the Polynesian Culture Center. Pool and private beach across the road. 4 complete PCC packages. (Write manager, 55–109 Laniloa Street, Laie, HI 96762; 293–9282.)

There are also privately owned summer homes along some of the beautiful beaches in rural Oahu available for rent on a weekly or monthly basis. Arrangements can be made through some of the larger real estate agencies who will often put you in touch with the owner. For Kahana Beach, for instance, telephone Four Star Service of Hawaii, 732–1121, or Pacific Island Adventures (262–2210).

Honolulu International Youth Hostel, Seaview Ave. across the street from the University of Hawaii, has lodgings at $6.50 a night for card-carrying members or $8.50 for non-members (946–0591). And a second facility in Waikiki for members only at 2417 Prince Edward St. (926–8313), for $9. Both facilities handle about 20 people. There's normally a minimum stay of 3 nights.

There is also a new bed and breakfast operation a block away, at the historic 8-bedroom **John Guild Inn,** 2001 Vancouver Dr. The home, built in 1915, recently underwent a $775,000 remodeling. Prices range from $80 a night to $145. Nothing like it anywhere in the Islands (947–6019). For more information on bed and breakfasts in Hawaii, see *Facts at Your Fingertips.*

RESTAURANTS. Waikiki offers a great variety of menus, although the rest of Honolulu in general leans to Chinese cooking. Further, many of the best restaurants in Waikiki have American or Continental cooking and are located in the large hotels. Otherwise anyone interested in Asian cooking has come to the right place. There are plenty of Japanese restaurants, and a number featuring Korean, Filipino, Thai, Vietnamese, and Malaysian cooking. French, Italian, and Mexican restaurants are popular. Rare are Hawaiian, German, or Indian cooking, and almost nonexistent are Eastern European or Middle-East cooking.

Parking is available at almost all, some valet service. Every restaurant listed accepts credit cards. As a rule, the only need for cash comes at small neighborhood Chinese restaurants and fast food snack stops. Reservations are necessary at the bigger, better restaurants. As for the dress code, only *Michels, LaMer,* and the *Maile Room* advise jackets (ties however are optional) and·they have jackets available.

The price ranges given are *Expensive,* over $15; *Moderate,* up to $15; *Inexpensive,* up to $8 for one person excluding tax, tips, beverages.

Here is a selected list of Honolulu's restaurants to guide you in your gastronomic researches.

American Continental

Canlis. *Expensive.* 2100 Kalakaua Ave. (923–2324). Part of the Waikiki scene longer than the others—since 1954. And one of the best.

Hy's. *Expensive.* 2440 Kuhio Ave. (922–5555). Canada's pride. A charbroil specialty steakhouse. Piano bar nightly.

JR's Upstairs. *Expensive.* Kilohana Square, Kapahulu Ave. (735–2204). Tiny, intimate, very special menu.

Maile. *Expensive.* In the *Kahala Hilton,* 5000 Kahala Ave. (734–2211). International, with dishes like tournedos Madagascar.

Monarch Room. *Expensive.* At the Royal Hawaiian, 2259 Kalakaua Ave. (923–7311). Long king of the hotel dining rooms, now more of a show room.

Orchids. *Expensive.* Halekulani Hotel, 2199 Kalia Rd. (923–2311). Dining in a lovely beachside setting.

Protea. *Expensive.* In the Prince Kuhio Hotel at 2500 Kuhio Ave. (922–0811). An elegant spot.

The Third Floor. *Expensive.* In the *Hawaiian Regent Hotel,* 2552 Kalakaua Ave. (922–6611). Has everything—great food, atmosphere, service, strolling musicians. A first-class operation and pricey.

Top of Waikiki. *Expensive.* 2270 Kalakaua Ave. (923–3877). Just as above the Waikiki Business Plaza. A little more expensive than Windows of Hawaii.

Alfred's. *Moderate.* 1750 Kalakaua Ave., Century Center (955–5353). Has oysters Rockefeller, even wiener schnitzel.

Cafe Colonnade. *Moderate.* In the Princess Kaiulani Hotel, 120 Kaiulani Ave. (922–5811). Mediterranean in decor with continental cuisine.

Columbia Inn. *Moderate.* 645 Kapiolani, at the "Top of the Boulevard" (531–3747). Likes newsmen and athletes and anyone who stays out late.

Hau Tree Lanai. *Moderate.* New Otani Kaimana Beach Hotel, 2863 Kalakaua Ave. (923–1555). A lovely beach setting near Sans Souci.

Peacock Room. *Moderate.* In the *Queen Kapiolani Hotel,* 150 Kapahulu Ave. (922–1941). Elegant, with Hawaiian royalty watching over the scene from their picture frames.

Pottery Steak and Seafood Restaurant. *Moderate.* 3574 Waialae in Kaimuki (735–5594). Here you can watch the potter's wheel spin while you wait.

Ranch House. *Moderate.* 5156 Kalanianaole Hwy. at the entrance to Aina Haina (373–2177). A family retreat with animals on the walls.

Spindrifter. *Moderate.* Kahala Mall (737–7944). Spanish motif, popular.

Stuart Anderson's Cattle Co. *Moderate.* Ward Warehouse, 1050 Ala Moana Blvd. (523–9692). Steakhouse.

Summery. *Moderate.* Downstairs at the Hawaiian Regent Hotel (922–6611). Has a Roman feast—a buffet for $12.50.

Summit. *Moderate.* Atop the *Ala Moana Americana,* 410 Atkinson Dr. (955–4811). Supplies a breathtaking view; entertainment.

Swiss Inn. *Moderate.* 5730 Kalanianaole Hwy., in Niu Valley (377–5447). Very popular with locals stepping out.

T.G.I. Friday. *Moderate.* 950 Ward Ave. (523–5841). Atmospheric with one of the largest menus in the city.

Willows. *Moderate.* 901 Hausten (946–4808). A long time at one address and under one owner, has a willow-shaped pool of carp in spring-fed waters.

Windows of Hawaii. *Moderate.* 1441 Kapiolani Blvd. (941–9138). 23 floors up, makes a turn in an hour, in the Ala Moana Building.

Bobby McGee's Conglomeration. *Inexpensive.* 2885 Kalakaua Ave. (922–1282). Pretty sporty at times. Lots of laughs.

Flamingo Chuckwagon. *Inexpensive.* 1015 Kapiolani (538–1161). Eat all you want, with roast prime rib the feature. It's popular with locals.

Moose McGillycuddy's. *Inexpensive.* 1035 University Ave. (944–5525) and 310 Lewers in Waikiki (923–0751). Hamburgers, omelettes, taco salads. College crowd.

Austro-Hungarian

Pallfy. *Moderate.* Pacific Grand Hotel, 747 Amana St. (942–8181).

British

Horatio's. *Moderate.* In the Ward Warehouse, 1050 Ala Moana Blvd. (521–5002). More of the same John Bull and much fish.

Cockney Fish and Chips. *Inexpensive.* 1010 University Ave. (949–8533). Tiny type near campus.

Chinese

Golden Dragon. *Moderate.* In the *Hilton Hawaiian Village,* 2005 Kalia Rd. (949–4321). May be the nicest Chinese restaurant in Waikiki.

King Tsin, *Moderate.* 1486 S. King St. (946–3273). Features Mandarin cooking in an intimate setting.

Wo Fat. *Moderate.* 115 N. Hotel St. (537–6260). Downtown, serving Cantonese cuisine. The restaurant is almost 100 years old.

Hee Hing. *Inexpensive.* 449 Kapahulu Ave. (735–5544). An old restauranteur in a new location, near Waikiki.

Maple Garden. *Inexpensive.* 909 Isenberg St. (941–6641). Has Mandarin dishes.

Mongolian Bar-B-Que. *Inexpensive.* 100 N. Beretania St. (533–7305). In the Cultural Plaza in Chinatown on the River Street Mall. Pour any or all 9 sauces over the 3 kinds of meat or turkey. Another is in the Kuhio Mall in Waikiki (923–2445).

Pacific Chop Suey. *Inexpensive.* 1997 Pauoa Rd. (536–4204). The best Won Ton Min and Cashew Nut Chicken this side of Hong Kong, served to a packed house of local residents until 8 P.M. nightly, when the cook emerges from the kitchen to hurry everybody out. Come early, bring friends, and by all means order the specials.

East Indian/Indonesian

The Bali Room. *Moderate.* In the Hilton Hawaiian Village, 2005 Kalia Rd. (949–4321). Superb sesame seed salad and other Indonesian foods served in a stunning oceanview atmosphere.

India House. *Moderate.* 2632 S. King St. (955–7552). Near the University. Has kebob.

Shalimar. *Moderate.* 450 Lewers in Waikiki (923–2693). Tries to meet Indian and Pakistani tastes.

Filipino

For your pork adobo go to **Nagong Filipino.** *Inexpensive.* 2 N. Hotel St. (531–1846). Downtown.

French

Bagwell's 2424. *Expensive.* In the *Hyatt Regency* complex 2424 Kalakaua Ave. (922–9292). Another of the more posh restaurants. French cuisine. A Travel/Holiday award winner.

Chez Michel. *Expensive.* On Eaton Square at 444 Hobron Ln. (955–7866). Michel himself holds forth.

La Mer. *Expensive.* 2199 Kalia Rd. (923–2311). In the new Halekulani Hotel. Plush, special.

Michel's. *Expensive.* In the *Colony Surf Hotel* at the foot of Diamond Head, 2895 Kalakaua Ave. (923–6552). French cuisine. It overlooks the ocean, requires men to wear a coat for dinner, and has earned 17 *Holiday* magazine awards for culinary greatness. Also open for breakfast and lunch.

Yacht Harbor. *Moderate.* Yacht Harbor Towers near Ala Moana Shopping Center, 359 Atkinson Dr. (946–2177). French, continental, with piano.

German

Braustub'l. *Moderate.* 1216 Kapiolani Blvd. (523–0951).

Greek

It's Greek to Me. *Moderate.* Royal Hawaiian Center, 2201 Kalakaua Ave. (922–2733). Baklava, gyros, souvlaki, spinach pie, no credit cards.

Hawaiian

Try **Helena's.** *Inexpensive.* 1364 N. King St. (845–8044). The works for a couple costs very little. Locals also crowd **Ono Hawaiian Foods.** *Inexpensive.* 726 Kapahulu (737–2275) not far from Waikiki.

Irish

Jameson's Irish Coffee House. *Moderate.* 12 Merchant St. downtown and in Waikiki, 342 Seaside (531–4666 or 922–3396). Mulligan stew, quiche Lorraine.

Italian

Matteo's. *Expensive.* 364 Seaside Ave. (922–5551). In Marine Surf Hotel in Waikiki. Very nice.

Andrew's. *Moderate.* Ward Centre, 2nd floor, 1200 Ala Moana Blvd. (523–8677). A throwback, polished brass, all pastas shown in the window.

Che Pasta. *Moderate.* 3571 Waialae Ave. (735–1777). A fancy little place in Kaimuki.

Renown Milano. *Moderate.* Discovery Bay Shopping Center, 1778 Ala Moana Blvd. (947–1933).

Trattoria. *Moderate.* 2165 Kalia Rd. (923–8415), in the Edgewater Hotel.

Castagnola's. *Inexpensive.* Manoa Marketplace, 2752 Woodlawn Dr. (988–2969). Popular with locals.

Il Fresco. *Inexpensive.* Ward Centre, 2nd floor, 1200 Ala Moana Blvd. (523–5191). Great pasta and other things.

Old Spaghetti House. *Inexpensive.* Ward Warehouse (531–1513). 19th Century streetcar inside.

Rudy's. *Inexpensive.* 2280 Kuhio Ave. (923–5949).

Japanese

Kobe Steak House. *Expensive.* Close to the Hilton Hawaiian Village at 1841 Ala Moana Blvd. (941–4444). Features first-class Japanese delicacies by expert cooks performing before your eyes.

Pagoda. *Moderate.* 1525 Rycroft. (941–6611). More carp, more water under diners, good atmosphere, good Oriental dishes.

Suehiro's. *Inexpensive.* 1842 S. King St. (949–4584). Again popular with locals, which says a lot.

To spend more and see different types of Japanese cooking—at some places, the cook puts on a show at your table—consider **Zen.** *Expensive.* In the *Waikiki Grand,* 134 Kapahulu Ave. (923–8878). **Maiko** in the *Westin Ilikai* (946–5151). *Expensive.* **Benihana of Tokyo** in the *Hilton Hawaiian Village,* at 2005 Kalia Rd. (955–5955). *Expensive.* Or **Chaco's** at 2888 Waialae (732–9333). *Moderate.*

Another Japanese novelty house is **House of Noodles Dairyu.** *Inexpensive.* In Chinatown's Cultural Plaza, 1610 S. King St. (941–1939).

Korean

Kal Bi. *Inexpensive.* 1145-C 12th Ave. in Kaimuki (732–3088). A tiny spot next to a pool hall, but what short ribs! One block *makai* of Waialae Ave. Another good one is **Kim Chee No. 3.** *Inexpensive.* at 1040 S. King St. (536–1426), in back and at four other locations.

Kosher

Lyn's Kosher-style Delicatessen. *Inexpensive.* In the Ala Moana Center (941–3388). Has good pastrami.

Mexican

Jose's. *Moderate.* In Kaimuki, 1134 Koko Head Ave. (932–1833).

Las Margaritas. *Moderate.* In the Royal Hawaiian Shopping Center, 2d floor, Waikiki. Newest Mexican restaurant in town, operated by the family whose grandfather invented the margarita. Ceviches and other Mexican seafood a specialty.

Most popular Mexican place is **Mama's Mexican Kitchen.** *Moderate.* 378 N. School St. Close to downtown in Waikiki at 478 Ena Rd. and the Moanalua Shopping Center near the airport. But bring your own beer.

Compadres. *Inexpensive.* Ward Centre, 1200 Ala Moana Blvd. (523–1307).

Seafood

John Dominis. *Expensive.* At Kewalo Basin, 43 Ahui St. (523–0955). One of the newest of Oahu's fine restaurants, specializes in seafood. Has a superb view. Really a class place.

Nick's Fishmarket. *Expensive.* in the Waikiki Gateway Hotel 2070 Kalakaua Ave. (955–6333). Also good for seafood, particularly fresh local products such as mahimahi or for crêpes Madagascar.

Bob's Bar-B-Que. *Moderate.* 12th Ave. and Harding in Kaimuki (732–2479). Has all-you-can-eat seafood buffet for $13.

Fisherman's Wharf. *Moderate.* 1009 Ala Moana Blvd. (538–3808). Long-time Spencecliff restaurant at Kewalo Basin. You can watch fishing and cruise boats pass while dining here.

Monterey Bay Canners. *Moderate.* At Ward Centre, 1208 Ala Moana Blvd. (536–6197), and Outrigger Waikiki Hotel, 2335 Kalakaua Ave. (922–5761). Fresh food from the deep.

Besides **Nick's,** try **Little George** 680 Ala Moana Blvd. (536–7344). **Pier 8.** *Moderate.* 133 Ala Moana (521–6893). **Orson's.** *Inexpensive.* 1050 Ala Moana Blvd. (521–5681) in the Ward Warehouse, or **Oceanarium.** *Moderate.* Pacific Beach Hotel, 2490 Kalakaua Ave. (922–1233), where there is a 280,000-gallon view.

Spanish

Casa Madrid. *Moderate.* 444 Hobron Ln. (953–3333). Has hanging plants, paella, plus Portuguese and Italian dishes.

Thai

Keo's Thai Cuisine. *Moderate.* 625 Kapahulu Ave. (737–8240) and Ward Centre. Delectable spring rolls and other goodies make this among the most popular restaurants (with two branches now) in town.

Mekong. *Moderate.* 1295 S. Beretania St. (521–2025). Has Southeast Asian spicy things to make you glow. The same menu at **Mekong II.** 1726 S. King St. (941–6184). Another good one, **Keo's Thai Cuisine.** *Inexpensive.* 625 Kapahulu Ave. (737–8240).

Vietnamese

There are several, but try **Vietnam House.** *Inexpensive.* 638 Keeaumoku St. (944–3796).

Wine Houses

Grape Escape Wine Bar & Cafe. 2255 Kuhio Ave. (923–0438). Waikiki Trade Center is a new concept—the specialty house that emphasizes wine.

Quick Snacks

Wailana and **Rigger** in Waikiki; **Yum Yum Tree** in the Kahala Mall, Ward Centre, and Kailua; and **Patti's Chinese Kitchen** in the Ala Moana Shopping Center and on Kalakaua Ave. in Waikiki. Another low budget spot is **the Sizzler** at 1945 Kalakaua Ave. and 5 other locations.

The Waikiki Shopping Plaza on Kalakaua Ave. between Seaside and Royal Hawaiian has a choice of fast-food places in the basement—tacos, pizza, Japanese, Chinese—and up the escalator and around the plunging waters are the more expensive dining delights such as **Waikiki Lau Yee Chai.** The Royal Hawaiian Shopping Center, a three-block complex on Kalakaua Avenue in Waikiki, has a number of fast food-style carts on different levels serving everything from crepes to sushi.

A number of excellent small sandwich shops have opened in the downtown area. One of the best is **Heidi's,** with European breads. A new pancake and crêpes house with some class is **Jake's** at the corner of Bishop and Hotel Sts. downtown. Popular with families is **Shakey's Pizza,** at many locations.

Another recent development is Tokyo-type drinking houses where you can drink *sake,* beer, or coffee, eat *sashimi,* peanuts, or shrimp tempura. There are about 150 of them, and most are run by Koreans. Many advertise in the newspapers, "Under New Management," or "First Anniversary." Taxi drivers know where these "Korean" bars are. A word of warning: some are alleged clip joints and game for crime lords. Be cautious.

There are also the usual drive-ins frequented by teenagers, and Hawaii boasts something the rest of the United States does not have—the *saimin* (Japanese soup) and plate lunch stand.

There are health food places around, but often they fold or change names. Ask around.

One of the most permanent is **Laulima Fine Vegetarian Food,** 2239 S. King St. Fresh fruit and vegetable salads, sandwiches made from fresh baked wheat bread, honey, ice cream from 6 P.M.

And there are certain places that seem to be everywhere: **McDonalds,** which has 46 outlets in the state, **Burger King, Big Boy, Taco Bell, Col. Sanders,** and other fast food places, as well as chop suey joints and little steak houses.

OUTSIDE THE CITY

If you are driving via Koko Head to Makapuu Point and need lunch, the first stop out in the middle of nowhere is the **Hawaii Kai Golf Course,** where a good sandwich can be had. Next stop is **The Galley** at Sea Life Park. Inexpensive meals and plenty of children running around, excited after seeing the porpoises leap.

Kailua is picking up in restaurant quality and turning French with: **L'Auberge's** (263–4663) crepes and **Orson's Bourbon House** (262–2306) with Creole gumbo. Quite different are **Florence's** (261–1987) and **Haiku Gardens** (247–6671) with its flowers and trees. All 4 are *moderate.*

On the long ride up the Windward Coast to Kahuku, the best spot is the Crouching Lion (237–8511) near Kahana Bay, a delightful inn 45 min. from town looking out over the water and offering broiled steaks, lobsters, and Slavonic steak continental. *Moderate.*

In Haleiwa on the North Shore one might try the **Pelican.** *Moderate.*
66–134 Kamehameha Hwy. (637–3514), where the owner also shows
photo travelogues while you eat. *Moderate.*

Coming back through the Schofield Barracks Plateau, the best by far
is **Kemoo Farm** (621–8481) where the steaks sizzle, the *mahimahi* sandwich is great, and the view overlooks Lake Wilson. Trout and prime rib
are a dinner favorite. The restaurant has been around for 50 years. *Moderate.*

Nearing Honolulu again, we come to the **Pearl City Tavern** (455–1045)
in Pearl City, which specializes in Maine lobster and caged monkeys, *moderate,* and **Round House,** in Waiau, which specializes in trains, one of
which moves. *Inexpensive.*

Cattle Company Restaurant. (487–0054) in Pearl City specializes in
prime rib angus steaks and seafood. *Inexpensive.*

Out in Waianae there are few places to eat, but we like **Fogcutter**
(695–9404) in Makaha. *Inexpensive.*

HOW TO GET AROUND. When you come out of the baggage claim
area at Honolulu International Airport all set for your ride to a Waikiki
hotel, you have a choice of getting on a van that will take you to your
waiting car rental (if it's waiting), an airport bus, such as *Gray Line* among
others, which costs about $5, or a metered taxi, which costs about $13.
Airport Transport (926–4747) makes the trip for $5; $3 for children. The
taxi and bus dispatchers are on the sidewalk outside baggage claim. The
distance to Waikiki is 9 mi. If driving, it may be smart to take Nimitz
Highway to Waikiki the first time and leave the freeway puzzles for later.
The bus services have hotel pickups when you are going the other way.
If you need to go to Windward Oahu, telephone *Windward Airport Trans-
portation Service,* 834–6884.

Public transportation in the capital is by modern *Mass Transit Lines*
buses. There are 30 different lines crisscrossing the city, cutting into the
residential valleys, and climbing to the heights which separate them. Adult
cash fares are 60¢ a ride, and students (high school age and under) can
ride for 25¢. No dollar bills. All buses carry signs showing their route number and destination, and the driver will issue a free transfer for another
route if it's necessary to change to get to where you're going. Visitors may
obtain a monthly unlimited ride bus pass for $15 at the MTL office, 725
Kapiolani Blvd., open 7:30 A.M.–3:30 P.M., Mon.–Fri. For schedule information, call The Bus, 531–1611. Bus rides are free for people 65 years and
older, although there is a one month wait for the ID cards. Senior citizens
must obtain their free pass at the MTL office in person with proof of age.
The blind also ride free. Service is from 4:30 A.M. to 1 A.M. A popular trip
is the one to Pearl Harbor. In Waikiki, board No. 20, ask for a transfer
because you'll stop at Ala Moana, and get off at Halawa Gate. Remember
that the boats to the *Arizona* don't operate on Monday. There is a $4 shut-
tle bus to the *Arizona* from Waikiki; 926–4747. The so-called *Beach Bus*
runs only on weekends from Monsarrat Ave. near the Zoo every hour
starting at 9:20 A.M. It stops at Hanauma Bay, Blow Hole, Sandy, and
Makapuu Beaches. No surfboards. To circle the island, get on No. 52 at
the Ala Moana Center. To get there from Waikiki, take No. 2 or No. 8.
The same buses will take you downtown if you are going in the other direction.

Taxi cabs are plentiful, driven by qualified drivers, and metered at 25¢ each sixth of a mile. It's 20¢ for each minute of waiting. Many of the drivers are picturesque Island "types," and many are not. Random cruising is not allowed; don't stand on a street corner, pick up a phone instead. Some cab companies are *The Cab* (536–1707) or *Aloha State* (847–3566). *SIDA* (836–0011) has the airport concession.

Rental Cars. The range of cars for hire runs just about the whole gamut of the automotive industry, both domestic and foreign. Often you can do better face-to-face over a counter rather than relying upon what you are told over the phone. *Avis* will rent to an 18-year-old who has a valid driver's license, a major credit card, or holds an Avis travel voucher. *Robert's Rent-A-Car* will rent to marrieds if 18. The State Consumer Protection Office suggests you ask, on fly/drive deals, 1) if the company will honor a reservation rate if only larger cars are available and 2) if there are credit card limitations. Many offer a batch of food or gift coupons to help you on your way. Hertz, Avis, National, and Dollar systems have tie-ins with Hawaiian Air.

Driving in Honolulu is much like driving in any Mainland city, except that there is more courtesy on the road here. It may exasperate you at first, but you'll get used to it. The Islands will eventually lower your blood pressure. Also you can turn right on red at most intersections. And try to keep your eyes on the white arrows in your lane. Lock your U-drive when you sightsee. Cars, purses, and cameras are popular with thieves. Traffic in Honolulu and on the freeway is heavy, bordering on the impossible much of the time, especially during the morning and afternoon rush hours. Allow plenty of time. Don't park at a red curb. Feed the meters or the tow truck will provide an unpleasant surprise.

Your Mainland driving license is good anywhere in Hawaii for 90 days. If you stay longer, you can pick up a Hawaii license for $3 from the Department of Motor Vehicles.

Most U-drive agencies have a deductible-collision insurance arrangement, and you can get complete protection on the spot for an additional fee of $5 a day. Every agency now requires the customer to pay for the gas and fill up before turning the car back in, Some Honolulu car-rental firms: *Avis,* Honolulu International Airport, Hilton Hawaiian Village or 148 Kaiulani Ave. (836–5511); *Budget,* 2379 Kuhio Ave. and other Waikiki locations as well as airport (922–3600); *Hertz,* Honolulu International Airport, Hilton Hawaiian Village, 6 other major hotels (836–2511); *Tropical* at the airport and Waikiki locations (836–1041).

Other rental car agencies: *Dollar Rent-A-Car, Sears.* Can use a Sears credit card, 922–3805, three locations on Oahu. If you need a van for 10 people or so check out *World Rent-A-Car* (833–1866).

Ugly Duckling Rent-A-Car, 655 Mapunapuna (263–3825) has Sprints for $15 a day.

If you have deluxe tastes, Kalani Simerson of *Royal VSP Services* (Very Special People), at 1777 Ala Moana Blvd. (949–7989) has Cadillacs for $30 an hour. *Silver Cloud Limousine Service* (524–7999) will provide red carpet treatment, even private yacht or air services. Mercedes 450SL convertibles for $100 a day.

King's Limousine Service, 2550 Kuhio Ave. (924–7774), will take you anywhere. You can also rent a driver at $10 per hour (924–6703).

For **Mopeds,** call *Moped Hawaii* at 926–5808, $12 for all day. To rent motorcycles, call *Aloha Funway* rentals at 942–9696, where a Kawasaki

250 goes for $27 for 24 hours, mopeds for $12, adults only, with the motorcycle insurance $10. Aloha Funway also rents bicycles for $10 to $15 a day. Pedicabs are available all over Kalakaua and will provide you with a slow-motion view of the tropics. This may appear like old Shanghai, but it's really new Waikiki—be wary about fares. Normally a trip from Lewers to Kapahulu will cost about $5, or $6 if going the other way against traffic. Get it ironed out in advance.

TOURIST INFORMATION. The *Hawaii Visitors Bureau* is the state's visitor promotional agency. For every type of information on Oahu, or the state, visit the main office on the eighth floor, 2270 Kalakaua Ave., Honolulu, HI 96815 (923–1811). Available are brochures, fliers, and people to answer questions. There are branch offices in New York, Washington, Chicago, San Francisco, Los Angeles, British Columbia, Tokyo, and the Neighbor Islands.

Once you've reached Waikiki you'll find free information booklets, such as *This Week* and *Guide to Oahu,* containing coupons for savings, stashed in racks on many street corners along Kalakaua Ave. Bookstores are another source of information.

If you want detailed maps of anything in Hawaii, check out *Maps and Miscellaneous,* 404 Piikoi, Suite 213 (538–7429), or the *Hawaii Geographic Society,* Arcade Bldg., 216 Merchant St., Suite 308 (538–3952).

For currency exchange: *Deak-Perera and Co.,* 841 Bishop St., Suite 140 (544–3100), and the larger banks.

SEASONAL EVENTS. For specific dates on the events listed here, check with the *Hawaii Visitors Bureau* (923–1811) or the weekly publications found in racks on street corners, particularly on Kalakaua Ave. in Waikiki:

January. The surf is at its best at Waikiki, and the temperature of the water hovers around 75 degrees. *Hula Bowl Football Game* at Aloha Stadium is a sports classic featuring many All-American college stars and a field full of hula girls at half time. The *Pro Bowl,* featuring the cream of the National Football League, a week after the Super Bowl.

The *Narcissus Festival,* a vigorous, colorful fête, celebrating the Chinese New Year takes place 3 weeks preceding and 5 days following the new lunar year. The entire Chinese community turns out to celebrate with flower and fashion shows, drama, a parade featuring Chinese dragons, the crowning of the Narcissus Queen, Coronation Ball, a fashion show, mandarin banquet, "Night in Chinatown," Chinese art shows, street dancing, and, of course, fireworks. Dates vary, so check in advance. Frequently extends into February.

On the third Wednesday the *Hawaii State Legislature* opens its annual session at the Capitol in Honolulu in a unique legislative program which includes music, the hula, prayers, sacred and secular music, much giving and receiving of *leis,* and more flowers than you'll see at the Nice Mardi Gras. Plan to get there early. By the time the legislators, their relatives, the hula dancers, and various secretaries, clerks, and choir boys crowd into the Capitol, there isn't much room left.

Robert Burns Night, a gathering of Scots and Scots-lovers to honor the poet, at the Westin Ilikai.

February. Continuation of the *Narcissus Festival.*

Hawaiian Open Golf Tournament is a P.G.A. tour regular with the big names shooting for $500,000 at Waialae Country Club near Waikiki.

Yacht Season opens with a parade of yachts off Waikiki. The Honolulu to Pokai Bay, 25 miles, is the first big event.

The *Punahou Carnival* at the private school founded in 1841 offers many crafts for sale and the flavor of a school fund-raiser.

Opera Festival at the Blaisdell Center Concert Hall features such favorites as *La Bohème* and *II Trovatore* with New York Metropolitan Opera stars, and the Honolulu Symphony Orchestra.

March. *Kuhio Day,* March 26, is a state holiday celebrating the birth of Prince Kuhio, Hawaii's first delegate to Congress (1902–1922). Hawaiian cultural programs are presented. Ancient chants at Royal Mausoleum in Nuuanu Valley and pageant and ball highlight the celebration in Lihue, Kauai. Memorial service at Kawaiahao Church, Honolulu.

Carole Kai Bed Race. A moment of hilarity and nonsense on Kalakaua Avenue in Waikiki. A country-time concert is held at the Waikiki Shell the night before the race. (Also held in Lihue, Kauai, a week earlier, and in Wailuku, Maui, in February. There's even a race on Guam.)

Kamehameha Schools Annual Song Festival at the Blaisdell Center arena.

Annual *Hawaiian Song Festival* usually takes place during the second week of this month with a contest to determine the best new Hawaiian songs and the winning songs presented by leading Island entertainers at a program in the Kapiolani Park Bandstand at Waikiki.

St. Patrick's Day Parade in Waikiki. Emerald Ball is at the Pacific Beach Hotel.

Outdoor Polo Season begins March 12 and runs to September 1. Matches are held at the Walter F. Dillingham Field bordering the ocean at Mokuleia on Oahu's north shore. Local teams compete against players from the Orient, South America, Europe. Admission is $4, children under 12, free.

Cherry Blossom Festival, a Japanese celebration of spring, has the whole Japanese community astir for weeks with the choice of a Cherry Blossom Queen and her court, Japanese cultural exhibitions, parades, dances, and often a big show like the Takarazuka Review imported from Japan. Sponsored by the Japanese Junior Chamber of Commerce in Honolulu, this is one of the most colorful and most highly organized of Hawaii's festivals.

Hawaiian and Scottish Games, with dancing, pipes, food, games, held at Punahou School in Honolulu.

April. *Wesak Day,* the birth of Gautama Buddha is celebrated by many Thousand Island Buddhists in Honolulu's Kapiolani Park on the nearest Sunday morning to April 8, usually the first Sunday in April. A sunrise ceremony is followed by a long program of Japanese music and dancing in honor of the Buddha. Japanese of all ages get out their most beautiful kimonos.

Bishop Museum Festival includes art, crafts, shows, and tours.

The Easter Sunrise Service at the National Memorial Cemetery of the Pacific, Punchbowl, in Honolulu draws thousands of residents and visitors. A moving and impressive ceremony.

Honolulu-to-Pearl Harbor Yacht Race is popular, drawing about 150 yachts, since the Navy base is closed to yachts the rest of the time.

Hawaiian Festival of Music, Waikiki Shell, features competing bands, choirs and such from other states.

Aloha Basketball Classic attracts the pro scouts by putting four teams of the nation's best players on the floor for a shootout at Blaisdell Center.

Kailua Madrigal Singers Concert at McKinley High School features talented high-school students who tour the world every year. The Christmas concert is held in December at the same place.

Foster Garden's Garden Fair offers demonstrations in weaving, ceramics, and a chance to purchase rare plants. But to take plants back to the Mainland you will have to knock the soil out of the roots. And some states will prohibit any plant importations.

May. May Day is *Lei Day* in Hawaii. On the first of the month, Honolulu throbs to the sound of the hula. Everybody wears a *lei*—it's practically obligatory; you'll feel undressed without one—and there are programs of music, dancing, *lei* display, and Island pageantry everywhere, especially at the Waikiki Shell in Kapiolani Park.

May 5 is *Japanese Boys Day.* You'll see big colorful paper carp kites flying from houses and stores all over Honolulu and in the rural areas too, honoring the male offspring of Japanese families. The carp is a symbol of courage.

Sea Spree at Haleiwa includes surfing, canoe race, torchlight pageant, art auction, carnival.

Pacific Handicrafters Guild Fair, Ala Moana Park. Arts and crafts.

Memorial Day. A service is held in the morning at the National Memorial Cemetery of the Pacific in Punchbowl Crater, and the 27,000 graves are covered with flower *leis* strung by Island children. A deeply moving display, colorful and solemn at the same time.

Historic Preservation Week includes parades, tours and films celebrating old structures and yesteryear in general.

Korean Heritage Week, trade show at Blaisdell Center, other events at East-West Center and elsewhere.

The *Maritime Day* yacht race around Ford Island in Pearl Harbor is followed later in the month by the race around Oahu.

Armed Forces Day. A parade through Waikiki and open house at several military bases. Chance to go aboard a few fighting ships.

June. The *50th State Fair* usually runs through the first 10 days of June, featuring exhibits of Island industry and agriculture, local arts and crafts, floral displays, music, dancing, and all the jams, jellies, and other preserves you'd expect to find at a state fair back home. Dates may vary, so check in advance. The midway is set up in the Aloha Stadium parking lot.

Kamehameha Day, June 11, honors Hawaii's greatest king and warrior with a pageant, outrigger canoe races, parades, and a spectacular floral display (the king's statue in downtown Honolulu is draped with leis that are 40 feet long). This is your chance to see pa'u riders in flowing Hawaiian riding skirts. In connection with Kamehameha Day celebrations is the *Holoku Ball* at a Waikiki hotel, a classic; ladies in their formal attire. At Kapiolani Park, Waikiki, classical hula and chant competition.

Miss Hawaii Scholarship Pageant at Blaisdell Center picks a contestant for the Miss America Pageant at Atlantic City in September.

Filipino Festival, usually mid-month, recalls a Spanish provincial fiesta with pretty girls in mestizo dresses, unusual stick dances, athletic competitions, and lots of music commemorating Philippine Independence and Rizal Day.

Hawaiian Festival of Music at the Waikiki Shell brings together high-school singing groups from around the country.

Yacht Races feature a spin around Oahu, followed by the Gaylord Dillingham Race from Honolulu to Kaneohe Bay.

State Farm Fair at McKinley High School features agricultural exhibits, country market, 4-H livestock show, and entertainment, and would interest anyone from Iowa, Manitoba, or other good soil areas.

Festival of Ethnic Music and Dance/Interacts, University of Hawaii.

Mission Houses Museum Fancy Fair in Honolulu, an open market of crafts.

Prince Lot Hula Festival at Moanalua Gardens on Oahu honors Prince Lot who became Kamehameha V.

July. *Japanese Bon Dances* are the outstanding attraction of this month and of August. They are held every weekend by Buddhist societies outdoors at temples and schools, and they are very impressive. *Bon odori* are dances in honor of the dead. The dancers wear white towels around their heads and kimonos which are the reverse of anything colorful or gay.

Foster Garden Midsummer Night's Gleam. Walk between the trees and plants along candlelit walks.

Fourth of July is celebrated as in most American communities, though perhaps with a little more patriotic fervor here. There are fireworks and a band concert at the Waikiki Shell after a day of entertainment and (after all, this is still Hawaii) outrigger canoe races, the Walter McFarland Championships off Waikiki, and the Oahu championship canoe races in Keehi Lagoon.

In odd-numbered years, July 4 is also the departure date for yachts in the *Trans-Pacific Race* from Los Angeles to Honolulu. The competing yachts cross the finish line at Diamond Head from 10 days to 3 weeks later and heave to at Ala Wai Yacht Basin, after which there are parties galore in honor of the visiting yachtsmen. Once all the yachts are in, and sometimes before, the dash to Hanalei Bay, Kauai, begins for the Transpac crews.

Pan Am Hawaiian Windsurfing World Cup in Kailua on Oahu.

August. Annual *Hula Festival* takes place on first 2 Sundays in Kapiolani Park. Hundreds of dancers participate, children as well as old timers, and the repertoire extends from ancient and sacred examples of this national dance down to the irreverent high jinks of The Princess Pupule and The Cockeyed Mayor of Kaunakakai.

State Canoe Championship Races are held at Keehi Lagoon.

Obon Festival. Bon dances, floating lanterns that drift out over the reef. Watch from the sand at midnight. A Buddhist commemoration for the dead. Haleiwa Jodo Mission.

Ukulele Festival at Kapiolani Park Bandstand.

Honolulu Zoo Day. Family entertainment around the animal areas.

Admission Day, on the 20th, celebrates the date in 1959 on which Hawaii became the 50th state.

Miss Chinatown Queen Pageant, in Honolulu; winner goes to San Francisco for more beauty competition.

Flora Pacifica features exotic Island plants, exotic food, dances, cooking, weaving, at the University of Hawaii's new Art Gallery. $2 adults, $1 students and seniors, children under 12 free.

September. *Labor Day* is observed in the 50th state pretty much as it is in the other forty-nine. There are banquets and speeches in honor of labor, and nobody works. The big Unity House picnic at Ala Moana park usually features pungent comments by top Island politicians.

Waikiki Rough Water Swim. A 2-mile race through deep water from Sans Souci to Duke Kahanamoku Beach for all ages, kids to oldies.

Aloha Week ushers in the fall season with a Hawaiian king and queen in the regal costumes of their ancestors presiding over 7 days of pageantry which only the Islands could put on. *Aloha* shirts, with bright Hawaiian prints are *de rigeur* even in the most sedate offices of Honolulu, and everyone gets into the spirit of the celebration. There is much dancing in the streets and a lot of friendly competition among the various ethnic groups. Programs of international dance and music are the order of the day. Grand climax is a terrific general parade in which all sections of the community outdo themselves in dramatizing their own contribution to the fascinating Island mélange. If you want a concentrated week of local color, plan to have your Honolulu sojourn coincide with Aloha Week. It is usually held in the second part of October. Check with the Hawaii Visitors Bureau for specific dates each year.

October. *Molokai-to-Oahu Canoe Race* is a 27.5-mile endurance test for men. The race from Molokai to Waikiki is completed in one morning, after about 100,000 paddle strokes. Teams from California and Tahiti also compete.

Orchid Show. For more than 30 years a popular attraction. More rare and hybrid cattleya, vanda, and dendrobium than imaginable. Blaisdell Center.

Festival at the Bishop Museum. Hawaiian dances, food, crafts.

Music and Drama Season starts in Honolulu with regularly scheduled concerts by Honolulu Symphony Orchestra and plays and musicals by the Honolulu Community Theater and University of Hawaii Theater Group.

Pan Am World International Rugby Tournament at Kapiolani Park, Waikiki, is held on odd years. The airline also sponsors soccer in March, yacht races and netball (at Princeville, Kauai) in September.

November. Festivity begins with the *All Islands Makahiki,* 4 days of music, dance, pageantry, and sporting events. The celebration is observed on the 4 major islands: Hawaii, Maui, Oahu, and Kauai.

Hunting Season for game birds opens the first Saturday in November and runs to the third Sunday in January on weekends and holidays only.

Hawaii International Film Festival, sponsored by the East-West Center.

Veterans Day Parade, from Ft. DeRussy to Kapiolani Park, Waikiki.

Thanksgiving Day is as you like it on the mainland with church services and family feasts with turkey and cranberry sauce.

Triple Crown Hawaiian Pro Surfing Championships. The best on big waves at Oahu's North Shore. A 2-day event, scheduled according to the best wave conditions. Since the big ones break around this time of the year, the *Men's Masters* is held at the Banzai Pipeline and the *Duke Kahanamoku Championship* at Sunset Beach, *World Cup* at Haleiwa.

December. *Bodhi Day* is celebrated on the nearest Sunday to December 7. This is the anniversary of the enlightenment of the Buddha and the establishment of the Buddhist religion.

Princess Bernice Pauahi Bishop's Birthday is celebrated on December 19 with solemn and impressive ceremonies at the Royal Mausoleum in Nuuanu Valley with various Hawaiian societies and the Kamehameha Schools participating.

Festival of Trees is an exhibit of Christmas trees, little exquisite ones and large brilliant ones, a benefit for Queen's Hospital held at the Blaisdell Center.

International Surfing and *Duke Kahanamoku Championships* usually are held in late December, at Makaha Beach. Both sexes and all ages ride 5- to 20-foot waves in competitions.

Honolulu Marathon is a mob scene of more than 10,000 runners, including former cardiac cases, who rise at 6 A.M. to run 26 miles from Aloha Tower through Waikiki to Hawaii Kai and back to Kapiolani Park. Maui, Kauai, and the Big Island have marathons at different times in the year.

Aloha Bowl pits top-ranked college football teams at Aloha Stadium.

Christmas is celebrated as on the mainland, except that Santa Claus arrives in Hawaii by airplane, outrigger canoe, or on a surfboard, and the poinsettias bloom by the thousand in fields instead of singly in pots.

Rainbow Classic. Eight of the nation's best college basketball teams go at it. Blaisdell Center.

New Year's Eve makes the celebration in the rest of America look like a meeting of the church auxiliary. Although recent legislation limiting the use of fireworks cut down on the size of firecrackers, there is still a lot of noise for several hours because police are unable to enforce the law. The din is deafening in the 15 minutes leading to midnight, and the next morning the city is awash with bits of red paper.

TOURS. Oahu can be toured by bus, mini-van, limousine, boat, helicopter, but not train. Most popular tours are one of the guided tours of the city, another that does the *Arizona* at Pearl Harbor, and a third the lengthy circle island tour.

Around Honolulu. Bus tours. Typically *Gray Line's City Tour* leaves from hotels in Waikiki at 8:30 A.M. daily. First come Iolani Palace and Barracks then St. Andrew's Cathedral, Kawaiahao Church, the National Cemetery in Punchbowl Crater for a view of the city, and finally the East–West Center in Manoa. Adults $10.50, and each adult can take one child free, though additional children are $5.25 each (834–1033). *Polynesian Express* has an *Arizona* and city, including Punchbowl, tour for $17.50, starting at 7 A.M. and noon (922–5577).

Walking tours. There are two guided tours that are offbeat and quite interesting, both downtown about 6 miles from Waikiki. The Mission Houses Museum at S. King St. and *Mission Lane tour* starts at 9:30 A.M., Mon. through Fri. and ends at noon. Major attractions are the oldest house on Oahu, famed Kawaiahao Church, the King Kamehameha Statue, Iolani Palace and Barracks, St. Andrew's Cathedral, the governor's house and the state Capitol. The fee is $5, children $2 (531–0481).

The other tour covers Chinatown. You'll see the rapidly changing inner city, actually many buildings are restored on the sites of structures razed in the Chinatown Fire of 1900, herb shops, noodle factories, temples, even a demonstration on the way opium was smoked. This *Chinese Chamber of Commerce* tour is 9:30 A.M. Tues. only starting at 42 N. King St., $3 ($4 with a Chinese lunch at Wo Fat's), 533–3181, or the *Hawaii Heritage Center* tour starts at 9:30 A.M., Wed., and Fri., at 1026 Nuuanu Ave. $5 (521–2749).

More specialized are free guided tours available at the *East–West Center* (at 1:30 P.M. at Jefferson Hall), a self-guided campus tour brochure of the University of Hawaii available at Bachman Hall on the corner of Dole St. and University Ave., Brigham Young University-Hawaii, Honolulu Academy of Arts at 11:00 A.M., Tues. through Sat., 2 P.M. Sun. and Lyon

Arboretum at 1 P.M. on the first Fri. of each month. *Foster Botanic Gardens* has a 1:30 P.M. tour, Mon. through Wed. ($1 entrance fee).

Sociological Tour. A chance to see offbeat Honolulu, the rarely seen ethnic curiosities of Manoa, Kalihi, and Nuuanu valleys and Chinatown. Tours are periodic. Write Hawaii Geographical Society, Arcade Bldg., 216 Merchant St., Suite 308, Honolulu, HI 96815 (538–3952).

Around the Island of Oahu. There are numerous daily **circle tours of Oahu with chauffeur-guides.** The trip, covering 110 miles and sometimes more, takes 6 to 8 hours and includes most of the points mentioned earlier.

Most tours stop for lunch, some at Pat's in Punaluu, others at the Turtle Bay Resort or Haleiwa Sands, but the cost of lunch is not included in the prices listed below. Better add $3 to $4 to the quoted price for lunch; or, better, take a picnic lunch along. Tickets for tours are available at most major Waikiki hotels.

Gray Line circles Oahu daily starting at 8:30 A.M. from the Waikiki hotels, by way of Nuuanu *pali* and the Windward Coast and then up to Kahuku and around to Pearl Harbor. Adults $18.50; same policy on children as city tour.

Akamai Tours offers a circle-island tour. Adults $35, children under 12, $29. 9 A.M. to 5 P.M. Phone 922–6485.

E Noa Tours offers a casual all-day (8–5) ride around the island with time for snorkeling and a picnic for $36 adults, $30 children under 12, $27 children under 7. Phone 941–6608. Both *E Noa* and *Akamai* operate mini-buses for those wanting a more intimate tour.

Polynesian Adventure Tours (923–8687), uses a van for a longer route, including lunch, for $36.50.

Trans Hawaiian Service (735–6467) has a Little Circle trip that includes Iolani Palace, $22.50 Wed. through Sat. twice daily 8:30 A.M. or 12:45 P.M. and without the Palace stop on Mon. and Tues. for $18.50. A North Shore trip for $48 includes swimming, horseback riding, and a dunecycle ride. Leaves at 8 A.M., returns at 4.

Gray Line's bus to Pearl Harbor for the free Navy boat ride is $12.50, leaving Waikiki at 8:30 A.M. or 12:30 P.M. There is a shuttle bus to the Arizona Memorial for $4 (834–1033).

Least expensive way to circle the island is to board the No. 52 bus at Ala Moana Shopping Center after getting a transfer on No. 2 or No. 8 in Waikiki. Your many-stop trip around Oahu will cost 60¢.

Boat tour. The only way to circle Oahu by ship is to book passage on *American Hawaii Cruises* but then you're talking 3- to 7-day excursions, all first class, that features Neighbor Island sightseeing stops.

There are, however, smaller cruise boats that go twice daily from Kewalo Basin near the Ala Moana Shopping Center to Pearl Harbor for a swing around Ford Island and the Arizona Memorial. The times are 9:15 A.M. and 1:15 P.M. and the round trip is $10 (with a bus pickup at your Waikiki hotel); call 536–3641.

Helicopter tour. *Hawaii Pacific Helicopters,* 228 Lagoon Dr. (836–1566) operates from a pad in Waikiki near the Ilikai Hotel. The circle island tour is $185, compared with a 7-mile quick look at Waikiki for $27. Popular also is a tour through the Nuuanu Pali and around Makapuu Point for $98.

PARKS. The two most popular parks in the minds of local people are **Kapiolani** in Waikiki and **Ala Moana** near the large shopping center of the same name. Both are filled on weekends. Kapiolani is for picnics, tennis, jogging, band concerts, big events at the Waikiki Shell (such as the New York Philharmonic), the popular Kodak Hula Show, a close-up view of Diamond Head, softball, and even rugby. To swim you have to cross the street where Waikiki Beach stretches to Sans Souci. Ala Moana is for picnics, fishing, tennis, a view of Waikiki, jogging, lawn bowling, softball, but the emphasis is on man-made lagoon swimming.

The 70-acre Ala Moana includes its newest addition, *Magic Island,* a peninsula built in 1963 that juts out into the ocean. In the last century Kapiolani served as a polo grounds and site of Camp McKinley (1898), the military's first installation in Hawaii.

The 200 acres of Kapiolani include the *Honolulu Zoo* and *Waikiki Aquarium.* The zoo is open daily from 8:30 A.M. to 4:15 P.M. Admission is $1; free for accompanied children under 12. A whole spectrum of 2,000 exotic animals and birds populates the zoo. It's the place to see beautiful Hawaiian people, fauna, and flora. The No. 8 bus from Ala Moana goes to the zoo (531–1611).

The *Waikiki Aquarium* is at 2777 Kalakaua Ave. opposite Kapiolani Park in Waikiki. Open daily from 9 A.M. to 5 P.M. Admission: $2.50; children under 16 free. A favorite spot with local kids as well as tourists, the aquarium is in its seventh decade of operation. There are a seal pool and salt-water tanks for viewing everything from the celebrated *humuhumunukunukuapuaa* (a small tropical fish) to huge monsters that will gnash their teeth at you through the glass. An excellent collection of tropical fish, exotic and colorful. The Natural Selection Shop features marine-related books and gifts, and offers special tours in English and Japanese.

The **Civic Center** downtown is a lovely green area with large shade trees that give it park-like qualities though it is not part of a park system. This open stretch features Iolani Palace and the State Capitol, and the contrast in the architecture of government from 1870 to the present.

Good picnicking and viewing are the features of the new **Sand Island Park** (the view is Honolulu Harbor, passing big ships and downtown highrises), **Keehi Lagoon Park** near the airport, and **Blaisdell Park** (for a view of Pearl Harbor). **Fort DeRussy** at Waikiki is an important open area in a hotel-congested neighborhood but of little service to the visitor except to walk along the beach. Both the hotel (Hale Koa), inside Fort DeRussy, and other facilities, except the Army Museum, are for military personnel only.

Three intimate parks of note: **Aala Park, Thomas Square,** and **Honolulu Stadium Park.** Aala was very familiar to earlier generations of immigrants and on a visit today you'll find skateboarders mixing with old Filipino men talking "story" about their life years ago in plantation camps. It borders on Nuuanu Stream and is for sitting. Thomas Square, across Beretania St. from the Honolulu Academy of Arts, has huge banyans and a fountain. It often is used for dog shows or exhibits of handicrafts. Honolulu Stadium Park, at S. King and Isenberg Sts., is for sitting and kids. This is quite in contrast to the period 1926–1976 when it was the site of a 23,700-seat stadium where Babe Ruth, O. J. Simpson, and Rocky Marciano, among thousands of others, performed.

For spectacular views, the best parks are mountain-top parks such as **Puu Ualakaa** on Tantalus and **Waahila** above St. Louis Heights. Puu

Ualakaa (pooh-oo-oo-ah-lah-kah-ah) is best reached by driving *mauka* on Makiki St. and turning right then left at the water pumping station to take Round Top Dr. The road, cut into the side of Round Top, girdles the mountain. Near the end of the valley you plunge left into a completely different world from the Waikiki area you left 15 minutes ago. It's a magic tropical forest, full of ferns and giant philodendron which flourish on the abundant rainfall here. It's at least 10° cooler than it was at the beach, and considerably damper. This is the lush forest that clings to the sides of 2,013-foot Tantalus, Honolulu's highest residential district. The people who live in the peace and quiet of this cool upland wouldn't change it for a waterfront estate. Also an excellent place for easy hikes along well-marked trails. Puu Ualakaa provides a breathtaking view of the city, from Diamond Head to Pearl Harbor. For picture taking the morning hours are preferable, the sun at your back. The park closes at 6:30 P.M.

Waahila offers a view of upper Manoa Valley and the mountainside where Puu Ualakaa is located. The setting is shaded with large Norfolk pines towering over picnic tables. Take St. Louis Dr. to Peter St., and left onto Ruth Pl. to the park, which also closes at 6:30 P.M.

Four interesting parks on the Windward side some 20 or more miles from Waikiki are **Hoomaluhia, Kualoa Point, Kahana Bay,** and **Malaeka-hana,** in that order driving north. Hoomaluhia is the city's largest regional park and is new. Located *mauka* of Kaneohe town, it is an inland setting with a reservoir close to the mountains. It was the child of a flood-control project. Kualoa Point at the north end of Kaneohe Bay on Kamehameha Hwy. (83) is for swimming and close to its shallow waters sits Mokolii, better known as Chinaman's Hat. Kahana Bay Beach Park also on Kamehameha Hwy. is a beautiful crescent beach of shallow waters, mild surf, ironwood trees, picnic benches, showers and a boat ramp and usually a breeze. It is an idyllic setting. Malaekahana, a new state recreation area, is on the makai side of Kamehameha Hwy. near the Mormon Temple at Laie. This campground and beach faces Mokuauia, also known as Goat Island.

Five well-known parks are commercial:

Sea Life Park, just beyond Makapuu Point lookout at Waimanalo, about a 40-minute drive along Oahu's dramatically scenic southern shoreline from Waikiki, is one of the world's finest marine parks. On a plateau of unspoiled and rugged terrain set against a backdrop of green, fluted Ko-olau Mountains that rise 1,000 feet vertically behind it, the park overlooks craggy Makapuu headlands that plunge to the sea, the open ocean, and seven small offshore islands. The setting is majestic.

The Hawaiian Reef Tank is a circular, 300,000-gallon glass tank which contains a "living recreation" of offshore Hawaii. You walk along a ramp which descends from the surface tunnels through an underwater lava flow and ends at the ocean floor from which you exit. The marine climate offers natural habitats for 2,000 ocean creatures.

There's a show every two hours in the glass Ocean Science Theater, where you see the sea animals perform both above and below the surface. The Park's dolphin trainers, incidentally, employ underwater electronic signals and SONAR rather than the usual voice and hand commands in working the agile and intelligent dolphins. Whaler's Cove is an open sea-water pool in which a replica of the square-rigged whaler *Essex,* five eighths actual size, is berthed. It is the historic ship whose voyages inspired Herman Melville's sea classic, *Moby Dick.* Pacific and Atlantic bottlenose dolphins, the only collection of the species on exhibit anywhere in the world, inhabit the pool along with two whales. At Sea Life Park is the small Pacific Whaling Museum, which houses the largest collection of whaling artifacts in the Pacific. The Rocky Shores simulates intertidal zones surrounding Hawaii.

Sea Life Park is unique among the world's oceanaria in that it is only part of a complex that includes an institute for marine research. The buildings of the institute adjoin the Park, but are not open to the public. Establishment of Sea Life Park, early in 1964, was fulfillment of a dream for marine biologist Taylor A. ("Tap") Pryor. It is now owned by Bishop Corporation of Honolulu.

The Park is open from 9:30 A.M. to 5 P.M. daily. Admission is $8.50 for adults, $6.50 for children 7–12; under 7, $2.75. For an additional $1.75 there is a tour, four times daily starting at 9:45 A.M., of the research aspects of the park. A visit to the Park is included in numerous regularly scheduled Oahu tours, but special tours can be arranged through any of the tour companies. A city bus makes hourly runs. From Ala Moana or Waikiki catch #57. The tour bus costs $12.

Polynesian Cultural Center. At Laie, a small rural town along Oahu's north shore, about a one-and-a-half-hour drive from Waikiki. Aside from summer homes that dot nearby beaches, the community is largely a center of Mormonism in Hawaii. It is the location of the Church's famous Hawaiian Temple (see *Exploring Oahu*) and the Brigham Young University–Hawaii. The Polynesian Cultural Center is a project of the Mormon Church.

The Center is a living museum of seven primitive South Sea village areas clustered on about 40 acres of carefully landscaped grounds and waterways. The native structures and the inhabitants are authentic, and the stated purpose is to exhibit and perpetuate the ancient culture—arts, crafts, skills, sports, and customs—of Polynesia. The six Polynesian groups represented are Hawaiian, Tahitian, Samoan, Fijian (though technically Melanesian), Tongan, and Maori. The most recent addition is a Marquesan village, depicting the islands described by Herman Melville in his novel *Typee*. Visitors can mingle with the Islanders, sample their food, ride in their canoes, observe them at work and at play—in effect, absorb a lot of early Polynesian atmosphere.

There's an outdoor theater that has a man-made lava-rock waterfall for a backdrop, sand for a stage, and, between stage and audience, a moat with fountains for a curtain. A covered semicircle of tiers accommodates an audience of 2,780. With as many as 150 Polynesian performers on stage, the entertainment can be quite spectacular. Massed dancing and singing, rarely seen outside the more remote islands of the South Pacific, are featured. Fijian performances are the most vigorous, Maori choral work the most moving. The purpose of PCC is to present and preserve the art and lifestyle of Pacific Island people, and to provide employment and scholarships for students at BYU-Hawaii.

Polynesian Cultural Center is open at 12:30 P.M. daily except Sunday. A Voyager Passport, for admission to all shows and an all-you-can-eat buffet, is $30 adults, $25 juniors (12–15), $10 children (5–11). The prices are $35, $18, and $11 in peak summer months. An afternoon only (without the evening *This Is Polynesia* extravaganza) is $20 adults, $10 juniors, $6 children. Private tours with a guide are offered for groups of 10 or more at a slightly higher price.

In 1979 the Center opened The Gateway restaurant, billed as the largest dining room in the Pacific, to accommodate visitors at lunch and dinner. Those arriving early see a musical orientation show at 1 P.M. Canoes depart from each village between 2 P.M. and 5 P.M.; at 6 P.M. the brass band enlivens the evening. One can walk the villages, take a tram, or ride in the canoes. Packages including a show and dinner are available from Polynesian Express, Akamai Tours, Roberts Hawaii, and others. Both Polynesian Adventure Tours and Polynesian Express stop at the center during trips around the island, but not for the evening show.

Reservations for the show must be made at the Center's Waikiki Office, 2222 Kalakaua Avenue (telephone 923–1861 or 293–3333 at Laie).

There is a free tram ride through Laie, the temple grounds, and Brigham Young University–Hawaii that takes 45 minutes.

Many scheduled Oahu tours include a stop at the Center. There are several tours to the Center from Waikiki. A typical one leaves Waikiki about 1 P.M. and returns at 10:30 P.M. There's a North Shore shuttle (fare: $2) that leaves the Moana Hotel daily at 9 A.M.

Abundant tropical flowers, plants, and trees can be seen along the mile-long pathway leading to the 45-foot falls at **Waimea Falls Park.** Many visitors to this private park ride the mini-bus from the park entrance to the falls, then walk back. Guided hikes are also available. The 1,800-acre park features labelled botanical collections as well as peacocks, guinea hens, ducks, and even Amazon birds. There are demonstrations of ancient Hawaiian games, hula dancing, and high dives at the falls. Proud Peacock is the park restaurant. Admission $8.50 adults, $5.25 juniors, $1.75 children ages 4–6. Open 10 A.M. to 5:30 P.M. (923–8448).

Located deep in lush Manoa Valley, **Paradise Park** is a tropical attraction that offers visitors trails through bamboo forests, fascinating hau tree jungles, fish ponds, a flamingo lagoon, and tame macaws. Oddly, the park combines 14 acres of greenery and many plants not native to Hawaii—they took decades to grow—with exotic birds brought from all over the world. Open daily from 9:30 A.M. to 5 P.M. with bird shows, duck shows, carp feeding, and puppet shows continuous from 10 A.M. to 4 P.M. Admission $7.50 for adults; children under 12, $3.75. A buffet lunch is served at the Henri Hawaii Restaurant ($10 adults; $7.50 children). *Magic In Paradise,* a new evening show, plus all of the above is $32 adults; $25 children. City bus # 5 connects with Waikiki, and the park has free shuttle bus service (988–2141).

Hawaii's first amusement park since the 1920s, **Castle Park Hawaii's** 16-acre attraction has five "activity centers" including water country, bumper boat lake, miniature golf courses, Castle Park Grand Prix and a fairy-tale arcade. Batting cages are also provided for those who fantasize about hitting home runs. Plenty of video games. Located at 4561 Salt Lake Boulevard near Aloha Stadium. Entrance is free but tickets must be purchased inside for whatever strikes your fancy. The arcade opens at 9:30 A.M. daily, the rest at 10 A.M. The water slide closes at 6 P.M., the park itself at 10:30 P.M. (488–7771).

GARDENS. If your timetable calls for one garden, it is best to pick **Foster Botanic Garden.** Located at 50 North Vineyard Boulevard. Open daily from 9 A.M. to 4 P.M. Adults $1, children under 12 free. This 15-acre oasis of century-old trees and rare tropicals was once the garden of Dr. William Hillebrand, a German physician who attended the royal family more than a century ago. Sent by the king to the tropics of Asia and America to find a labor source for Hawaii's new sugar industry and to secure plants of economic value, Hillebrand introduced a variety of tropical timber and resin-producing trees, many of which now tower majestically over the shaded lawns and walks. The County Arborist Advisory Committee has nominated 117 trees on Oahu and Kauai for lifetime protection. Foster Garden has 21, including the largest doum palm in the nation. Sometimes called the gingerbread palm, its seeds were brought from Egypt. Other plants of special interest include collections of tropical palms, hybrid and species orchids, cycads, and a wealth of brilliantly flowering trees. Special indeed are the Austrel Kauri, Bo, Cabbage Palm, Cannonball, Chicle, Elephant Ear, Hog Plum, Kapok, Pilinut, and Pogada. A free self-guide tour booklet is available from volunteers at the entry desk. Free guided tours are conducted each Mon., Tues., and Wed. at 1:30 P.M.

Next best, and quite different, is the old but free **Moanalua Gardens.** On Moanalua Road, accessible by bus, the No. 13 Tripler, from King and Umi Street terminal in Kalihi (two-block walk from bus stop on Ala Mahamoe to back entrance; 3/4 mile walk from bus stop in Mapunapuna). Privately owned and maintained for public use and enjoyment by the Estate of S. M. Damon, who was given the area by Princess Bernice Pauahi Bishop in 1884. The gardens are full of beautiful old trees, including the Bo tree, a scion of the tree in Ceylon where the Buddha received enlightenment, as well as specimens of the monkey-pod or "rain tree," called the most perfectly-shaped in the world by *Ripley's Believe It or Not.* The annual Prince Lot Hula Festival is staged on a hula mound in front of the cottage the third Saturday in July. Picnicking allowed.

Lyon Arboretum (988–7378), is deep in Manoa Valley. Drive through Paradise Park to reach it. The view of the Koolau range from the parking lot and greenhouse is very special, mountains almost close enough to touch. The 124 acres hosts 200 endemic plants.

Liliuokalani Gardens. Adjacent to Foster Botanical Garden at School Street and Waikahalulu Lane, is a 5-acre public park is cooled by shade trees and the Nuuanu Stream, which tumbles over the rocks at this point to form Waikahalulu Falls and a swimming hole. A cool spot for picnicking and swimming, far from the tourist trade.

Koko Crater Botanic Garden is 200 acres of dryland tropical wonders where there is little rainfall. Many plants from South America, India, and Australia. To reach this free retreat, turn left off Kalanianaole Hwy. at Kealahou and go along the golf course before turning left where the road leads to the Koko Crater Stables.

Haiku Gardens, 46–336 Haiku Rd., Kaneohe is open daily except Mondays. Five acres of beautiful tropical gardens, nature run wild, with a lily pond, flowers, and tropical trees. More than 1,000 plants. No admission charge. A restaurant serves lunch and dinner except on Mondays.

There is also the **Wahiawa Botanical Garden,** an oasis of tropical trees and shrubs, at the end of California Ave., open 9 A.M. to 4 P.M. daily.

BEACHES. Oahu has dozens of beaches but we're only going to talk about 18. **Waikiki,** though the most familiar, is smaller in size than many. A beach is not just a beach. Each has a personality. While Waikiki, on any given sunny day, may have bodies only inches apart, some place like **Mokuleia** on the North Shore may not have a living soul for a stretch of several miles. Mokuleia's isolation requires a warning: the water is shallow, prominent coral can cut, beautiful tropical fish abound unbothered, the silence is sometimes broken by the eerie whine of overhead gliders, and hoodlums think it's a nice beach to bury victims in the dead of night.

Waikiki stretches from the helicopter pad off the Westin Ilikai Hotel in the northwest to Sans Souci to the southeast. By Australian standards it's a midget. The breakers are quite uniform and not too large to handle. A majority of Waikiki hotels are a short walk to the beach, usually through a private beach elevator specifically for this purpose. For those driving, there is free parking at Kapiolani Park. Best swimming is in the Kuhio Beach area of Waikiki at the end of Kapahulu Ave., or fronting the Royal Hawaiian Hotel. One advantage to Waikiki are the beach concessions. You can rent or purchase rides or instructions from the famed beachboys. Concessionaires offer surfboards, windsurfing gear, boogie boards, outrigger canoe rides, catamaran rides, pediboats, and parasail flights. Along the beach are snack bars, even people selling burn lotions. You'll see hotels slicing off a little private turf for beach chairs for their own guests, but don't worry, the beaches are free for all.

Ala Moana is where you'll find the locals. The water in the man-made lagoon is smooth for serious swimmers. There's free parking and food concessions.

Bellows Beach is where the locals go on weekends because it's the best, and weekends because that's the only time the Air Force allows civilians to use this small military facility on the Windward Coast. The waves are perfect for bodysurfing; park and picnic under the cool ironwood trees. No snack bars. The sand is fine, preferable to Waikiki, which can be coarse. Adjacent to Bellows on either side are 3 other great beaches, all with the same nifty wave action: **Kailua, Lanikai,** and **Waimanalo.** Both Kailua and Waimanalo have beach park facilities and there are public rights-of-way between beach homes, all well marked, at both Kailua and Lanikai. Parking is troublesome except at the park facilities. A word of warning at Waimanalo: there are frequent thefts from parked automobiles, even when the doors and trunk are locked.

Farther north on the Windward Coast are the excellent beaches at **Kualoa Point, Kahana Bay,** and **Malaekahana,** (see "Parks" above). Another fine swimming place is the beach at **Laie.** The numerous other beaches from Kualoa north to Laie are often uncrowded but shallow and with plenty of coral reef. **Haleiwa** has a fairly nice beach, protected from wave action with complete park facilities for softball, picnicking, and parking.

Hanauma Bay is in a class by itself as a skindiver's paradise. One of the most idyllic of tropical beaches: white sand, palm trees, and transparent turquoise water in a volcanic crater at the base of Koko Head. Maintained as a public park, this splendid cove is ideal for swimming, skindiving, and picnicking. A paved path leads from the parking area down to the beach; it's a steep climb back, but worth it. Even if you don't feel like exercise, don't miss the view of this jewel-like bay from the slopes of Koko Head. Many like either to hike to the top of Koko Head for the view or to take the path to the left from the beach, along the rocky ledge that leads to the "Bath Tub." Here water surges in a hole in the lava, delighting bathers of all ages. Hanauma Bay Beach Park provides a shuttle from the parking lot to the beach, 50¢ a ride, daily, 8 A.M. to 5 P.M.

Five other beaches feature huge waves and huge courage to ride them. They are **Sandy Beach, Makapuu, Sunset** (a large area of many named breaks including the Bonzai Pipeline), **Waimea Bay,** and **Makaha.** These are somewhat reserved for young men of athletic skills. Bodysurfing is good at Sandy almost anytime. Prince Charles tried it in a 1985 visit. Big waves at Sunset, Waimea, and Makaha arrive only in the winter months. Professional championship events at Sunset attract surfers from foreign countries and gaping visitors from Waikiki. In December 1985 an event at Sunset was cancelled—the waves had reached 30 feet, which is too much even for the best. One more warning: there are many lovely beaches on the Leeward Coast from Kahe Point to Kaena Point. But the police report frequent cases of harassment and thefts. It's tragic. But admiring **Yokohama Beach,** just beyond Kaneana Cave, from your U-drive is an idea.

PARTICIPANT SPORTS. Nothing compares with swimming, surfing, riding the waves, or skindiving under them in the cobalt waters that surround Oahu. Because of almost year-round perfect weather it is difficult to beat the golf and tennis facilities on Oahu. Honolulu also lays claim to being the running–jogging capital of the nation. Because of the two mountain ranges that make Oahu what it is geologically, hiking can be extraordinary, particularly when there are no snakes to scare you. Fishing is largely confined to the deepsea variety. Other sports from hang gliding, to kite flying, to bowling on the green are available. Winter sports are unavailable except for one ice rink. The best swimming is described in "Beaches" above.

Waikiki is your center for **surfing.** You'll find surfboards for rent at $3 an hour on the beach near the *Royal Hawaiian* and at the *ewa* end of Kuhio Beach at Hale Au Au, near the *Moana Ocean Lanai.* If you like, you can arrange for professional lessons from a beachboy teacher. If you can't manage the board and ride the waves with a reasonable standard of grace after the third lesson, our advice is to forget the whole thing. To check surf conditions, telephone 836–1952.

On the Waikiki beach you can also join in an **outrigger canoe ride.** Cost: $5 for three rides.

Hawaii has excellent guides and instructors for **skindiving** and **aqualunging:** In Honolulu check out *South Sea Aquatics* at 1050 Ala Moana (538–3854). A half day in the water is $45. All gear available to rent or buy. Surfboard, moped, wind-surf and snorkel gear for rent at *Waikiki Sport and Moped Hawaii,* 337 Lewers St. Newest water-thrill is jet skiing. *Paradise Jet Ski* operates from the beach at Moanalua Bay in Hawaii Kai, $25 for half hour, $35 an hour (734–0717); *Offshore Sports Hawaii* (395–3434) has similar water fun. *Suyderhoud's Water Ski Center* works in the nearby Koko Marina lagoon for about $50 a half day (395–3773). For windsurfing there's a van that takes you from Waikiki to Kailua Bay; this and the equipment run to $40. Lessons are $7. Call *Aloha Windsurfing* at 926–1185. For snorkeling, *Hanauma Bay Snorkel* (944–8828), goes to Hanauma for a half day or full day; an early bird special at 7 A.M. is $7. *Blue Water* (926–4485) has an early for $5, plus underwater camera and film for $9. *Budget Snorkel,* 234 Beachwalk (947–2447) has a trip for $10. *Vehon Diving Ventures,* Kuapa Kai Shopping Center, Hawaii Kai (396–9738) offers one tank for Hanauma, $40, two for $50.

Windsurfing lessons are available at 156C Hamakua Dr., Kailua (261–3539). *Tropical Water Ski Tours* (923–4434) has **parasail** outings at Waikiki for $40, from 8 A.M. to 10 P.M., and water skis for $50, and both for $80. To learn about kayak club activity and chances to take part, call Wendy Arbeit of the Hui Wa'a Kaukahi Club (524–5411).

There are 28 good **golf** courses on Oahu. The pro tour plays Waialae, an oceanside layout, but you can't get on unless you know someone, and that goes for guests of the posh Kahala Hilton.

The Ala Wai Golf Course runs along the Ala Wai Canal just across the water from Waikiki. The Oahu Country Club is a lush, hilly course in the heart of Nuuanu Valley but the problem here is the same as it is for Waialae. The Moanalua Golf Club has a 9-holer and welcomes visitors. Weekday greens fees, $8. The Pali Golf Course has sweeping vistas at the windward foot of Nuuanu Pali. Makalena, another city-owned course at Waipio alongside Pearl Harbor, is flat. Hawaii-Kai, out beyond the Blow Hole near Makapuu Point, has both a regulation-length course and a par 3. Courses built in the last 15 years include two courses in Makaha Valley, the Sheraton Makaha and the Makaha Valley, the Turtle Bay hotel course at the north end of Oahu, the Mililani Golf Club near Schofield Barracks, the Olomana Club in Waimanalo, and the Pearl Country Club on Halawa Heights, with a great view of Pearl Harbor. There is a sporty course at Kunia, the Hawaii Country Club, a city-owned course at Kahuku, and a lighted little par 3 called Bay View in Kaneohe. You may also play at certain weekday times at the Mid-Pacific Country Club at Lanikai, but it's expensive. The military has nine courses (you must have a connection).

Rates vary from about $5 to walk the four city courses to over $20 at nicer layouts. Another way is the complete golf package tour offered by Kato's, or Makaha's Golf Tours that run about $45 including van pickups in Waikiki.

There are 80 public **tennis** courts on the island, many are lighted. Visitors are welcome to play any of them. There are ten courts at Ala Moana Park, nine at the Diamond Head Tennis Center, six at Koko Head, another four in Kapiolani Park in the Waikiki area.

Would you believe the Kapiolani courts are open until 4 A.M.? Other courts for play are 12 at Punahou School, and the lighted Kailua Racquet Club, with bar and pool for those holding reciprocity arrangements cards between private clubs. There are 7 courts at the Westin Ilikai, 10 at Turtle Bay and 4 at Sheraton Makaha. Heightened interest in tennis means getting a court is tougher every year. Another four courts sit atop Pay 'N Save, 2220 S. King S., and are open from 7 A.M. to midnight. The International Fitness and Racquetball Center, 1680 Kapiolani Blvd., can get you in top shape.

Jogging. Visitors often are surprised by the hundreds of people of all ages they see running. Two jogging meccas are Kapiolani Park near Waikiki and Ala Moana Park near the large shopping center. But almost any district has its joggers, particularly along Pearl Harbor, on the quiet residential streets where there are few traffic light crossings to contend with. Jogging in the middle of Waikiki is difficult because the sidewalks and streets are jammed to capacity already and there are so many traffic lights because the blocks are short. The enthusiasm for jogging on Oahu since 1970 is directly related to the huge success of the Honolulu Marathon in December which has drawn more than 10,000 from every state and upwards of 40 countries. Other races, from 4 miles up to 13.1-mile half-marathons are run every weekend of the year and welcome out-of-state entries. Check in at any running apparel shop and you'll find stacks of entry blanks and details.

There are about two dozen **hiking** trails on Oahu listed by the State Forestry Division, at 1151 Punchbowl St., Honolulu. Maps showing the trails are being revised. The city publishes an 18-page booklet to acquaint hikers with the beauties and dangers of hiking in Hawaii. There are hikes scheduled nearly every Sunday by the *Hawaiian Trail and Mountain Club* (734–5515). In recent years the *Sierra Club* has been offering hikes. They meet at 8 Sunday morning at the Church of the Crossroads in Manoa Valley. Foster Garden also has guided walks on Oahu, Maui, and Molokai in the summer. Another great hike is at Moanalua Valley; contact the *Moanalua Gardens Foundation,* 1352 Pineapple Pl. (839–5334). *Lyon Arboretum,* deep in Manoa Valley (988–7378), offers hikes up Koko Crater and other sights.

Best waters for **deep-sea fishing** are off the Waianae Coast (mahimahi, marlin, ulua, ahi, sailfish*),* off Koko Head *(aku, marlin, mahimahi),* off Kaneohe Bay *(ahi, aku, ono* and *mahimahi),* and along the Penguin Banks southwest of Molokai across the Kaiwi Channel from Oahu. Charter boats available in Kewalo Basin. Cost: about $350 for a party of six, some at $70 a share, all day, including equipment. This is an early starters' adventure. Boats leave Kewalo at 7 A.M. Fresh-water fishing is possible in the Wilson Reservoir at Wahiawa, but there are no boats for rent.

Sailing. The Waikiki and Hawaii Yacht Clubs (Ala Wai Harbor, Honolulu) welcome members of mainland clubs and extend guest privileges. So does the Kaneohe Yacht Club in Kaneohe Bay, windward Oahu.

The Navy and Air Force have clubs. If you don't know how to sail, *Hawaiiana Yacht Charters* (521–6305) at pier 12, will show you. Sailboats between 22 and 40 feet in length can be rented in Kewalo Basin. *Hawaii's Sailing Center* (396–8226) offers a 2-hour yacht ride Koko Marina to Diamond Head for $50. *World By The Tail* (422–2521) has half days in a 50-footer for $350. There's a 2-hour catamaran sail off the North Shore for $20 with lunch and snorkeling also available. These charters operate out of *Haleiwa Harbor* (638–8279).

Hunting. There's not much hunting activity on Oahu. For an assessment of conditions, game and seasons, telephone the State Department of Land and Natural Resources in Honolulu, 548–2861. Most of the happy hunting grounds are on the Neighbor Islands. The state license is $15. If you want to hunt boar, go to it. Every island wants to get rid of these destructive, hairy, black critters.

Bicycling. Waikiki is no place to bicycle. In fact, most of Oahu's streets are too narrow or congested for safe biking. Unlike European cities, Honolulu has few bonafide bikeways. However, there are bike shops, rentals, and a few places to go. Endurance speed biking is gaining popularity, usually along the Honolulu Marathon route of Kalanianaole Hwy., and bikers circle the island in competition. One place to obtain information on this type of serious biking is *Island Triathlon and Bike, Inc.,* 569 Kapahulu Ave. (732–7227).

Hawaiian canoeing (not American Indian canoeing). For information telephone Michael Tong at 526–1969 or Moku Froseith at 732–2719. **Hang-gliding** at Makapuu. Telephone 396–8557 ($75 for dual instruction with an hour's flight) for these dangerous thrills. **Gliding.** Mokuleia, $32 for a ride, or 2 together for $45, telephone 623–6711. **Kite-flying.** Check out *Kite Fantasy* at the New Otani Kaimana Beach Hotel. The place to fly them is across the street in Kapiolani Park. **Ti-Leaf Sliding.** Contact the Hawaii Trail and Mountain Club for information on this ancient Hawaiian sport. **Riding** is available at Kualoa Ranch, 531–8531, or Koko Crater Stables, 395–2628. Turtle Bay Resort rents horses at $12 an hour.

More horses are at Gunstock's Ranch, 488–1593. And if you need your usual sweaty workout, check out the racquetball at the Honolulu Club, International Fitness Club, or Oahu Athletic Club. Certainly a border sport is Hawaii Paint Games, at Marconi Road in Kahuku (293–1590), an outdoor war game "sport" with concealment and a need for sharp wits. 9 A.M. to 5:30 P.M. Same place has dunecycles.

Equipment shops are everywhere and there are specialty shops for skindiving in Waikiki, or more general purpose stores such as Sears or Honsport in the Ala Moana Shopping Center.

Finally, you've come to Oahu to **ice skate.** Go to Ice Palace, 4510 Salt Lake Blvd. (487–9921), $5 includes skate rentals; children $3.75, operates 7 days a week.

SPECTATOR SPORTS. College football is king on Oahu and the place to see it is Aloha Stadium, a major feature near Pearl Harbor and Aiea. The stadium, after numerous delays and lawsuits, was finished in 1975 at a cost of nearly $30 million.

The ballpark is the home of the University of Hawaii Rainbow Warriors football team; the Pro Bowl has found a home at Aloha. The stadium hosts the annual *Aloha Bowl* in late December featuring teams like Notre Dame and Alabama and the *Hula Bowl,* an all All-American all-star format, in January and the *Pro Bowl* in February. Parking is impossible at games because the Aloha Stadium parking lot fills for tailgate parties. Charter buses, however, take fans to the stadium from several city locations.

In recent years top college basketball teams like Georgetown, Louisville, and Kentucky have come to Oahu for early season tournaments or the annual Rainbow Classic during Christmas week. Local opponents besides the University of Hawaii are University of Hawaii-Hilo, Chaminade, Brigham Young University-Hawaii, Hawaii Pacific College, and Hawaii Loa. Most tournaments are held at Neal Blaisdell Center.

In the spring **college baseball** is popular at the new University of Hawaii Stadium on campus in Moiliili Quarry. University ticket information is available at 949–2085. The baseball park seats 4,000 and is just about the best in the nation. Baseball tickets run $2.50 and $3.50, basketball $4.50 and $5.50, and football $9 and $10. Increasingly popular, too, is *wahine* (women's) volleyball. The University of Hawaii wahine volleyball team has come close to the national collegiate championship twice in recent years.

Two **PGA tour events** are held in Hawaii, the *Hawaiian Open* at Waialae in February and the *Kapalua Invitational* on Maui in November. Tickets for the Hawaiian Open are available at several gates to the fairways and cost about $5.

Other spectator sports on Oahu include **boxing, karate tournaments, tennis, sumo and professional wrestling, polo, college volleyball, auto and drag racing, canoe and yacht racing, and high school sports.** There is no horse racing in Hawaii. Honolulu has hosted a few world championship prizefights in years past.

CAMPING. There are 16 parks on Oahu: 13 Honolulu County beach parks (contact the city Parks Department, 650 S. King St. Honolulu, HI 96813; 523–4525) and three state parks—Aiea Heights, Sand Island, and Malaekahana (contact state Park Department, 1151 Punchbowl St., Honolulu, HI 96813; 548–7455). Locals love to tent out on the beach, so there may not be much space left for outsiders. Free permits are good for a week—starting at 8 A.M. Fri. mornings, ending 8 A.M. Thurs. mornings—at both beach and state parks.

There is a wide range of vehicles available on all islands, from pick-up trucks to deluxe homes on wheels for rent. Airport pick-up arrangements are possible. Two suggested camper operators: *Beach Boy Campers* of Honolulu and *Travel/Camp, Inc.,* based in Hilo. Beach Boy is reachable at 955–6381, Travel/Camp at 935–7406. Some of the facilities have showers and toilets and are big enough to sleep six.

Note: Discuss security with officials you are dealing with. A few areas, such as the Waianae Coast have known scenes of harassment and violence; but most campsites are safe.

HISTORIC SITES. (See also "Exploring Honolulu" earlier in this chapter.)

Pearl Harbor. America's great naval bastion which was asleep one memorable Sunday morning in 1941, may be visited with its tragic reminders of that "day of infamy": the sunken battleship *Arizona,* with 1,177 sailors entombed in its watery hulk, and the *Utah* with 58. These are sobering sights.

There are 5 basic ways to see the navy yard. Cruise boats make a twice-daily boat trip out of it, leaving Kewalo Basin near the Ala Moana Center at 9:30 A.M. and 1:30 P.M. Round trip is $8 to $15 depending on the type of boat, or if a Waikiki hotel pickup is included.

The Navy operates a shuttle boat to the *Arizona Memorial* every half hour between 8 A.M. and 3 P.M., daily. Children under 6 are not allowed and there is some waiting. If you know someone working or stationed in the base a visit may be possible by showing an ID card (passport if necessary) at Nimitz Gate. This is not necessary if you are taking a boat trip.

The tour has drawn more than a million people a year for several years, and the Navy has built the new Arizona Memorial Visitors Center to better accommodate tourists. The facility, on Kamehameha Highway, is operated by the National Park Service, and features two comfortable theaters where a 20-minute film helps put the 1941 events in historic perspective. The center opens at 8 A.M. in case you drive out on your own. Free tickets are first-come, first-served. No reservations. Gray Line has a bus trip to Pearl Harbor for the boat ride for $11.90 (children half price) leaving Waikiki 8:30 A.M. or 12:30 P.M.

The fourth way is to take the #8 bus from Waikiki to Ala Moana Center and #50 or #51 to the center; or drive your car to the park, there's plenty of parking. There's also an Arizona shuttle bus from Waikiki for $4, telephone 926–4747. The Park Service number is 471–3901. Next door to the Arizona Visitors Center is the diesel sub *Bowfin,* a veteran of many World War II patrols in the Western Pacific, open Tues. through Sun., 9:30 A.M. to 4:30 P.M., admission $3.

A historical note of interest on the yard: originally called *Wai Momi* (Pearl Waters) by the Hawaiians because of the presence of pearl oysters, the harbor is actually the double estuary of the Pearl River. The harbor's potential value first became known in 1840, when Lt. Charles Wilkes of the U.S. Navy made a geodetic survey of the islands and reported that the coral bar at the entrance to the Wai Momi lochs could be dredged to provide passage for large ships. In 1873, the United States acquired permission from the Hawaiian Kingdom to blast out the entrance channel, but this work was not accomplished until 1898, when attention focused on the Pacific during the Spanish-American war. America's first dry dock at Pearl Harbor collapsed when the foundation gave way as work neared completion in 1913. This was Pearl's first major disaster. The Hawaiians ascribed it to the anger of Kaahupahau, Queen of the Sharks, and her brother, whose home happened to be a cavern right under the dry dock. In subsequent construction, the Navy was more circumspect.

Today, Pearl Harbor is a vast and bristling installation, nerve center of the Pacific Fleet, with a responsibility for 85 million square miles. A visit to this impressive base provides a close contact with recent history. Battleship Row is parallel with the Ford Island shoreline. The island is the headquarters for the 3rd Fleet, but island visiting is discouraged. A warship is open to public visits at noon on the first Saturday of every month. Enter Nimitz Gate. The Submarine Base invites visitors to a free tour of the Pacific Submarine Museum Wed. and Sun. from 9:30 A.M. to 5 P.M. Telephone 471–0632.

The Mission Houses are at Mission Lane and S. King St. close to Kawaiahao Church and across from City Hall. Open daily 9 A.M.–4 P.M. This ensemble of early houses makes up a corner of Hawaii which is forever New England. The oldest house was actually "prefabricated," built from ready-cut lumber which was brought from Boston around Cape Horn to Honolulu on the ship *Tartar* in 1820. On August 23, 1821, Mr. and Mrs. Daniel Chamberlain moved into the typical two-story New England frame house, 6,000 miles from home. Later the missionaries constructed a small bedroom addition built of coral stone (17 by 28 feet). Today the addition accommodates a replica of the first printing press in the Hawaiian Islands. Within 5 years, the press in this tiny house turned out some 30 million pages of biblical text, primers, spellers, geographies, and other books, primarily in Hawaiian, to aid the missionaries in spreading the gospel among the heathens. The building is the oldest printing house west of the Rocky Mountains. A third house, built in 1831, of hand-hewn coral stone, followed the classical New England pattern. It is known as "Chamberlain House" after its first occupant, Levi Chamberlain, business agent for the mission.

The Mission Houses are maintained by descendants of the missionaries, organized as the Hawaiian Mission Children's Society. There are two important libraries of Hawaiiana, their own and that of the Hawaiian Historical Society, on the property. The Mission Houses are museums, full of household utensils, pictures, family mementos, and other relics of the missionaries' adjustment to Hawaii and vice versa. Fascinating history. Adults $5.30, children $1 to tour the houses. A guided tour to historical sites in the area leaves the Mission Houses on weekdays at 9:30 A.M. and returns at noon. $7 for adults, $2 for children. The downtown walk, not including the Mission Houses, starts at 10:30 A.M. weekdays and costs $3 for adults and $1 for children. Reservations in advance are required (531–0481).

Kawaiahao Church. Hawaii's first church was designed by the missionary pastor Hiram Bingham and built of coral blocks in 1841. The proportions and classic dignity of the church are a tribute to the pastor's simple New England taste. He is honored by a memorial tablet to *Binamu* (the Hawaiian equivalent of his name) in the vestibule, along with other missionaries and Hawaiians (like Queen Kaahumanu) who helped to spread the new faith in the islands. The church, opened for worship July 21, 1842, was the royal chapel of Hawaiian monarchs for two decades. Their portraits hang on the balcony. Scene of coronation ceremonies, state funerals, and even legislative sessions, Kawaiahao Church is steeped in Hawaiian history. Sunday morning services (Congregational) are still conducted in English and Hawaiian. Programs are printed, sermons are preached, and hymns are sung in both languages. The result of this duality is a long service (from 10:30 to noon), but a moving Hawaiian experience. The church is open to the public at times during the week but a series of thefts ended its traditional open door policy—a sad comment on the times.

If historical places are of interest, and you want to know more, a little research may be in order. Aside from a room full of Hawaiiana and Hawaii history books in the Library of Hawaii, and photographs of old Oahu at Bishop Museum, you could check out the Archives of Hawaii on the Lolani Palace Grounds. Open Mon.–Fri. from 7:45 A.M. to 4:30 P.M. Closed on Sat. and Sun.

MUSEUMS. The Bishop Museum at 1525 Bernice St. (848–4129). Open Mon. through Sat. and the first Sun. of every month from 9 A.M. to 5 P.M. Admission to both exhibits and the planetarium show is $4.95 for adults; $2.50 for youths 6–17. Under 6 free. Planetarium shows are at 11 A.M. and 3:15 P.M. Tickets can be purchased separately for $1.50, adults; 75¢, youths 6–17. Six and under are admitted only on Sat. and Sun. and are free on those days. Guided tours of Hawaii Hall daily at 10 A.M., noon, and 2 P.M. From Waikiki you can ride the minibus or take city bus No. 2 for 60¢.

Founded in 1889 by Charles R. Bishop as a memorial to his wife, Princess Bernice Pauahi, the Bishop Museum began as a repository for the royal possessions of this last direct descendant of Kamehameha the Great. Under the direction of such noted anthropologists as Sir Peter Buck and Dr. Alexander Spoehr, the museum achieved world fame as a center of research into the archaeology, ethnology, and natural history of Polynesia. The average visitor should not be put off by the museum's armory-like exterior. The building is a Victorian monument in its own right. Within its forbidding stone walls are enough treasures to make your eyes bulge, a marvelous visual recreation of how the ancient Hawaiians lived, dressed, and worshipped.

At Hawaiian Hall you will find some of the museum's feather capes and cloaks once worn by Hawaiian chiefs. Hand-made from the feathers of birds now extinct, these red and yellow cloaks were often years in the making, since each bird furnished only one feather of sufficient brilliance to adorn a chiefly cloak. The museum's collection of cloaks is so rare as to provide no basis for comparison. One of the cloaks, which once graced the broad shoulders of Kamehameha I, is currently valued at $1 million. Complementing the cloaks and capes is a collection of beautiful feather *leis* and the crested Hawaiian helmets.

Relics of the darker side of ancient Hawaiian life include a fierce idol of carved *ohia* wood, one of three known to have been used at a *heiau* devoted to human sacrifice; a temple drum of wood and sharkskin ornamented with human teeth; clubs, slings, spears, strangling cords, and other weapons of Hawaiian warriors; and the personal plates and platters of Kamehameha the Great, studded with the teeth of his enemies.

Among the most striking exhibits is a miniature *heiau*, showing how the Hawaiians worshipped their ancient gods before the missionaries brought new ones to their attention.

There are splendid examples of the outrigger canoes in which the Polynesians traveled the highroads of the sea.

In the new second-story gallery you will see a collection of calabashes and other Polynesian, Melanesian, and Micronesian artifacts of whalebone, tortoise shell, and beautifully carved wood, a striking contrast to the false Gothic splendors of the *authentic* thrones of the Hawaiian kingdom, which are also housed in this museum.

There also are innumerable specimens of the flora and fauna of the Pacific, including a marvelous whale, which hangs from the ceiling of Hawaiian Hall.

Outside is a replica of an Easter Island face (but this 6-ton idol came from New York). The idol was unveiled on Easter Sunday 1975. The island was discovered the same day in 1722. Newest attraction inside is the Ray Jerome Baker Room, third floor Paki Hall, where the famed photographer's collection of 360,000 pictures of Hawaii, dating back to 1845, can be seen. Baker's own photos number 20,000, done between 1910 and 1959. Reprints can be ordered.

With the addition of *Kilolani Planetarium* in 1961, even the space element in the Polynesian story is not overlooked at Bishop Museum's Science Center. A "theater of the sky" adjoins the scientific observatory, and the visual presentations there are splendid. The space exhibits vary, but the emphasis is on the celestial aspects of the Pacific and their influence on its history and evolution.

Iolani Palace. At King and Richards St. Tours only Wed. through Sat. 9 A.M.–2:15 P.M. Tours begin every 15 minutes and last 45 minutes. Admission $4 for adults; children 5–12 years, $1. Children under 5 years not permitted. Reservations necessary days in advance, phone 523–0141. The only royal palace on American soil, Iolani, or "Heavenly Hawk," was formerly the seat of the Hawaii Republic, territorial, and later state government legislature. The Senate met in what was once the royal dining room, the House of Representatives in the throne room. The cornerstone of the palace was laid on New Year's Eve in 1879, and the structure was completed in 1882 at a cost in excess of $350,000, big money in those days. King Kalakaua, the Merry Monarch, was the only king to occupy the palace. A thirty-third degree Mason, he had a Masonic dinner party for 120, his first official banquet, soon after he moved in 1882. Eleven years later, the Hawaiian monarchy was overthrown, and the Stars and Stripes flew from the central flagpole.

The architectural inspiration and execution of Kalakaua's palace are confused. Architects and contractors were changed midway in the construction of the building, and nobody is quite sure who is responsible for what. The palace is Continental and Victorian in appearance and looks rather like a casino at some fashionable European watering place.

The interior is more interesting than the exterior with its lavish use of Hawaiian *koa, ohia, kamani,* and *kou* wood, in addition to white cedar and walnut. To the right of this stairway on the ground floor is the throne room where King Kalakaua and his successor Queen Liliuokalani, the only Hawaiian monarchs to inhabit Iolani Palace, received and entertained. Royal *kahilis* lined the walls; the original crystal chandeliers, purchased by King Kalakaua from his European tour in 1882, still dip from the ceiling. The dais is flanked by huge feather *kahilis* in the colors of Kalakaua's sister, Queen Liliuokalani, last sovereign of Hawaii. Kalakaua's coat of arms, a crown with crossed spears, forms the decoration above the pediment of doors and windows. Portraits of Hawaiian royalty complete the decor. These are a post-monarchy addition; the original decorations consisted of gilded mirrors and thrones and 16 royal escutcheons. The originals were all removed in 1973. Replica thrones and portraits will be returned eventually.

Across the hallway from the throne room was the royal state dining room and its antechamber, the Blue Room, once decorated in blue mohair plush and serving as a lounge and music room. The second floor, which once contained four bedrooms, a library, a music room and other rooms housed the governor, lieutenant governor, and attorney general for many years. Of the portraits once in the Blue Room, most interesting is that of Louis Philippe, presented by the French monarch to Kamehameha III in 1848. It has a bullet hole in it, result of a wild shot in the Hawaiian revolution in 1893. The former royal bedroom of Kalakaua was used by the governor until 1968.

The royal bedroom is across the hall from a suite once occupied by a queen. This was the wilful Liliuokalani, who brooded here for nine months under house arrest after the revolution that toppled her throne. A few weeks earlier, the queen had held a *luau* down in the basement where Kalakaua had once tinkered in his workshop and played a few hands of poker over drinks and cigars with his buddies. Those merry days are gone forever.

● **The Academy of Arts,** at 900 S. Beretania St. (538–3693), faces Thomas Square. 10 minutes by taxi from Waikiki, 20 minutes by bus. Open Tues., Wed., Fri., and Sat. 10 A.M.–4:30 P.M.; Thurs. 11 A.M.–8 P.M.; Sun. afternoons from 2 to 5 P.M. Closed on Mon. No admission charge.

The Honolulu Academy of Arts, cultural center of Hawaii, is one of the most beautiful art museums anywhere. Endowed by Mrs. Charles M. Cooke and her family, descendants of early missionary teachers, the museum was dedicated in 1927 and reflects the racial and cultural complexity of Hawaii.

The building itself, designed by the noted New York architectural firm of Bertram Goodhue and Associates, translates these ideals into stone and tile, utilizing Occidental, Oriental, and Polynesian forms to create a striking new style. Behind the Academy's "Hawaiian face," suggested by the simple mass and steeply-pitched roof lines of early Hawaiian houses, there is a series of charming patios, of which the Chinese court, reminiscent of a Peking garden, is one of the most beautiful and tranquil spots in all of Honolulu. The exhibition galleries open onto these inviting courts, and the whole arrangement is a far cry from the exhausting perspective of endless galleries frequently found at other museums, which are enough to lay most travelers low with an acute case of psychosomatic athlete's foot.

One of the few art museums of a general comprehensive nature in the Asian-Pacific world, the Academy offers a very special opportunity to Westerners to become acquainted with the art of the Orient. Likewise, for many Asian residents and visitors, it provides an introduction to Western art. The Academy has set a pace for the growing community of Hawaii, and has gone beyond any parochialism to achieve world renown in certain departments. Art historians as well as less specialized visitors come from far away to this "remote" island to see such masterpieces of Chinese painting as the 100 Geese Scroll traditionally attributed to Ma Fen. The collection of Korean ceramics is one of the most distinguished outside the Orient, and the Japanese collection, augmented by a comprehensive selection of Japanese prints from the early masters to the modern, donated by James A. Michener, has made the Academy a mecca for world scholars.

In 1976 the Academy added a new gallery of sculpture from India. In addition, there are interesting examples of Chinese furniture, ceramics, and bronzes, Japanese screens, and Buddhist art. And in 1982 a new director, George R. Ellis, was named.

The history of Western Art is traced through notable examples of Persian, Egyptian, Greek, and Roman art down through the centuries to such modern masters as Van Gogh, Matisse, Picasso, and Cézanne. The Kress Collection of Italian Renaissance Painting is a small, choice synopsis.

The program at the Academy has expanded rapidly, and now there is a graphic arts center, galleries for 19th- and 20th-century European, American, and a small collection of Hawaiian art, and an educational wing to accommodate the roster of 50,000 children annually who have their first contact with art in these precincts. The fastest-growing part of the collection is as contemporary as Robert Rauschenberg, Kenneth Noland, and Morris Louis, and is now exhibited in the new Clare Boothe Luce wing. On the average, the Academy mounts 30 temporary exhibits a year. Its extension program takes exhibitions, film and visual presentations, lectures, and counseling services to art groups on the Neighbor Islands.

To help mark its 50th anniversary in April 1977, the Academy constructed a wing with a large gallery for the contemporary collection and a multi-media lecture hall called the Academy Theatre at a cost of $1.5 million. The hall hosts a regular diet of film classics and concerts. The new structural addition provides space for showing collections now in storage and serves the museum's expanded education and community activity programs. The Academy has also opened new exhibits of African, pre-Colombian, and Oceanic art. There is a small restaurant offering gourmet sandwiches at two sittings: 11:45 A.M. and 1 P.M. Tues.-Fri. A light supper is available Thurs. from 6:30–7:30 P.M. Reservations necessary (531–8865), except during the summer months, when a buffet is available.

● **Queen Emma Summer Palace Museum,** called Hanaikalamalama, is at 2913 Pali Hwy. Open 9 A.M. to 4 P.M. every day except holidays. Admission: $4 for adults; 12–18 years, $1; under 12, 50¢. This very delightful summer home of Hawaii's beloved Queen Emma (1836–1885, wife of Kamehameha IV) has been restored by the Daughters of Hawaii as a perfect setting for her personal belongings and other royal relics. You will see the queen's huge bed, carved of Hawaiian wood in the height of Victorian taste; the silver font which Queen Victoria sent to Hawaii for the christening of her godson, the attractive and ill-fated Prince of Hawaii; the Edinburgh Room, elegantly furnished to receive the Duke of Edinburgh on his visit to Hawaii in 1869; royal *kahili;* Queen Emma's silver service; and the gowns and jewelry she wore when the Hawaiian court was in its heyday.

There are 4 **military museums.** At Fort DeRussy in Waikiki is the *Army Museum* inside the concrete of Battery Randolph which has 2-inch-square steel-bar-reinforced cement walls up to 10 feet thick on the seaward side. Under the gun mounts the concrete is 22 feet thick. The battery housed 14-inch coastal rifles from 1911 until December 7, 1941, when the attack came from a different direction. After the fort withstood a battering by demolition crews, the Army had second thoughts, and a museum was created within. Displayed are tanks, guns, vehicles, uniforms and medals, ranging from a German World War I helmet to a Viet Cong flag. But the stress is on the war in the Pacific, 1941–45, with contributions by Hawaii's

442nd Regimental Combat Team and some earlier Hawaii military artifacts. Open 10 A.M. to 4:30 P.M. Tues.-Sun. Free; donations welcomed.

Inside Schofield Barracks near Wahiawa is the free *Tropic Lightning Historical Center*, open 7 days a week from 10 A.M. to 4 P.M. Closed on national holidays. There is an assortment of artifacts from World War II and Korean War days, many banners, photographs, and a large collection of Viet Cong rifles, mortars, and punji traps.

The 2 Navy museums are at Pearl Harbor. The small *Pacific Submarine Museum* has free tours Wed. and Sun., 9:30 A.M. to 5 P.M., inside the naval base (471–0632). The World War II diesel sub *Bowfin*, which sank a great many Japanese ships, is located adjacent to the Arizona Memorial Visitors Center, open Tues. through Sun., 9:30 A.M. to 4:30 P.M., $3.

Another museum that floats, à la Queen Mary, is the **Falls of Clyde.** Step back in time and visit the 100-year-old world's only surviving full-rigged 4-masted sailing ship. It is permanently at Pier 7, Honolulu Harbor.

Built in Scotland, in 1878, the *Falls* sailed the world on 70 voyages for the Glasgow Falls Line until, converted to a bark rig flying the Hawaiian and Matson flags, it made 60 trips on the regular San Francisco-Hilo cargo and passenger run. The crossing took 17 days. She hauled oil from 1907–20, then was tied up in Ketchikan and Seattle for 41 years before coming back to Honolulu for restoration and conversion as a maritime museum by the Bishop Museum. The people of Hawaii raised $25,000 in a month to buy her only weeks before she was to be sunk at Vancouver B.C. for use as a log breakwater.

Admission $3 for adults; children 6 to 12, $1; under 6 free. Open 11 A.M. to 11 P.M. daily. Worth inspecting is the Hokule'a, a replica of the ancient Polynesian raft. It made round-trips to Tahiti in 1976 and 1980. On the other side of the parking lot is a floating Chinese restaurant that was towed to the harbor from Hong Kong.

Friends of Waipahu Cultural Garden Park at 94–515 Waipahu St., near the sugar mill (677–0110) has artifacts of plantation life and many early 20th-century artifacts from the different ethnic groups who worked the fields.

The **Elvis Museum** is on the third floor of the Waikiki Shopping Plaza, 2250 Kalakaua Ave., Room 320 (926–1147); open 10 A.M. to 10 P.M., $3.

Taking shape slowly are museums to honor Hawaii's aviation, maritime, and railroad history.

The **Pacific Aerospace Museum** is due to open in mid-1988 at Honolulu International Airport with exhibits of everything from props to space vehicles.

The **Aloha Tower Maritime Museum** is on the 9th floor of the downtown tower, 606 Fort St., Pier 7. Open 9:30 A.M. to 4 P.M., Mon. through Fri. (548–5433).

The **Hawaiian Railway Society** (681–5461) as 91–1001 Renton Rd. in Ewa has several locomotives left over from the 1920s on display. No fee. When going *makai* or south on Ft. Weaver Rd., turn right at the second light. There were 140 locomotives working in the sugar industry in the old days.

The **Bottle Museum** has 18 exhibits of bottles from Captain James Cook's time up to annexation in 1898. The exhibits rotate to libraries. A newsletter and information is available from Hawaii Bottle Museum, Box 25153, Honolulu, HI 96825 (395–4671).

FILMS. An **International Film Festival** features new creations from Asia that are shown all day and evening at the Varsity Theater near the University of Hawaii campus and simultaneously at a number of other theaters during a week in late November. Producers and directors discuss their work at these showings. A film from China, *Yellow Earth,* was the 1985 winner. Tickets are free. Parking around the Varsity is difficult during the daylight hours. Information at 944–7666.

The only "art" film house in Honolulu is the **Honolulu Academy of Arts Theater** (entrance from Kinau St.) where, throughout the year, a series of movies from many nations are shown along with standard Hollywood silents from the 1920s, the complete Astaire–Rogers series, and similar sets. Admission $2; call 538–1006 for information. Parking is in a small lot off Kinau St. near the Admiral Thomas Apartments.

MUSIC. The **Honolulu Symphony Orchestra** schedule includes 2 performances of 10 concerts, Sunday afternoons, and Tuesday evenings at the magnificent Concert Hall of the Blaisdell Center at Ward Ave. and King St.: Sept. through Apr. Tickets range in price from $8.50 to $18.00. And the budget is up to $2 million a year. Schedules and advance reservations may be obtained by writing to the Honolulu Symphony Society, 1000 Bishop St., Honolulu, HI 96813 (537–6171). On Friday nights there is lighter fare, often featuring Island musicians. In the summer months the symphony has a Starlight series outdoor at the Waikiki Shell. There is a pre-subscription season series of Mozart, Haydn, and Bach at the Fort Ruger Theater.

Three operas produced by the **Hawaii Opera Theater** are performed each spring. *Merry Widow* (February), *Don Giovanni* (February), and *Carmen* (March) are on tap for 1989 (521–6537).

Chamber Music Hawaii (531–6617) sponsors 25 concerts a year, usually at the Lutheran Church across the street from Punahou School, or at the Honolulu Academy of Arts or at Lanikai and Kailua on the Windward side, and other places.

Honolulu Chamber Music Series brings in the Budapest String Quartet and others to Orvis Auditorium on the University of Hawaii campus.

Newest organization to offer a season of symphonic music is the **Honolulu Philharmonic Society** (734–0397). **The University of Hawaii Music Department** also has faculty concerts at Orvis through the school year (948–7756). Admission $5. **The Honolulu Chorale** and various church singing ensembles perform cantatas at church sites, sometimes free, sometimes for a fee. Rock groups and other contemporaries perform either at Neal Blaisdell Center Arena (521–2911) or Aloha Stadium (488–7731). NBC box office hours, Mon. through Sat. is 10 A.M. to 6 P.M.

DANCE. Each autumn the Honolulu Symphony sponsors the **San Francisco Ballet.** Other outside dance groups, like **Ballet West** or **Alvin Ailey,** make occasional visits. The major local company is **Ballet Hawaii** (988–7578), which puts on *Nutcracker* each year, or *Cinderella.* A number of private dance studios put on classic ballet and modern dance programs, and the **University of Hawaii Dance Department** has several shows a year at the Kennedy Theater. **The Chamber Ballet** from New York performed there in 1985. The University number, for more information, is 948–7677.

STAGE. The **Honolulu Community Theater,** an outstanding amateur group, holds center stage in Hawaii, though outdone by other good amateur groups for the entertainment dollar. The HCT remains busy all year round at the Fort Ruger Theater (5 minutes from Waikiki). Tickets are $4.50–$7.75. Telephone 734–0274.

University theater is always excellent and open to the public. Its home is the John F. Kennedy Theater at the East-West Center campus. And there are active drama programs at Chaminade College, Brigham Young University-Hawaii, and Hawaii Loa College.

Other successes include the **Honolulu Theater for Youth** (all around the state), and the **Windward Theater Guild** at the Kailua Elementary cafetorium. There is other intimate theater in Manoa Valley, the **Hawaii Performing Arts Company** (HPAC), 2833 E. Manoa Rd. (988–6131), and at Schofield Barracks. Occasionally companies from Broadway put on large musical productions at the Neal Blaisdell Concert Hall. Success has been elusive at best. **American Contemporary Theater of San Francisco** has performed at Kennedy and Ruger theaters with moderate success. Asian theatrical groups appear less often.

ART GALLERIES. The Honolulu Academy of Arts is the queen of the art galleries (see "Museums," above). Next best are the Contemporary Arts Center and the Tennent Art Foundation.

The **Contemporary Arts Center** at 605 Kapiolani Blvd. (in the News Building) is open from 8 to 5 weekdays and Sat. from 8 to 12. There is a monthly art show. Some of the most exciting works of Island artists are displayed. After leaving the gallery, walk upstairs and examine Erica Karawina's stained-glass window in the second-floor foyer. Then feel free to stroll throughout the building and enjoy the 900 other fine examples of Island art displayed. Eventually, the Center hopes to create a museum that will occupy the entire building.

The **Tennent Art Foundation** is at 201–203 Prospect St. Open Tues. through Sat. from 10 A.M. to noon. Sun., 2 to 4 P.M. Or by special appointment: phone 531–1987. There is no admission charge.

Any visitor interested in fine art should see this gallery in a lovely Hawaiian garden on the *ewa* slope of Punchbowl. Completed in 1954, it was designed by Vladimir Ossipoff for the express purpose of housing the paintings of Hawaii's foremost artist, Madge Tennent (1889–1972). Paris-trained as a child prodigy, London-born Madge Tennent, came to the Islands from South Africa early in the century. She found her métier in painting the Hawaiian people—great, noble, voluminous portraits of a race, so infused with understanding, so vital in concept and execution that one critic observed: "Even if the Hawaiians were to vanish as a race they would live forever in the paintings of Madge Tennent." No other artist in Hawaii has made such an original contribution to the arts or one which is so peculiarly Hawaiian.

In addition to the major works in the main gallery, there are smaller paintings and drawings by Madge Tennent in other rooms. There is also a library and a selection of pictures by other Island artists, either bought by the Foundation or donated by the painters in recognition of the encouragement which Madge Tennent always gave to young artists.

One of the best new art centers anywhere is the **Amfac Center Plaza,** an exhibition area at 745 Fort St. (Fort St. Mall at Queen St.). Operated as a public service, the Center features exhibits by Hawaii's best painters, sculptors, and photographers. Other items of general and visual interest are also displayed, such as contemporary interior design, architecture, and historical exhibits.

Island art can be seen at the *Ala Moana Center,* with the most popular art display area anywhere located on the ground level, *mauka* side.

Island art can also be seen at many other locations, some commercial, some not. The following have shows in all media: *Territorial Savings and Loan* downtown at the Financial Plaza; the *Gallery at the First Unitarian Church,* 2500 Pali Hwy.; *Central Pacific Bank,* 220 S. King; *Bishop Square,* second-floor show space, reach via escalator, at 1001 Bishop St.; the *Croissanterie,* 222 Merchant St.; the *Designer's Emporium,* 1044 Nuuanu Ave.; *The Pegge Hopper Gallery,* 1160A Nuuanu Ave.; *The Louis Pohl Studio and Gallery,* 3507 N. Pali Dr.; *The Ramsay Downtown Gallery,* 119 Merchant St.; *Gallery EAS,* Makaloa Sq.; the *Marinda Lee Gallery,* Hawaii Loa College; the *Prince Kuhio Federal Building,* 300 Ala Moana Blvd., which has a gallery managed by the Arts Council of Hawaii; *City Hall,* corner Punchbowl and S. King St.; the *Queen Emma Gallery,* in a wing of Queen's Hospital; and the *Church of the Crossroads* near the University, which also sells ceramics. The *University of Hawaii's Art Department* has the newest gallery, an excellent exhibition facility near Varney Circle in midcampus. Other places to view and purchase Island art are the *ArtLoft,* 186 N. King St. (523–0489), 11 A.M. to 5 P.M., Mon. through Fri. *Ward Centre Gallery,* 1200 Ala Moana Blvd. (531–2652), handles two dozen local artists. Nearby in the *Ward Warehouse,* 1050 Ala Moana, is the Artists Guild, where 65 local artists display work that is a little less expensive. Ceramics, oils, lithos, photos, glass, sculpture, jewelry, and koa. Another place to buy local art is at the *Art Mart* where paintings, new works sometimes still wet, hang on the Honolulu Zoo fence on Monsarrat Ave. in Kapiolani Park. The painters sit in folding chairs and discuss their works, which frequently are idealized seascapes. Things start about 10 A.M. on Sat. and Sun. (524–7910).

SHOPPING. It's fun to shop in Hawaii! Honolulu and Waikiki shops offer an exotic potpourri of wares, some Polynesian-inspired, others deriving from the Islands' Oriental background, still others imported from all over the world, a cosmopolitan array to suit international tastes. The Neighboring Islands also boast shopping markets, malls, villages, and resort hotel shops, many of which are branches of Honolulu stores. And watch for the tiny specialty shops, roadside merchants, and factories along the roads on all the Islands.

Wise travelers bring lightly-packed luggage and plan to fill out their wardrobes with Island attire. Surely a large part of the pleasure of a holiday in Hawaii is immediately donning casual, comfortable clothes, appropriate to this idyllic setting.

For shopping suggestions, four big malls come to mind for browsing and buying: At the **Ala Moana Shopping Center,** near Waikiki at 1450 Ala Moana Blvd., you will find Hawaiian arts and crafts, as well as more Mainlandish merchandise, in the center's 155 stores. (Sears Roebuck and Co. has a solid-value roundup of Hawaiian-made items at excellent prices.) The upscale **Kahala Mall,** 2 miles from Waikiki has 58 stores. The new **Windward Mall** is in Kaneohe at the corner of Kamehameha Hwy. and Kaiku Rd. The **Pearlridge Shopping Center** overlooks Pearl Harbor in the military complex.

In Waikiki there is also the **International Market Place** at 2330 Kalakaua Ave., created expressly to provide visitors with an entertaining smorgasbord of arts and crafts of the Pacific. The **Atrium Shops** at the elegant Hyatt Regency Hotel boasts over 70 shops on 3 levels. **King's Village,** next door, is a quaint complex with a Changing of the Guard each night. The **Waikiki Shopping Plaza** with its 75-foot water fountain is an attractive place to browse. The Plaza presents a free Waikiki Calls dance show daily at 6:30 P.M. and 8 P.M. Exotic is the best way to describe the colorful **Rainbow Bazaar** at the Hilton Hawaiian Village. Close by is the new **Eaton Square,** a small shopping center with appealing shops and restaurants. The **Royal Hawaiian Center** has 120 stores in a 3-building, 4-level complex constructed of lava and coral on Kalakaua Ave. The **Kuhio Mall,** just behind the International Market Place, has a decidedly Polynesian atmosphere and offers products of the Islands as well as international shops and eating places. Their free evening Polynesian show is a delightful pause for shoppers.

Three other malls that are special: **Kilohana Square** at 1016 Kapahulu is a miniature of San Francisco's Ghirardelli Square. A 2-story complex that is tasteful, attracting the young. At the **Ward Warehouse** near Ala Moana you'll find more than 65 shops, simple to elegant, offering contemporary merchandise, creations of local artists, and specialty items from around the world. There are 14 restaurants where evening patrons can enjoy Hawaii's glorious sunsets with Kewalo Basin in the foreground. Its addition, **Ward Center,** has another 50 shops—many very chic and expensive—and restaurants. The **Fort Street Mall,** downtown, is a stroller's delight.

All sales add a 4% state tax. The shopping malls have abundant free parking; the Waikiki sites are largely for the walk-in trade and all are surrounded by hotels. For general information on the malls above and a few others:

Ala Moana Shopping Center, 1450 Ala Moana Blvd. (946–2811); Kahala Mall, 4211 Waialae Ave. (732–7736); Windward Mall, 46–056 Kamehameha Hwy. (235–1143); Pearlridge, Moanalua Rd. (488–0981); International Market Place, 2330 Kalakaua Ave. (923–9871); Hemmeter Center, 2424 Kalakaua Ave. (922–5522); King's Village, 131 Kaiulani Ave. (922–1288).

Also Eaton Square, 444 Hobron Lane (544–1852); Hilton Hawaiian Village, 2005 Kalia Rd. (949–4321); Royal Hawaiian Shopping Center, 2201 Kalakaua Ave. (922–0588); Kilohana Square, 1016 Kapahulu Ave. (732–6658).

And Ward Warehouse, 1050 Ala Moana Blvd. (531–6411); Ward Centre, 1200 Ala Moana Blvd. (531–6441); Waikiki Shopping Plaza, 2270 Kalakaua Ave. (923–1191); Kuhio Mall, 2301 Kuhio Ave. (922–2724); Chinatown Cultural Plaza, 100 N. Beretania St. (521–4934); Koko Marina Shopping Center, 7192 Kalanianaole Hwy. (395–4737); Manoa Marketplace, 2752 Woodlawn Dr. (988–7081); Stadium Mall, 4510 Salt Lake Blvd. (488–3037).

Before discussing specific stores in and out of these main areas, let us first put in a strong plea for the Hawaiian *muumuu,* that particularly Hawaiian garment that is often laughingly referred to as a flowered nightshirt. That it emphatically is not, but rather a gracious, graceful garment. When beautifully designed, *muumuus* are truly distinctive; some of the best sell for $100.

Most visitors begin by deriding them, wear one timidly, and end up living in them. Hawaii's garment industry today is a $75 million a year operation.

Fashion and Fabrics

Alfred Shaheen (949–5311) is, and has been for a number of years, a major Hawaiian manufacturer. The firm designs and handscreens its own textiles, which, we are told, is rare. The Waikiki retail outlets are at the Hyatt Regency, the Hilton Hawaiian Village, the Ilikai, Sheraton-Waikiki, and King's Village and feature the creations of the parent company exclusively. Other stores at the Kona Inn, The Wharf in Lahaina, and in the Kapalua Bay Hotel on Maui.

Alion has a very nice selection of women's clothing, designers' lines, a boutique and fragrance section, and things for the children. Located within Carol & Mary's at the Kahala Mall, 4211 Waialae Ave. (735–7878). Très chic.

Andrade. Started in 1919 as a gentlemen's store, it is now one of Hawaii's finest resort apparel store chains, with jewelry and gifts as well. There are 39 shops throughout the Islands. The main store is located at the Royal Hawaiian Center (926–1211) and boasts an entire floor of products from China, from the inexpensive to items costing thousands. Other shops are at the Ala Moana Center and Kahala Mall. Resort shops are in King's Village and numerous hotels, including the Royal Hawaiian, Moana, Halekulani, Sheraton-Waikiki, Hyatt Regency, Princess Kaiulani, and Hawaiian Monarch. Also on Kauai, Maui, and in Lailua-Kona and Hilo on the Big Island.

Carol & Mary is headquarters, so to speak, for the city's white-gloves set. The shops are in the Kahala Hilton, Kahala Mall, downtown in the new Amfac building, at the Royal Lahaina Hotel, and at Wailea on Maui.

Cherry Blossom at 2184 Kalakaua Ave. is the real *kamaaina* for Hawaiian fabrics along the beach strip. There are many fabrics at low prices. In addition, Cherry Blossom carries shirts and muumuus (923–5844).

Crazy Shirts, popular with residents and visitors, is at 11 locations throughout the Islands, and offers an array of custom-made screen-printed T-shirts for the whole family (949–6900).

Hawaii Mitsukoshi's has moved to the Hyatt Regency, 2424 Kalakaua Ave. (926–8877). Firm handles Tiffany, Loewe, Trusardi, Dunhill, Carlia, and Fontana. This Japanese retailer, a 300-year-old firm, figures to be 10% below Tokyo prices.

Hilo Hattie's Fashion Center has hosted over one million visitors. In addition to a free bus and tour (their brightly colored bus passes through Waikiki four times a day), visitors can enjoy shopping for garments at factory prices. For information call 537–2926. The center is located at 700 N. Nimitz Hwy.

J. C. Penney Hawaiian print fashions will match couples for $17 for the *aloha* shirt and $38 for the short *muumuu*. Stores at the Ala Moana Center, Kahala Mall, Windward Mall, and the Pearlridge Shopping Center (946–8068).

Kaimuki Dry Goods, Ltd. has the largest selection of fabrics in Hawaii, including domestics, Hawaiian prints, and Oriental and European imports. It is a great place to browse and dream. Located at 1144 10th Ave. in Kaimuki (734–2141).

Liberty House, known as "the store in the middle of the rainbow," is one of the Island's oldest and largest retailers. Its Waikiki branch at 2314 Kalakaua caters to vacationers with lively selections of east–west gifts. There are 18 stores including 10 in Waikiki. Others are in the Hilton, Hawaiian Village, Ilikai, King's Village, Kuilima, Sheraton-Waikiki, Kahala Mall, Neighbor Islands. The main store in Ala Moana Center (941–2345) carries complete selections of china, linens, gifts, and men's, women's, and children's ready-to-wear and accessories, topped with the most comprehensive collection of *couture* fashions in the Islands. Its excellent restaurant and bar encourage shopping at lunch or teatime. (Dinner is served on open evenings, Mon. through Fri.)

McInerny, in the Islands since 1850, carries Hawaiian wear from local designers for men, women, and children, men's and women's sportswear, men's clothing, dresses, accessories, fine jewelry and shoes. Located in Waikiki at the Royal Hawaiian Center and at the Hilton Hawaiian Village (947–7811).

Reyn's, with 6 stores throughout the islands, including the Kahala Mall, Ala Moana Shopping Center, and Kahala Hilton, has an excellent selection of men's things in good taste. If your Aloha-wear tastes are conservative, this is the place (949–5929).

Rika's Slippers in the International Market Place will put you in step with casual Island fashions (923–2473).

Ritz features apparel for the family. The new, two-floor store in the Royal Hawaiian Center on Kalakaua is called The Ritz at The Royal. Other stores are located in The Ala Moana Center, one for men's and boy's, the original store on the Fort Street Mall, dating to 1938, and another at Pearlridge (531–6421).

San Francisco Rag Shop, Ala Moana Shopping Center, 946–2808, and at Pearlridge, is a swinging shop with young styles, colors, tastes and clerks.

The Slipper House in the Ala Moana Center offers a wide selection of comfortable footwear for the whole family (949–0155).

Watumull Stores are scattered around Oahu and Maui and, being the largest retailers of Hawaiian wear in the Islands, they have excellent selections of authentic Hawaiian apparel for the entire family at reasonable prices. In addition to apparel, they carry Hawaiian jewelry, accessories, perfumes, and souvenirs. You'll find their Waikiki stores on Kalakaua Ave., at the Ilikai, Outrigger Hotels, King's Village, Hyatt Regency, and the new Royal Hawaiian Center, Sheraton-Waikiki, Hawaiian Village, Cinerama Reef, Holiday Inn hotels, the Princess Kaiulani Hotels, in the Ala Moana Center, and Lahaina, Maui (955–1144).

Oriental Ware and Gifts

Antiques Pacifica in the Royal Hawaiian Hotel carries the finest of Oriental antique and art objects, including many museum-quality screens, scrolls, bronzes, jade carvings, snuff bottles, *netsukes, obis,* lacquers, porcelains dating from Han Dynasty through Ching, antique Chinese and Oriental rugs, and rare jewelry. Gallery Two of Antiques Pacifica has Early American, European and Hawaiian antiques, including silver, porcelain, glass, crystal, paintings and objets d'art, as well as fine antique Chinese, Japanese, and English furniture. A lovely spot to browse (923–5101).

Fabulous Things, in the Kahala Mall, offers a large selection of Thai silk, Bangkok cotton yardage, and hand-waxed Javanese batiks. Asian treasures include teak temple carvings, Chinese porcelains, genuine (guaranteed) Asian antiques, and many other items priced for every pocketbook (735–7622).

Hotei Ya is an Ala Moana Center shop dealing in Japanese imports and Hawaiian souvenir items. Pottery, china, and mountains of lacquer bowls, trays, and tables comprise the bulk of the merchandise. The store has that "volume turnover" look which suggests that bargains may abound. The appearance is not misleading. For $1.15 you can get a paper carp (fish), 30 inches long, to fly on Boy's Day, May 5 (949–6838).

Iida S M Ltd. (946–0888) offers a fine collection of Japanese wares in the Ala Moana Center.

There are cups and plates, porcelain rice bowls in a bewildering number of designs, bamboo flower vases lined with tin, *bonsai* dishes, pots, tubs, baskets, and everything to delight the heart of the flower arranger and dish gardener. Look sharp and you'll see some terrific glazed earthenware casseroles, in grey or muted ochre, which you can pop right into the oven and bring piping hot to the table. The hanging lanterns of bronze or forged iron are light and cheap, and the classic Japanese paper lanterns are the lightest and cheapest of all. There are some real bargains, a *sake* set, a tea bowl complete with flying crane, and those amusing folded paper birds and Japanese fans and dolls that delight the heart of any child.

India Imports International has stores in the Ala Moana Center, Kahala Mall, and Pearlridge. Imports from all over include clothing, toys and games, jewelry, household items, and baskets. Items from India, Pakistan, Nepal, Thailand, Hong Kong, Japan, Latin America, Africa, Belgium, Denmark, and Italy are found here (946–7707).

Joji's. For a more intimate atmosphere and selective Japanese merchandise, try this studio at 2514 Rainbow Drive in Manoa. Joji has such good taste that you can safely purchase any item there.

Bargains in Mashiko ceramic tableware and heavy cotton Happi coats. Joji also has an excellent eye for ceramics, and features pieces by the world-famous Japanese potter Hamada in a price range from $250 on up. They also carry Japanese antique art. Call 988–3942 for an appointment.

Mills Gallery, 701 Bishop St., downtown (536–3527) is new but one of the largest dealers in Chinese and Japanese antiques, furnishings, screens, bronze, and porcelains. Located within the shop is Past Era (533–6313), which deals in estate jewelry, Victorian, art deco, artnouveau.

Shirokiya is a small-scale Tokyo department store in the middle of Ala Moana Center and Pearlridge with everything from food to fine arts. Except for a token stock of Hawaiian sportswear, everything is imported from Japan.

For unusual gifts, be sure to examine some of the fine lacquerware, ceramics, and hand-painted screens and scrolls. For the gourmet on your list, there are Japanese delicacies in the food department, fresh baked goods, and for the small fry a vast assortment of Japanese-made toys, which are both inexpensive and ingenious (941–9111).

Treasures of the East, 1320 Makaloa St. (945–7877), Mon. through Sat., 10 A.M. to 5 P.M., has oriental arts and antiques from Asia, Southeast Asia, India, and Turkey.

Of the 24 Oahu listings in the Hawaii Antique Dealers Association guide, 6—T. Fujii, The Carriage House, Max H. Davis Assoc., the Lantern Shop, the French Quarter, and Pacific Book House (rare books)—are located inside Kilohana Square, 1016 Kapahulu Ave. Most hours are Mon. through Sat., 10 A.M. to 4 P.M.

Hawaiian Woodcarving

Blair's is perhaps the best known name in Island woodcarving. The shops offer a wide variety of wooden bowls, trays, and other objects, most of it carved from monkey pod, koa, and milo wood. Shops are located at 404A Ward Ave. (536–4907) Outrigger Hotel, Outrigger East, and the airport Holiday Inn.

House of Kalai belongs to Tommy Leong, a superior craftsman in local hardwoods. His showrooms include the Sheraton-Waikiki Hotel and the factory at 1727 Mary St., way out in Kalihi Kai (841–2623). A trip to the factory can mean a considerable saving, as well as a chance to tour the establishment. Mr. Leong experiments with smooth and rough finishes, but rough or smooth, round or rectangular, this man's work is always beautiful. If you are looking for a major present for somebody back home—or yourself—you might consider one of his original and gracefully carved trays and bowls.

Irene's Hawaiian Gifts, on the street level at Ala Moana Center, is a must for those who love beautiful and rare handcarvings. These are fashioned from native milo wood, and some are collector's items. Other items include unusual Hawaiian dolls, ceramics, and inexpensive jewelry (946–6818).

To visit a factory that makes polished kukui nut jewelry, go to 66–935 Kaukonahua Rd. in Waialua on the North Shore, Kukui Nuts of Hawaii Inc. (637–5620).

Jewelry Shops

B.D. Howes and Son bought out two of Honolulu's Establishment jewelry firms, and later consolidated in one shop in the Royal Hawaiian Hotel. Besides precious gems, Howes has watches, clocks, and silver. With stores in California and Arizona, Howes has established its reputation in the course of 104 years (923–5756).

The Coral Grotto shops feature a wide selection of beautiful coral jewelry, mastercrafted in the Islands by *Maui divers of Hawaii.* Black, pink, and gold coral are offered in many one-of-a-kind items. Locations are at Ala Moana Center, the Sheraton Waikiki, Hilton Hawaiian Village, Hemmeter Center, and in the Royal Hawaiian Center in Waikiki (955–6760).

The Jade Market, also at 1600 Kapiolani in the Pan Am Building, is where many Islanders go for their fine jade jewelry. Open Mon. through Sat., 9 A.M.–5 P.M. (949–5001).

Food Stores

Big supermarkets are the best sources for quality Island specialties, name brands you know, or gourmet items from around the world. Then, if you want to look into Japanese specialties, try the smaller family groceries in districts such as Kapahulu, Kaimuki, or Kalihi, or the Chinese specialty markets in Chinatown downtown.

No food shop can be more unique to Hawaii than the **Crackseed Center** in the Ala Moana near the escalator (949–7200). These oriental fruit preserves will be an experience. There are many similar stores around the city.

Ice cream shops can be found in many places, especially at Ala Moana Shopping Center and along Kalakaua Ave. in Waikiki. MacNuttery, 2098 Kalakaua Ave. (942–7798) is the newest and biggest entrant in this field, open 11 A.M. to 11 P.M. Major dealers, some with as many as 10 shops and 31 flavors, include Baskin-Robbins, Copenhagen Cones, Dairy Queen, Dave's Ice Cream Parlor, Farrell's Ice Cream Parlours, Haagen-Dazs, and Swensen's.

Macadamia Nut Factory specialty shops at 2200 and 2430 Kalakaua Ave. If you're a nut for this kind of nut, you're in good company. Gourmets call it "the perfect nut," and these shops have it in more than 100 different forms, ranging from chocolate-coated to finely-ground for cooking (923–9811).

Tropical Fruit. How about taking home some delicious island fruit? Several companies pack agriculturally inspected pineapple and papaya and provide free airport delivery. **Tropical Fruits Distributors** is located at 429 Waiakamilo Rd. (847–3234). **St. Louis Florist and Fruits** also provides coconuts, Maui's famous sweet onions in season, and some tropical plants (732–1454). **Island King** will ship pineapple, papaya, coconuts, and island-grown avocados, as well as other local specialties. A pack of 6 pineapples costs $10 to $14 depending upon the size (836–3821).

Vintage Wine Cellar. The most attractive wine, beer, and spirit shops around are four cellars, one at 625 Keawe Street, one located in the Makiki Village Market at 1249 Wilder Ave. one in the Davies Pacific Center building downtown at 178 Queen St., and the fourth at Pearlridge Shopping Center, Wines from around the world are featured.

NIGHTLIFE. Waikiki is not quite Las Vegas but it's jumping, mostly to the disco beat. Still, flashy Polynesian shows are popular, and entertainment also is available outside Waikiki, from *the Brothers Cazimero* at the Royal Hotel on down to the strip shows on Hotel Street in Chinatown.

Disco development in the 1970s was rapid and exciting, but then went into gradual decline. Still, the younger set gravitates to *Anabelle's* atop the Ilikai, 1777 Ala Moana (949–3811); *Bobby McGee's Conglomeration,* near the Colony Surf, 2885 Kalakaua Ave. (922–1282).

Hula's Bar and *Lei Stand,* 2103 Kuhio Ave. (923–0669) are popular gay hangouts. For more suggestions, you might ask a taxi driver.

For the young-at-heart, *Hard Rock Cafe,* 1837 Kalakaua Ave. (955–7383), came to town in 1987 and is a popular gathering site for Australian visitors (mostly male) and the airline set in search of dancing and companionship.

Don Ho is king of the Waikiki strip and performs nightly, except Saturday, at the Hilton Hawaiian Village Dome. Dinner at 6:30 P.M. and show starts at 10:30 P.M. Dinner show charge of $40.50 includes the show, steak and mahimahi, and 2 drinks. Cocktail show is $24, seating at 7:30 P.M. Sun. through Fri. (949–4321).

Entertainers move around, but the following summaries tell the story: The Royal Hawaiian Hotel has a dinner show at 8:30 P.M. in the Monarch Room, featuring *The Brothers Cazimero* currently, Tues. through Sat. $46.50 dinner/$18.50 cocktails (923–7311). The Royal's show is one of the few in Waikiki that is primarily Hawaiian in mood and focus; others in town promoted as Polynesian are just that, featuring Samoan, Tahitian and Maori and a modicum of Hawaiian costuming and dances.

Sheraton Spectacular Polynesian Revue, Princess Kaiulani Hotel, 120 Kaiulani Ave., is a rousing roundup of authentic Polynesian entertainment, with a first-class buffet dinner at 6:30 P.M., show at 8:30 P.M., $40.50/cocktails $20.50 (922–5811).

For an evening change of pace there's *Hawaiian Hoe-Down Country Barbecue* on Olomana Ranch at the foot of the Koolau Mts. Dancing by the Paniolo Country Kickers, hula, buffet barbecue; $37 includes roundtrip transportation from Waikiki (259–9300).

Al Harrington, a reformed Samoan football player, is highly entertaining at the Outrigger Reef Towers, 227 Lewers (923–9861). Cocktail show for $39.

Tropical Heatwave at the Hula Hut, 286 Beachwalk, show at 9:15 P.M., or dinner first at 8 P.M., cocktail show at 11:15 P.M. (923–8411). The dinner show is $35.

For jazz, try *Trappers* in the Hyatt Regency. Top 40 contemporary is recorded at the *Bluewater Cafe,* 2350 Kuhio Ave. (926–2191).

The *Aliis,* at the Best Western Waikiki Plaza, 2045 Kalakaua, $32 (941–8684), and *Society of Seven* in the Outrigger Waikiki Hotel, 2335 Kalakaua, $34 (923–0711), are two long-running vocal/variety dinner shows popular with local crowds.

Danny Kaleikini headlines the Hawaiian show at the Kahala Hilton's *Hala Terrace* at 9:30 P.M. (734–2211). Dinner is at 7:30; the lot is $53.

For dancing, try the *Garden Bar,* at the Hilton Hawaiian Village Hotel (949–4321); *Nicholas Nikolas,* at the top of the Ala Moana Hotel (955–4466); *The Surf Room;* or the *Monarch Room*'s Monday afternoon tea dances at 5:30 P.M. to Del Courtney's orchestra at the Royal Hawaiian.

For more rock dancing consider the *Jazz Cellar,* 205 Lewers St. (923–9952), where there's no jazz. *Spats* in the Hyatt Regency (922–9292) is another disco. And there's dancing next to the pool at the same hotel, at *Scruples* in the Waikiki Market Place at 2310 Kuhio Ave. (923–9530), and *Angles* at the Ilikai. For the opposite of a rock-blast joint, how about a Japanese tea ceremony, free, at Urasenke Foundation, 245 Saratoga in Waikiki, 10 A.M. to noon, Wed. and Fri. For reservations, 923–3059.

Sellouts are not uncommon at the 8,400-seat Neal Blaisdell Center arena for top-name acts, 777 Ward Ave. (527–5400) for information. Another full house covered the grass at the *Waikiki Shell* to hear Johnny Cash. Locals love Charles K. L. Davis, formerly of the Metropolitan Opera, who belts out Hawaiian and Broadway hits Wednesday and Sunday noon at Kemoo Farm across the street from Schofield Barracks, 1718 Wilikina Dr. (621–8481).

There are plenty of servicemen's bars on Hotel Street and environs downtown. Some of these feature strippers and other artists of dubious talent, and the general atmosphere is somewhere between the lurid and the tawdry. Club Hubba Hubba, 25 North Hotel St., is in this category and dates back more than one generation, 536–7698. Want to be the entertainer yourself? No trouble. Go to the *Kabuki Restaurant* in Waimalu, 98–020 Kamehameha Hwy. (487–2424). where patrons may sing solo on stage.

Less bouncy are the piano or guitar bars such as the *Bali,* Hilton Hawaiian Village Tapa Tower (949–4321), 7 to 11 P.M., Mon. through Sat.; *Hanohano Room* at the Sheraton-Waikiki (922–4422), from 6:30 to 10:30 P.M.; *Tanghut Restaurant,* 1910 Ala Moana (942–7771), from 4 to 6 P.M.

Masquerade has pop stuff from 9 P.M. to 2 A.M. at 1900 Kalakaua Ave. at McCully (949–6337).

A fun Thursday noon of Hawaiian music and hijinks hosted by Irmgard Aluli is featured at the *Willows,* 901 Hausten St. (946–4808).

If you want to swing away from the Waikiki hubbub, try *Fast Eddie's* disco at 52 Oneawa St., Kailua (261–8561).

To rock its *Gussie L'Amour's,* 3251 N. Nimitz (836–7883), which old-timers will remember as a place that once had male strippers.

SUNSET DINNER CRUISES. Any evening you'll see colored lights bobbing in waters off Waikiki as the sun drops below the Waianae Mountains, often with spectacular, romantic effect. You too can be out there where the dinner-dance package consists of bus pickups at all hotels, transportation to Kewalo Basin or elsewhere, where you step on deck for a salty evening phantasy. What follows is a buffet dinner, all the drinks you want, dancing, a Polynesian show of dancing girls, all to help with a new romance or to rekindle banked fires.

A few ideas:

Adventure V (923–2061), ($29.95) or ($23 for children under 12), and hotel pickup.

Aikane Catamarans (538–3680), sunset ($37), moonlight ($35), rock 'n' roll ($20), combo ($37.50).

Alii Kai Catamaran (524–1800), sunset ($38), a show and buffet.

Hawaiian Love Boat, (538–7733), double-hulled Polynesian canoe ($19.99), table service.

Hilton Rainbow I Catamaran, (949–4321), ($37) twilight buffet dinner sail, open bar, dancing, entertainment.

Rella Mae (922–1200), a big one, three decks, buffet, show ($39).

Several of these prices drop at certain times or if you present a discount coupon from one of the free publications found in street racks in Waikiki.

HAWAII

Nature's Primeval Showplace

By
JODI PARRY BELKNAP

Jodi Parry Belknap has worked as a journalist in Hawaii since 1970. She writes extensively about Hawaii and other Pacific islands for a variety of local and national publications and is the author of several books about Hawaii.

The island of Hawaii is a land of startling contrasts where nature busily pursues a primeval course. Here, slalom skiers hurtle down the snowy slopes of Mauna Kea beside an ancient adze quarry where ti-leaf cloaked Hawaiians once searched reverently for stone tools with which to shape their voyaging canoes. A few miles away the volcanic vents of Kilauea Iki continue to disgorge molten red rivers of lava drawn from the earth's deepest core.

At 4,034 square miles, Hawaii is twice the size of all the other Hawaiian Islands combined. That's larger than the 132 other atolls, islets, and islands in an archipelago stretched across 1,523 miles of Pacific Ocean to Johnston Island. Hawaii's most frequently applied nickname, naturally enough, is the Big Island.

But Hawaii is sometimes called the Volcano Island, too, and not without good reason. Five volcanos—Kohala, Hualalai, Mauna Kea, Mauna Loa, and Kilauea—helped create the island. The process began about half a million years ago and still is continuing. Fiery flows slowly built the island 19,680 feet up from the ocean floor to the surface, and then 13,796 feet more to the lofty top of Mauna Kea, now known as the world's tallest seamount. Neighboring Mauna Loa is the world's most massive mountain, though not the highest. Both Mauna Loa, which last erupted in 1984, and Kilauea are active today. In the mid-1980s Kilauea entered a highly active stage, erupting 42 times in a two-year period. Fountaining reached 1,200 feet in January 1986. In modern times Hawaii's volcanoes have been considered the safest in the world for observation, since their gently sloping flanks do not explode suddenly or spew lethal ashes like steep-sided Vesuvius or Mount St. Helens.

One more nickname occasionally is applied to the island, and that is the Orchid Isle. More than 22,000 varieties of the exotic flower are grown on the island. At nurseries in and around Hilo, which is known as the orchid capital of the Pacific, as many as 30 million blooms have been harvested in one year.

The Big Island is divided into six districts with distinctive characteristics. In Puna, beaches of jet black sand flank moss-covered ruins of ancient *heiau.* In southern *Ka'u,* an occasional oasis of green ferns fed by a concealed spring breaks the pattern of arid lava-strewn dessert. Nurseries with fields of lavendar orchids and bright red anthuriums thrive in the rich soil of the Hilo district. Along the island's northeast coast green fields of sugarcane flourish in the wetlands of Hamakua. In West Hawaii's thriving Kona district, new condominiums and resorts contrast sharply with a stone-age past carefully preserved at Puuhonua O Honaunau National Historic Park. In northern Kohala world famous luxury resorts sit atop lava beds on the coast, while in the rolling uplands of 250,000-acre Parker Ranch, waterfalls plunge into ravines beside beavertail cactus.

The Big Island attracts more and more visitors, and understandably so. Once the state's undiscovered resource when it comes to tourism, the Big Island is fast becoming an attractive and exciting destination. There's more to do and see on it than on any other Hawaiian Island.

Exploring Hawaii

There's more to the Big Island than can be seen in one or two visits. For those who have limited time, tour companies on the island offer a variety of introductory tours. If you want to see the island on your own in a rental car or four-wheel drive, several side trips of a day's length or more are possible from home bases in either Hilo or Kona. It's possible to swoop around the southern point of the island from Hilo to Kona or vice versa in one day, but you won't have time to see or do much on the way. One recommendation is to stay in Hilo long enough to explore the city and drive up the Hamakua Coast to Waipio Valley on one day and take separate day-long side trips to the volcano and into Puna on additional days. Then, on the third or fourth day, you can drive around the island to a new base in Kona or Kohala, stopping en route to thoroughly explore South Point in the Ka'u district and Puuhonua Honaunau (City of Refuge) National Historic Park in south Kona. You'll need an equal amount of time to explore the historic town of Kailua-Kona, the Kohala Coast, and Waimea in the same way.

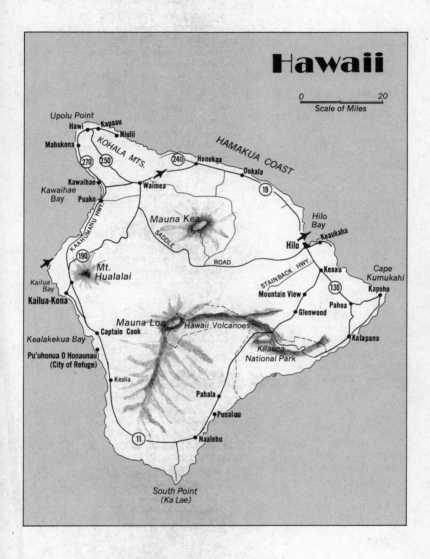

Hawaii

0   20
Scale of Miles

Upolu Point
Hawi   Kapaau
Mahukona   Niulii
KOHALA MTS.
270   250   240   Honokaa
HAMAKUA COAST
Kawaihae   Ookala
Kawaihae
Bay   Waimea
Puako   19
Mauna Kea
KAAHUMANU HWY.
SADDLE   Hilo
Bay
190   ROAD   Hilo   Keaukaha
Mt.
Hualalai   Keaau   Cape
Kumukahi
STAINBACK HWY.   130
Kailua
Bay   Mountain View   Kapoho
Kailua-Kona   Glenwood   Pahoa
Mauna Loa
Kealakekua Bay   Captain Cook   Hawaii Volcanoes   Kalapana
Pu'uhonua O Honaunau   Kilauea
(City of Refuge)   National Park
Kealia
Pahala
11   Punaluu
Naalehu

South Point
(Ka Lae)

The Big Island has a lot to offer to those with special interests. For a change of pace with a four-wheel drive and good hiking shoes you can actually find white, gold, green, gray, and black sand beaches on the island. If you're an amateur or, for that matter, a professional archeologist, by all means take time to search out the many ruins of Hawaiian *heiau* (places of worship) and petroglyph fields on the island. Several are part of public parks. Ask around and you may even find a local resident willing to take you to sites where you can see burial caves or unusual petroglyphs of 18th-century western sailing ships or marching soldiers.

Visiting the Volcano

There are two ways to get to the main part of Hawaii Volcanoes National Park, the Big Island's most popular attraction, which is about 30 miles southwest of Hilo. The direct route is via Highway 11 leading to Kilauea Visitor Center, where you can pick up maps and books on wildlife and plants, from 8 A.M. to 5 P.M. daily. A longer drive through Puna offers a chance to learn about Hawaiian civilizations in the Kalapana coastal area at the park's Wahaula Visitor Center, which is open from 9 A.M. to 4 P.M. From here you can drive up the Chain of Craters road into the main part of the park.

Kilauea, the most active of two live volcanoes in the park, is in the midst of its longest-running eruption ever, one that began in 1983. If you're fortunate, you may be in the park during either a fountaining or lava flow phase. If so, rangers will help you find the best and safest viewing points. Excellent background information may be found in the park's new Thomas A. Jagger Museum.

Even if there's no fiery display, there's plenty to see in the 344-square-mile park, which was established in 1916. It includes the summit caldera and gently sloping northeast flank of 13,680-foot Mauna Loa, most of Kilauea, and a section of Kalapana coast in the southern Puna district of the Big Island. Within it are lava tubes, cinder cones and odd mineral formations, oases of giant ferns and trees, stone ruins of a Hawaiian sacrificial temple, and trails beside steaming vents and across crater floors.

The only hotel in the park is Volcano House, which is an excellent place for a late lunch or dinner or cocktails by the picture window. The first Volcano House was a hut of wooden poles and *pili* grass thatch built in 1846. The current 37-room inn was built in 1941. Part of an older Volcano House now houses the Volcano Art Center next to Kilauea Visitor Center where photographers, writers, and artists inspired by the beauty of the Big Island display their work.

Crater Rim Drive is an 11.1-mile drive around Kilauea Volcano with turnouts and exhibits at major park features. For an orientation drive start at Kilauea Visitor Center and drive counterclockwise to points of interest where markers direct you to walking and hiking trails.

Walks

An easy circle walk beginning at Volcano House leads first past Sulphur Banks, an area where escaping gases have deposited large amounts of yellow, and quite odorous, sulfur. Next, the trail passes through a section known as Steam Vents, where foggy vapor wafting through scraggly trees creates an eerie, otherwordly effect something like the set of an old horror movie. The trail continues across the highway and up to the edge of Kilauea Crater, then along a ledge past some rare specimens of sandalwood.

Kipuka Puaulu, or Bird Park, accessible via the Mauna Loa Strip Road leading off Crater Rim Drive to Mauna Loa, is a 100-acre *kipuka* (oasis) of indigenous plants and trees left intact when a Mauna Loa lava flow split and bypassed it. With a folder provided at picnic grounds where an exhibit describes native birds and plants to look for, you can take an hour's self-guided walk on a mile-long trail through the park. Watch for a giant koa tree (Hawaiians made outrigger canoes from the best of these).

Devastation Trail, one of the most photographed sites in the park, leads through the skeletal remains of an *'ohi'a* tree forest burned out in 1959 by cinder falls from Kilauea Iki's lava fountains. A .06-mile walk on a boardwalk across the cinders begins at Kilauea Iki Overlook and ends at Puu Puai, the cone built during that eruption.

At the far northeast end of Crater Rim Drive are Fern Jungle and Thurston Lava Tube. Huge tree ferns, some just unfurling their delicate branches, grow amid a forest of gnarled ohia trees beside a short trail leading to the tube. It's a natural tunnel about 10 feet high that formed when the cooling top and sides of a lava flow hardened and the lava inside drained away. Lorrin A. Thurston, for whom the tube is named, was a descendant of New England protestant missionaries and a Honolulu newspaper publisher who helped establish the park. You can walk 450 feet into the tube.

Hikes

A good exploratory hike is along 3.2-mile Halemaumau Trail. It leads from a point near Volcano House across Kilauea Caldera to the edge of Halemaumau Crater, a steaming, half-mile wide pit inside Kilauea caldera that is the principal vent for Kilauea volcano. Reserve about half a day or more for the hike, beginning in the cool of morning if you can. Hawaiians named the pit *hale amaumaa,* or house of ferns, because its sides were covered with ferns until the eruptions of 1790 destroyed them. To Hawaiians Halemaumau is the traditional home of Pele, the volcano goddess. Pick up a self-guiding pamphlet at the Visitor Center to find out about useful plants and geologic features you'll see along the way. You can walk out of the crater and back to Volcano House three and one-half miles on Byron Ledge Trail, or stop at Halemaumau Overlook if you've arranged for someone to come pick you up.

For an even more remarkable experience, try watching a film of the spectacular 1959 eruption of Kilauea Iki (little Kilauea, a second vent for the volcano) shown in the evening at Volcano House, and follow it with a morning hike directly into Kilauea Iki crater. From the parking lot at Thurston Lava Tube an easy four-mile switchback trail leads to the blackened floor of Kilauea Iki crater where ferns and other plants are beginning to poke through cracks. Walk across the still smoldering crust, which was a boiling lake of lava a quarter of a century ago, to Puu Puai, the 400-foot cone created when lava fountains shot 1,900 feet into the air during that eruption. Return the way you came, or if you're up to it, climb out the rugged Byron Ledge side of the crater.

Experienced backpackers in excellent shape may want to try the 18-mile Mauna Loa Trail. It rises 7,000 feet to Mokuaweoweo (fire pit), Mauna Loa's summit caldera. It begins at the end of Mauna Loa Strip Road, a drive to a mountain shelter and overlook at 6,662 feet. Hikers can acclimatize at Red Hill, an overnight shelter with blankets and other supplies at 10,035 feet. In March 1984, Mauna Loa poured lava from a vent near Red

Hill for the first time in 103 years. Hikers must check in at Kilauea Visitor Center for a required permit before starting out.

From the center of the park you can take Chain of Craters Road 25 miles through lava beds and past Mauna Ulu (growing mountain) to the Kalapana coast. Highway 130 takes you east along the coast to Wahaula Visitor Center. Lava from the December 1986 eruption covered roads in Kalapana. Check at the Visitor Center on which roads are open. Next to the center are the ruins of a *heiau* first built around A.D. 1250 by Paao, a powerful *kahuna* (priest) from Tahiti said to have introduced human sacrifice to Hawaii.

Hilo, City of Rainbows

With a population of only about 37,000 of the island's 98,050 residents, Hilo nevertheless is the fourth largest city in the state. Spread around a curving bay, it is the county seat as well as the center of business and shipping activity on the island. The state's second international airport and the only Neighbor Island branch of the University of Hawaii are here, too.

Hilo is a calm and friendly community reflecting the amalgam of cultural influences operating in Hawaii today. In and around town you can taste Portuguese malasadas or good Japanese miso soup, listen to choirs singing in Hawaiian at Haili Church or Malamalama Church, or ponder the Chinese architecture of United Community Church, built in 1937 as Hilo Chinese Christian Church, but with a mix of membership now.

It's no accident that a wide green belt extends along much of Hilo Bay and several blocks inland across what might seem to be prime business property in any other waterfront community. On an early morning in May 1960 a *tsunami* took the lives of 61 people when a series of high waves hit the waterfront. Many of those lost had returned to stores and shops facing the bay in spite of warnings. If high waves should come again, they will damage only the lawns and gardens of a new park. At Wailoa Visitor Center, a round building near Waiakea Pond in the park, you can see photos of the damage wrought by this *tsunami* and one that struck on April 1, 1946.

East Hawaii's main resort destination is on Hilo's Banyan Drive, where several hotels and condominiums are located. On clear days the view from many *lanais* is of snow-capped Mauna Kea in the distance. Most of the shady banyan trees that line the drive were planted in 1935 by notables such as Franklin Delano Roosevelt, King George V, Amelia Earhart, and Fannie Hurst.

Hilo receives an average of 139 inches of rain a year, mostly at night and in the early morning. One result is that gardens in the area flourish. Most of the state's anthuriums, and many of its orchids—including the little vanda hybrid seen so often in leis—are grown in Hilo nurseries. If you're in town at the beginning of July, don't miss the annual orchid show at Hilo Orchidarium, at 575 Manono Street. It's worth visiting throughout the year to see orchids growing in its landscaped gardens.

Hilo's other must-see sights include Lyman House Museum and Rainbow Falls, both on the west end of town. Residents often point out the large and lengthy Naha and Pinao stones in front of the library on Waianuenue Avenue, too. Tradition has it that anyone who could overturn the Naha stone would rule the islands. Kamehameha is said to have accomplished the feat in the late 18th century when he was a teenager.

Puna, Pele's Playground

The district south of Hilo, reached via Highway 13 from Hilo, is a laboratory for the 20th-century handiwork of the volcano goddess Pele. In 1955 and 1960, after a century of inactivity, lava flows from a Kilauea rift covered homes and farms in the district. And in the 1980s flows have several times threatened homes in Kalapana as well as in one of several new Puna subdivisions that have sprung up under the sponsorship of real estate speculators.

Puna's main attraction, a somewhat nicer result of Pele's handiwork, is the area's many black sand beaches. These are formed when hot *aa* lava hits the cold sea and explodes into millions of tiny granules that wash back to shore creating new beaches of black sand.

One of the best known black sand beaches, a favorite of photographers because of the coconut grove that rings it, is at Kaimu in Puna. In 1975 a major earthquake permanently changed its appearance by causing the ocean floor to drop three feet, thus bringing the water in among the palms, many of which now have toppled into the sea.

Exploratory trips on side roads in Puna will take you to other examples of Pele's whimsy. On Highway 132, just past Pahoa, is Lava Tree State Park, with its amazing collection of stone tree trunks, actually the encrusted shells of an ohia forest engulfed by lava during the island's major 1790 volcanic flow. Continuing toward the coast the road passes over Kapoho, a village totally obliterated by the 1960 Puna lava flow. Amazingly, beach lots and property in the area are now being sold as vacation property. At the end of the road, the spot where the lava flow stopped six feet short of automated Cape Kumukahi lighthouse is clearly evident.

Double back up from the lighthouse to Highway 137, which leads south along the coast past beach parks and one of two well-known painted churches on the island, tiny Star of the Sea Painted Church. Go inside to see a trompe l'oeil effect of columns supporting vaulted ceilings. This historic church barely escaped destruction by the 1986 flow.

At the end of the highway, just before you reach the south entrance to Hawaii Volcanoes National Park and its Wahaula Visitor Center, is another site worth visiting, accessible via a short side road. Queen's Bath, or Punaluu, as it once was known, is a 15- by 150-foot rockwalled freshwater swimming hole about 10 feet deep. Shaded by large mango trees and other vegetation, it's a cool swimming spot. Recent lava flows came within a stone's throw of this landmark.

Ka'u and South Point

The most interesting place to explore in the Big Island's southernmost district is South Point, an area settled by early Polynesian voyagers. Before you reach the turnoff to it on Highway 11, you'll pass through Punaluu, home of a major resort, a condominium and golf course behind a black sand beach. It's a good place to stop for lunch. A visitor center at the beach has exhibits from the area. You can climb up an abandoned sugarcane loading site at the northeast end of the beach to explore the ruins of Kaneeleele Heiau or go across the street to a small outdoor chapel honoring Henry Opukahaia. Opukahaia was an adventurous Punaluu orphan whose fate changed the course of Hawaiian history. In 1809 he swam out to a fur-trading ship anchored in Punaluu Harbor and asked to be taken on board as cabin boy. He sailed with the ship to New England, adopted Christianity, and entered the Foreign Mission School in Cornwallis, Connecticut. He died of typhoid fever in 1818 before he could return to the Islands, but his zeal inspired the American Board of Missions to send the first Protestant missionaries to Hawaii in 1820.

Naalehu, beyond Punaluu, is the last place to buy gas for the drive to South Point or around to Kona. Beyond is Waiohinu, a village that has been continuously inhabited for many centuries. Look for the Mark Twain Monkeypod Tree, a new tree growing from the original roots of one blown down in 1957 that is said to have been planted by the writer when he visited the Islands in 1866. Also at Waiohinu is prettily-trimmed Kauahaao Church, built in the steepled New England Congregationalist style in 1842.

The turnoff to South Point, or Ka Lae, its Hawaiian name, is about three miles beyond Waiohinu. The narrow road to it slopes gently downhill through pasture land for about 10 miles to the southernmost point in the United States where sheer cliffs meet the sea. There are no facilities of any kind in this remote and seldom-visited site, much of which recently was set aside for eventual development as South Point Park. Local fishermen come to the treeless, windswept spot to cast or take out outriggers and small boats moored in the sea beneath the cliffs.

Archeologists believe that Ka Lae may have been populated as early as A.D. 750, most likely by settlers from Tahiti who arrived in their great voyaging canoes. If you have a good eye, you can see the evidence of former civilization everywhere. Begin by looking carefully for old canoe mooring holes carved through rocks beside and below the cliffs. About 80 of them remain. Small Kalalea Heiau is readily visible beside a 32-foot tower with a marine navigational marker on top of it. Within the *heiau* you may see small stones wrapped in fresh ti leaves left as an offering by a contemporary Hawaiian fisherman. If you decide to walk or use a four-wheel drive to go south to the green sand beach, there are more sites to discover. Makalei Cave, marked by a ring of stones overgrown with sticker-packed lantana, is not so easy to find, but if you do locate it you may flush out a *pueo* or two, the indigenous brown and gray Hawaiian owl. Lua o Palahemo, a brine-filled well about 30 feet wide within an old lava tube, is a little easier to find. It's marked by six stone cairns visible on the *mauka* (mountain) side of the road leading to the green sand beach. The entire South Point area is an important archeological site that has yielded much information about how Hawaiians lived.

The Kona Coast

From the South Point turnoff it's about a 54-mile drive up the West Hawaii coast to the town of Kailua-Kona. It's a drive to take leisurely, stopping to explore what interests you. At first the road leads across a hundred years' worth of Mauna Loa lava flows, many of them dated and marked with a Hawaii Visitors Bureau warrior sign. About 10 miles up the road is Manuka State Park, which looks like a roadside rest area easily passed up. If you're at all interested in trees that grow in the tropics, stop for a brief walk through this cool park. A sausage tree, grass tree, coffee tree, royal poinciana, and others you've probably been wondering about are all identified for non-botanists.

A special place to stop next for those who have the time and temperament is Milolii, reached by a very windy, one-car road that juts off Highway 11 down to the coast. Milolii is Hawaii's last working fishing village. You can park in a churchyard at the far end of town, then walk back through the village to watch outrigger canoe fishermen bringing in the day's catch. Stop at the community store set behind a vintage glass gas pump for a cool drink and to talk story with soft-spoken mayor Eugene Kaupiko, who was born in Milolii and remembers the old ways well.

Puuhonua O Honaunau

For 400 years before the old ways were discarded in 1819, Hawaiian *kapu* breakers, conscientious objectors, and defeated warriors who reached this remarkable coastal site were granted refuge and then purified by powerful priests who practiced here. Now a 180-acre National Historic Park, it includes the restored Hale-o-Keawe Heiau, built in 1650, for Keawe, a Hawaiian chief who was the major patron of the *puuhonua* (place of refuge). The bones of Keawe and more than 20 other chiefs deified after death were kept here until their removal to secret hiding places in 1929. Their *mana,* or spiritual power, was so great that Hale-o-Keawe was left intact for some time after the general razing of Hawaiian temples that occured in 1819. Hawaiian historians have authentically reproduced the *puuhonua* structures and wooden images of Hawaiian gods from drawings made by early European visitors. A self-guiding map folder and recordings introduce exhibits. Frequent demonstrations of poi pounding, Hawaiian games, canoe making, and other crafts are presented.

Captain Cook and Coffee Farms

In 1778, when Captain James Cook first put into Kealakekua Bay, it was Makahiki season, a traditional Hawaiian feast time honoring a god-chief who had sailed away centuries earlier and was expected to return. Controversy still continues about why Cook allowed local priests to welcome him as the long-awaited god Lonoikamakahiki. In any event, the local population lavished gifts on Cook and his men who took thorough advantage of the situation, even desecrating the *heiau* sacred to Lono by taking its wooden railing for firewood. After a short exploratory visit, Cook sailed away. Unfortunately, he had to return a month later when the foremast of the *Resolution* broke in a storm. Makahiki past, this time the welcome was not nearly so friendly. A resentful Hawaiian stole a longboat. In retaliation, Cook came ashore on February 14, 1779 to take an elderly chief hostage for return of the boat. Fearing for the chief's life, warriors fought for his release. Captain Cook was killed during the fight. The flesh was stripped from his body and the bones taken for their *mana* to a *heiau* behind the site at Kealakekua Bay where the Captain Cook monument, a 27-foot white obelisk erected by the British Commonwealth in 1874, now stands. Cook's sailing master, Captain William Bligh (who would be infamous later as Captain of the *HMS. Bounty*) asked for the return of the bones. He received only those of Captain Cook's skull, hands, arms, and legs for burial. You can visit Hikiau Heiau where Captain Cook was welcomed. Take Highway 16 from Honaunau or Keokea off Highway 11 to Napoopoo. This *heiau* is in the beach park beside Kealakekua Bay. Look across the bay to see the monument.

After this tour into the past you can see what's going on in the present in this area at the Royal Kona Coffee Mill and Museum. A side road near the town of Captain Cook leads to it. Kona's cool upland coffee country is a strip of land between the town of Honokohau in north Kona roughly to Kealia south of Kealakekua Bay. Hawaii's Ellison Onisuka, one of the seven astronauts killed when the shuttle Challenger exploded in January 1986, grew up in this area.

Most Kona coffee is grown above 1,200 feet. The plants sport clusters of white flowers in spring, then produce round green beans which ripen to harvest-ready red by fall. Kona school vacations still coincide with harvest season so the children of family-owned coffee farms can help with picking.

Other sites to see in the area include St. Benedict's painted church just off Highway 16 above Napoopoo. Father John Berchmans Velghe of Belgium, who served the parish from 1899 to 1904, painted the interior of the church to resemble a European Gothic cathedral. He also decorated churches in Tahiti and the Marquesas. The church is on the register of National Historic Sites. Also on Highway 16 is Barry's Nut Farm, a botanical garden within a macadamia nut orchard; it is worth a stop, too, if only to see the unusual collection of bonsai plants. It's open daily and there's no admission charge.

Keauhou Resort

For a change of scenery you can swing down to the burgeoning resort area of Keauhou, on the coast about 10 miles from Captain Cook. A growing cluster of luxury hotels and condominiums is situated here beside Keauhou Golf Course. There's a shopping center and historical Kona Gardens, as well as plenty of places to have lunch.

Kailua-Kona: A Historic Town

Big Island residents call this town simply Kailua, but there are two other towns with the same name in Hawaii, one on Oahu and the other on Maui. This one may well be the prettiest, resting as it does beside a blue bay at the foot of 8,271-foot Hualalai, a dormant volcano. King Kamehameha the Great must have found it so. He spent the final years of his life here between 1813 and 1819, ruling from an area known as Kamakahonu in the north part of town where Amfac's Hotel King Kamehameha stands now. Ahuena Heiau, beside the hotel has been restored. Free ethnobotanical and historical tours of the area are offered by the hotel staff at scheduled times. Check with the front desk to find out when.

Protestant New England missionaries selected Kona as one of their first landfalls in 1820. Their first church in the Islands, imposing Mokuaikaua, was started in 1823 and finished in 1827 with the help of Hawaiian parishioners and the island's governor, Kuakini, who ordered huge ohia wood trunks brought down from the slopes of Mauna Loa for it. The walls of the church are made of heavy stones from an abandoned *heiau* held together with mortared coral. The interior posts and beams are hand-hewn ohia wood fitted together with ohia pins. You can't miss the church. Its white steeple is decidedly New England Congregational.

Across the street from the first Western church in the Islands is Hulihee Palace, a two-story structure with wide verandas built in the middle of town in 1837 by Kuakini. It served as King David Kalakaua's summer palace in the 1880s. Its restored interior and elegant furnishings reflect the splendor of that era. Glass cases downstairs hold Hawaiian artifacts. A highly-polished hatbox made from the broad base of a Samoa palm upstairs held the outsize headgear of another era.

Catholic missionaries had a far rougher time gaining initial acceptance among Hawaiians than did Protestants, who happened to arrive at a propitious moment. The latter arrived just a year after Kamehameha's favorite wife Kaahumanu, in collusion with her son, the weak-willed new ruler Liholiho, had engineered the banning of the old religion and its restrictive *kapus,* many of which applied to women exclusively. Kaahumanu embraced the new Christianity, but it was the Protestant version that she accepted. When Catholic missionaries first arrived in the Islands in 1827, she made things very tough for them, even condoning torture of converts in spite of the vehement protests of her Protestant missionary mentors. Nevertheless, the Catholic mission prevailed and Kailua got the first Catholic Church built in the Islands in 1848 on the site of the first mission established on the Neighbor Islands. St. Michael's Church on Alii Drive at the south end of town has a coral grotto shrine.

The Kohala Coast and Waimea

Two routes lead north of Kailua-Kona. Highway 19, Queen Kaahumanu Highway, and later Highway 270 follow the Kohala Coast all the way to the tiny community of Hawi at the island's northern end. Beyond award-winning Keahole Airport with its pavilion-like check-in stations resembling an ancient Hawaiian village, the road passes between long miles of rust-colored clinkers left by old Kohala volcano lava flows. The monotony of the landscape is broken by the often whimsical graffiti messages local residents create with white stones against the piles of red beside the highway.

The 20 miles north from Kaupulehu to Kawaihae Harbor along this coast is the true Gold Coast of Hawaii. Here, on their own expanses of private acreage, are super luxury resorts like no others in the Islands. Kona Village in the south and Mauna Kea Beach Resort in the north were the first world-class resorts of their kind in Hawaii when they were built more than 20 years ago. Two more resorts have been built since, each with its own beautiful white sand beach and rolling golf greens, and none within sight of another. More luxury resorts are planned for the next few years. Most notably, the $360-million, 1,260-room Hyatt Regency Waikoloa, which is scheduled for a 1988 opening, sprawls over 60 oceanfront Kohala Coast acres.

In addition to the resorts and their golf courses, restaurants and shops, there are some very explorable sites in Kohala. At Puako, a small coastal town beyond the Mauna Lani Bay Hotel, is one of the most interesting petroglyph fields on the island. A Hawaiian warrior marker in midtown points the way to an old field of smooth pahoehoe lava, where three different groups of petroglyphs, including one of stacked marching warriors, may be found.

Even if you never go swimming, you must stop at Hapuna State Recreation area, north of Puako. It has one of the most beautiful and biggest white sand beaches anywhere. At Kawaihae two restored stone *heiau* invite exploration. One is the spot where Kamehameha sacrificed the chief of Kauai. Beyond pretty Kawaihae Harbor, where local residents and sports fishermen keep luxury boats, Highway 270 hugs the sunny coast to Lapakahi State Historical Park, site of a 600-year-old fishing village now restored and open for self-guided walking tours. If you've caught the amateur archeologist bug by now, continue on to Hawi, where the road to Upolu Airfield leads to massive, goose-bump-producing Mookini Heiau, on a solitary rise in the middle of a cane field. Watch for a Hawaii Visitors Bureau marker to show the way down a dirt road. Kamehameha was born at a site nearby, marked by a plaque.

Beyond Hawi, Highway 27 leads to Kapaau, where a statue of Kamehameha just like the one in Honolulu stands in front of the courthouse. This, however, is the original statue which was completed in 1880 in Italy but lost at sea off the Falkland Islands when the German ship carrying it to Hawaii sank. The Hawaiian legislature ordered a new statue with $10,000 in insurance money which was placed in Honolulu. Two years after the sinking, an American sea captain on the way to Hawaii found the original statue in a Port Stanley junk yard and brought it to Honolulu. The legislature decided to put it near Kamehameha's birthplace.

Waimea, Town with Two Names

From Hawi, you can loop inland across the green Kohala mountain ridge to the cattle ranch town of Waimea, which is sometimes called Kamuela, the Hawaiian word for Samuel, after Samuel Parker most people believe, the son of the founder of 250,000-acre Parker Ranch. The name Kamuela originally was given to the town's post office, but now is used for the town itself. A second route to Waimea is the 39-mile drive from Kailua-Kona inland on Highway 190.

Enclosed by green pastures, Kamuela is a town of 1,250 residents. Its appearance is something of a surprise. Part ranching town and part quaint community of picket fences and gingerbread trimmed houses, it has something of the feel of an Alpine village. This is the place to live for many Big Island residents and for many fugitives from Honolulu who can manage to move here. Kamuela has shopping centers, restaurants, an inn, and a lodge. Parker Ranch operates a museum and there's an excellent theater. Richard Smart, present owner of the ranch, had a long Broadway career and is a moving force behind the theater here.

John Palmer Parker, a young seaman who arrived in Hawaii in 1809, began his ranching career by rounding up wild Spanish longhorn cattle for Kamehameha. The longhorns were descendants of some animals given to the chief by Captain George Vancouver when he wintered in Hawaii between 1792 and 1794. Parker used the cattle as basic stock when he established his ranch around 1815. He later married Kamehameha's granddaughter. Today about 50,000 Herefords are run on the ranch, kept in shape by Hawaiian *paniolos,* some of whom are descendants of the ranch hands who worked alongside Parker. With the King Ranch in Texas, Parker Ranch remains one of the largest privately held spreads in the United States.

To Waipio Valley and Hamakua

From Waimea, Highway 19 crosses to the east Hamakua Coast of the Big Island and can be followed back to Hilo. At Honokaa, the first coastal community, is the Hawaiian Holiday Macadamia Nut Farm and Factory, renamed and revitalized in the 1980s by members of the same family that developed Ghiradelli Square in San Francisco. A store and factory next door are open for tours and free samples are given out. Macadamias were brought to Hawaii by William Purvis, an Australian, for planting in 1882. The nutritious nut can be used in all kinds of recipes, and is becoming an important crop in Hawaii. Honokaa is a community originally settled by immigrants from Portugal and Madeira. If you catch the fragrant aroma of fresh bread or rolls in Honokaa, stop at the bakery to buy fresh malasadas, delicious, dumpling-shaped Portuguese donuts that are best when eaten warm.

Highway 24 branches off north at Honokaa to Waipio Valley Lookout, where the view is of a green Hawaiian valley against 1,800-foot cliffs where taro farmers still use the same cultivating methods their ancestors did. You can hike down the steep road into the valley or take a popular four-wheel drive tour, the Waipio Valley Shuttle, which must be arranged in advance.

The drive into Hilo along the Hamakua Coast passes cane fields and waterfalls. Laupahoehoe State Park is about 20 miles down the road from Honokaa. From a lookout here you can gaze down on a site where school children and three of their four teachers from the mainland were swept out to sea by a *tsunami* that hit this coast in 1946. A plaque marks the spot. At Honomu take the scenic drive that meanders a few miles beside the coast through canopies of trees. Look for spreading monkeypods and the shimmering silverish leaves of the kukui tree, which was far more important to Hawaiians than the macadamia nut in its shell is to us. Kukui nuts were used for necklaces, dye, and purgatives. Their oil was used for lights at night.

The Saddle Road

The high road that crosses the saddle between the Big Island's two largest volcanoes, Mauna Kea and Mauna Loa, makes a fascinating side trip. A jeep, camper, other four-wheel drive, or friend's car is probably best for the 60-mile trip between Waimea and Hilo on the Saddle Road (Highway 20). Rental car companies on the island discourage use of their automobiles on the lonely road, although it is well paved for the U.S. Army and Marine vehicles that frequently transport troops to a camp at Pohakuloa for practice maneuvers.

The Saddle Road turns off Highway 190 about six miles south of Waimea. For the first 12 miles you climb gradually to 3,000 feet through lava beds and game bird country with views of three volcanoes, Hualalai, Mauna Loa, and Mauna Kea. Watch for pheasant and quail darting among the clinkers of *aa* on either side of the road. This rocky terrain is said to resemble that on the surface of the moon. Apollo astronauts came here to train.

Mauna Kea State Park, better known locally as Pohakuloa, is the main destination here. At 6,500 feet, this is the place to break out your jackets. The park's rustic cabins are popular as acclimatizing sites for Mauna Kea skiers, hikers bound for the summit of Mauna Loa, and hunters. Reservations must be made well in advance through the Department of Land and Natural Resources' Division of State Parks in Hilo. The cabins offer basic amenities, including hot showers. Pens at the park contain the rare Hawaiian *nene,* an indigenous goose that the State Division of Fish and Game is bringing back from near extinction. Several hundred have been released between the 5,000- and 8,000-foot levels on the slopes of Mauna Loa and Hualalai.

On weekends and holidays between November 1 and January 15, hunters come to the state-maintained game management area here for chukar partridge, pheasant, and quail. Mammals, mostly wild pig, Mouflon sheep, and goats, are hunted year-round, but it is advisable to have guides if you are unfamiliar with the many wandering jeep roads.

You can drive to the 13,796-foot summit of Mauna Kea in a four-wheel drive. A well-tuned passenger car will make it six miles up a paved road from Humuula junction beyond Pohakuloa to Hale Pohaku, a view point at 9,200 feet in the park. From here you can hike six miles up to Lake Waiau at 13,200 feet on a trail paralleling the jeep road. The very chilly lake is 400 feet across and 15 feet deep most of the year. More interesting even than the lake or summit is Keanakakoi Cave, passed at the 12,400-foot level, actually a series of caves used by Hawaiians as basalt quarries for adzes. Koa for canoes was cut and carved with the hewn stone tool, and many other purposes were found for it. Partially completed adzes lie on the ground here.

At Mauna Kea's summit are $60 million worth of observatories with seven telescopes operated by the U.S. Air Force, NASA, the University of Hawaii, Cal Tech, and assorted European countries. The clear atmosphere provides views of the heavens that are excellent for study through telescopes of 24, 88, 144, 150, and a recently installed one of 400 inches. Tours are offered on weekends and holidays between May and September, from 9 A.M. to 3 P.M. Saturday evening viewing is offered after 6:30 P.M. in summer.

Depending on the year's quantity of snow, winter skiing can be excellent from points just below the observatory on white slopes with names like the Poi Bowl, Pele's Parlor, and the King Kam run. A ski shop in Waimea has complete equipment to rent and will arrange rides back up the mountain in a four-wheel drive vehicle.

The adventurous can consider taking another gravel road that winds northeast up Mauna Kea from Humuula Junction through tall stands of koa and ohia. At 7,000 feet it becomes a four-wheel-drive trail that passes near a monument for botanist David Douglas, who was found dead under mysterious circumstances in a cattle trap at this point in 1834. The Douglas fir was named for him. The road, which passes through multiple gates that require opening and closing, finally turns on to a graveled road again near Mana before coming out on Highway 190 near Waimea.

On the other side of Highway 20 is a 17-mile paved road leading to Mauna Loa Observatory known as the highest passenger car route in the Pacific. During weekdays a locked chain at the nine-mile point bars the road to cars in order to protect sensitive equipment at the observatory, but hikers are welcome to come up to see the bizarrely formed and colored lava flows along the way.

The Saddle Road continues from this point uneventfully across old lava flows into Hilo. One of them threatened Hilo during a 1935 eruption until its route was diverted by aerial bombing.

PRACTICAL INFORMATION FOR HAWAII

HOW TO GET THERE. There are more than a dozen flights daily from Honolulu to the Big Island, plus a number of special weekend flights. *Aloha and Hawaiian* offer jet flights; Hawaiian also has daily flights on its Dash prop. Midday rates one way to Hilo are about $45; lower rates are available. Flying time by jet between Honolulu and Hilo, a 214-mile distance, is 35 minutes; between Honolulu and Kona 45 minutes. *United Airlines* operates daily flights to Hilo Airport and Keahole Airport from Los Angeles, Chicago, and San Francisco. Commuter carriers, such as *Princeville Airways* has 2 trips daily from Honolulu during the week, 3 on Fri. and Sun.; weekly roundtrip is $68; weekend $72. *Big Island Air* has two commuter flights daily on a 9-passenger Cessna between Kona and Hilo beginning in Kona at 6:45 A.M.; $25 one-way, $50 roundtrip.

Airport shuttle service from Keahole Airport to Keahou-Kona is $7.50; from Hilo International Airport to Banyan Drive Hotels is about $3.

A taxi from Keahole Airport to Keauhou-Kona is about $20.

ACCOMMODATIONS. The Big Island, with its steaming volcanoes and balmy Kohala Coast beaches, offers the widest range of accommodations of any Hawaiian island. There are 3 main resort destination areas on the island: along the Kohala Coast, at Keauhou-Kona, and on Banyan Drive in Hilo. The island's major self-contained luxury resorts, offering a full range of activities and facilities such as tennis, gardens, and golf courses are on the Kohala Coast and in north Kona. The newest addition to the scene is the Hyatt Regency Waikoloa Hotel on the Kohala Coast, scheduled to open in August 1988. Additionally, there are specialty properties at other prime locations on the island. Of the 7,511 vacation units available, 2,279 are in condominiums.

Package arrangements offered at some resorts in cooperation with airlines and tour operators may include peak season (winter) supplement charges. At least 2 of the island's luxury resorts have MAP rates exclusively. Most major credit cards are accepted at hotels (check when making reservations).

Accommodation price categories based on double occupancy are: $185 and up, *Super Deluxe;* $65 to $110, *Deluxe;* $34 to $65, *Moderate;* $14 to $34, *Inexpensive.* Hotels and condominiums are listed by geographic area.

Hilo

Moderate

Country Club Apartment Hotel. 121 Banyan Dr., Hilo, HI 96720 (935–7171). A pleasant bayfront hotel with 149 air-conditioned rooms, a cocktail lounge, pool, restaurant, and golf course.

Hawaii Naniloa Hotel 93 Banyan Dr., Hilo, HI 96720 (800–367–5360 or 969–3333). Hilo's nicest hotel on the bay, with 386 air-conditioned rooms. Seven- and 12-story hotel towers overlook the harbor and offer superb views of Mauna Kea. Sandalwood Room for fine dining, plus tennis, golf, and convention facilities. Children under 12 free.

Hilo Bay. 87 Banyan Dr., Hilo, HI 96720 (800–367–5102 or 935–0861). 150 air-conditioned rooms, most with kitchenettes. The charm of this hotel popular with Neighbor Islanders lies in proprietor Uncle Billy Kimi, who stages a nightly hula show with Hawaiian entertainment during dinner. Kimi's restaurant, coffee shop, cocktail lounge, nightly entertainment, shopping arcade, pool.

✦ **Hilo Hawaiian.** 71 Banyan Dr. on Hilo Bay (800–367–5004 or 935–9361). All air-conditioned, TV. Queen's Court restaurant, pool, shops, meeting room, and cocktail lounge. 290 units.

Hilo Hukilau. 126 Banyan Dr., Hilo, HI 96720 (800–367–7100 or 935–0821). A bayfront property with 139 rooms cooled by ceiling fans, a restaurant, cocktail lounge, shops, and freshwater swimming pool.

Inexpensive

Dolphin Bay Hotel. 333 Iliahi St., Hilo, HI 96720 (935–1466). A clean, homey 18-unit property 4 blocks from Hilo Bay, with a banana patch out back. No telephones.

Hilo Hotel. 142 Kinoole St., Hilo, HI 96720 (961–3733). This spartan, 35-room hotel has 2-bedroom suites and family rooms for 6, a restaurant and cocktail lounge, and is frequented by visitors from Japan.

Lanikai Hotel. 100 Puueo St., Hilo, HI 96720 (935–5556). This is Hilo's least expensive hostelry, 2 blocks from the heart of town. 35 rooms, caters to local residents and Japanese tourists.

Hamakua Coast

Inexpensive

Hotel Honokaa Club. Box 185, Honokaa, HI 96727 (775–0678). Operated by the same family since 1908, this quiet place has 20 rooms catering mostly to those enroute to Waipio Valley. Good dining.

Waipio Hotel. 25 Malana Pl., Hilo, HI 96720 (775–0368). Reservations are required if you want to rough it at this kerosene-lamp-lit, 5-room building on the floor of Waipio Valley. There's a community kitchen and bath. Bring your own food to cook and plenty of insect repellent for the mosquitoes.

Volcano-South Point

Deluxe

Sea Mountain at Punaluu. Box 70, Pahala, HI 96777 (800–367–804 or 928–8301). C. Brewer plans a major resort eventually at Punaluu, near the southern tip of the Big Island. For now, there are 33 studio, 1- and 2-bedroom vacation units available in the 76-unit Colony I condominium complex. It's all surrounded by the incredible vistas of tabletop volcanic formations and the sweeping greens of a championship golf course. The Aspen Institute, a think-tank-style meeting facility, is located on property. Golf course, tennis courts, swimming pool, restaurant, cocktail lounge, maid service. Minimum 2-day stay.

Volcano House. Box 53, Hawaii Volcanoes National Park, HI 96718 (967–7321). One of the most atmospheric places to stay in Hawaii, this 2-story inn has 37 cozy double rooms in a vintage structure that sits beside steaming Halemaumau Crater in the national park. There's even a steam room supplied by the volcano. The hotel will put up a box lunch if you want to explore. Sightseeing crowds are bussed in for lunch, but for a quieter atmosphere you can dine later in the bar on splendid sandwiches made with Portuguese sweet bread. At night there's nothing like a candlelight dinner beside the eerie aspect of the volcano. Reservations in advance are a must.

Inexpensive

Shirakawa Motel. Box 467, Naalehu, HI 96772 (929–7462). This modest but very clean 13-unit motel not far from the Mark Twain monkeypod tree in Naalehu, near the southern tip of Hawaii, has been offering friendly service to visitors making an around-the-island trip since 1928. Dining is at 2 drive-ins and a coffee shop in tiny Naalehu. No telephones.

Captain Cook

Inexpensive

Manago Hotel. Box 145, Captain Cook, Kona, HI 96704 (323–2642). There are 42 comfortable if spartan rooms in this old hotel in the foothills above Kealakekua Bay. The building dates from 1917. The least expensive rooms have a community bath; rooms with private baths are available too. Japanese food and good views of the bay.

Keauhou-Kona

Deluxe

Kanaloa at Kona. 78–261 Manukai, Kailua-Kona, HI 96740 (800–367–6046 or 322–9625). This 62-unit condominium complex borders the golf course. There's a swimming pool, tennis courts, a whirlpool, and a recreation center.

Kona Surf. 78–128 Ehukai St., Kailua-Kona, HI 96740 (800–367–8011 or 322–3411). Built on a black lava rock promontory, this 535-room hotel is the showplace around which Keauhou-Kona Resort is growing so quickly. Recently sold to a Japanese investor, it has 4 bougainvillea-bedecked wings, a gourmet dining room, other dining facilities, cocktail lounges, 2 swimming pools, a tennis complex, shops, meeting rooms, and play on a championship golf course.

Moderate

Keauhou Beach Hotel. 78–6740 Alii Dr., Kailua-Kona, HI 96740 (800–227–4700 or 322–3441). A 317-room hotel in a single, 7-story building overlooking the Pacific Ocean. Two restaurants, cocktail lounges, tennis courts, swimming pool, shops, access to a championship golf course.

Keauhou Resort Condominiums. 78–7039 Kamehameha III Rd., Kailua-Kona, HI 96740 (800–367–5286 or 322–9122). There are 39 vacation units available in townhouses with *lanai* views of the ocean and golf course fairways. Swimming pools, access to golf course. Minimum 5-day stay.

Keauhou-Kona Surf & Racquet Club. 78–6831 Alii Dr., Keauhou-Kona, HI 96740 (322–6696). This 190-unit oceanfront condominium complex has 1-, 2-, and 3-bedroom vacation units, a swimming pool, tennis courts, and access to a championship golf course.

Kona Lagoon. 78–6780 Alii Dr., Keauhou-Kona, HI 96740 (800–367–5004 or 322–2727). A 454-unit oceanfront hotel in 3 wings, with a restaurant, cocktail lounges, tennis courts, shops, meeting room, swimming pool, and access to a championship golf course.

Kailua-Kona

Super Deluxe

Kona Village Resort. Box 1299, Kaupulehu-Kona, HI 96745
(800–367–5290 or 325–5555). There is no other resort in Hawaii quite like
this one, on its own private white sand beach somewhere at the end of
a private road across the lava fields north of Kailua-Kona town. In fact,
privacy is almost as important an element as relaxation at this village of
115 thatched-roof *hales* (houses) inspired by South Pacific island homes
but recently redecorated and refurbished by the best U.S. designers available. This is the ultimate retreat from the workaday world, where all recreational activities—and there are a lot, from glassbottom boat rides to guided historic walks and authentic Hawaiian luaus—and all meals are
included in the rates. No newspapers, no television, radios, or phones in
the room by deliberate choice. Lots of good, friendly pampering service.
Once you've stayed here, chances are you'll be determined to return at
least once in this lifetime, no matter what your income bracket.

Deluxe

Kona By the Sea. 75–6106 Alii Dr., Kailua-Kona, HI 96740
(800–367–5124 or 329–0200). One of the nicer oceanfront condominiums
in Kailua-Kona. There are 80 air-condintioned 1- and 2-bedroom units,
all with lanais, and 2 swimming pools.

Kona Hilton Beach & Tennis Resort. Box 1179, Kailua-Kona, HI
96745 (800–452–4411 or 329–3111). This 452-room oceanfront hotel in
the heart of Kailua-Kona recently has been completely refurbished and
redecorated. There is a swimming pool, coconut grove, and saltwater lagoon. Fine cuisine, including kosher meals, is in the Hele Mai dining room.
There are cocktail lounges, shops, meeting rooms, and an extensive tennis
complex.

Kona Reef. 75–5888 Alii Dr., Kailua-Kona, HI 96740 (800–367–7040
or 329–4780). About 50 vacation units are available in this oceanfront 120-
unit condominium. It has a Jacuzzi and swimming pool, too.

Royal Sea-Cliff Resort. 75–6040 Alii Dr., Kailua-Kona, HI 96740
(800–367–5124 or 329–0200). One- and 2-bedroom apartments are available in this 154-unit oceanfront condominium. About 150 of the units are
vacation rentals. There are 2 swimming pools and a tennis court on property.

Moderate

Casa de Emdeko Resort. 75–6082 Alii Dr., Kailua-Kona, HI 96740
(800–367–5168 or 329–6488). This 106-unit oceanfront condominium
complex is very attractively landscaped. All of 30 available 1- and 2-
bedroom vacation units are air-conditioned. There is a saltwater and a
freshwater swimming pool and a sauna.

Hale Kona Kai. 75–5870 Kahakai Rd., Kailua-Kona, HI 96740
(329–2155). There are 24 1-bedroom vacation rentals in this 39-unit condominium on the ocean in Kona. Swimming pool, maid service on request,
3-day minimum.

Hotel King Kamehameha. 75–5660 Palani Rd., Kailua-Kona, HI 96740
(800–227–4700 or 329–2911). History surrounds this 460-room hotel on
the shores of Kailua Bay at the north end of town, which has recently
suffered from uneven upkeep. Hawaii's great chief, Kamehameha, proba-

bly swam in the sandy cove, which is the only really swimmable ocean spot in town. Events of his time are reenacted in weekly evening pageantry at the hotel. Restaurants, cocktail lounges, swimming pool, tennis courts, sauna, shopping mall, and meeting rooms.

Kona Bali Kai. 76–6246 Alii Dr., Kailua-Kona, HI 96740 (329–9381 or 800–367–6046).There are 97 1- and 2-bedroom vacation rentals in this 155-unit Colony Resort-managed condominium apartment on Holualoa Bay in Kona. Swimming pool.

Kona Hukilau Hotel. 75–5646 Palani Rd., Kailua-Kona, HI 96740 (800– 367–7000 or 329–1655). This modest 100-room property in the heart of town is popular with Neighbor Island residents. For a small extra charge, a Budget automatic compact rental car is available at this hotel and the Kona Seaside.

Kona Islander Inn. 75–5776 Kuakini Hwy., Kailua-Kona, HI 96740 (800–367–5124 or 329–3181). Some 100 of 140 studios are available for vacation rental in this older, but pleasant low-rise apartment hotel across the street from Kailua Bay.

Kona Seaside Hotel. 75–5646 Palani Rd., Kailua-Kona, HI 96740 (329–2455). Four categories of rooms are available in this 125-unit local-style hotel across the street from Kailua Bay. Restaurant, cocktail lounge, swimming pools, meeting rooms, and shopping plaza.

Sea Village. 75–6002 Alii Dr., Kailua-Kona, HI 96740 (800–367–5205 or 329–1000). About 63 1- and 2-bedroom units are available for vacation rentals in this 131-room oceanfront condominium apartment hotel. Swimming pool, tennis court, weekly maid service, minimum 3-day stay.

Inexpensive

Kona Tiki Hotel. Box 1567, Kailua-Kona, HI 96745 (329–1425). There are 15 hotel units—some with kitchen facilities—in this simple 17-unit property about a mile south of Kailua town. No telephones in rooms. Minimum 3-day stay.

Puako-Waimea (Kamuela)

Moderate

Parker Ranch Lodge. Box 458, Kamuela, HI 96743 (885–4100). In the high country of Parker Ranch, in the heart of its central cowboy town, is a 10-unit motel–lodge with spacious junior suite rooms suitable for families. Great base for exploring this green country.

Kohala Coast

Super Deluxe

Hyatt Regency Waikoloa. 2424 Kalakaua Ave., Honolulu, HI 96815 (800–228–9000 or 922–9292). Opened in August 1988, this is a one-of-a-kind $360-million Kohala property, created by Honolulu developer Chris Hemmeter. On a wide expanse of oceanfront, it is surrounded by sparkling lagoons, meandering waterways, sprawling gardens, and lagoon atriums. 1,244 guest rooms in three 6-story buildings. Nine tennis courts with an exhibition center court, 4 racquetball courts, whirlpools, catamaran cruises, fishing charters, golf, an acre of free-form swimming pool complete with slides and a grotto bar, plus 9 restaurants serving seafood and broiler specialties, continental, French, Italian, and Japanese health food.

Mauna Kea Beach Resort. Box 218, Kamuela, HI 96743 (800–228–3000 or 882–7222). One of the great plusses of this world-class hotel is its general manager, Adi Kohler, who is as much at home with guests of modest achievement as he is with the greats of the world who so often vacation here. Located on one of the whitest and longest soft sand beaches in Hawaii, the hotel is a fully self-contained resort with modified American plan rates. Laurence S. Rockefeller developed the resort, now owned by United Air Lines and managed by Westin. It nestles in the brow of a hill at the foot of a majestic extinct volcano, Mauna Kea. Swimming, snorkeling, sailing, and surfing are superb in crystal waters of broad Mauna Kea Beach. Sportfishing—including black marlin weighing in at 1,000 pounds or more—is available at Kawaihae Marina, 1½ miles from the hotel. Golf is world-famous on the challenging Robert Trent Jones-designed championship course; tennis on 13 championship Lay-Kold and Plexipave courts. There's a world of riding-hunting-ranching just 12 miles away in the crisp mountain air of the Ranch House, where hotel guests enjoy exclusive hunting rights for the famous Parker Ranch's wild boar, bighorn sheep, pheasant, quail, and partridge. The hotel, a stunning architectural form, has 310 mountain- and ocean-view rooms. The *Dining Pavilion* and *Batik Room* provide beautiful settings for superb international cuisine.

Mauna Lani Bay Hotel. Box 4000, Kawaihae, HI 96743 (800–367–2323 or 885–6622). This glittering 351-room luxury hotel is the flagship of the Emerald Hotels line.

Shaped like a 6-story arrowhead aimed at the beach along Makaiwa Bay, this superb hotel sits atop black lava flows; 40 acres of ancient Hawaiian fishponds and walking trails are preserved. Almost all rooms have a view of the ocean. There are 10 plexipave tennis courts, boating, pools, whirlpool, a fitness jungle, and a $6.7-million golf course.

Deluxe

Sheraton Royal Waikoloa. Box 5000, Waikoloa, HI 96743 (800–325–3535 or 885–6789). This quite luxurious, 543-room hotel is situated behind a royal fishing lagoon fronted by a coconut-palm-ringed white sand beach. The self-contained resort has a full complement of recreational activities including golf on a championship course, tennis, hiking across lava beds and in search of petroglyphs, swimming, windsurfing, and snorkeling. Lots of nice shops, too.

Moderate

Waikoloa Villas. Box 3066, Kamuela, HI 96743 (800–367–7042 or 883–9588). There are 55 rental units among this 104-unit complex at Waikoloa Resort on the lower slopes of dormant Hualalai volcano in south Kohala. Golf on championship courses, tennis, horseback riding, swimming pools, weekly maid service. Three-day minimum.

Hawi

Inexpensive

Luke's. Box 308, Hawi, HI 96719 (889–5577). With 23 rooms in the heart of this country town, 22 miles from Waimea. On the central plaza, facing the closed cinema.

Old Hawaii Lodging Co. Box 521, Kapaau, HI 96755 (889–5577). This very modest 23-unit property near Hawi has a restaurant, cocktail lounge, and swimming pool; phone in the lobby.

RESTAURANTS. On the Big Island you can dine on veal Oscar, Parker Ranch steak, ahi sashimi, or, if you're fortunate, fresh-caught *opihi* (limpet), a Hawaiian delicacy, and top it all off with an aromatic cup of Kona coffee. The star among Big Island dining experiences is still the luncheon buffet at the Westin Mauna Kea Beach Hotel, but there are other memorable dining experiences on the island, too. Some exploring on your own in Hilo may turn up just the right place for local-style Japanese cuisine; in Kailua-Kona you may find fresh *opakapaka, aku, ono,* mahimahi, or *ulaula* on the menus. By all means try these Island fish. They are all delicious. (You may recognize them more easily as pink snapper, tuna, wahoo, dolphin fish, and red snapper.) Casual dress is the norm almost everywhere (no sandals or tank tops). At finer hotel restaurants women will feel comfortable in long or short dresses; men in better Aloha shirts.

We consider $40 and up to be *Deluxe;* $25–$40, *Expensive;* $15–$25, *Moderate;* and under $15, *Inexpensive* for a 3-course meal for one, excluding tip and beverage. Calling ahead for reservations always is a good idea.

Kohala-Kona-Keauhou

Batik Room. *Deluxe.* Mauna Kea Beach Hotel, Kawaihae (882–7222). World-class Continental cuisine is served in an Indonesian setting in this Mauna Kea Beach Hotel dining room. Of course, the curries are a specialty. Gourmets praise the curried chicken in coconut milk with cashew nuts and fried bananas. Other favorites include veal Oscar, tournedos of beef, and broiled Pacific lobster. Extensive wine list. Dinner only. No credit cards.

Dining Pavilion. *Deluxe.* Mauna Kea Beach Hotel, Kawaihae. (882–7222). A talented executive chef, Kim Dietrich oversees the international cuisine served in this award-winning Mauna Kea Beach Hotel dining room. The menu varies each night. Try the roast capon with piñon nut stuffing. Breakfast and dinner served here and in the adjacent, more intimate Garden Pavilion. The hotel's renowned smorgasbord-style Luncheon Buffet is served in the Cafe Terrace daily, $16.50 non-guests, $15.50 guests. A weekly *luau* in the North Point oceanside garden offers traditional Hawaiian fare such as *lau lau* (fish and pork steamed in ti leaves), *huli huli* pig, baked bananas and taro, and *haupia* (coconut pudding).

The Third Floor. *Deluxe.* Mauna Lani Bay Hotel, Kalahuipua. (885–6622). Continental cuisine with a French touch is served in this supra-elegant restaurant in the glittering Mauna Lani Bay Hotel. Try the Casserole of Pacific Seafood "Noilly Pratt," tender island *opakapaka* and assorted tasty fish baked in a vermouth cream sauce. Meals here should always begin with "Promising Start," a generous array of hot and cold hors d'oeuvres. Dinner only. Major credit cards.

Bay Terrace. *Expensive.* Mauna Lani Bay Hotel, Kalahuipuaa. (885–6622). Dine outdoors under the stars or beside a rainbow at this lovely Mauna Lani Bay Hotel location. Breakfast, lunch, dinner, late supper. Major credit cards.

Club Restaurant. *Expensive.* Mauna Lani Bay Hotel, Kalahuipuaa. (885–6622). American cuisine is served at lunch and dinner in this pleasant Mauna Lani Bay Hotel dining room. Major credit cards.

Hele Mai. *Expensive.* Kona Hilton Beach and Tennis Resort, 75–5852 Alii Dr., Kailua-Kona. (329–3111). Continental cuisine is served in this Kona Hilton Beach & Tennis Resort dining room. Dinner only. Major credit cards.

Huggo's. *Moderate.* 75–5828 Kahakai St. Kailua-Kona. (329–1493). Everybody goes to this Kailua-Kona waterfront restaurant with a glorious ocean view. As you might expect, fresh seafood is the main attraction, though the menu is not limited to *opakapaka* and mahimahi. Nevertheless, that's what's best here. Open daily for dinner; weekdays for lunch. Major credit cards.

Royal Terrace. *Moderate.* Sheraton Royal Waikoloa Hotel, Waikoloa. (885–6789). Fine American food is served in this relaxing Sheraton Royal Waikoloa dining room. Dinner only. Major credit cards.

S.S. James Makee. *Moderate.* Kona Surf Resort, Keauhou-Kona. (322–3411). It's worth the drive to Keahou-Kona if you're not staying in the vicinity for the fine Continental cuisine served in this Kona Surf Resort dining room with a decor reminiscent of interisland steamship days. Dinner only. Major credit cards.

Plantation Lanai. *Inexpensive.* Kona Ranch House, 75–5633 Kuakini Hwy., Kailua-Kona. (329–7061). Fresh Kona-caught seafood and fine quality steaks are served in this candlelit dining room at the Kona Ranch House, a turn-of-the-century-style building atop a hill in the town of Kailua-Kona. Take-out orders. Dinner. Major credit cards. Good barbecue ribs and combination plates are served in the adjoining *Paniolo Room.*

Teshima-Kealakekua-Kona Restaurant. *Inexpensive.* Highway 11, Honalo. (322–9140). If you like good Japanese food, this popular local restaurant on Highway 11 just beyond Keauhou-Kona is the place for you. As she has since 1943, family matriarch Mrs. Teshima leads diners to booths where she first serves them complimentary sake. House specialties are shrimp tempura and sukiyaki. Open daily for breakfast, lunch, and dinner. No credit cards.

Volcano

Ka Ohelo Room. *Moderate.* Volcano House, Hawaii Volcanos National Park. (967–7321). The crowds come by bus for the noon buffet in this Volcano House main dining room, where huge windows offer views of steaming Halemaumau Crater. By evening the mood changes as checkered tablecloths are exchanged for white to create a special dining experience. Leave room for cheesecake topped with tiny red ohelo berries indigenous to the Hawaii volcano area. During the day, try lunch after 2 P.M. in *Uncle George's Lounge* where you can order Portuguese-style hot dogs and other delicious sandwiches. Breakfast, lunch, and dinner. Major credit cards.

Hilo

Sandalwood Room. *Expensive.* Naniloa Hotel, 93 Banyon Dr., Hilo. (935–0831). Dine in an intimate atmosphere that recalls the years of the Hawaiian monarchy in this Naniloa Hotel dining room. Dinner only. Major credit cards.

Dick's Coffee House. *Inexpensive.* Hilo Shopping Center, Hilo. (935–2769). This Hilo Shopping Center restaurant is popular with local residents. Breakfast, lunch, dinner. Master Card and Visa.

K.K. Tei Restaurant. *Inexpensive.* 1550 Kamehameha Ave., Hilo. (961–3791). Tempura, teriyaki steak, miso soup, and other traditional Japanese foods in a garden setting. Lunch and dinner. Major credit cards.

HOW TO GET AROUND. Hilo-based **buses** make a minimum of 2 roundtrips daily to Puna, Hamakua, and Kona (via Honokaa and Waimea). The bus terminal is at Mooheau Park on Kamehameha Avenue. Shuttle service runs daily except Sunday between Hilo's Banyan Drive hotels, shopping centers, and visitor attractions. A *Hele-On* bus runs from Hilo to Kailua-Kona daily, except Sunday; fare is $4. In West Hawaii a free double-decker bus runs between Kailua-Kona and Keauhou-Kona daily, from 9 A.M. to 5 P.M. A shuttle bus runs on Alii Drive between Kailua-Kona and Keauhou-Kona and small towns in between.

Taxis in and around Hilo are about $1.35 per mile.

Limousine service with chauffeur–guides is available from about $35 an hour. *Big Island Limousine Service,* Box 5560, Kailua-Kona, HI 96745 (325–1088) is based on the island. *Carey Limousine of Hawaii,* Box 29638, Honolulu, HI 96820 (800–367–2669), has Cadillac limos on the island, too.

Almost two dozen **car rental** firms serve the island; most have desks at or service both Hilo International Airport and Keahole Airport. The drive around the island from Hilo through Hawaii Volcanoes National Park, and around South Point to Kailua-Kona, is about 135 miles; to loop back to Hilo through Waimea and down the Hamakua coast, is about 225 miles. Many side trips to interesting sites are possible depending on your hotel or condominium base. Major car rental companies such as *Alamo, Avis, Budget, Dollar, Hertz, National, Thrifty,* and *Tropical* serve the island. Hawaii-based companies include *Harper* (969–1478); *Phillip's* (935–1936); *Rent & Drive* (329–3033); *Roberts* (947–3939); *Travel/Camp* (935–7506); *United* (935–2115); and *World* (329–1006). Four-wheel drive vehicles for exploring the Saddle Road and other sites are available from *Harper, Hertz,* and *Travel/Camp.*

Mopeds for use in Kailua-Kona are available from *Continental Rental* (329–3250), or *Kona Fun-N-Sun* (329–6068).

TOURIST INFORMATION SERVICES. Free brochures, maps, and general information are available at *Hawaii Visitors Bureau-operated booths* at both Keahole Airport and Hilo International Airport. If you have a real problem, the Big Island branch of the HVB is located in Hilo Plaza, at 180 Kinoole St., Suite 104 (961–5797). General office hours are 8 A.M. to 12 noon and 1 to 4 P.M. weekdays. The office in Kailua-Kona, with the same hours, is at 75–5719 W. Alii Dr., Kailua-Kona 96740 (329–7787). An excellent and thorough brochure, *A Guide to Ocean Recreation on the Big Island of Hawaii,* is available by sending a stamped, self-addressed business-size envelope and $1 to University of Hawaii Sea Grant Extension Service, Marine Science Bldg., 1000 Pope Rd., Room 213, Honolulu, HI 96822.

SEASONAL EVENTS. January. Athletes congregate for the *Volcano Wilderness Marathon and Rim Runs* that include 5.5-, 10-, and 26.2-mile runs into Kilauea caldera and back.

February brings annual *Great Waikoloa Rodeo and Horse Races* on a flat track in Kohala. Later, there's the *Captain Cook Festival* including a town party in Waimea and a reenactment of the British explorer's landing in Kealakekua.

March. More athletic events such as the grueling *Keauhou-Kona Triathlon* gets underway. It's followed by the *Hawaii Ski Cup* meet atop snowy Mauna Kea. For less outdoorsy folks there's the *Ikebana Show* in

Hilo highlighting Japanese flower arranging. Then it's horses during the annual *Kona Stampede,* a full range of rodeo events in Honaunau.

April. The island's most popular annual event, the *Merrie Monarch Festival,* honoring King David Kalakaua, Hawaii's last king, runs throughout the first week of the month in Hilo. Islanders reserve tickets a year or two in advance for the hula contests that are the highlight of this gala affair.

May brings more sports events beginning with the 2-week *Kona Sports Festival* at the beginning of the month. Then there's *Western Week* in Honokaa, a series of events including a rodeo and a *Portuguese Bean Soup* contest in Honokaa.

June. In this month, the Big Island honors the memory of its native son, King Kamehameha, with a *parade and hoolaulea* (celebration), a statue draping, and a foot race in Hilo and Kona. At the end of the month Hawaiian arts are featured during the *Puna Cultural Festival.*

July. A busy month begins with the annual *Hilo Orchid Society and Bonsai shows,* both in Hilo. On the Fourth there's the *Parker Ranch Rodeo* in Waimea and the 45th annual *Naalehu Rodeo.* Later there's the *Big Island Marathon,* the *Sheraton Royal Waikoloa Brantley tennis tournament,* the *International Festival of the Pacific*—a pageant of nations—and the *Mauna Kea Beach Hotel's Pro-Am golf tournament.*

August. The annual *Kona Billfish Tournament* gets underway at the end of July and extends into August. It's followed immediately by the *Annual Hawaiian International Billfish Tournament.* Later in the month there is a cultural festival and a macadamia festival as well as an anthurium show in Hilo and the *Parker Ranch Roundup Rodeo* in Waimea.

September. The month begins with the *Million Dollar Golden Marlin Fishing tournament.* Then it's *Aloha Week* in the Islands. Celebrations on the Big Island are scheduled at midmonth.

October. This is *Ironman World Triathlon Championship month* on the Big Island. It gets underway at midmonth in Kailua-Kona.

November. The *Annual Kona Coffee Festival* features ethnic events, a recipe contest and parade at the beginning of the month. Later there's the Annual *lei-making contest* at Kilauea Volcano Art Center, which is followed at the end of the month and extending to the day before Christmas by the annual *Christmas in the Country festival exhibit,* also at Volcano Art Center. The Big Island *Ultraman National Championship,* one of the world's toughest endurance contests is held later in the month, too.

December. At midmonth the Waimea-Kawaihae Community Association holds its *Annual Christmas Parade and Musical Festival.* Also at midmonth Hilo's Lyman House Museum holds its *Christmas Tradition observance* as held by Hawaii's early New England missionaries.

TOURS. *Gray Line Hawaii* conducts 6 different tours with limousines, custom-built Grayliners, or vans with the friendliest Hawaiian chauffeurs as guides. Their tours include one-day coverage of Hilo and the Volcano; another of Hilo, the Volcano, and the Kona Coast; a tour of Hilo, the Hamakua Coast, and Kona; a Kona special of historical sites; and a trip featuring Waipio Valley and Waimea. There's also a historical Kona tour that looks at coffee and Honaunau, takes 3 hours and costs $12, leaving hotels in Kailua-Kona at 1 P.M. An 8-hour, half-island tour, starting either in Hilo or Kailua-Kona, costs $30.95. Call 800–367–2420.

Akamai Tours (800–922–6485), using vans, circles the Island in 10 hours, a 260-mile trip, for $34, children under 12 for $32. Or there's a look around Kohala for $26 that takes 8 hours. An afternoon tour of Kona costs $14. *The Waipio Valley Shuttle* runs an hour-and-a-half Jeep trip for $15, children under 12, $5 (775–7121). *The Pacific Whale Foundation,* 75–5702 Alii Dr. in Kailua-Kona (329–3255), offers seasonal whale-watching cruises ($25) with researchers working with humpbacks, as well as off-season trips to see other area cetaceans.

Hawaiian Cruises (329–3811), 3½ hours, leave the Kailua-Kona wharf every morning at 9 and cover all historic points of Kealakekua Bay where Captain Cook landed and was killed. The trip including snorkel time costs $18.00 for adults, $9 for children under 12. If you want to see what's under the surface of Kailua Bay take the *Captain Cook VII* glass-bottom boat. It leaves the Kailua pier 3 times daily, $5. *Capt. Bean's* 150–ft. Polynesian canoe has a $38 adults-only moonlight cruise.

If you want to feel what's under the surface of Kailua Bay check out scuba tanks and snorkels with *Sea Dreams Hawaii* (329–8744). The yacht *Fair Wind* has a scuba-snorkel cruise with lunch, leaving Kailua-Kona at 9 A.M. daily, for $30, children $22; $12 toddlers (2–4), 78–7128 Kaleopapa Rd. (322–2788).

If the volcano is erupting, *Anuenue Aviation* (961–5591) has air tours of the area for $85 in a Cessna. *Kenai Helicopters* (885–7361) has assorted flightseeing tours in 4- and 6-passenger Bell Ranger helicopters beginning at $160. *Papillon Helicopters,* based on Kauai (669–4884), offers a Mauna Loa Odyssey for $175.

Kona Activities Center can book you into many water outings (329–3171); they also rent bicycles. *Kona Coast Activities* (329–2971) has horseback riding, flightseeing, and water activities, too.

PARKS AND GARDENS. Akaka Falls State Park. Gorgeous Akaka Falls drop 442 feet into a deep, rockbound pool in this verdant park accessible via a short drive inland from Honomu, about 10 miles north of Hilo on Hwy. 190. A 66-acre tropical garden filled with ginger, ferns, orchids, and other tropical growth surrounds the falls.

Hawaii Tropical Botanical Garden. This 17-acre nonprofit working botanical garden on Onomea Bay is a scenic drive north of Hilo and has a mile of trails leading through an assortment of fruits and plants. For $6 a shuttle takes visitors from a reception center by the highway to the garden a mile inland. (Call 964–5233 for information.)

Hawaii Volcanoes National Park. The Big Island's most interesting site includes 2 active volcanoes, Mauna Loa, which doesn't erupt much (but did in 1984) and far more active Kilauea, which in 1988 entered the fifth year of its current eruptive phase, the longest in its history, according to geologists. On its 220,000 acres the park also has campgrounds, hiking trails, a museum, a hotel, the Volcano Art Center, a rain forest, and all kinds of unusual lava formations to visit up close. The National Park Service operates 2 Visitor Centers in the park where you can pick up brochures. Kilauea Visitor Center is open from 8 A.M. to 5 P.M. and is devoted to information about the volcanoes. Wahaula Visitor Center at the south end of the park is open from 9 A.M. to 4 P.M. Its exhibits concentrate on Hawaiian history and archeology. As of Feb. 1987 there is a $5 vehicle entry fee and $2 fee for those on foot. For up-to-date volcano eruption information, call 967–7977.

Kona Gardens. Petroglyphs, Hawaiian home sites, lava formations, burial platforms, and an ancient *heiau* are found in this privately operated Keauhou-Kona area park. $5 adults. 78–6739 Alii Dr. (322–2751).

Kualoa Farms. All kinds of anthuriums—from palest pink to deep magenta—are grown on this 62-acre farm, as are orchids and other exportable plants. There's a collection of rare palms, too. Off Highway 11 in south Hilo. Guided tours. Open daily 8 A.M. to 4 P.M. (959–4565). Admission.

Lapakahi State Historical Park. Excavations cleared the 600-year-old Hawaiian fishing village that is the heart of this 265-acre park on the north Kohala coast. A self-guided walking tour gives you an unusual opportunity to see what life was like for the average resident of old Hawaii at Koiae village, which was occupied through the 18th century. Open daily, except Sun. 8 A.M. to 4 P.M. On Hwy. 27 in Mahu-Kona (889–5566).

Lava Tree State Park. In 1790 a lava flow inched slowly through a forest of ohia trees in this Puna district park (on Hwy. 132), burning off their tops and encrusting their trunks with lava. Now, nearly 2 centuries later, the remaining gray lava stumps create an eerie scene in the midst of a new tropical forest. Look for orchids blooming on the lava trunks.

Liliuokalani Gardens. This beautifully sculpted Japanese-style garden on Hilo Bay's Waiakea Peninsula was built after the devastating 1960 *tsunami* cleared the waterfront area of buildings. Named for Hawaii's last queen, it covers nearly 30 acres with pagodas, mondo grass, Hawaiian plants, and trees.

Nani Mau Gardens. More than 100 varieties of tropical fruit trees and more than 2,000 varieties of ginger, orchids, and anthuriums are displayed in a 20-acre commercial garden. Tours. 421 Makalika St., Hilo, HI 96720 (959–9442). Open daily 8 A.M. to 5 P.M. Admission $3.95.

Panaewa Rainforest Zoo. On Stainback Highway at the south edge of Hilo. Children of all ages will enjoy animals and plants found in the world's tropical rain forests living here. Open daily 9 A.M. to 4:30 P.M.

Puuhonua O Honaunau National Historic Park. This former place of refuge for Hawaiian *kapu*-breakers where priests protected even those who had committed great crimes, is now a 180-acre park. Wooden replicas of original images of Hawaiian gods are at Hale-o-Keawe, the most recent of 3 sacred *heiau*. A self-guiding map and recordings introduce the park. Frequent demonstrations of Hawaiian crafts are held. Open daily 7:30 A.M. to 5:30 P.M. Off Hwy. 11 (328–2326).

Wailoa River State Park. A visitor center in the heart of this north Hilo state recreation area has exhibits on Big Island culture and history. Open daily, except Sun. 8 A.M. to 4:30 P.M. (961–7360).

Wailuku River State Park. Two Hilo area sights, beautiful Rainbow Falls, and "Boiling Pots," several 20–40-foot-wide pools filled by waterfalls are located in this park just northwest of town.

BEACHES. Broad beaches of smooth white sand buffeted by gentle 2- to 4-foot waves flank the northwest coast of the Big Island. It's no accident that more super-luxury hotels are located on this coast than anywhere else in Hawaii, for these are the best looking beaches in much of the Pacific. Elsewhere on the island are beaches with black and even green sand, tide pools big enough to swim in, and historic sites to explore. As on the other Hawaiian Islands, winter months bring higher surf and intermittent hazardous swimming conditions. At any time of year it's a good idea to swim only where the sea is calm and when local residents are in the water. The Big Island has more than 80 accessible beaches. Those on the western coast generally are more appealing to visitors for swimming. Here are some of the better known beaches and some suggestions on what to do at them.

They are grouped geographically from northwest to northeast around the island.

Kohala-Kona-Keauhou
(West Coast)

Lapakahi State Historical Park. If you are a snorkeler, in summer when the surf is calmer, combine a visit to this intriguing site of an ancient Hawaiian village with a swim in Koaie Cove, a Marine Life Conservation District that is part of the park. Enter the water on the sandless beach where canoeists once launched to catch *ama ama* (mullet) and other fish running along the coast.

Spencer Beach Park. One of the safest year-round swimming and snorkeling beaches on the Big Island is protected by a long shallow reef offshore. Facilities in the park are very complete and include large shade trees, picnic tables, showers, and even some tennis courts. It's a good beach for small children.

Mauna Kea Beach. Known locally as Kauanoa Beach, this lengthy crescent of white sand around a bay is one of the best sunning beaches on the island. Swimming amid gentle waves here is very pleasant. It has been the site of the world-famous hotel of the same name since 1965. Public access is provided by the hotel at the south end of its parking lot.

Hapuna Beach State Recreation Area. Surely a higher being created this primevally perfect beach for the pleasure of humanity. A gleaming, sunny, white plank of sand stretches beside the bluest of seas here for more than a half mile. In summer it may be 200 feet wide. At sea it slopes gradually into deeper waters ideal for swimming and snorkeling in summer months, but with frequent hazardous conditions in winter. Not a good idea to swim here if the surf is up.

Puako Beach. In summer combine a walk along this very explorable beach with a visit to the petroglyph field accessible from the main road through the town of Puako. (Look for a Hawaiian warrior sign.) Lots of tide pools and inlets. Good snorkeling near the reef about 30 feet offshore for those who've had some experience. Watch out for sea urchins in shallow water.

Anaehoomalu Beach. The name may be difficult to pronounce but a visit to this easily accessible curve of white sand beach fronting the Sheraton Royal Waikoloa Hotel is well worth it. Windsurfers like this beach, which is also excellent for snorkeling. Take time to explore the Hawaiian petroglyphs and fishponds preserved in the area.

Kiholo Bay. Black sand beaches front this wide 2-mile bay popular with local residents for swimming and fishing. A superlative experience for visitor or resident is a swim in Luahinewai, a deep, spring-fed freshwater pool right next to the south shore of the bay. Beaches along the bay are good for exploring. Green sea turtles may sometimes be seen at the north end of the bay.

White Sands Beach Park. Known locally as Disappearing Sands Beach, this small white beach on Alii Drive in Kona is a popular bodysurfing and boardsurfing site. It is not a good swimming site.

Kahaluu Beach Park. Coconut palms ring this large, white sand swimming beach between Kailua and Keauhou. Good snorkeling just offshore for beginners, including children. Ruins of Hawaiian house sites and petroglyphs to explore.

South Point-Kalapana-Kapoho-Laupahoehoe
(East Coast)

Papakolea Green Sand Beach. Four-wheel drive vehicles may reach the remote location of this unusual beach via a bumpy, 2.5-mile ride along an unimproved dirt road northeast of the boat ramp at South Point Park. The beach, at the base of a steep cliff, attracts swimmers and bodysurfers during calm periods. Its distinctive olive-green tint is caused by an accumulation of large deposits of olivine crystals on the surface of the sand. It is often very stormy here in winter.

Punalu'u Beach Park. A black sand beach at the south end of a small bay along which many Hawaiians once lived. Ruins of a *heiau* and a large flat-topped sacrificial stone are on top of a point at the far north end of the beach. Some swimming close to shore at the beach park, but there is a potentially dangerous offshore current near the boat ramp. Good exploring.

Harry K. Brown Beach Park. A black sand beach park popular locally with sunbathers, surfers, and families (children can swim safely in a shallow area at the southwest end of the beach). Swimming directly off the beach is frequently hazardous.

Kaimu Black Sand Beach Park. This often-photographed black sand beach fringed with a grove of coconut palms is a good place to stop for a roadside breather on a drive around the island. The beach is beautiful to look at but unsafe for swimming.

MacKenzie State Recreation Area. This 13-acre beach park has an unusually peaceful aspect because of the many tall ironwood trees growing here. There is no swimming beach but it is a good place to picnic and explore. It is said that campers and others who remain after dark should be wary of the night marches Hawaiian spirits are believed to make in the area.

Kapoho. The snorkeling here is wonderful in a series of clear, deep tidepools situated along the shoreline of Kapoho Bay accessible via Vacationland Drive. There is no beach or public facility, however.

Leleiwi Beach Park. A well-developed beach park about 3 miles south of Hilo with picnic pavilions, a small sunbathing beach, and very good snorkeling in shallow waters protected by a point of land jutting into the sea.

Onekahakaha Beach Park. Hilo's most popular ocean wading pool has a sandy bottom and small white sand beach that attracts families with young children. Swimming beyond the breakwater is not recommended because of a rip current.

Coconut Island Park. Reached by a pedestrian bridge off Waiakea Peninsula on the south side of Hilo Bay, this sunny islet is a popular and very pleasant picnic and swimming spot.

Laupahoehoe Point Park. This small park on top of a point of land overlooking the sea is a good place from which to watch the surf and to contemplate the power of natural forces. The site below is famous as the location of a 20th-century tragedy. Early on the morning of April 1, 1946, a *tsunami* that hit the northeast coast of the island took the lives of 32 people here. Many of those lost were schoolchildren swept out to sea along with 4 of their teachers. Only 2 of the children and 1 teacher could be rescued that night.

PARTICIPANT SPORTS. The Big Island offers an almost unlimited selection of sports activities for beginners through experts. Kona is world famous for its deep-sea fishing opportunities. An unexpected sport on the island is snow skiing, possible most years from December through May atop 13,796-foot Mauna Kea.

Deep-Sea Fishing. The waters off the Kona Coast teem with marlin, mahimahi, tuna, wahoo, and other fighting game fish, and everything is available here for the fisherman's pleasure. Diesel and gas-powered boats leave the Kailua-Kona pier every morning about 8, and you can arrange to go fishing either on the spot or through your hotel desk. The *Kona Activities Center* (800–367–5288 or 329–3171) is headquarters for information. The 50 boats, averaging 36 to 42 feet, and accommodating 1 to 6 persons, can be chartered for $280–$450 for a full day, $85–$350 for a half day, less if you're sharing a charter with others. Fishing tackle and soft drinks are furnished; you bring your own box lunch (your hotel will provide that) and hard liquor if you want it. Boat captains know the fishing grounds, and all boats are licensed by the U.S. Coast Guard and are equipped with ship-to-shore radios.

Diving. There are many excellent dive sites both on the island and off-shore. Operators offer excursions for beginners to experts starting at $45. Five- to 7-day open-water certification courses begin at $275. Operators provide equipment, but you may prefer to bring your own snorkel and mask. Make arrangements with the following companies among others: *Dive Makai Charters,* Box 2955, Kailua-Kona, HI 96745 (329–2025); *Fair Wind Sail & Dive,* 78–7128 Kaleopapa Rd., Keauhou-Kona, HI 96740 (322–2788); *Gold Coast Divers,* 75–5660 Palani Rd., Ste. Pl, Kailua-Kona, HI 96740 (329–1328).

Golf. There are 10 courses on the island. Two miles from *Volcano House* is a good, though sometimes wet and misty 18-hole course through ohia woods. Green fees are $14.50. *Hilo* has a fine municipal course on Haihai Street; green fees are $6 weekdays, $8 weekends. There is a small, criss-cross 9-hole course at *Hamakua Country Club* in Honokaa (green fees $10) and another 9-holer at the *Country Club Apartment Hotel* on Banyan Drive in Hilo (green fees $8).

By far the best courses to play on the island, however, are the lengthy resort links where cart riding is mandatory. At *Seamountain Golf Course,* designed by Arthur Jack Snyder, on the island's southern tip, the sweeping views are as much of a challenge as any hole (green fees with required cart are $43), *Kona Country Club golf course* offers play on greens built around a lava field. Green fees for guests at affiliated accommodations are $47 with required cart; $59 for non-guests. At the spectacular *Francis H. I'I. Brown* course, opened in 1981 at Mauna Lani Resort, golfers must lob the ball over open ocean at one hole in order to play the entire course. Green fees and shared carts are $50 guests; $60 non-guests. At Waikoloa the choice of challenges is either an 18-hole beach or 18-hole upland village course, both designed by Robert Trent Jones, Jr. At the beach course, which is affiliated with the *Sheraton Royal Waikoloa,* guest green fees with carts are $45; for non-guests $60. At the village course green fees with cart are $40. You can play both Waikoloa courses for one fee, too. Robert Trent Jones, Sr. designed the *Mauna Kea Beach Hotel's* renowned course more than two decades ago. It's had plenty of time to season and to gain fame. Mauna Kea No. 3 is known as the bane or blessing of golfers every-where. How you play the 175 yards of craggy cliff and Pacific ocean in between tees can make or break a reputation. Green fees are $30 guests, carts $24 per round; non-guests pay $60 plus cart. Be sure to check out play at the new Hyatt Regency Waikoloa courses, as well.

Horseback Riding. There are horses to rent for trail rides at 3 stables in Kohala. They are: *Waikoloa Countryside Stables* (883–9335), offering rides on Parker Ranch land; *Mauna Kea Beach Hotel's stables,* offering rides to guests only in pastures above Waimea; and *Ironwood Outfitters,* on Kohala Mountain Road, Hwy. 250 at the 13-mile marker, with guides at $18 an hour (885–4941). *Waipio Ranch* operates a guided ride into Waipio Valley twice daily, 4 hours for a party of up to 6, including a swim and lunch, $40. Pickup point is the Waipio Woodworker Art Gallery in Kukuihaele, 9 A.M. and 2 P.M. (775–0373 or 775–7425). More horses are for rent at *Waiono Meadow Ranch* at Hualalai, free pickup at Kona hotels (329–0888). Kona Coast Trail Rides offers guided rides several times a day; an 8:30 A.M. to 10:30 A.M. ride is $30.

Hunting. Arrangements for hunting Mauna Kea sheep, Spanish goat, wild boar, and a wide variety of bird game on private grounds can be made through *Hawaii Hunting Tours,* Box 58, Paauilo, HI 96766 (776–1666). Bow hunting is available through *Wayne Matthews' Gray Fox Outfitters,* Box 266, Papaikou, HI 96781 (961–5943). Current rates for a day's hunt run about $350, or less if there's a group, equipment extra. Bow hunting rates are lower.

The State Department of Land and National Resources in Hilo issues annual hunting licenses and free but required daily permits for mammal hunting. Season for birds and mammals runs from first weekend in November to third weekend in January, with some variations. Representatives of the Department's bureau of game are in Hilo (961–7307 weekdays) and at Pohakuloa and Kona.

Skiing. An avid group of Hawaii residents pursues skiing atop snowy Mauna Kea with determination. At *Ski Shop Hawaii* on Parker Ranch Road in Waimea (885–4188) you can rent equipment and arrange for a guide and shuttle service during years when the snow is heavy enough. A day trip is $86 plus a $10 membership in the Ski Association of Hawaii, all equipment and shuttle lift service included. An overnight trip including meals, lodging, all equipment, and shuttle lift service is $126, plus $10 membership fee. Mauna Kea's ski runs are at a very high altitude—nearly 14,000 feet—so this experience is for the physically fit. Take plenty of sunblock, too.

Tennis. Almost two dozen sites on the island offer opportunities to play tennis. Resort hotels and clubs with 2 or more courts that restrict play to guests only include Country Club Villas, Kona Lagoon, Kona Makai, and White Sands Village in Kailua-Kona. At the *Hotel King Kamehameha* in Kailua-Kona non-guests may purchase memberships to play. The Kanaloa at Kona, the Keauhou-Kona Surf & Racquet Club, Kona Village Resort, Mauna Lani Bay Hotel, and the Mauna Kea Beach Hotel also restrict play to guests. The *Keauhou-Beach Hotel* has 6 courts, rates are $4 per day. The *Kona Hilton Beach & Tennis Resort* has 4 courts, rentals and instruction. Rates are $5 guests; $6 non-guests per day. The *Kona Surf Racquet Club* has 3 courts, rentals and instruction. Rates are $6 per day guests, $7 non-guests. The *Sheraton Royal Waikoloa* has 6 courts, rentals and instruction. Rates are $4 per hour per person; $2 for non-prime time. At the *Seamountain Tennis Center* which has 4 courts, rates are $4 per hour. And in Hilo, the *Naniloa Racquet Club* has 2 courts, rentals and instruction with rates set at $8 per day. Those who have their own equipment may take their chances getting play time on more than 4 dozen school and park courts all around the island. The beautiful *Hilo Tennis Stadium* at Piilani and Kalanikoa Sts. has 8 courts, 3 of them nightlighted, and charges a small fee.

Windsurfing. The *Sheraton Royal Waikoloa* offers windsurfing and hobie cat lessons through its beach services desk at Anaehoomalu Bay (885–6789). *West Hawaii Sailboards,* on Kaiwi St. in Kailua-Kona, rents boards and provides windsurfing lessons, too (329–3669).

CAMPING AND HIKING. The Elysian fields for these activities are in the *Volcano district,* and source of trail information and permission to camp and hike is the National Park Headquarters opposite the Volcano House. If you are planning to climb Mauna Loa, you can avail yourself of two fully equipped overnight cabins, one at 10,000 feet, the other at the summit. Write, well in advance, to Superintendent, Hawaii Volcanoes National Park, HI 96713. Keys and instructions provided at National Park Headquarters. The cabins are free, but the park service wants you to sign up first. If you are less ambitious, there are plenty of trails around the Volcano House and in the Mauna Ulu vent area. Many are guided walks that range from 2 to 14 hours. The Kilauea sector has three campgrounds and one, Namakani Paio, has unfurnished cabins that rent for $14 a night, plus $3.12 for bedding and deposit. At the 7 state parks, cabins rent for $8 per person, or $4 each if there are 6. A-frames at Hapuna are $7. Barracks rates are $3 if there are 3 for 3 nights. Information on parks is available from the Department of Parks and Recreation, 25 Aupuni St., Hilo, HI 96720, (961–8311); or the Division of Parks, Department of Land and Natural Resources, Box 936 Hilo, HI 96720 (961–7200).

Trek Hawaii, 677 Ala Moana Blvd., Honolulu, HI 96813 (523–1302), and *Wilderness Hawaii,* Box 61692, Honolulu, HI 96822 (737–4697) offer treks and educational camping tours of varying lengths to the Big Island. An assortment of campers ranging from simple cabovers to posh motorhomes with showers and full kitchens may be rented from *Travel/Camp Hawaii,* Box 11, Hilo, HI 96721 (800–367–8047). The company offers a slide show orientation to parks and camping sites on the island. A motorhome sleeping up to 6 people may be rented for $279 per week with 500 free miles and a small mileage charge thereafter.

HISTORIC SITES AND MUSEUMS. Captain Cook Monument. From Hikiau Heiau, an imposing stone platform beside the sea at Napoopoo in Kona, look across Kealakekua Bay to see an obelisk erected in 1874 in memory of Captain James Cook. Although Cook was welcomed at a ceremony in the *heiau* in 1778 by priests who mistook him for the Hawaiian god Lono, he was killed at quiet Kealakekua Bay after he returned to the island in 1779. Take Hwy. 16 off Hwy. 11 to reach Napoopoo.

Hulihee Palace. Built in 1838 as a summer retreat for Hawaiian royalty, this elegantly furnished 2-story structure in the heart of Kailua-Kona offers a glimpse into the splendor of the 19th-century period of the monarchy in Hawaii. Continuous tours; the last is at 3 P.M. (329–1877). Open 9 A.M. to 4 P.M. daily. Admission is $4 adults; $1 students; 50¢ children 6–12.

Kamuela Museum. At the Kawaihae and Kohala junction in Kamuela (Waimea), this privately owned museum has a fascinating collection of

Hawaiian memorabilia and artifacts dating from the period of the monarchy (885–4724). Open daily 8 A.M. to 5 P.M. Admission is $2.50.

Lyman Mission House & Museum. A house built by New England missionaries in 1839 and a modern museum beside it house exhibits on the cultures of Hawaii and its geology. At 276 Haili St. in Hilo (935–5021). Open 10 A.M. to 4 P.M. daily, except Sun. Admission: $3 adults; $1.50 children 6–18.

Mookini Heiau. By far the most impressive ancient *luakini* (sacrificial) *heiau* in Hawaii, this massive structure built in A.D. 480 sits in 20th-century solitude in a sugarcane field near Upolu Point at the northern tip of Hawaii.

Parker Ranch Visitor Center and Museum. Hawaii's largest working ranch, established by John Palmer Parker in 1815, is located on 250,000 acres largely in the northern district of Kohala. The history of the ranch is explained through a multi-media show and memorabilia displayed in a museum at the Parker Ranch Shopping Center in Waimea. Open daily, except Sun., 9:30 A.M. to 3:30 P.M. Admission $2.25; with lunch, $10.50 (reserved only).

Puukohola and Mailekini Heiau. In 1791, as he began the battles that would unite the Islands of Hawaii for the first time, Kamehameha had huge Puukohola, a 224- by 100-foot stone sacrificial *heiau* built and dedicated to his war god, Kukailimoku. Situated on a hillside overlooking the sea south of Kawaihae, it's an impressive sight. Together with an older *heiau* across the street, it is part of a National Historic Site.

Royal Kona Coffee Mill and Museum. On a side road that winds down to the ocean from the town of Captain Cook is a spot you can't miss because of the aroma of freshly brewed coffee around it. Have a free cup while you walk about reading signs that explain the history of Big Island coffee growing. Open daily, 8 A.M. to 4:30 P.M.

St. Benedict's Painted Church. Branch off onto Hwy. 16 at Keokea to find a side road leading to a tiny white gable-roofed church built in 1902. Father John Berchmans Velghe, a Belgian priest who served here, painted the interior with religious scenes that have Hawaiian motifs.

South Point. A narrow, but paved road off Hwy. 11 leads to one of the most interesting historic sites in Hawaii. The southernmost point in the United States, the area was heavily populated as early as A.D. 750. Mooring rings, Palahemo Well, house platforms, small Kalalea Heiau, and other archeological sites located beside sheer cliffs abutting the sea are part of a national historic landmark.

Suisan Fish Market. It's worth getting up very early to go to this bustling open market at 85 Lihiwai St. in Hilo where local shopkeepers bid in pidgin for the day's catch. The action is at its height around 7:30 A.M.

Thomas A. Jaggar Museum. In Hawaii Volcanoes National Park. Displays and videos explore Hawaii's origins and how interpretive material is gathered by geologists. Free with $5 per car park entry (967–7643).

Waipio Valley. A 50-mile drive through green Hamakua coast sugarcane fields north of Hilo leads to an overlook above a beautiful valley where Hawaiians still farm taro much as they have continuously for several centuries. Hiilawe Falls drops 1,200 feet to the valley floor here when water from it is not needed for sugarcane irrigation. You can hike into the valley or arrange to see it via a guided 4-wheel drive tour, the Waipio Valley Shuttle (775–7121).

SHOPPING. There are no vast shopping complexes on the Big Island. Stores in Hilo and Kailua-Kona for the most part retain the flavor of rural Hawaii. Nevertheless there are some special products you may want to take home from the island. The heritage of an older civilization so evident on the Big Island inspires artwork, from the sophisticated paintings of historic Hawaiian events by Herb Kawainui Kane (stop by his studio in the **Keauhou Beach Hotel**) to objects created in native *milo* or *koa* wood by lesser known artists available at **Kamaaina Woods** in Honokaa. At **Volcano Art Center,** housed in the original Volcano House at the park, original works in a variety of media by island artists are displayed and sold. As you might expect, flowers grown on the island—especially anthurium—are sold at gardens in and around Hilo for prices you won't see at Honolulu International Airport. Other products to look for include macadamia nuts (both Mauna Loa's macadamia nut farms in Puna and Hawaiian Holiday's in Honokaa offer visitors free samples) and unusual jellies—from guava to lilikoi. Fine specialty shops with resort wear and jewelry tend to be located in resort hotels, but even in these you may find work by local artists that you'll want to take home.

NIGHTLIFE. There has never been much need for lavish evening entertainment on the Big Island since there's so much to do by day. Several of the major resort hotels do offer luaus and shows with a decidedly Hawaiian motif that are well worth trying.

The **Hotel King Kamehameha** in Kona holds a pageant featuring authentically costumed performers who arrive in Hawaiian outrigger canoes before dinner. Held on Tues., Thurs., and Sun. at 6 P.M., it's $31. The hotel also offers Hawaiian entertainment nightly from 5 to 10 P.M. in the Billfish Bar (329–2911). At the **Kona Hilton Beach & Tennis Club** you can take in the West Hawaii Revue on Mon., Wed., and Fri., with cocktails outdoors and dinner inside, priced at $31. There's live music for dancing nightly in the Windjammer Lounge at the hotel (329–3111).

The **Kona Surf Hotel** in Keauhou-Kona offers a variety of lounge entertainment at different sites plus a Polynesian revue 2 nights a week at 7:45 P.M. (322–3411).

The **Naniloa Hotel** in Hilo has a disco with a disc jockey that's popular with local young people. It's open from 8 P.M. to closing (935–0831).

Resorts on the Kohala coast offer luaus and Hawaiian shows. At the **Sheraton Royal Waikoloa,** there's a Sun. luau for $38. On the Royal Terrace Wed. night there is a Waikoloa Roundup featuring western music and food; Fri. night is Sunset Swing Slack Sax night; there's also dancing in the Vanda Lounge Wed. through Sun. from 9:30 P.M. to 1 A.M. (885–6789). The **Mauna Lani Bay Hotel** has a strolling Hawaiian trio and a duo playing light tunes in the Bay Terrace on alternate nights, as well as a classical guitarist in the Club Restaurant and a pianist in The Third Floor restaurant (885–6622). At the **Westin Mauna Kea Beach Resort,** there's a luau with authentic Hawaiian food at 6 P.M. on Tues., $46, nonguests. Both dining rooms—The Batik Room and Pavilion—have live music for dancing on most evenings (882–7222).

MAUI

Roses, Romance, and Rainbows

By
JODI BELKNAP

The official flower of the second largest Hawaiian Island is a small, very pink rose, the *lokelani*. It is traditionally worn intertwined by the dozen or so in a *lei* resting on the bosom of a lovely Maui girl, be she 18 or 80. The rose is an apt symbol for an island where romance seems to be so much a part of daily life.

Maui even takes its name from a famous Polynesian demigod with an adventuresome spirit. Among other feats, he is said to have lassoed the sun, forcing that celestial body to pass more slowly over the island so his mother's *kapa* (bark cloth) could dry faster. To many, the sun does seem to shine longer on Maui. It takes its daily leave reluctantly, too, often lingering to create a splendid tropical sunset.

Two volcanoes shaped Maui. Haleakala Crater, the remnant of one, rises to 10,023 feet in the middle of the eastern part of the island. It is the largest crater in the world. Smaller 5,800-foot Puu Kukui in the northwest flanks sugarcane fields and the long beaches of a famous resort at Kaanapali. The two dormant volcanoes are connected by a low and narrow isthmus, thus giving Maui its nickname, the Valley Isle. At 38.4 miles from east to west, and 25 miles from north to south, the island is longer than it is wide.

There are about 75,000 permanent residents on Maui, a figure that always is swelled by part-time residents, as visitors to this island rightfully believe themselves to be. Maui is a very popular island to visit; about 2 million people call the island home temporarily each year, staying in one of more than 7,800 condominium units or 5,000 hotel rooms.

Some choose East Maui, the area flanking much of Haleakala. It's a lot like the tiny Hawaiian community of Hana on the island's east coast—quiet, green, and banked in rainbows. More visitors select West Maui as a base. It's a bustling, sunny stretch of beachfront perhaps personified best by the lively former whaling town of Lahaina that crowns it.

Even the whales know that Maui is an island for lovers of all ages. Every winter the number of rare humpback whales who come down from polar seas to sojourn in the deep waters of West Maui's warm Maalaea Bay increases. If you're fortunate, you may see a playful humpback or two with a new calf born in Hawaiian seas. Even they seem to agree with an old Hawaiian saying often applied to the island, *Maui no kai oi,* Maui is the best.

Exploring Maui

The best way to explore Maui in depth is to take short trips in different directions from one or more bases on the island. A complete drive around the island is not recommended, nor is it possible much of the time, since roads on the extreme northeast and southeast coasts are unimproved and can be treacherous in places. The southeast coast in particular requires a four-wheel drive. Otherwise, Maui's roads are in very good condition. From Kahului, where the main airport is located, some trips to consider are an 18-mile drive to Kula, a 40-mile morning trip to the summit overlook at Haleakala National Park, a 22-mile lowland drive to Lahaina, and the 50-mile drive along a very winding road to Hana; the latter is best taken when you plan to stay overnight in Hana. Depending on time, interests, and your base, Maui offers all kinds of exploratory experiences from a walk through Kula Botanic Garden to a wine-tasting at Ulupalakua Ranch, train ride to Lahaina, whale watch along the West Maui coast, rodeo in Makawao, or visit to a new sugar museum in Puunene.

Kahului: A Harbor Town

Maui's largest town is situated beside deep Kahului Bay, just west of Kahului Airport. It has an estimated population of about 15,000 and is a fast-growing port city with lots of new houses among the old. As a harbor town that once existed primarily to serve the shipping needs of Maui's sugar plantations, it has a distinctive island aspect in architecture that reflects the tastes of the many ethnic groups who have worked in the sugar industry and made their homes here.

Several hotels and three shopping centers are located on the main thoroughfare, Kaahumanu Avenue, named for the favorite Maui-born wife of Hawaii's best known king, Kamehameha I. At Maui Mall or Kaahumanu Center, the largest shopping center in East Maui, you can buy poi in a plastic bag at a supermarket or an elegant dress in a fine boutique. Older Kahului Shopping Center offers pleasant outdoor seating beneath shady

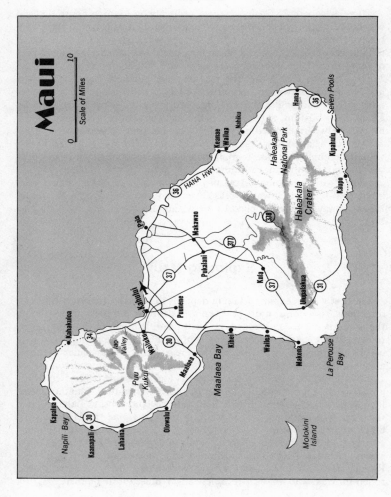

monkeypod trees. This is the place to sample that island institution, a plate lunch, which can be purchased from one of several takeout stands. It's your choice of entrees—lamb curry, beef tomato, or stew are the local favorites—always served with a "scoop rice" and macaroni salad.

Another place of interest in the Kahului environs is Kanaha Pond, beside the road on the way in from the airport, where you are likely to see the black-necked Hawaiian stilt, a rare species now protected in what was once a royal fishpond. At Maui Zoo, across from the War Memorial complex in town, you can stop to see indigenous Hawaiian birds, the *nene* goose and *koloa* duck. The zoo is part of a huge 190-acre Central Maui Park project being completed in phases over the next 10 to 20 years. Anyone interested in Hawaiian history should stop at Halekii and Pihana Heiaus, two 18th-century Hawaiian ceremonial and sacrificial sites accessible by following markers just past the Iao Stream bridge on Kahului's beach road.

Before leaving Kahului, take a two-mile side trip from Kaahumanu Avenue up monkeypod-lined Puunene Avenue to the Hawaiian Commercial and Sugar Company, and the new Alexander & Baldwin Sugar Museum across the street, the only museum about sugar in the islands. Director Gaylord Kubota is a Maui boy who went to Japan on a Fulbright Scholarship after college and ended up in ethnic studies at Bishop Museum in Honolulu before returning to Maui to open the sugar museum.

Wailuku: Maui's County Seat

Maui, Molokai, and Lanai are all governed from this charming older town of hilly streets just three miles from Kahului. White-steepled Kaahumanu Church on High Street, built in 1837 by Congregationalist missionaries from New England and their Hawaiian converts, is a town landmark. Also on High Street is the 1907 Court House. The Wailuku Historic district, encompassing the west side of the street, is worth a walk-through to see spacious, carefully landscaped homes.

Iao Valley

Iao Needle, a green-clad 2,250-foot spire, threads the sky in this quiet, waterfall-carved gorge sacred to Hawaiians. The road to it is an extension of Wailuku's main street. On it is Hale Hoikeike, a museum housed in an old seminary for girls where koa calabashes and silver punchbowls displayed side by side with other artifacts offer a good introduction to Hawaiian history. Also on the road is Kepaniwai Heritage Gardens, where pavilions and formal gardens represent cultures introduced to Hawaii by its different ethnic groups. The garden's Hawaiian name, which means variously "the water dam" or "water of destruction," comes from a gruesome 18th-century battle in which the forces of Kahekili, chief of Maui, nearly annihilated the army of a chief from the Big Island. So many Big Island warriors were slain that their broken bodies are said to have blocked Iao Stream causing it to run red with their blood.

In Iao Valley Park, at the end of the road, well-marked paths lead through various plantings to the stream and to a sheltered overlook where you can see deep into the valley and as far as Kahului Bay.

Lahaina: Model for Historic Preservation

Highway 30 takes you from Wailuku across Maui's narrow isthmus to Maalaea Bay and then up the coast to Lahaina, now a "lively relic from Hawaii's turbulent past," according to James C. Luckey, executive director of the Lahaina Restoration Foundation. Luckey should know. The foundation he directs has been responsible for the renovation and maintenance of so many historic structures in and around town that a folder with a map and walking tour outlined on it is necessary for anyone who wants to really see Lahaina. It's available free from any of the Foundation's museums, such as Baldwin House or the Brig Carthaginian. Numbered sites on the map are keyed to signs that help you locate structures.

Between 1852 and 1859 as many as 100 whaling ships at a time stood off Lahaina while their crews raised various kinds of havoc ashore. Life for sailors on a whaling ship was anything but easy. Even Herman Melville, author of *Moby Dick,* once jumped ship for three days in Lahaina.

On shore the crews often ran amok of the Christian morality brought to the islands by New England Protestant missionaries. Evidence of those tumultuous days is well preserved in the 33-acre portion of Lahaina designated a National Historic Landmark in 1966.

Among more interesting sites on the Foundation's walking tour is the Baldwin House Museum, home of a medical missionary to the Islands from 1836 to 1868; the Carthaginian, a square-rigged sailing ship in Lahaina Harbor; and Hale Paahao, the prison where errant sailors were kept in irons.

Also of interest is Lahainaluna School, the oldest school west of the Rockies, which celebrated its 150th anniversary with fanfare and speeches by well-known graduates in 1981. On the quiet campus, a mile and a half from Lahaina toward Puu Kukui, is another completed Lahaina Restoration Foundation project; Hale Pai, an old printing house now open to the public as a museum. The first American newspaper published west of the Mississippi, *Ka Lama Hawaii,* the "Torch of Hawaii," was printed here in February 1834.

Lahaina was important in pre-western times, too, as the site of a great sacrifical *heiau.* In later times many members of ruling Hawaiian families made Lahaina home. The graves of several can be seen in Wainee Church cemetery.

In addition to its colorful past, Lahaina has two other attractions today. It's the best place on Maui to dine in an open-air restaurant where a spectacular sunset comes free with your meal. It's also a good place to shop for inexpensive gifts to take back home, whether it's a T-shirt that says "Here Today, Gone to Maui," or a piece of original art purchased during the Sunday display by artists under Lahaina's enormous banyan tree. (This tree was planted in 1873 to commemorate the 50th anniversary of the arrival of Protestant missionaries on Maui.)

Kaanapali: Successful Super Resort

On a 1,200-acre site fronting two long white sand beaches north of Lahaina is a resort development first thought about in the 1950s by board members of Lahaina's Pioneer Sugar Mill, a subsidiary of Amfac Inc., and opened to guests first in 1962. Today there are seven condominiums and six hotels, surrounded by two championship golf courses, a shopping center and a narrow-gauge train to ride at Kaanapali Beach Resort. Among the hotels is one with a whale-shaped swimming pool and another with a hair-raising water slide. Whaler's Village and Museum shopping complex is probably the only shopping mall in the world with a 40-foot whale skeleton hung over a reflecting pool outside and a museum with more than 100 whaling artifacts inside. Kaanapali Beach Resort, a successful project of one of Hawaii's old "Big Five" companies, is now a model for similar projects in Hawaii and around the world.

A jitney bus stops at all hotels at the resort to take you to Whaler's Village and Museum and to the only working railroad in Hawaii. Guests can ride into Lahaina on the Lahaina, Kaanapali & Pacific Railroad, which runs on a 36-inch, narrow-gauge track formerly used by the Kahului Railroad. Part of the route followed by the train is on the roadbed used to haul sugarcane to and from Pioneer Mill from the 1880s until 1952. The steam engine Anaka pulls the train through sugarcane fields and over a wooden trestle as a conductor sings about sights along the way. Depar-

tures from the Puukolii Station at the north end of Kaanapali begin at
9:35 A.M. daily.

Napili and Kapalua: Beautiful Bays

North of Kaanapali the coastline is fronted by white sand beaches for
a long way. The road just north of Kaanapali skirts quiet condominiums
near fine beaches at Honokowai and Kahana before coming to Napili Bay.
Here several pleasant low-rise vacation condominiums are packed shoulder to shoulder around a beautiful swimming and snorkeling beach. Further north at Kapalua Beach is an elegant 750-acre complex originally developed by Maui Land & Pineapple Company. It has a fine hotel, private
villas (some available to vacationers), a tennis garden, and twin golf
courses in a challenging hillside and waterfront layout.

Beyond Kapalua, Highway 30 meanders beside some beautiful beaches,
not all of which are suitable for swimming and none with lifeguards. At
Honolua Bay, an area designated as an underwater marine life conservation district, snorkeling is good along the rocks and reef at the left side
of the bay. This beach is the point from which Hawaii's famed Polynesian
canoe, the *Hokulea,* first set sail on its maiden voyage to Tahiti in 1976.
The paved road ends about two miles farther on at Honokohau. It is possible to drive all the way around the northeast end of the island to Wailuku,
but not in wet weather and not without a four-wheel drive and permission
from your rental car company. Most car firms on the island prefer
that you turn around just beyond Honokohau at a high point where you
can see Haleakala looming in the southwest. If you do make the trip
around this coast by jeep, stop at Kahakuloa village on the coast where
local families still farm taro and live much as they did before the arrival
of westerners in Hawaii. From Kahakuloa to Waihee above Wailuku, it's
a nine-mile drive along high cliffs on an unsurfaced road. This section of
the island is not the place to stop at a beach for a swim, although you
may be tempted to do so.

Maalaea Bay: Baby Boom in Humpbacks

From Kahului it's an eight-mile drive directly across Maui's narrow
isthmus to the shores of Maalaea Bay. During winter many of the world's
remaining humpback whales come down from the North Pacific to breed
and bear their young in this warm, deep, Hawaiian bay. About 400 to 600
humpbacks arrive in Hawaii annually. The Pacific Whale Foundation and
the University of Hawaii are doing research studies with them.

One of the best experiences on Maui is seeing a whale breach or spy
hop (peeking above the surface of the sea), either from the shore or from
an authorized whale-watching boat. Whales are protected in Hawaiian waters and approaching them is carefully regulated so that their normal activity will not be disturbed.

When baby whales are born off the island they measure about 10 to 15
feet in length and do not have much fat. They quickly gain a protective
layer of blubber from their mother's milk—as much as 100 pounds a day.
Eventually they may reach 45 feet and weigh over 40 tons.

Kihei: Beautiful Beaches

Two highways cross Maui's narrow valley between the low flanks of
Puu Kukui and Haleakala. From Kahului, take the southern route, High-

way 350, across green sugarcane fields to the south side of Maalaea Bay. Just as you turn south to start down the coast, you will come to Mai Poina Oe Lau Beach Park. The melodious Hawaiian name means "Forget me not." A memorial plaque in the park pavilion is dedicated to those who have died in recent American wars. At the south end of the park across the street from Kihei's first major resort, the Maui Lu, is a monument to British sea-captain George Vancouver, who went ashore with his men here in 1792 and briefly explored the island. J. Gordon Gibson, the original owner of the Maui Lu, designed and erected the monument to commemorate the visit.

The rest of the drive south on Kihei Road passes beach park after beach park, including a trio with the same name, Kamaole I, II, and III. Kihei is the condominium capital of Maui, if not of Hawaii. Packed in and around these beautiful swimming beaches are more than 45 condominiums, many of them high-rises. Rates at most are moderate, which makes this a popular destination for families. If you should see the red Canadian maple leaf flag here and there, don't be surprised. Kihei attracts many Canadians who come down from their cold country to stay a month or so to soak up the slow Maui sun.

Wonderful Wailea

Down the road from Kihei is Wailea, Alexander & Baldwin's tasteful 1,450-acre resort. Only two luxury hotels and a number of low-rise condominiums are situated on this acreage, which is three times the size of Waikiki. Its spaciousness is further enhanced by sloping green lawns and lots of coconut palms. No fewer than five beaches—Keawakapu, Mokapu, Ulua, Wailea, and Polo—front the resort. All are good swimming and sunbathing beaches. When Wailea was being built in the 1970s, A & B, Maui's largest employer, and its co-developer, Northwestern Mutual Life Insurance Company of Milwaukee, were required to put in public parking and facilities for each beach. They did so embracing wholeheartedly the spirit of a law in effect in Hawaii since the time of King Kamehameha, that beaches belong to all the people. As a result it's much easier to find public beach parking at Wailea than at other major resorts on the island. Additionally, Wailea resort has two championship golf courses, 11 paved and three grass tennis courts, and a Town Center where art exhibits often are held. For a nice change of pace, ask at Stouffer Wailea Beach Hotel for a walking tour map of the hotel's lush tropical garden. This is also the spot where one of the best half-day snorkeling cruises in Hawaii takes off to tiny Molokini Island offshore. (Call ahead to Ocean Activities Center, which maintains an office in a Wailea condominium.) Off this coast you frequently can see whales in season, or hear them if you're under water. The islands of Kahoolawe and Lanai are also clearly visible offshore.

Makena and Beyond

South of Wailea, at Makena Bay, giant Seibu Corporation of Japan has built a resort on 1,000 acres. An 18-hole golf course was completed in 1981, condominiums marketed for $350,000 and up have been built, and a 300-unit luxury resort, the Maui Prince, opened in 1986.

A four-wheel drive vehicle is recommended for access to two interesting points beyond Makena—Ahihi-Kinau Natural Area Reserve and La Perouse Bay, where the state of Hawaii eventually plans to build a park that will include Hawaiian archeological sites in the area. Ahihi Bay and tidal pools atop Cape Kinau, a squarish butt of coast created in 1790 by Maui's last lava flow, contain rare larval fish, corals, and other unusual species of marine life protected from harvesting.

The first westerner known to have set foot on Maui was a Frenchman, the Comte de la Perouse, a skilled navigator who went ashore with a landing party on May 30, 1786 at the bay that now bears his name. This is a popular site with local shoreline fishermen, but it is not for swimmers because of strong currents and coral-strewn beaches. The navigable road ends at La Perouse Bay.

Upcountry Maui: Paniolos and Proteas

A duchess and a prince live in cool Kula, the name islanders give to this upland area on the higher slopes of Haleakala that includes a town of the same name, a state park in the middle of a rain forest, and a famous rodeo town. The duchess, the prince, and their assorted relatives actually are the names given to varieties of *proteas,* the exotic plant grown so successfully in the volcanic soil and cool climate of upcountry Maui. Longlasting proteas make excellent gifts to take home, since many varieties retain their beauty for months as dried blooms. While proteas are more beautiful than the other well-known Kula agricultural product, they have not replaced Maui onions in popularity. The sweet Maui onions sold in Hawaii's airports for visitors to take home invariably are Kula onions. Other notables who thrive in Kula are well-known citizens of Hawaii who find the cool climate ideal for the site of a vacation or retirement home.

Kula may be reached on Highways 37 or 377. At the little community of Pukalani on Highway 37, Highway 400 branches off northeast to Maui's cow and cowboy town, Makawao. On July 4th every year Makawao is packed with residents and visitors who've come to see Hawaii's *paniolos* compete in the state's best known rodeo. For the rest of the year Makawao is a sleepy, but photogenic country town with some interesting local shops to explore. Farther up Highway 37 at Pulehu is Kula's area landmark, the octagonal Church of the Holy Ghost. It was built by Portuguese settlers in 1897; lovely gilded bas-reliefs and an altar shipped around the Horn grace its interior.

At Pulehu, take Highway 377, a short loop road, to visit Kula Botanical Garden, which has more than 700 kinds of plants. If you have a four-wheel drive vehicle, Polipoli Road branches off just beyond the garden to twist upward seven miles through stands of eucalyptus, Norfolk pines, and redwoods to the 6,476-foot summit of Polipoli cinder cone. From the summit the sweeping view of the West Maui coast, and of the islands of Lanai, Molokai, and Kahoolawe in the sea beyond it is well worth the spine-jarring drive.

Ulupalakua Ranch: Maui's Wine Country

Beyond Kula, Highway 37 continues on for about 10 miles to Ulupalakua Ranch, an 18,000-acre working cattle and sheep ranch on the slopes of Haleakala Crater. Ulupalakua Ranch got its start in the 1850s when a former whaling ship captain, James Makee, grew sugarcane here. Today the ranch lands are diversified. In place of sugarcane there are vineyards of Carnelian grapes. Wines produced here as a result of a partnership formed more than a decade ago between Ulupalakua Ranch owner C.

Pardee Erdman and Napa Valley-bred Emil Tedeschi include a pink champagne and the 1985 Maui Nouveau. Tedeschi Winery, housed in a cool, thick-walled former prison built in 1856, has a tasting room and tours. Not far from it are the ruins of Makee Sugar Mill dating from 1878.

Highway 31 continues as an inland road paralleling Maui's southeast coast for a while before coming down to the shoreline en route to Hana. It's a seldom-traveled, though view-filled, 35-mile drive in this direction and probably is not advisable unless you plan to spend the night in Hana. Points of interest worth exploring along the way are described in the section on Hana.

Haleakala: House of the Sun (W/HANA BY HELICOPTER)

One good way to appreciate one of the most unusual volcanic formations in the world is to get down into it. If you're agile and have on good trudging shoes, from just beyond Haleakala Visitor Center walk a short way down steep Sliding Sands Trail until your head is below the crater's rim. From here, fantastically colored slopes in mixed hues of rust, red, brown, gray, and yellow stretch before you. Suddenly the Hawaiian legend about how the House of the Sun was created seems logical. Angered because his mother's bark cloth took too long to dry, the Polynesian demigod Maui snared the sun with a lasso to slow it down. The fused sands of Haleakala Crater were shaped when the sun slowed down a little too much at first.

The best time to visit is usually in the morning, or on one of many clear days during the year. Before leaving call the park's hotline, 572–7749, to hear a recorded message about the day's weather conditions. Whether you go in the morning or afternoon, take a warm jacket, as the temperature at the summit may get as low as 14°, cold for Hawaii.

From Kahului, the 26-mile drive to the entrance of Haleakala National Park takes about an hour and a half. You can take Puulehu Road, Highway 377, to Kula. From here, switchback Highway 378 gradually climbs through pastures and low-lying clouds. At the entrance there is a $3 fee for vehicles and $1 fee for those on foot.

Just inside the park entrance a side road leads to Hosmer Grove, a picnic, rest, and campground area surrounded by trees that thrive in the cool atmosphere, including eucalyptus, cedar, juniper, spruce, and Indian deodar.

Park headquarters is about a mile beyond the entrance at 7,030 feet. Here rangers provide help in planning camping and hiking trips into the crater. Pick up a free map guide to sites in Haleakala.

From headquarters it's a 10-mile drive to visitor centers at the summit. On the way are the entrance (or exit) to Halemauu Trail, which crosses the crater floor, and two overlooks, Leleiwi at 8,800 feet and Kalahaku at 9,324 feet. If you are at the overlooks in late afternoon when there is some mist and clouds in the crater, you may be able to see a rare phenomenon, the Specter of the Brocken, your own shadow projected against the clouds within a circular rainbow.

Take the short side road to Kalahaku Overlook to see a garden of silverswords, an extraordinary-looking plant related to the sunflower, and only found here. Silverswords are short, round, spike-covered plants when they are young, aged four to 20 years. At maturity they send up a single six to eight-foot stalk covered with up to 100 brilliant yellow and purple blossoms, a startling sight. After about a week the blossoms fade, seeds for new plants fall to the volcanic soil where they seem to thrive, and the original plant dies.

At Haleakala Visitor Center, at 9,745 feet, exhibits explain the geological formation and features of the crater. From the center it's a half-mile drive farther up to Puu Ulaula Visitor Center, a shelter at the actual 10,023-foot summit, where on a clear day you may get a panoramic view of Maui and the islands beyond it, including Oahu.

Beyond the center is Science City, not open to visitors, where astronomers and engineers from the Universities of Michigan and Hawaii, the U.S. Air Force, and the North American Air Defense Command carry out missile tracking, space and light refracting studies, and operate a satellite tracking station.

More than 30 miles of trails are maintained in 27,350-acre Haleakala National Park, which includes an eight-mile strip of land extending through Kipahulu Valley to the east coast of the island below Hana. Part of the lower region of the park is accessible from Hana.

Three cabins at different points on the crater floor are available to hikers and campers by lottery when reservations are made 90 days in advance. Only two consecutive nights are allowed in any one cabin. Kapalaoa, Paliku, and Holua cabins each accommodate 12 people in wooden bunk beds. Bring your own sleeping bag. A wood-burning stove with a store of pressed logs in each is a much welcome item during Haleakala's very cold nights. With a permit gotten at park headquarters, you may also camp outside at Holu and Paliku, but you'll want a down sleeping bag that covers your head.

A good introductory exploring trip for those who don't hike all the time is down Sliding Sands Trail and northwest across the crater floor on Ka Moa O Pele Trail to Holua Cabin, leaving plenty of time to explore Pele's Paint Pot, Pele's Pig Pen (a spatter vent), and Silversword Loop en route. After a night spent in the cabin, you can hike out on Halemauu Trail up the cliff side and back up the highway. Sliding Sands Trail is too steep for the return trip for most people. Overnight trips are also recommended for exploring trails to the northeast side of the crater. At Paliku you'll find a small rain forest of native trees and ferns. Those with plenty of time and experience can arrange to hike from here out Kaupo Gap through the east end of the park.

A pleasant and less rigorous way to explore the crater floor is on a guided horseback trip. Pony Express Tours conducts several.

A popular Haleakala trip is a sunrise visit, available from several companies that operate van tours on the island. Depending on where you are staying, you should be ready to leave at around 3 A.M.

Heavenly Hana

Tiny Hana, population 700, on Maui's eastern shore, is a special place. A bit of old Hawaii thrives in the pleasant community where everyone seems a little friendlier than elsewhere in Hawaii.

It's best to arrange to stay overnight in Hana if you can, because the 50-mile drive along the coast from Kahului deserves and demands exploring and pausing time. At first you drive past beaches and through sleepy country communities—Spreckelsville, Lower Paia, and Pauwela. If you have plenty of time, take a side trip up to Mama's Fish House in Paia for lunch where you can order your entree prepared in one of six ways. Farther on, be sure to watch for windsurfers at Hookipa Beach Park. Near the tiny communities of Huelo and Kailua the road begins to wind in and out of no fewer than 33 little gulches packed with ferns, breadfruit, guava, bamboo, and a tangle of tropical trees and plants often situated beside small waterfalls. Look for the giant leaves of the *ape* plant, some of them four or five feet wide. If the air seems heady with a hypnotically fragrant odor, it's probably ginger in bloom. Watch for the fragile pale yellow and white flowers protruding in bunches from green corn-like stalks along the road.

Good places to stop briefly on the way are Kuamahina State Park, a shady spot on a cliff above Honomanu black sand beach about 25 miles from Kahului, and Keanae Lookout above a peninsula neatly laid out with taro patches cultivated as they have been for 600 years. If you still have plenty of time, a side road here leads to the village of Keanae, which will give you a sense of the peaceful life enjoyed by East Maui residents. Similar side roads over the next 10 miles lead to the villages of Wailua and Nahiku, where tiny churches and other bucolic settings make good photographic subjects.

Four miles outside of Hana a fourth side road you should take leads to Waianapanapa State Park, where you'll find two lava tube caves near the sea that are filled with water. They are said to be connected by those courageous enough to dive with lights in the cold water. A Hawaiian legend probably based on fact is told about this site. A cruel chief suspected his wife was having an affair with her younger brother. She hid in Waianapanapa Cave but the shadow of a feather staff waved by her attendant betrayed her whereabouts and the chief killed them both. Now, it is said, you can hear her sobs echoing in the cave. In April the water in the caves runs red, which some say is her blood, but others know to be newborn brine shrimp. Walking trails and cabins for campers are maintained in the park.

Hawaiians, part-Hawaiians, and a few famous mainlanders live in quiet Hana Town, at the base of a valley on the eastern flank of Haleakala. The town has a distinctive history in that it has been inhabited by Hawaiians for many centuries, as stone terraces in the valley reveal. Much of the surrounding acreage is now used as grazing land for the Hereford cattle of 4,500-acre Hana Ranch. Hana is the location of the luxurious Hotel Hana-Maui.

Everyone still goes to the Hasegawa General Store, where you can get a bumper sticker that's better than any far more expensive designer-initialed product. Here shelves overflow with everything anyone could possibly need in the remote community.

At 100-year-old Wananalua Church, services are conducted in Hawaiian and English. Part of the thick lava wall used to construct this church over a 20-year period came from a nearby Hawaiian *heiau*.

Atop Kauiki Head, the cliff that guards Hana Bay, you can search for smooth stones once used in slingshot battles between the warriors of Maui's chief Kahekili and those of Kamehameha. You can also get a good grasp of this area's insular history at the Hana Cultural Center.

Kipahulu

From Hana, Highway 31 continues 10 miles to Kipahulu, the eastern edge of Haleakala National Park. On the way stop at gray sand Hamoa

Beach, where swimming is usually safe inshore. At Wailua Cove, just before Kipahulu, twin waterfalls cascade hundreds of feet over the cliffs of
Haleakala when Maui has had plenty of rain. Unfortunately, in the last
couple of years dry weather has reduced the falls to a trickle. A concrete
cross here is dedicated to Helio, a Hawaiian convert to Catholicism who
preached his new faith and converted hundreds in the 1840s in spite of
a law against the new faith.

Three miles south inside the park is one of Maui's loveliest sites, Oheo
Gulch, which also is called Seven Pools. Seven large pools, and a number
of small ones—the result of an unusual volcanic flow—stairstep down to
the sea. When there's ample water on Maui, waterfalls cascade downward
from one pool into another. A path descends along one bank to accessible
pools for swimming and picnicking. Rangers lead walks and hikes in the
park throughout the year.

The paved road ends at Kipahulu Ranch. Near here look for restored
Palapala Hoomau Church, a short walk away from the road. Among famous 20th-century personages who found peace in Hana was Charles A.
Lindbergh, whose gravestone is in the clifftop Hoomau Church graveyard.
It carries the Old Testament quotation beginning, "If I take the wings of
the morning, and dwell in the uttermost parts of the sea," which seems
as fitting for the site as for the man.

Kipahulu to Ulupalakua Ranch

It's an eight-mile drive on a gravel road between Kipahulu and the town
of Kaupo, which is a base for hikers entering and exiting Halekala National Park. The sea is very close on this road, so close that you should not
drive it if the surf is up. At Kaupo you can explore the ruins of a mission
school and *heiau* near recently restored Huialoha Church. The road hugs
the coastline beyond Kaupo for about eight miles. The view across the
sea may include the Big Island, 30 miles away.

At old Nuu Landing you dip down to the sea where there are village
ruins. From here the road is paved again and swings away from the coast.
The view out to sea is even more spectacular as you rise gradually toward
Ulupalakua Ranch. Kahoolawe, the U.S. military target island and the
semicircle of tiny Molokini Island, are visible in blue seas offshore.

PRACTICAL INFORMATION FOR MAUI

HOW TO GET THERE. Kahului Airport is served by more than 90 flights a day on 9 airlines, including 3 commuter carriers operating small planes. About half that number of daily small-plane flights service the Kapalua-West Maui Airport, which services resort destinations on the island's west side.

American Airlines has arrivals daily from Los Angeles and Dallas, *United Airlines* has direct daily flights from Chicago, Los Angeles, and San Francisco; *Suntrips* flies daily charters from San Francisco aboard Hawaiian Air; *Ward Air* operates weekly flights from Canada.

From Honolulu to Kahului *Aloha Airlines* has 30 daily flights aboard Boeing 737s; *Hawaiian Air* offers a varying but comparable number aboard jets and props.

Three commuter airlines also serve the island. *Air Molokai* has 3 daily flights from Honolulu aboard Cessnas. *Princeville Airways* has four flights a day from Honolulu.

Nonstop flying time between Honolulu and Kahului is 18 minutes. *Gray Line Hawaii* runs a shuttle between Kahului Airport and Kaanapali Beach Resort for $5 (reservations only). Taxis from Kahului to resorts on the western side of the island are $20 and up. Royal Hawaiian Air services Hana Airport with 5 flights a day in peak season.

ACCOMMODATIONS. Maui's many hotels and condominiums range in type from the atmospheric Pioneer Inn in historic Lahaina to several very luxurious resorts at Kapalua, Kaanapali, and Wailea. A brand-new Westin Maui is due to open in Kaanapali in August 1987. Package arrangements offered at resorts in cooperation with airlines and tour operators may include peak season (winter) supplement charges. Most major credit cards are accepted at hotels (check when making reservations). The majority of accommodations, whether in hotel or condominium, are situated along the island's sunny, western coast. Several separate pocket destinations on the island offer a choice in hotels and condominiums and common use of semi-private beaches, championship golf courses, tennis stadiums, shopping centers, and other amenities. Among them are Kaanapali Beach Resort, Kapalua, and Wailea Resort.

Price categories based on double occupancy are $135–$1,400, *Super Deluxe;* $80–$134, *Deluxe;* $60–$79, *Expensive;* $40–$59, *Moderate;* $25–$39, *Inexpensive.*

Super Deluxe

Hotel Hana-Maui. Reserve direct: Box 8 (I), Hana, Maui, HI 96713 (in Hawaii call 248–8211 or on the Mainland, 800–421–0000). This 80-room luxury retreat in the middle of a 4,500-acre working ranch and its nearby Hana Ranch town center have just undergone a $16 million renovation to add touches like French windows and trellised verandas to guest rooms, and a new porte cochere and arts and crafts gallery to the main building. There are 22 double-unit, oceanview Garden Cottages, suites with private lanais, standard, superior, and deluxe rooms. There's a swimming pool and pitch and putt golf course. Guests have access to a secluded gray sand beach where Friday night luaus attended by members of the surrounding Hawaiian community are held. There are moonlight wagon and trail rides and barbecues, too. Rates include meals. Access is by small plane or, less conveniently, by 40-mile drive from Kahului, 30 miles of it along a very winding, but waterfall- and garden-banked road.

Hyatt Regency Maui. 200 Nohea Kai Dr., Lahaina, Maui, HI 96761 (in Hawaii 667–7474, on the Mainland 800–228–9000). A glittering and exciting beachfront playground surrounds this 815-room luxury resort. There's an art gallery and many elegant shops, and a 130-foot waterslide that leads to huge twin swimming pools with a Grotto Bar between them that's accessible only by swimming under a waterfall. Restaurants include the award-winning Swan Court, Lahaina Provision Company, the Pavillion, and Sunset Terrace. Five tennis courts, a health club, regular excursions on a sailing yacht and catamaran, hobie cat and laser rentals, snorkeling, and scuba lessons. Golf on Kaanapali's 2 courses.

Kapalua Bay Hotel & Villas. One Bay Dr., Kapalua, Maui, HI 96761 (in Hawaii 669–5656, on the Mainland 800–367–8000). This very tasteful 750-acre luxury resort with a total of 327 available units, 194 of them in a world-class hotel, is becoming internationally known for its golf and tennis tournaments. Spacious rooms at the Kapalua Bay Hotel feature walk-in closets and "his and her" bath units. There are 2 dining rooms in the hotel—The Dining Room and The Plantation Veranda—and one on the beach—The Bay Club. Complete tennis facilities with 10 courts; 2 Arnold Palmer-designed golf courses. EP rates.

Maui Marriott Resort. Reserve direct: 100 Nohea Kai Dr., Lahaina, Maui, HI 96761 (in Hawaii 667–1200, on the Mainland 800–228–9290). Marriott's flagship luxury hotel in Hawaii has 720 rooms in 2 9-story wings with a connecting promenade housing many shops, 4 restaurants, and 3 cocktail lounges. On the ocean in the southern part of Kaanapali Beach Resort, the hotel has tennis courts, a swimming pool, and access to the 2 championship Kaanapali golf courses.

Maui Prince. 5400 Makena Alanui, Kihei, HI 96753 (874–1111, 800–321–MAUI). On one of Maui's finest and sunniest beaches, this elegant, activity-oriented resort has 300 rooms all facing the ocean, lots of pampering and elegant relaxation. Four restaurants, championship golf course.

Stouffer Wailea Beach Resort. 3550 Wailea Alanui Dr., Wailea, Maui, HI 96753 (879–4900 or 800–468–3571). A serene atmosphere prevails in this low-rise, 350-room hotel at Wailea where sloping lawns roll down before it to 5 good swimming beaches. Open-air dining is downstairs in The Palm Court, and award-winning dining is upstairs at Raffles restaurant. Guests have use of a swimming pool with whirlpool, Wailea's tennis courts and clubhouse, and 2 challenging championship golf courses, the Blue and the Orange. Besides excellent ocean swimming, wading, and sunbathing, there are excursions to tiny offshore Molokini Island where the snorkeling is among the best in Hawaii.

The Westin Maui. Reserve direct: 1777 Ala Moana Blvd., Honolulu, HI 96815 (942–8855, 800–228–3000). This $70-million hotel has 9 restaurants and cocktail lounges, 5 swimming pools with waterfalls and man-made slides built on different levels around a central island, a European-style health club, a shopping arcade, and $2 million worth of fine art. There are 762 rooms, including 28 suites and 43 Royal Beach Club units where guests are pampered with a multitude of extra services and amenities.

Deluxe

Hoholani Condo Resort. 4401 Honoapiilani Rd., Lahaina, Maui, HI 96761 (in Hawaii 669–8021, on the Mainland 800–367–5032). Has 22 2-bedroom units with kitchens, maid service on request, on the beach at Kahana Bay. Pool, shop, and 3-day minimum.

Honokeana Cove. 5255 Lower Honoapiilani Rd., Lahaina, Maui, HI 96761 (669–6441). Has 36 1-bedroom, 2-bedroom, and townhouse units on the ocean; swimming pool, weekly maid service, minimum 3-day stay.

Kaanapali Alii. 50 Nohea Kai Dr., Kaanapali, Maui, HI 96761 (in Hawaii 667–1400, on the Mainland 800–367–6090). A luxury beachfront condominium at Kaanapali Beach Resort with 264 air-conditioned 1- and 2-bedroom apartments available. Swimming pools, tennis courts, access to Kaanapali golf courses.

Kaanapali Beach Hotel. 2525 Kaanapali Pkwy., Lahaina, Maui, HI 96761 (in Hawaii 661–0011, on the Mainland 800–227–4700). All 431 rooms in this waterfront Kaanapali Beach Resort hotel are oceanview. Water sport activities. Whale-shaped swimming pool. Restaurants, cocktail lounges. Golf on Kaanapali courses. Optional European Plan rates.

Kaanapali Plantation. 150 Puukolii Rd., Lahaina, Maui, HI 96761 (661–4446). A 62-unit condominium ¼ mile from the beach at Kaanapali Beach Resort. Swimming pool, tennis court, minimum 3-day stay.

Kaanapali Shores Resort. 100 Kaanapali Shores Pl., Lahaina, Maui, HI 96761 (in Hawaii 667–2211, on the Mainland 800–367–5124). Luxury, 463-unit beachfront condominium in a 9-floor complex on Maui's northwest shore. Not part of Kaanapali Beach Resort in spite of its name. Whirlpool, swimming pool, tennis courts, restaurant, and cocktail lounge. Studios, 1- and 2-bedroom units.

Kahana Sunset. Box 10219, Lahaina, Maui, HI 96761 (669–8011 or 800–426–0494). Oceanfront at Kahana. 79 1-bedroom, 2-bedroom, and executive units. Swimming pool.

Kahana Villa. 4242 Lower Honoapiilani Hwy., Lahaina, Maui, HI 96761 (in Hawaii 669–5613, on the Mainland 800–367–6046). This condominium on the beach at Kahana Bay has 92 units with ceiling fans, a restaurant, cocktail lounge, tennis court, and swimming pool.

Kapalua Villas. One Bay Dr., Kapalua, HI 96741 (in Hawaii 669–5656, on the Mainland 800–367–8000). Vacation condos on the beach. Swimming pools, tennis courts, golf.

Lahaina Shores. 475 Front St., Lahaina, Maui, HI 96761 (in Hawaii 661–4835, on the Mainland 800–367–2972). There are 150 condominium units in this property with a surprising 20th-century rendition of an 1880s facade on the southern side of Lahaina. Air-conditioning, swimming pool, tennis court, and—all-important in crowded Lahaina—parking.

Mahana. 110 Kaanapali Shores Pl., Lahaina, Maui, HI 96761 (in Hawaii 661–8751, on the Mainland 800–367–5124). About 150 units are available in this beachfront condominium on Maui's northwest shore. Swimming pool, tennis courts, minimum 3-day stay.

Maui Eldorado Resort. 2661 Kekaa Dr., Lahaina, Maui, HI 96761 (in Hawaii 661–0021, on the Mainland 800–367–2967). This is one of the more seasoned condominium resorts at Kaanapali. It abuts the golf course. 120 hotel units available. Swimming pool, maid service on request, golf on Kaanapali course; shuttle to beach with private cabanas.

Maui Hill. 2881 S. Kihei Rd., Kihei, Maui, HI 96753 (879–6321 or 800–367–2363). A well-equipped 140-unit condominium next to the Wailea golf courses. Swimming pool, tennis court, maid service every other day.

Maui Inter-Continental Wailea. Box 779, Wailea, Maui, HI 96753 (in Hawaii 879–1922, on the Mainland 800–367–2960). This 600-room hotel offers many amenities, the best of which is its prime location on the beach at Wailea. Restaurants include the award-winning La Perouse. Three swimming pools. Jogging map. Classes in scuba-diving, snorkeling, Hawaiian arts; lots of ocean activities.

Maui Kaanapali Villas. 2805 Honoapiilani Hwy., Lahaina, Maui, HI 96761 (667–7791 or 800–367–7040). The 200 refurbished condominium units in semi-private 2-story units at Kaanapali Beach Resort date from the Resort's early days when they were part of the Royal Lahaina Hotel. Access to resort activities; minimum stay 3 nights.

Napili Kai Beach Club. 5900 Honoapiilani Rd., Lahaina, Maui, HI 96761 (in Hawaii 669–6271, on the Mainland 800–367–5030). This is the nicest of the apartment hotels clustered around lovely and eminently swimmable Napili Bay on Maui's northwest coast. The total of 136 units each comes equipped with a kitchen and has a lanai facing the beach. One-bedroom units are available. Four swimming pools, shuffleboard, putting, tennis, and a huge whirlpool. Entertainment 6 nights a week and full dining service daily in The Teahouse of the August Moon.

Napili Point. 5295 Honoapiilani Hwy., Lahaina, Maui, HI 96761 (in Hawaii 669–9222, on the Mainland 800–367–5124). A condominium with 84 hotel units on Napili Bay. Two swimming pools.

Papakea Beach Resort. 3543 Honoapiilani Hwy., Lahaina, Maui, HI 96761 (in Hawaii 669–4848, on the Mainland 800–367–5637). There are 364 units in this well-managed beachside condominium just north of Kaanapali Beach Resort. Tennis courts, swimming pool, putting green. Studios, 1- and 2-bedroom units, and garden suites.

Royal Lahaina Hotel. 2780 Kekaa Dr., Lahaina, Maui, HI 96761 (in Hawaii 661–3611, on the Mainland 800–227–4700). The atmosphere in this 514-room newly renovated hotel at Kaanapali Beach Resort is laid-back South Seas by design. Royal Court Shopping Arcade. Four restaurants offering steak, seafood, and elegant dining. Tennis courts, swimming pools. Golf on Kaanapali's courses. Standard, superior, deluxe rooms, cottages, and suites.

Sheraton Maui Hotel. Kaanapali Beach, Lahaina, Maui, HI 96761 (in Hawaii 661–0031, on the Mainland 800–325–3535). Perched atop and down the side of Kaanapali Beach Resort's best known landmark, Black Rock, this 503-room hotel had all of its rooms completely renovated in 1985. The garden, swimming pools, cocktail lounge, and dining rooms are on the top of the hotel overlooking the beach. The lobby is at the bottom of the cliff; elevators go up to rooms. Sunset reenactment of a Hawaiian king's dive off this once-sacred cliff followed by a spectacular Polynesian show in the Discovery Room. *SNORKELING MEHT BELOW HOTEL*

Wailea Condominiums and Villas. 3750 Wailea Alanui, Wailea, Maui, HI 96753 (in Hawaii 879–1595, on the Mainland 800–367–5246). A total of 598 condominium units in 3 separate complexes are available, many on the beach or golf course. All the amenities of Wailea, from golf to tennis, are available.

The Whaler on Kaanapali Beach. 2481 Kaanapali Pkwy., Lahaina, Maui, HI 96761 (in Hawaii 661–4861, on the Mainland 800–367–7052). There are 360 units available for guests in this twin-towered beachfront condominium at Kaanapali Beach Resort. All units are air-conditioned. Tennis court, swimming pool; golf on Kaanapali's courses. Maid service on request. Minimum stay 3 days.

Expensive

Aston's Maui Lu Resort. 575 S. Kihei Rd., Kihei, Maui, HI 96753 (in Hawaii 879–5881, from the Mainland 800–367–5124). A Polynesian-style low-rise across from the beach at Kihei. 170 units; many with kitchens. Swimming pool, tennis courts. Longhouse restaurant and bar with nightly entertainment.

Coconut Inn. Box 10517, Napili, Maui, HI 96761 (in Hawaii 669–5712, on the Mainland 800–367–8006). A 41-unit condominium of studios, 1-bedrooms, and loft units with access to Napili Bay. Swimming pool.

Hale Kai Condominium Apartments. 3691 Honoapiilani Rd., Lahaina, Maui, HI 96761 (669–6333). On the beach at Honokawai north of Kaanapali, with 40 units, a pool, maid service on request. Minimum 3-day stay.

Hana Bay Vacation Rentals. Box 318, Hana, Maui, HI 96713 (248–7727). Eight private oceanfront homes in Hana. Maid service on request.

Hana Kai Resort Apartments. Box 38, Hana, Maui, HI 96713 (248–8426). On the water between the airport and village. 19 studio and 1-bedroom units with kitchens, no telephones.

Kamaole Sands. 2695 S. Kihei Rd., Kihei, Maui, HI 96753 (in Hawaii 879–0666, from the Mainland 800–367–6046). Across the road from Kamaole Beach. 440 1-, 2-, and 3-bedroom units. Swimming pool. Tennis courts. Whirlpool.

Kanai A Nalu. 2145 Wells St., Suite 205, Wailuku, Maui, HI 96793 (242–4466 or 800–367–5234). An 80-unit condominium with 2-bedroom suites for up to 6 people on the beach at Maalaea. Swimming pool. Five-day minimum.

Kihei Surfside Resort. 2936 S. Kihei Rd., Kihei, Maui, HI 96753 (in Hawaii 879–1488, from the Mainland 800–367–5240). Oceanfront with 83 1- and 2-bedroom hotel units. No telephones. Swimming pool. Maid service every 4th day. Three-day minimum.

Luana Kai. 940 S. Kihei Rd., Kihei, Maui, HI 96753 (in Hawaii 879–1268, from the Mainland 800–367–7042). Nicely managed condominium with 114 1-, 2-, and 3-bedroom rental units. Tennis court. Swimming pool. Putting service. Maid service every 3rd day.

Makani Kai-Maui. 2960 S. Kihei Rd., Kihei, Maui, HI 96753 (in Hawaii 879–1561, from the Mainland 800–525–2025). A 160-unit condominium on the beach at Kihei. Restaurant, shops, cocktail lounge, swimming pool. Bedroom (studio), 1-, and 2-bedroom units.

Makani Sands. 3765 Lower Honoapiilani Rd., Lahaina, Maui, HI 96761 (669–8223). On the beach at Honokowai. 30 1- to 3-bedroom hotel units. Pool. Weekly maid service. Three-day minimum.

The Mauian Hotel. 5441 Honoapiilani Rd., Lahaina, Maui, HI 96761 (669–6205 or 800–367–5034). A 46-unit low-rise hotel on the beach at Napili Bay. Each unit has a kitchenette and private lanai. The beach is steps away from this well-managed little hotel with a friendly staff. Freshwater swimming pool. Shuffleboard, croquet, maid service. Three-day minimum.

Maui Kai. 106 Kaanapali Shores, Lahaina, Maui, HI 96761 (in Hawaii 661–0002; from the Mainland 800–367–5635). A condominium with 80 air-conditioned kitchen units for rentals on the beach above Kaanapali Beach Resort. Swimming pool. Twice weekly maid service. Minimum stay 2 days.

Maui Sunset. 1032 Kihei Rd., Kihei, Maui, HI 96753 (in Hawaii 879–9272, from the Mainland 800–367–2954). A popular beachfront condominium with 225 units, including suites and studios. Swimming pool.

Napili Shores Resort. 5315 Honoapiilani Hwy., Lahaina, Maui, HI 96761 (in Hawaii 669–8061, from the Mainland 800–367–6046). On Kaelelii Point overlooking Napili Bay, this well-managed condominium has 107 studios and 1-bedroom units with kitchens and ceiling fans. Two swimming pools, putting green, Orient Express restaurant.

Napili Surf Beach Resort. 50 Napili Pl., Lahaina, Maui, HI 96761 (669–8002). On Napili Bay with 53 studios and 1-bedroom kitchen units. Two swimming pools, shuffleboard.

Polynesian Shores. 3975 Honoapiilani Hwy., Lahaina, Maui, HI 96761 (669–6065). This small condominium on the beach at Mahinahina north of Kaanapali has 52 1- and 2-bedroom rental units with kitchens and ocean views. Swimming pool, minimum 3-day stay.

Moderate

Haleakala Shores Resort. 2619 S. Kihei Rd., Kihei, Maui, HI 96753 (879–1218). A condominium across the street from the beach with 76 kitchen units. Pool and shuffleboard. No telephones. Three-day minimum.

Hale Kai O Kihei. 1310 Uluniu Rd., Kihei, Maui, HI 96753 (879–2757). A 59-unit condominium on the beach at Kihei with 1- and 2-bedroom rental units with kitchens. Swimming pool. Children 6 or older only. Maid service on request. One week minimum stay.

Hale Ono Loa. 3823 L. Honoapiilani Rd., Lahaina, Maui, HI 96761 (in Hawaii 669–6362, from the Mainland 800–367–5108). Oceanfront at Honokawai with 67 apartment hotel units, all of which have kitchens and lanais. Swimming pool. Weekly maid service. Three-day minimum.

Hono Kai Resort. R.R. 1, Box 389, Wailuku, Maui, HI 96793 (in Hawaii 244–7012, from the Mainland 800–367–6084). A 46-unit condominium at Maalaea Village on the beach with 1-, 2-, and 3-bedroom units to rent. Some air-conditioning. Swimming pool. Maid service on request. No phones. Five-day minimum stay.

Kahana Reef. 4471 Honoapiilani Rd., Lahaina, Maui, HI 96761 (669–6491). On the beach at Kahana. 88 kitchen units. Swimming pool.

Kauhale Makai. 2145 Wells St., Suite 205, Wailuku, Maui, HI 96793 (242–4466 or 800–367–5234). A 168-unit condominium at Kihei Beach. Air-conditioning, swimming pools. Four-day minimum summer; five-day minimum winter.

Kealia. 191 N. Kihei Rd., Apt. 104, Kihei, Maui, HI 96753 (879–9159 or 800–367–5222). A 36-unit condominium on the beach at Kihei. Air-conditioned, swimming pool.

Lihi Kai Cottages. 2121 Iliili Rd., Kihei, Maui, HI 96753 (879–2335). 25 studios and 1-bedroom cottages across the street from the beach at Kihei. Three-day minimum.

Maalaea Banyans. 2145 Wells St., Suite 205, Wailuku, Maui, HI 96793 (in Hawaii 242–4466, from the Mainland 800–367–5234). A 76-unit condominium on the ocean at Maalaea. Swimming pool. Five-day minimum.

Makani A Kai. R.R. 1, Box 400, Maalaea Village, Maui, HI 96793 (in Hawaii 244–5627, from the Mainland 800–367–6084). A 24-unit condominium with 17 hotel rental units on the beach at Maalaea. Partial air-conditioning. Swimming pools. Maid service on request. Five-day minimum.

Makani Sands. 3765 Honoapiilani Rd., Lahaina, Maui, HI 96761 (669–8223). On the beach at Honokowai. 30 1- to 3-bedroom hotel units. Pool, weekly maid service. Three-day minimum.

Maui Beach Hotel. 170 Kaahumanu Ave., Kahului, Maui, HI 96732 (in Hawaii 877–0051, from the Mainland 800–367–5004). A 154-unit, 2-level hotel on Kahului Bay run by Hawaiian Pacific Resorts. Air-conditioned. Red Dragon Chinese restaurant and cocktail lounge. Swimming pool. Standard, superior, deluxe, superior deluxe rooms, and Jr. Suite.

Maui Sands. 3559 Lower Honoapiilani Rd., Lahaina, Maui, HI 96761 (in Hawaii 669–4811, from the Mainland 800–367–5037). A 76-unit condominium with 56 1- and 2-bedroom rental units in a quiet setting at Honokowai. Electric kitchens, dishwashers, ceiling fans. Swimming pool. Seven-night minimum winter; four nights summer.

Nani Kai Hale. 73 N. Kihei Rd., Kihei, Maui, HI 96753 (in Hawaii 879–9120, from the Mainland 800–367–6032). A 46-unit condominium on the beach at Kihei with 30 studio, 1- and 2-bedroom rental units. Swimming pool. Three-day minimum.

Napili Village Resort Hotel. 5425 Honoapiilani Rd., Lahaina, Maui, HI 96761 (669–6228 or 800–336–2185). A 28-unit condominium next to the grocery store and a short stroll away from Napili Bay. Swimming pool.

Puamana. Box 515, Lahaina, Maui, HI 96767 (in Hawaii 667–2551, from the Mainland 800–367–5630). A 226-unit condominium apartment complex with 69 hotel rental units with kitchens on a beachfront near Lahaina. Swimming pool, tennis court. Maid service every third day. Three-day minimum.

Shores of Maui. 2075 S. Kihei Rd., Kihei, Maui, HI 96753 (in Hawaii 879–9140, from the Mainland 800–367–8002). A 50-unit condominium at Kihei Beach with 38 1- and 2-bedroom rental units. Swimming pool, tennis court. Three-day minimum.

Inexpensive

Maui Hukilau Hotel. 2222 Kalakaua Ave., Honolulu, HI 96815 (in Hawaii 877–3311, from the Mainland 800–367–7000). A pleasant 2-story hotel on Kahului Bay that is popular with Hawaii residents. All 89 rooms have lanais. Cocktail lounge, dining room, swimming pool. Shopping plaza. A compact rental car with unlimited mileage is available for $10 extra.

Maui Palms. 170 Kaahumanu Ave., Kahului, Maui, HI 96732 (in Hawaii 877–0071, from the Mainland 800–367–5004). A very pleasant 103-unit inn built around a freshwater swimming pool minutes from the airport in Kahului. Hawaiian decorative motifs add to the comfortable meals served on Lanai Terrace overlooking Kahului Bay.

Pioneer Inn. 658 Wharf St., Lahaina, Maui, HI 96761 (661–3636). A 48-room, 2-story hotel in the heart of busy Lahaina overlooking the harbor. Built in 1901, its turn-of-the-century architectural look harks back to the days when Lahaina's liveliness was the result of sailors in port, not tourists. An exciting place to stay. Two restaurants, one with fresh-air seating on the groundfloor deck, and the Whaler's Saloon. Partial air-conditioning. Swimming pool.

Silversword Inn. R.R. 1, Box 469, Kula, Maui, HI 96790 (878–1232). Six attractive chalet-style cottages perched high beside the road on the way to Haleakala Crater. This is cool country at night at 3,300 feet, but a fireside lounge helps. Breakfast and lunch available.

TraveLodge at Lahaina. 888 Wainee St., Lahaina, Maui, HI 96761 (in Hawaii 661–3661, from the Mainland 800–542–6823). A 58-unit, 2-story Polynesian-style property in Lahaina. Swimming pool. Restaurant.

RESTAURANTS Superb dining experiences are possible on Maui, whether it's the quality of the cuisine or the tropical atmosphere that appeals. There are award-winning restaurants as well as those frequented by the rich and famous who so often choose this island for their holidays. Worth trying, too, are the Mom 'n Pop enterprises popular with local residents where two scoops of rice and one of macaroni salad is served with a slab of broiled fish or steak. Dress is generally casual but not too casual; a good Aloha shirt suffices for men in the finest of hotel dining rooms.

We consider $40 and up *Deluxe,* $25–$40 *Expensive,* $15–$25 *Moderate,* and under $15 Inexpensive for a three-course meal for one, excluding tip and beverage. Be sure to call ahead for reservations, especially at restaurants not located within a hotel.

Kapalua-Kaanapali-Lahaina

Swan Court. *Deluxe.* Hyatt Regency Maui, Kaanapali Beach Resort (667–7474). This is dining at its best on Maui for both the food and the setting are superb. Guests at this al fresco dining room in the Hyatt Regency Maui look out on a peaceful lagoon and garden where swans play. The sauteed veal with morel mushrooms, Tiger prawns with black bean sauce, and shrimp bisque flavored with cognac are a few of the entrees that have earned consistent raves from discriminating dinner guests. Lavish breakfast buffet and dinner. Major credit cards.

The Bay Club. *Expensive.* Kapalua Bay Hotel, One Bay Drive, Kapalua (669–8044). Hearty dining at a popular beachside location where seafood is a specialty. Lunch, dinner, cocktails. All major credit cards.

Lokelani. *Expensive.* Maui Marriott Resort, 100 Nohea Kai Drive, Kaanapali Beach Resort (667–1200). Superb salads and the best in fresh seafood selections in a pleasant setting at the Maui Marriott Resort. Try the mahimahi sauteed in herb sauce; order a tossed salad with pepper cream dressing, too. Dinner only. Major credit cards.

Longhi's. *Expensive.* 888 Front Street, Lahaina (667–2288). Among Lahaina's most popular dining spots since 1977. No printed menus; instead waiters recite the daily fare prepared with an Italian touch. Noted for its prawns Amaretto, scallops combination plate and chocolate orange cheesecake, but other dishes are equally tasty. Breakfast, lunch, and dinner. No reservations. Major credit cards.

The Plantation Veranda. *Expensive.* Kapalua Bay Hotel, One Bay Drive, Kapalua (669–8044). Kiawe-broiled *opakapaka* (a delicious local white fish) garnished with macadamia nuts and other entrees prepared in the French manner with the freshest local ingredients are the hallmark of this formal dining spot in the Kapalua Bay Hotel. The wine list includes fine California vintages first introduced to Maui at this hotel. Closed Tues. Dinner and cocktails only. All major credit cards.

Teahouse of the Maui Moon. *Moderate.* Napili Kai Beach Club, 5900 Honoapiilani Rd., Napili Bay (669–6271). This is down-home Maui for the visitor in an open-air dining spot right on the surf. Good French fries and Maui potato chips. Breakfast, lunch, dinner, cocktails. Dancing at night. Major credit cards.

Kimo's Restaurant. *Inexpensive.* 845 Front Street, Lahaina (661–4811). The friendly Hawaiian atmosphere is as good as the fish and steaks served at this popular Front St. restaurant in the heart of Lahaina. Lunch, dinner, and cocktails. Major credit cards.

Wailea

La Perouse. *Deluxe.* Maui Inter-Continental Wailea Hotel, Wailea (879–1922). From a window table in this elegant restaurant in the Maui Inter-Continental Wailea you can see the islands of Lanai and Molokai, but you won't be looking at them much because the superb Continental cuisine focusing on seafood will demand your full attention. The Callaloo crabmeat soup made with coconut milk is a must and any kind of fish entree is bound to be a pleasing choice here. The wilted spinach salad is a satisfying option, too. But by all means leave room for the pastry cart to which no 19th-century dining room in Dresden or Paris could have held a candle. Dinner only. Major credit cards.

Raffles. *Deluxe.* Stouffer Wailea Beach Hotel, Wailea (879–4900). This restaurant doesn't need to borrow an image from Sir Stamford Raffles' namesake in Singapore; it has an atmosphere all its own that's decidedly Mauian. Among the culinary delights are the vegetable tempura and mulligatawny dip appetizer, poached *ono* (mackerel) with ginger and avocado, and noisette of lamb for two with red currant glaze. All-you-can-eat Sunday brunch buffet (you'll want to fill up at the $19.50 price, one of the highest in Hawaii); otherwise, dinner only. Major credit cards.

Paia

Mama's Fish House. *Moderate.* 799 Kaiholo Pl., Paia (579–9672). People drive from miles around to dine here beside the blue Pacific on abalone flown in from Baja California as well as on the freshest of island fish prepared local-style and served with a house teriyaki sauce enhanced with Maui onions and Hana ginger. Try the chilled papaya and coconut soup, too. Sunday brunch, lunch, and dinner daily. Major credit cards.

Kahului

East-West Dining Room. *Moderate.* Maui Palms Hotel, 170 Kaahumanu Ave., Kahului (877–0071). A generous and delicious Japanese teppanyaki buffet is served nightly from 5:30 to 8:30 P.M. in this Maui Palms Hotel dining room. Chefs prepare teriyaki steak, scallops and other items teppanyaki style to your order at the buffet. Popular with local residents. Dinner only. For breakfast and lunch, there are several other dining rooms in the hotel and the adjoining Maui Beach Hotel. Major credit cards.

HOW TO GET AROUND. Rental cars are by far the best means of transportation on this island which has no public bus system, although *Shoreline Transportation,* a private company, runs scheduled **bus service** between Kapalua and Wailea on 28- to 55-passenger buses. (Two trips a day between Lahaina and Kihei-Wailea, one-way fare is $3.75; trips on the hour between Kapalua and Lahaina until 10 P.M.; one-way fare is $1.50, roundtrip $2.40.) All of the better hotels provide pickup at Kahului Airport. The many tour packages sold for the island include airport transfers. *Gray Line Hawaii* provides shuttle service from Kahului Airport to hotels on the western coast for $5. Metered **taxis** charge about $1 a mile, which makes the rate $20 and up to the Kaanapali area. Call Alii Cab, 661–3688 or Red & White Cabs, 242–6404.

Rental cars. Car rental companies charge a flat day rate, usually without a mileage charge. Reservations, particularly in winter, are necessary. Many tour packages to the island include use of a rental car at a rate far less than charged directly. About two dozen rental car companies, including most of the major national chains, operate on the island. More than a dozen have desks at Kahului Airport and the Kapalua-West Maui Airport; most others provide airport pickup service. Prices for a diversity of vehicles range from $25 to $110. It's possible, for example, to rent a luxury Cadillac or economy compact Toyota from *Budget Rent-A-Car* (800–527–0707); *Tropical Rent-A-Car* has a wide variety of cars and many special package arrangements (800–367–5140); limousines and other luxury cars can be rented from *V.I.P. Car Rentals* (946–1671).

Limousines or private cars. Many transportation companies on the island can provide limousine or private car service. *Gray Line Hawaii* (800–367–2420) charges $15 per person from Kahului to Honokowai; $17.50 per person to Kapalua. Private car rental to Hana is $33 an hour for a total of about 7 hours. It's about a 3-hour drive to Hana from Kahului, but the driver must return alone, so that time is charged, too.

TOURIST INFORMATION SERVICES. The *Hawaii Visitors Bureau* (HVB) maintains an office on Maui though unfortunately, the office is not so easy to find. It's at 172 Alamaha St., Kahului, Maui, HI 96732 (871–8691). Open 8 to 4:30 weekdays. Free brochures for everything from hotels to snorkeling trips as well as maps are available at the Kahului Airport HVB information booth, however. It's open whenever planes are arriving. You can also write in advance to the HVB for a wide variety of free material.

SEASONAL EVENTS. February. Island girls compete in the *Miss Maui Pageant* held at Baldwin High Auditorium in Wailuku in mid-February.

March. Runners congregate for the *Annual Maui Marathon.* The course runs from Maui Mall in Kahului to Whaler's Village in Kaanapali on a Saturday early in the month.

April. Wind and sea conditions usually are ideal this month for windsurfing. Champions in the sport from around the world come to Maui for the 2-week *O'Neil Invitational* held at Hookipa Beach Park. Later in the month there's a chance to see beautiful flower leis displayed during the Maui Inter-Continental Wailea's annual *Lei Day Celebration.*

May. In mid-month, Seabury Hall in Makawao hosts an arts and crafts fair. Elsewhere, athletes gather for the *Valley Isle Triathlon* and equestrians congregate for an annual champagne brunch and polo game at Haleakala Polo Field.

June. Maui Island holds its annual *Kamehameha Day Parade* on the first Saturday in June in Lahaina. The annual upcountry fun fair follows at midmonth when 4H kids display products and other events occur at the Eddie Tam Center in Makawao.

July. This month's big event is always the statewide *Makawao Rodeo* held the weekend following July 4th. Parker Ranch in Waimea town also sponsors a rodeo as well as horse races.

August. Chamber music enthusiasts and performers from around the world gather for the *Kapalua Music Festival* held at the Kapalua Bay Hotel during the first 2 weeks of the month. There's a challenging way to work off calories later in the Haleakala Run to the Sun, a 36-mile uphill race finishing at the top of the crater. Athletes can top it off with the *Maui Channel Relays Swim* beginning on Lanai and finishing at Lahaina at the end of the month.

September. *The Maui Country Rodeo* is held at Makawao at the beginning of the month. The *Annual Windsurfing for the Whales* meet gets under way at the Maui Inter-Continental Wailea at about the same time. Then more runners come to Maui to take on the 54-mile *Hana Relays* usually held at midmonth.

October. The *Maui County Fair* is held on the fairground in Kahului this month.

November. A festival of Hawaiiana in music, dance, and song with craft exhibits and a luau, the *Na Mele O Maui Festival* is the not-to-be-missed annual ethnic event on the island. It's held in Lahaina. If you need some unusual gifts for the holidays, the *Hui Noeau Christmas Craft Fair* has many decorative items. It's held at Kaluanui Museum in Makawao at midmonth in plenty of time for shoppers. There's another run this month, too. It's the *Turkey Trot Fun Run* in Kula on Thanksgiving Day.

December. The public is welcome when Buddhist temples in Lahaina and Kahului celebrate *Bodhi Day* on Dec. 8, commemorating Buddha's "Day of Enlightenment."

TOURS. Several different kinds of tours are available on the island, including driving tours with guides, offshore snorkeling, scuba and sailing tours (some to Lanai), walking tours of historic sites, bicycle tours, horseback tours, guided treks, whale-watching boat tours in season, helicopter flightseeing tours, and even a sightseeing ride aboard a train that runs along a narrow-gauge track.

A wide variety of tours may be booked direct, at hotel desks, or through several activity centers specializing in bookings on the island: *Aloha Activity Center,* 2435 Kaanapali Pkwy., Bldg. A., Lahaina, HI 96761 (808–667–9564); *Maui Activity Guide,* Box 12091, Lahaina, HI 96761 (808–667–9747); *Kaanapali Shores Travel,* Box 11476, Lahaina, HI 96761 (808–667–2202); *Maui Sightseeing Center,* Maui Lu Resort, 575 Kihei Rd., Kihei, HI 96753 (808–879–3374); *Maui Sunshine Activities & Tours,* Box 493, Lahaina, HI 96761 (808–661–0619); and *Ocean Activities Center,* 3750 Wailea Alanui D-2, Wailea, HI 96753 (800–367–8047, ext. 448).

Standard **ground tours** in small vans and limousines offered on the island include half- and full-day tours with a driver–guide to Iao Needle, Haleakala Crater and Hana among others, at rates regulated by the Public Utilities Commission. For example, Gray Line Hawaii's Hana Highlights is $40; Kula-Iao-Lahaina $18.50; Iao-Valley-Lahaina $15; Haleakala Special $17.50; Upcountry Maui $25, all with slight variations depending on pickup point. To book driving tours direct: *Akamai Tours,* 546 Keolani Pl., Kahului, HI 96732 (800–922–6485); *Diamond Head Tours,* 400 Hilo

St., Kahului, HI 96732 (808–922–0544); *Gray Line Hawaii,* 273 Dairy Rd., Kahului, HI 96732 (800–367–2420); *Holo Holo Maui Tours,* Box 1591, Lahaina, HI 96761 (808–661–4858); *Maui Island Tours,* Box 247, Kahului, HI 96732 (808–877–5581); *Robert's Hawaii Tours,* Box 1563, Kahului, HI 96732 (808–871–6226); *Trans Hawaiian Services,* 3111 Castle St., Honolulu, HI 96815 (808–735–6467). More than 100 tour wholesalers package tours to Hawaii that include Maui; many utilize the services of about 40 additional local transportation companies to provide tours on the island. A travel agent can provide details.

Cruise companies provide **snorkeling** (from $40), **glassbottom boat rides** (from $9.50), **scuba-diving** (from $45), **whale-watching** (from $20), **dinner cruises** (from $42) or all-day **sailing trips** (from $89). They include: *Alihilani,* Box 1286, Lahaina, HI 96761 (808–661–3047); *Captain Nemo's Ocean Emporium,* 700 Front St., Lahaina, HI 96761 (800–367–8088); *Coral See,* Box 596, Lahaina, HI 96761 (800–367–8088); *Lin Wa Cruises,* Box 1376, Lahaina, HI 96761 (808–661–3392); *Scotch Mist Charters,* Box 845, Lahaina, HI 96767 (808–661–0386); *Seabird Cruises,* Box 1553, Lahaina, HI 96767 (800–442–7245); *Spirit of Windjammer,* Box 218, Lahaina, HI 96761 (800–367–4753); *Trilogy Excursions,* Box 1121, Lahaina, HI 96767 (800–874–2666).

Historic tours of Lahaina in combination with a glassbottom boat ride and train ride are offered by: *Lahaina-Kaanapali & Pacific Railroad,* Box 816, Lahaina, HI 96761 (800–367–4753).

Bicycle tours with equipment included begin at $78 for a morning coasting tour from the summit of Haleakala to sea level. They may be booked direct with: *Cruiser Bob's Haleakala Downhill,* 505 Front St. #131, Lahaina, HI 96761 (808–667–7717); *Maui Downhill,* 440A Alamaha St., Kahului, HI 96732 (808–871–2155).

Horseback tours ($80 half day; $120 full day) with a guide into Haleakala Crater for a maximum of 6 riders at a time can be arranged through *Pony Express Tours,* Box 507, Makawao, Maui, HI 96768 (808–667–2202). At Kaanapali 2-hour horseback tours ($38) may be booked from *Kaanapali Kau Lio,* Box 10656, Lahaina, HI 96761 (808–667–7896). A variety of guided rides beginning at $15 for a 1-hour beginner's plantation ride may be booked in the Kapalua area from *Rainbow Ranch,* Box 10066, Lahaina, HI 96761 (808–669–4991); in Kula from *Thompson Stables,* Thompson Rd., Kula, HI 96790 (808–878–1910).

Helicopter flightseeing tours (from $75–$200) of Haleakala Crater, the Seven Pools in Hana and other sites may be booked through: *Kenai Helicopters,* Box 11358, Lahaina, HI 96761 (800–367–2603); *Maui Helicopters,* Box 1002, Kihei, HI 96753 (800–367–8003); *Papillon Helicopters,* Box 339, Hanalei, HI 96714 (800–367–7095); *South Sea Helicopters,* Box 11618, Lahaina, HI 96761 (800–367–2914).

Tedeschi Winery. Visitors are welcome at this winery on Ulupalakua Ranch in upcountry Maui which markets Hawaii's first wine, 1985 Maui Nouveau, as well as pineapple wine and Hawaiian champagne. The winery is open weekdays from 7 A.M. to 3:30 P.M. for self-guided tours; or a $2 per person guided walking tour with wine tasting may be arranged in advance. A Tasting Room is open to walk-in visitors weekdays from 9 to 5, and weekends from 10 to 5. Ulupalakua Ranch, Ulupalakua, HI 96790 (808–878–6058).

PARKS AND GARDENS. Haleakala National Park. Maui's most famous landmark, a dormant volcanic crater at 10,023 feet in the south central part of the island, extends southward to include the Seven Pools in Hana. The 42-mile drive from Wailuku to the top is along a winding road and is best taken in the early morning before the frequent mist has a chance to settle in. The House of the Sun Visitor Center is open from 9 A.M. to 3 P.M. weekdays; talks are given here on the unusual flora and geology of the crater. There is also an extensive network of trails, some easy, some very challenging. The rare silversword plant can be seen at Kalahaku Overlook. Visitors frequently come to see the sunrise which is spectacular. Details regarding weather conditions including time of sunrise and sunset are recorded daily for visitors (572–7749).

Halekii and Pihana Heiau State Monument. Ruins of Halekii, a large temple of worship used during the time of Maui's last great chief, Kahekili (1765–1795), and Pihana, a sacrificial temple dating from 1779, are preserved at a hilltop site near Iao Stream about 2 miles from Kahului.

Iao Valley State Park. A green gorge with an unusual spire threading the sky, 2,250-foot Iao Needle, this park sacred to Hawaiians is just outside of Wailuku. Kepaniwai Heritage Gardens, just below Iao Needle, is a series of 6 gardens representing the different ethnic groups in Hawaii.

Kanaha Pond. Located between the airport and Kahului, this former royal fishpond is now Hawaii's most important refuge for migratory waterfowls. Watch for Hawaiian stilts.

Kula Botanical Garden. On Highway 377 in Kula is a pleasant garden with more than 700 types of plants grown in tropical climates, including many varieties of protea. A self-guiding tour takes about a half hour. Open 9 A.M. to 4 P.M. daily (878–1715). Admission $3 teenagers and adults, 50¢ children.

Maui Plantation. A 60-acre garden of Hawaiian plants such as sugarcane, pineapple, star fruit, papayas, protea, anthurium, orchids, and guava in Waikapu. Visitor Center, restaurant, and plant nursery. A 30-minute narrated tour is conducted aboard a tram. Open 8 A.M. to 5 P.M. daily (244–7643). Tram ride is $5. General admission is free.

Maui Zoo. A 5-acre zoo in Kahului across from the War Memorial has 50 mammals and lots of tropical birds, including the rare Hawaiian goose (*nene*) and duck (*koloa*). Open daily from 9 A.M. to 4 P.M. Admission free (244–3276).

Polipoli State Park. This recreation area 10 miles from Kula in upcountry Maui is accessible only via 4-wheel drive vehicle. For an incredible view you can hike 1,000 feet up to the top of Polipoli Cone or just explore the many trails through the forest of 35,000 redwood trees planted here in 1927. (For camping permits, call 244–5514.)

Waianapanapa State Park. At this park just south of Hana Town, a path through a lush tropical growth leads to 2 lava tubes near the sea, known as Waianapanapa Cave and Waiomao Cave. Other sights in the park are a natural arch, a blowhole, a black sand beach, and a portion of an ancient Hawaiian trail around the island south of the beach. (For camping permits, call 572–8122.)

BEACHES. Many of Maui's hotels and condominiums are located on beautiful beaches or provide access to them. Gorgeous, rockless, golden sand beaches offering excellent wading, swimming, windsurfing, and snorkeling may be found at Kaanapali, Napili Bay, Kapalua, Kihei, and Wailea—and it isn't necessary to be staying in these areas in order to use them. There are about 80 beaches on the island, but by no means are all safe, in spite of the sometimes inviting aspect of a crescent of white sand. Unless local residents who know the currents and reefs are swimming, you should not go in the water. Here are highlights about some of Maui's better-known beaches, which are grouped geographically.

Kahului-Hana

Waiehu Beach Park. A narrow but beautiful beach just north of Kahului with a shallow inshore reef and good swimming in calm water.

Hookipa Beach Park. This beach south of Kahului on the upper part of Hana Highway is not a good swimming beach, but when the winds are up it is the place to go on Maui and perhaps in the world to watch windsurfers jumping the waves.

Seven Pools Park. It is often hard for visitors to Hana to resist going into these freshwater pools created during an ancient lava flow and fed now by Oheo stream; it's a thrilling experience to swim here, but you should be very careful of slippery sides and submerged rocks. Often, during a prolonged dry spell, the waterfalls that fill these pools have not been flowing, so the swimming is not good. Ocean swimming at the point where the stream reaches the sea should not be attempted, as there is a very dangerous rip current.

Kapalua-Kihei-Wailea

D.T. Fleming Beach Park. This popular beach park north of Kapalua Beach is flanked by shady ironwood trees and is a popular picnic site, though the swimming is sometimes dangerous when rip currents are created by heavy swells.

Kapalua Beach. The crescent of white beach in front of Kapalua Bay Hotel fronts one of the safest and best swimming areas on Maui. Snorkeling is very good in the clear waters, too. Public access and parking is provided at the south end of the beach.

Napili Bay. This lovely sloping beach flanked by many vacation condominiums is an excellent place for swimming and snorkeling on calm days. Plentiful public access.

Kaanapali Beach. Actually 2 very long, white sand beaches front Kaanapali Beach Resort, one extending north of Black Rock, the promontory atop which the Sheraton Maui is situated, the other south. In waters close to shore both offer excellent snorkeling and swimming in usually wonderfully calm seas. The area just south of Black Rock offers especially good snorkeling.

Kamaole III Beach Park. This is the most popular of a series of 3 easily accessible beach parks on south Kihei Road. This is a good swimming beach except during heavy surf or storms; it's also a popular picnic site.

Wailea Beach. Five separate beaches actually are found at Wailea Beach Resort. All 5 are among the best swimming and sunning beaches on the island. The resort developers have provided a public mini-park, parking lot, and walkway to each beach.

SPORTS. There's something about Maui that brings out the sports enthusiast in the most confirmed sideline kibitzer. Perhaps it's the constant balmy weather, or the careful design of resorts with tennis court, golf green, and beach just steps away. Whatever the cause, there is an activity for everyone.

Deep-Sea Fishing. Marlin, blue-nose dolphin, yellowfin tuna, and more have been caught at sights like Penguin Banks accessible from Maui via charter fishing vessel. *No Ka Oi III,* 3750 Wailea Alanui, Wailea, HI 96753 (800–367–8047 ext. 448), runs shared and exclusive charters beginning at $70 for a half-day shared trip aboard a 38-foot Bertram, the Blue Max. *Lahaina Charter Boats,* Box 12, Lahaina, HI 96767 (808–667–6672), runs charters beginning at $50 for a half-day trip on a shared basis aboard 2 sportfishing boats.

Golf. There are seven prime 18-hole resort courses on Maui designed by the best in the field, Arnold Palmer (Kapalua), Robert Trent Jones, Jr. (Makena), Robert Trent Jones, Sr. (Kaanapali North), Arthur Jack Snyder (Kaanapali South and Wailea Blue and Orange). There is also an 18-hole municipal course and 2 9-hole country club courses. At *Kapalua's Bay and Village courses* green fees are $35 for guests, higher for visitors. Carts, clubs, and lessons from head pro Gary Planos are extra. At the *Makena course* south of Wailea green fees with a shared cart are $50. At the 2 *Royal Kaanapali courses* fees vary depending on accommodations; resort guests get priority starting times, but both courses are open to the public. Green fees at the seaside *Waiehu Municipal Course* are $15 weekdays, $20 weekends and holidays, carts are extra. *Maui Country Club's* 9-hole course in Paia is open to the public on Mon. or you can get a guest card from better resort hotels; green fees for 9 holes are $20; more for 18 holes. At the new 18-hole, Bill Newis–designed Silversword Golf Course in Kihei, fees with required cart are $40. At the *Wailea Blue and Orange courses,* low season May–Nov. green fees are $30 guests, $50 non-guests including shared cart; clubs and shoes extra. Dec.–Apr. fees are $45 guests, $80 non-guests. A 2-day advance preferential time is given to resort guests.

Hiking. *Haleakala National Park* offers the best-maintained hiking trails. Suggestions include an easy 2-mile walk just below the crater rim, a half-day hike in Kipahulu Valley near Hana at the south end of the park, or for the experienced hiker, a 2-day trip from the summit across the crater floor to Kipahulu, a drop of 10,000 feet in elevation. At the *Seven Pools* in Hana park, rangers conduct a 4-hour nature walk on Sat. at 9 A.M. Write for a required hiking permit to Haleakala National Park, Box 537, Makawao, HI 96768.

Experts say the easiest hikes on Maui are to Twin Falls on the Hana Road, Redwood Trail at Polipoli, and LaPerouse Bay. For tougher folks, try Waimoku Falls, the St. Anthony cross above Wailuku, or the Lahaina "L." For the rugged, the Skyline Trail near Science City, Poohahoahoa Stream in Iao, Lauulu Trail in the crater, and Puu Kukui in West Maui.

Hunting. You can take pheasants, quail, and doves during the mid-October to year's end season in the Kula Game Management Area with permission from the Department of Land and Natural Resources (244–4352). Wild pigs and goats may be hunted all year long. A hunting license and permit are required for any activity.

Scuba-Diving. Opportunities for shore and boat dives are plentiful on Maui. A fascinating variety of marine life—manta rays, lobsters, and sea turtles among them—may be seen by day or night at dive sites around the island. Operators offer excursions for beginners as well as experts at rates starting from $45–$75. In Hawaii operators provide all equipment. Five-day certification training beginning at about $185 is also offered by several operators. Arrangements can be made through the following shops: *Captain Nemo's Ocean Emporium,* 700 Front St., Lahaina, HI 96761 (800–367–8088); *Central Pacific Divers,* 780 Front St., Lahaina, HI 96761 (800–821–6670); *Dive Maui,* Lahaina Marketplace, Lahainaluna Rd., Lahaina, HI 96761 (808–667–2080); *Hawaiian Reef Divers,* 129 Lahainaluna Rd., Lahaina, HI 96761 (808–667–7647); *Lahaina Divers,* 710 Front St., Lahaina, HI 96761 (800–367–8047 ext. 102); *Maui Dive Shop,* Box 1018, Kihei, HI 96753 (808–879–3388); *Dive Shop of Kihei,* 1975 S. Kihei Rd., Kihei, HI 96753 (808–879–5172); *Ocean Activities Center,* 3750 Wailea Alanui D-2, Wailea, HI 96753 (800–367–8047, ext. 448).

Tennis. If Superman had to give up flying he could comfort himself by playing tennis on Maui, which is almost as good an experience. There are some major tennis centers on the island and dozens of courts at different properties. The *Wailea Tennis Club,* open to the public, has 14 courts, 11 paved, and 3 lawn. There are daily programs, night play, rentals, and several levels of instruction. Rates are $10 to $12 a day for general play. The *Royal Lahaina Tennis Ranch* at Kaanapali Beach Resort has 11 courts, 6 of them night-lighted, daily clinics and instruction, rentals. Daily guest rate per court is $6 singles, $10 doubles, $2 more for night play. Non-guests at the resort pay $1 more. Also at Kaanapali, the *Hyatt Regency Maui* has 5 courts, rentals and instruction; rates are $12 per hour singles, $15 doubles for both guests and non-guests. The *Maui Marriott Resort* has 5 courts, rentals and instruction at the same rates. The *Sheraton-Maui* has 3 courts, night-lighting, rentals. Rates are $5.25 per hour for guests and non-guests. Up the road a bit, *Napili Kai Beach Club* has 2 courts; guests pay $5, non-guests $6. *Kapalua Tennis Gardens* farther up the coast, is an airy complex of 10 courts with night-lighting on 4 of them, rentals and instruction. Rates are $8 per day for guests, $9 for non-guests; $4 per person noon to 3 P.M. There are 2 public courts at the *Luana Kai* and also at the *Maui Sunset* in Kihei. A couple of dozen other properties on the island have courts where guests may play free of charge.

Windsurfing. The best place to watch and participate in this graceful but deceptively rigorous sport is along the island's northern coastline, from Kahului east to Hookipa Beach Park. In fact, this is the windsurfing capital of Hawaii, if not America. Rentals and instruction are becoming more available as the popularity of windsurfing grows. Best on the island is Mike Waltze's *Sailboards Maui* (871–7954), 201 Dairy Road, Kahului.

CAMPING. Two companies provide elaborate camping excursions on Maui: *Island Odysseys,* 677 Ala Moana Blvd., Honolulu, HI 96813 (800–367–5696); *Wilderness Hawaii,* Box 61692, Honolulu, HI 96822 (808–737–4697); rates begin at $255 for a 4-day 1-island trip. *Beach Boy Campers,* 1720 Ala Moana Blvd., Honolulu, HI 96815 (808–955–6381), rents a 2-person sleeper truck for $45 plus 6¢ a mile or larger campers with showers and toilets for up to $70.

Otherwise you may camp on your own at several county parks and in Haleakala Crater, where cabins are available by lottery; write Haleakala National Park, Box 537, Makawao, HI 96768. Permits and a small daily fee are required to camp at any county park or to use mountain cabins at Polipoli Springs, which is in the middle of a tropical rain forest, or at Waianapanapa near Hana. These facilities are maintained by the Department of Land and Natural Resources, 54 High St., Wailuku, Maui, HI 96793 (808–244–4354). The cabin at 6,000-foot Polipoli Springs is $5 a night for 6 people or $10 single. Two-bedroom cabins at Waianapanapa, near lava tubes and sea cliffs, begin at $10 a day for 1 up to a maximum of 6 for $30. Another good camping spot is at Kaumahina, in a rain forest overlooking the Hana coast.

HISTORIC SITES AND MUSEUMS. Alexander & Baldwin Sugar Museum. Opened at the end of 1986 in Puunene, across from the C & H Sugar Mill. Photo exhibits, artifacts, and a working scale model of sugar processing machinery are among exhibits housed in the largest old plantation overseer's house in Hawaii. A restored steam locomotive dating from 1882, the former Kahului Railroad's No. 1, is exhibited outdoors. Box 125, Puunene, HI 96784 (871–8058). Admission $2.

Baldwin Home Museum. The 150-year-old clapboard private residence of the Rev. Dwight Baldwin, a missionary doctor, on Front St. in the center of Lahaina. The narrated tour is an excellent introduction to Maui history. Open daily 9:30 A.M. to 5 P.M. Admission $2.50. (661–3262).

Brig Carthaginian. Permanently berthed in Lahaina Harbor is a 93-foot vessel maintained as a maritime museum by the Lahaina Restoration Foundation (661–3262), an organization responsible for the recovery and maintenance of most of the area's historic buildings. Tape and video show about the whaling life in the 19th century. Open daily 8:30 A.M. to 4:30 P.M. Admission $2.50.

Hale Hoikeike. An historical museum in Wailuku housed in a thick-walled building erected in 1832 as a school for girls and now on the National Register of Historic Houses. Koa calabashes, kapa, and other Hawaiian archeological implements are displayed. Open 9 A.M. to 3:30 P.M. daily. Admission $2. 2375 A Main St. (244–3326). Kaahumanu Church, the oldest church on the island, built in 1837, is nearby.

Hale Paahao. "Stuck-in-irons house," at the corner of Prison Rd. and Wainee St. in Lahaina, is fascinating for the look it affords into the rough life whalers knew in the 1850s when this coral block prison's rusty iron shackles and balls and chains were in regular use. (Call Lahaina Restoration Foundation, 661–3262.)

Hale Pa'i. A restored coral block printing house built in 1834 on the campus of Lahainaluna School above Lahaina. Open daily, except Sun., 10 A.M. to 4 P.M. Free. (Call Lahaina Restoration Foundation, 661–3262.)

Hana Cultural Center. A new museum not far from the courthouse in Hana is small but very well designed and organized. The old photos of Hana displayed are intriguing, and there are Hawaiian artifacts, too. Open daily, except Sunday, 11 A.M. to 4 P.M. Admission. Uakea Rd. (248–8622).

Wainee Church and Churchyard. A block and a half from Baldwin House is the first stone church built in Hawaii (1828). It has been rebuilt several times. The adjoining church graveyard provides a trip back into time. Here lie the graves and gravestones of chiefs and commoners, seamen and missionary children, many of whom died in infancy. Kamehameha III is buried here among other Hawaiian notables.

Whaler's Village Museum. A collection of more than 100 whaling implements and artifacts is housed in this museum in Whaler's Village Shopping complex at Kaanapali Beach Resort. Surgeon's tools of the era— including assorted hacksaws with which to amputate limbs—are among the fascinating displays, as is a 6-foot model of a whaling ship. Movies on whales are shown throughout the day. Free. (661–5992).

Wo Hing Temple. A recently restored Chinese temple in Lahaina now houses a museum with a Buddhist shrine upstairs, photo exhibits and displays about the heritage of island Chinese residents. Open daily. Free. (Call Lahaina Restoration Foundation, 661–3262.)

SHOPPING. Maui has elegant boutiques in several of the major resort hotels, as well as tiny T-shirt and souvenir shops packed along narrow Wharf St. across from the seawall in Lahaina. **Kaahumanu Center** in Kahului has dozens of shops selling Hawaiian, Oriental, and Mainland goods. **Whaler's Market Place** in the south part of Lahaina has jewelry and souvenir shops in a series of wooden frame structures built to resemble New England houses of the 1880s. Lahaina has other, smaller shopping centers: **The Wharf, Lahaina Square, Lahaina Market Place,** and **Lahaina Shopping Center. Whaler's Village Shopping Center** at Kaanapali Beach Resort has 50 restaurants and gift and souvenir shops, Maui potato chips, sweet Maui onions grown in Kula and sold in bags at the airport, scrimshaw created in the authentic manner, and exotic protea blossoms from upcountry Maui are some distinctive items to take home. Art galleries at Kapalua and Wailea offer the works of Robert Lyn Nelson, famous for his portraits of whales, and Guy Buffet, whose country Hawaiian scenes are delightful, among others. Discriminating buyers will be able to find many items to take home at prices the same or slightly higher than on the Mainland.

NIGHTLIFE. A very satisfying evening's entertainment on Maui may consist simply of a leisurely meal somewhere beside the sea highlighted by a view of red-gold washes spread across the sky by a setting sun. For something more exciting, several resorts on the island offer lavish shows, many with a Polynesian motif. The traditional Hawaiian event, the *luau,* a feast usually accompanied by singing and performances of the hula, is held outdoors at several hotels, too.

Anton's Maui Lu Resort. In Kihei the place to go is the luau at the Maui Lu, held at 5 P.M. Sat., $32 adults. For reservations call 879–5811.

Hyatt Regency Maui. "Drums of the Pacific," a rousing Polynesian revue, is staged every night except Sun. as a dinner show featuring kiawe-grilled fish, prime rib, chicken, or Hawaiian food. Dinner seating at 5:30 P.M.; cocktail seating at 7:15 P.M. $36 dinner; $30 cocktails. There is changing musical entertainment in the Pavilion, Swan Court, and Weeping Banyan, too. Dance off the calories later at Spats II, a roaring disco. For reservations call 667–7474.

Kapalua Bay Hotel & Villas. Musical entertainment, some appropriate for dancing, is offered in the Kapalua Room, Plantation Veranda, Bay Lounge and at the Bay Club on the beach. For reservations call 669–5656.

Maui Beach. In the Kahului-Wailuku area local residents congregate in the Red Dragon Disco from 10 P.M. to 2 A.M. on Fri. and Sat. for live music and dancing. Cover charge plus 2-drink minimum. For reservations call 877–0051.

Maui Inter-Continental Wailea. "Maui's Merriest Luau" is held each Thurs. on special luau grounds at the hotel, with a sunset *imu* ceremony, rum punch, buffet, and show for $37 adults. The Inu Inu Lounge offers dancing to live music 9 P.M. to 1 A.M. nightly, and from 5:30 to 7:30 P.M. on Sun. "Swing is King" is offered. La Perouse has piano music at dinner and local entertainment is offered during the Champagne Sun. brunch from 8 A.M. to 1 P.M. For reservations call 879–1922.

Maui Marriott Resort. There's contemporary entertainment in the Makai and Poolside Bars, plus piano styling in the Lobby Bar. The hotel has 2 dance floors with an in-house deejay and backgammon tables in its popular Banana Moon disco.

Maui Palms. After dinner there's dancing to live music in the dining room from 9:30 P.M. until closing on Fri. and Sat. For reservations call 877–0071.

Royal Lahaina Hotel. A buffet and Polynesian show follow the nightly luau beginning at 5:30 P.M. Charge is $38. Happy Hour and evening entertainment is offered nightly on the Ocean Terrace. On Sun. a Champagne Brunch is held from 9 A.M. to 2 P.M. For reservations call 661–3611.

Sheraton Maui. Sun. through Thurs. the Aloha Luau begins with a reenactment of a Hawaiian king's dive off Black Rock at 5:15 P.M. Guests also receive shell leis and view Hawaiian crafts at the $37.50 feast. "Maui, Moonlight & Magic" is the dinner show here held twice nightly, except Tues., and featuring Rodney Arias. Seating for dinner is at 6:30 P.M.; cocktail show seating at 10 P.M. There is a cover charge and dining is off the menu. A $3 cover plus 2-drink minimum applies for the cocktail show. From 8 P.M. to 11 P.M. Wed. through Sun. a trio plays contemporary Hawaiian music in the Sundowner Bar. For reservations call 661–0031.

Stouffer Wailea Beach Resort. Local music groups play from 5:30 to 8:30 P.M. weeknights and 6 P.M. to 10 P.M. weekends on the Sunset Terrace. A pianist performs nightly during dinner and for Sun. brunch at Raffles. A live quartet plays for dancing in the Lost Horizon nightclub from 9 P.M. to 1 A.M., nightly, except Sun. For reservations call 879–4900.

MOLOKAI

Friendly, Easy-Going, and Traditional

By
THELMA T. CHANG

Born and raised in Hawaii, Thelma Chang has traveled extensively throughout the world. She has worked as a free-lance writer since 1983 and has written for national and international publications including Westways, Essence, *and* Pacific.

It's hard to believe that Molokai—often referred to as the island most exemplifying "old Hawaii"—is just a 20-minute flight from Honolulu's hustle and bustle. As soon as you land at the island's Hoolehua Aiport, just eight miles from the main town of Kaunakakai, you begin to see why Molokai is known as "The Friendly Isle." The tiny airport with its single, main building is an example of Molokai's easy-going, relaxed pace as tour drivers, airline personnel, and baggage handlers wave to each other, often engaging in "talk story" sessions as they come and go.

The camaraderie manifested at the airport is evident not only in Molokai's 6,000 people, but also in the island's environment.

You can drive from one end of the island to the other, a distance of about 50 miles from the Kaluakoi Resort complex on the west side to Halawa Valley in the east, without encountering a single traffic light. (If you think of Molokai as slipper-shaped, the west side is at its heel, Halawa is at its toes, while such landmarks as Kaunakakai and Kalaupapa are at its center, with Kaunakakai on the south shore and Kalaupapa lying toward the north.)

Other modern trappings such as a chain store, elevator, or buildings more than three stories high are yet to be found on Molokai, the fifth largest island in the Hawaiian chain. Instead, the island offers physical and psychological balms such as sheer cliffs etched by time, deep valleys with forest pools, rolling hills teeming with wildlife, and secluded white sand beaches that delightfully surprise unsuspecting visitors who drive along the island's narrow, curvy road that hugs the southeastern shoreline. At the same time, there is no pressure to compress a long list of "things to do." Molokai—10 miles wide and 38 miles long—invites residents and visitors alike to relax with outdoor activities and sightseeing, ranging from fishing and mule rides to boat cruises and hiking trips.

However you choose to explore Molokai, it is hard to ignore the overall mystery of an island filled with *heiau* (sacred sites) and surrounded by ancient fishponds along the southern coast. The ponds, used for fish farming, exist much as they did in the 13th century, when ancient Hawaiians looked to the sea for some of their bounty, constructing sophisticated stone-walled enclosures that were unique to the Hawaiian Islands.

Indeed, many residents and visitors report a feeling that a certain site has chosen to view and receive them rather than the reverse. Collectively, Molokai remains a place steeped in spirituality and far removed in time and feeling from much of the outside world.

But Molokai wasn't always "The Friendly Isle." Before Western contact, powerful *kahuna* (Hawaiian priests) protected the 261-square-mile island from invasion partly through spiritual prestige. Thus, ancient ways were preserved to a greater degree on Molokai than on any of the other major islands.

In 1792 Molokai became part of the unified kingdom of Hawaii upon its conquest by King Kamehameha I. Later, in the 1870s and 1880s, the island became synonymous with Father Damien, the once-shunned Hansen's Disease settlement at Kalaupapa, and the Belgian priest's beloved patients who suffered in physical and emotional ways. Those who contracted what was then referred to as "ma'i Pake," (the "Chinese disease," although no one knows for sure its exact origins) also endured heartbreaking separation from loved ones on neighboring islands.

Molokai's "lonely island" label no longer applied with the dawn of the 20th century and the annexation of the Hawaiian Islands to the United States.

Several key events led the island out of isolation, including the construction of Molokai's first east-to-west water system in 1911 and, later, the rise of the pineapple industry. Until recently, pineapples filled Kaunakakai's dockside wharf for shipment to Honolulu canneries. However, with the closing of Dole's plantation at Maunaloa in 1975 and the phasing down of Del Monte's acreage at Kualapuu in 1983, unemployment on the island shot up to 20 percent, the highest in the state. The 60-year-old plantation shut down fully in late 1988.

Spurred mainly by this crisis, residents, the private sector, and government took a hard look at Molokai's future. The process often generated heated debate among native Hawaiian activists and "outsiders," as concerned parties mulled over the consequences of development and tourism. In its present state, Molokai is free from the stress of dense traffic, high-rises, and general congestion. Most visitors and residents don't want "another Waikiki."

A 1983 State report, recognizing the spread of urban sprawl especially on Oahu and Maui, expressed the importance of maintaining Molokai's rural lifestyle and environment. Available data suggested a balance of diversified agriculture—Molokai farms provide most of the state's watermelons, green beans, and bell peppers, for example—and tourism as having the greatest hope for economic recovery. As for the latter alternative, most local residents are aware of tourism's job potential. (To date, there are seven hotels and condominiums providing 900 units for visitors.) At the same time, the people are understandably protective of their open spaces, natural tranquility, and friendly lifestyle.

There is only one major resort on Molokai—Kaluakoi on the island's hilly west side. Developed by Kaluakoi Corporation, a subsidiary of the Louisiana Land and Exploration Company, the resort complex encompasses 6,700 acres and includes two bungalow-style condominums and a hotel. 1987 brought two changes to Kaluakoi. In April the Sheraton Molokai Hotel became the Kaluakoi Hotel and Golf Club, and in October Louisiana Land sold the resort to Tokyo Kosan Co. Ltd.

As you head toward Kaluakoi from the airport, visually soak in the rolling plains, farmlands, and cattle pastures of the 60,000-acre Molokai Ranch, the island's largest local landholder. Kaluakoi itself stretches along the coast for more than five miles, including the two-and-a-half-mile-long Papohaku Beach, the largest expanse of white sand beach in Hawaii.

If you choose, just relax, or participate in a variety of activities that can be conveniently arranged from the hotel, ranging from surfing and skindiving to fishing and horseback riding. (For Hawaiian waters in general, check with hotel personnel or others who know about ocean conditions, such as sharp coral and undertow, before venturing offshore.) On a clear night, stroll the beach, look across the 25-mile Kaiwi Channel, and take in the sparkling lights of Oahu and Diamond Head.

A trip to Kaluakoi wouldn't be complete without seeing some of the estimated 500 animals that reside at Molokai Ranch Wildlife Park, a 2,000-acre slice of the Serengeti that borders the resort. In the early 1970s the ranch introduced rare and endangered species from Africa and Asia, including crown cranes, Barbary sheep, Indian black buck, eland, rhea, and ostriches. Today, camera safaris depart regularly from the Kaluakoi Hotel and Golf Club for the bumpy, but scenically beautiful, hour-and-a-half ride through the preserve.

Exploring Molokai

Above the Kaluakoi Resort, at the westernmost end of the main highway (Route 460), lies Maunaloa, a former Dole plantation town filled today with quaint arts-and-crafts galleries in old-style buildings. Take a look at the handful of shops and people who occupy the quiet stage that is the town's one-block-long "main street." For example, the unusual collection of kites at the Big Wind Kite Factory and fine, silk-screened T-shirts at the Molokai Red Dirt Shirt Shop share neighborhood space with stores that sell handmade dolls and native wood works. Hungry? Drop

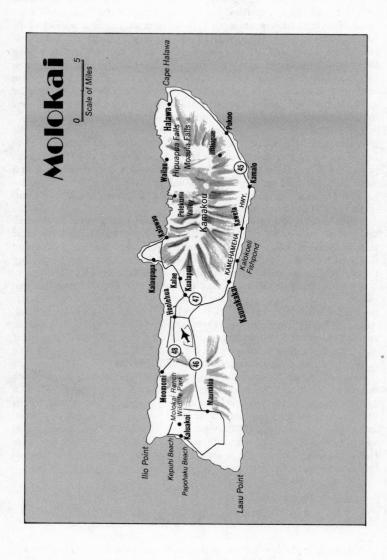

Molokai

Scale of Miles

0 5

Cape Halawa
Halawa
Hipuapua Falls
Wailau
Moaula Falls
Pukoo
Iliiliopae
Pelekunu Valley
45
Kamalo
Kalawao
Kamakou
Kawela HWY.
Kawela
KAMEHAMEHA
Kalaupapa
Kalae
Hoolehua
Kalokoeli Fishpond
Kualapuu
47
Kaunakakai
48
Moomomi
46
Molokai Ranch Wildlife Park
Maunaloa
Ilio Point
Kepuhi Beach
Kaluakoi
Papohaku Beach
Laau Point

in at Jojo's for Korean-style short ribs or their popular fresh fish of the day.

If you happen to be on Molokai during October, check to see exactly when one of the island's biggest events takes place: At Hale-o-Lono, a rocky, coastal harbor southwest of Maunaloa amid Molokai's famous red dust and kiawe trees, outrigger canoes and their paddlers get prepped for the annual Molokai to Oahu canoe race, a 42-mile endeavor that ends up near Ft. DeRussy in Honolulu amid much hoopla and celebration.

On the drive from Maunaloa town toward the south shore and just before you reach Kaunakakai, be on the lookout for what seems, at first glance, to be an ocean of coconut trees planted relatively close to each other. That's the Kapuaiwa Coconut Grove, a symbol of the economic and aesthetic value of the plant and one of the last surviving royal groves planted by Prince Lot, who later became Hawaii's King Kamehameha V in 1863. Before his reign, the young prince lived on Molokai. Across the street from the grove is Church Row, where missionary influences can be seen in the quaint, wooden churches that stand side by side.

You're soon in Kaunakaki, Molokai's "big" small town, and the island's other "operations base" if you choose to stay at one of the two charming, cottage-style hotels here: The Hotel Molokai and the Pau Hana Inn. ("Pau Hana," essentially meaning "done with work for the day," is a popular 50th state term.) For a home-away-from-home, get a condo at Molokai Shores, which is also oceanfront.

Kaunakakai is the island's "commercial center," but don't let the term discourage you. Kaunakakai is like a colorful one-block-long "Old West" movie set of delightful sights, smells, and sounds, a place where it's easy to imagine Clint Eastwood drifting into town from the plains. It hasn't changed much since the 1930s, when pineapple reigned supreme and clogged the docks for shipment to Honolulu canneries. Today, at Kaunakakai's dockside wharf, which extends far out to sea, pineapple is joined by other Molokai products such as watermelons, cattle, herbs, and honey. The wharf is also home for deep-sea fishing boats, some of which also offer sailing, snorkeling, whale watching, photographic, and diving expeditions.

A microcosm of Hawaii's diverse cultures exists within that one block of Kaunakakai town. Here, as you pass horses tethered to trees while waiting for their owners, you'll find freshly baked Molokai bread and cookies at Kanemitsu Bakery. *Paniolo,* Hawaiian cowboys, often stroll in not only for baked goods, but also for the fresh fish located behind another counter. If you're lucky, you might get to hear one of Molokai's spirited "talk story" sessions in the bakery—for example, when Molokaians, including *paniolo,* discuss the best way to steam their fish, for steaming is a popular way of cooking in the Islands.

Food is one indicator of the fact that a large portion of Molokai's population is Hawaiian, Asian, or a mixture. In town, for example, you can find reasonably priced Chinese dishes at Hop Inn, Filipino cuisine at Oviedo's Lunch Counter or Rabang's, and Hawaiian-style fish at the Mid-Nite Inn.

All the while, the environment is spiritually warm, filled with people who may be related to each other, people who are dressed in colorful aloha shirts, boots, or long flowing muumuus, people who laugh as they talk to each other, often in pidgin and often with their hands.

Kalaupapa

There is a mood distinctly different from Kaunakakai as you head north toward Kalaupapa and the world-famous Hansen's Disease settlement. James Michener, the author of *Hawaii,* a 1959 best-selling novel, described Kalaupapa Peninsula this way: "In the previous history of the world no such hellish spot had ever stood in such heavenly surroundings." Kalaupapa, meaning "Flat Leaf," is cut off from the rest of the world by natural barriers of ocean and sheer sea cliffs.

In 1980, more than 100 years after the government schooner *Warwick* began transporting leprosy victims to the peninsula in 1866, this isolated but beautiful community was designated a National Historic Park.

The tranquility of the place today makes it difficult to comprehend the fact that at one time, when ignorance and fear about the disease were rife, Hawaiians were torn from families, dumped into the ocean, and left to fend for themselves in huge swells. Those who didn't drown or give up in despair existed under the harshest of wilderness conditions imaginable until a Roman Catholic priest, sickened by what he saw, committed himself to the humane care of the sufferers. At one time there were more than 1,000 patients. Today, thanks to the miracle of medical science and general knowledge, there are fewer than 100 residents who are now free to come and go as they please. Most choose to stay in their beautiful setting.

The priest, Father Damien Joseph De Veuster, lived in the colony from 1873 to 1889, when he, too, died from the disease of a people he grew to love.

That love has been returned in fullest measure. Books and movies have celebrated the man. Damien's memorial in the cemetery next to Kalaupapa's St. Philomena Church is a shrine. His statue fronts the State Capitol in Honolulu. However, missing from Kalaupapa are Father Damien's remains, which were returned to his native Belgium in 1936.

Many come to Molokai just to visit the once-sorrowful site. You can reach Kalaupapa through regularly scheduled mule rides or flights—there is a small airport at the peninsula to accommodate flights from topside Molokai, Oahu, and Maui—but permission is required from the Hawaii State Department of Health ahead of time if you decide to hike in on an unscheduled basis.

The Molokai Mule Ride to Kalaupapa provides a thrilling experience for those who are physically fit and at least 16 years of age. Allow a full day and sensible clothing for the adventure that starts at Kalae Stables, a corral 1,600 feet above Kalaupapa. With an experienced guide and sure-footed mules (as one guide remarked, "These mules are smart—they won't commit suicide") you meander down the rocky, winding, three-mile trail with its 26 switchbacks. The view from the sea cliff is unforgettable: lush rain forests, the Pacific Ocean, and vistas of the distant peninsula getting closer and closer.

At the bottom of the cliff and after a short ride along the sandy beach, you board a mini-bus for the settlement. No one is allowed to roam unattended, but residents themselves give you a personalized tour, taking you through the village that includes small wooden houses, medical facilities, Father Damien's church, Mother Marianne's memorial, and lonely graveyards.

The tour includes a marvelous box lunch picnic at Kalawao Park, which offers views of the north coast, home of the world's highest sea cliffs.

Kalawao was the original site of the Hansen's Disease colony, but with the installation of a water pipeline in 1888, the residents moved to the less windy side at Kalaupapa.

You may decide to skip the ride if you're not comfortable with scaling heights on four-footed transportation. Instead, at Palaau State Park, a few hundred yards past the Kalae Stables, another magnificent view of the 1,600-foot cliff and Kalaupapa can be seen from Kalaupapa Overlook. The park also offers Kauleonanahoa, an unabashed six-foot-high Phallic Rock, a natural formation that is believed by some to possess fertility powers.

East to Halawa and Beyond

Along Molokai's southern shore, just 30 miles separate Kaunakakai from Halawa, but numbers can be deceiving. There is so much scenic and spiritual beauty to enjoy on this side of the island, you should allow at least a half-day for a lazy, round-trip drive. If you decide to picnic, swim, hike, or go horseback riding at a leisurely pace, allow a full day for this trip to the east side so that you may still negotiate the drive back to town during daylight hours.

Makai, or oceanside, of the paved two-lane road, which later evolves into a narrow, rocky strip, you'll see secluded white sand beaches, historic churches, including two built by Father Damien, and numerous fishponds. Because fishponds, a vital source of life for ancient Hawaiians, are so prevalent along the coast, they deserve more than passing mention.

Such fishponds were typically built by constructing an encircling wall out of stone or coral, or by connecting with a wall two points of land. Wooden gratings that allowed small fish to enter were placed at strategic points in each pond to ensure circulation of fresh seawater and to keep predators out. As fish fattened, and thus grew too large to escape, they were caught in nets. To the degree that sensitivity to one's environment can be measured by a people's balanced approach to natural resources, ancient Hawaiians were highly intelligent and developed. They fashioned such a natural yet sophisticated kind of aquaculture by the 13th century.

Today, many of these ponds have been virtually destroyed by a variety of factors, including tidal activity, silt accumulation, and man. The remaining few have since become aquaculture experiments or commercial operations.

Ancient Hawaiians were also spiritually sensitive, and this dimension can be seen in such places as Kawela, meaning "heat of the battle," where caves, petroglyphs, burials, and *pu'u honua* (places of refuge) are located. Here, high on an inaccessible ridge, King Kamehameha I successfully fought for the inclusion of Molokai into his kingdom.

At Kamalo, one of Molokai's few natural harbors, stop by one of the two churches built by Father Damien—he also had a reputation as an excellent carpenter—in the late 1800s. Kamalo's harbor was once a stopping place for small ships carrying cargo along the coasts in the 19th century. Within the Kamalo vicinity you'll also spot a monument that marks the spot where Ernest Smith and Emory Bronte completed the first trans-Pacific flight by a civilian crew in 1927, a time when such a feat garnered world headlines.

While in the vicinity, look toward Mount Kamakou, the island's highest point at 4,970 feet. Hidden within the mountain is Nature Conservancy of Hawaii's Kamakou Preserve, a 2,774-acre refuge for endangered birds, plants, and other wildlife.

After passing Ualapue and the 216-room Wavecrest Apartments (43 are set aside for visitor rentals), it's not too long before you'll reach the road to Iliiliopae (ee-lee-ee-lee-oh-pie), a major Hawaiian *heiau* listed on the National Registry of Historic Places. You may park your car by the side of the road which leads to the *heiau,* about a 10-minute walk inland from the Wailau Trail sign. The *heiau's* massive stone platform—286 feet west to east and 87 feet north to south—is a breathtaking sight. Be sure to heed the surrounding Private Property signs.

If you get hungry while driving along the main road, stop at the "last chance" Neighborhood Store & Snack Bar at Pukoo and pick up an order of Chicken Papaya if it's available that day. The chicken is flavored with green papaya and lemon grass that the Quinones family grows on their adjacent property. If the pictures on the store's walls are still there, you'll see how the Quinoneses, a local Filipino family, built up a prosperous business that today sits in a modest but "regular" building. For many years before, the Neighborhood Store was a simple lean-to, with its wares and produce displayed in front.

In the Pukoo area the character of the coastline changes—it has been rocky or muddy up to this point. Now, stretches of white, sandy beaches and picturesque bays seem to pop into view from nowhere. Near Honouli-wai Bay, where many Hawaiians lived peacefully with their fishpond and wet-land taro agriculture, the road becomes rugged, but the scenic rewards are great for those who navigate their Toyotas or Chevies forward.

Soon you're climbing through the Puu-o-Hoku ("Hill of Stars") Ranch and Lodge, one of the best sites from which to view West Maui and the turtle-shaped Mokuhooniki Island, a place used by the U.S. military for bombing practice during World War II.

Past the ranch's entrance is a sacred kukui tree grove that has long been regarded with veneration. The area was once the home of Lanikaula, a powerful *kahuna,* who planted the gray-barked trees of silver-green leaves. The *mana,* or spiritual force, of the site is taken very seriously. For example, laborers once refused to help a commercial company clear the place, respecting the belief that virtually nothing in the vicinity, the burial place of Lanikaula, should be disturbed. "Do not touch," still applies.

Just before you descend into Halawa Valley and reach the end of the road, there's a marvelous view of the mountains, sea, and valley itself. From this vantage point it's easy to imagine a geological time eons ago when all of the Hawaiian Islands, including this spot, lay under the ocean.

Halawa Valley (A.D. 650) itself is the oldest recorded habitation site on Molokai and the home of a large agricultural and fishing community until it was struck by a devastating tidal wave in 1946. Today the valley, which is four miles long and half a mile wide, is home for a riding stable, a few animals, and a handful of people who find much of their daily sustenance in the food of their ancestors—fish, poi, taro, and fruit.

There are dirt roads throughout the valley floor, but because of mud-holes and other factors it is advisable to walk, not drive, through. Depending on weather conditions, it is often possible to drive toward the sandy beach, where you may picnic or simply sit and absorb the beauty around you.

Park your car at a clearing opposite the tiny church in the valley if you choose to make the hike inland to reach Moula Falls, the legendary home of the *mo'o* (mo-oh) or giant lizard. Hikers who make the muddy, hour-long trek by foot—mosquito spray is advised for the sensitive-skinned—

experience the sight of taro patches, lush forests, sweet-smelling ginger and, for those wishing to indulge, a refreshing swim at the base of the 250-foot fall that cascades into a glorious mountain pool. Moula is one of two waterfalls in the rear of the valley that feed a stream flowing into the sea.

Beyond Halawa are some of the most spectacular valleys, sea cliffs, and wilderness areas in the state but, with the exception of Kalaupapa Peninsula and Halawa Valley, most of the north coast is inaccessible for viewing except by pre-arranged tours via helicopter, boat, or kayak. The latter two usually run during the summer months, from May through September, when weather and seas permit.

The area has no roads, just rugged trails that even the most experienced hikers have learned to respect. The beauty of Molokai is that you don't have to go to extraordinary lengths to see and hear the heart and soul of Hawaii. They can be found everywhere on the island for those willing to look and listen, from the friendly "talk story" people at shops, hotels, and restaurants to the mystique that emanates from the silent, awesome cliffs at Halawa. In the words of a lifetime resident, "At times I haven't been sure whether I chose a particular site or the site chose me."

PRACTICAL INFORMATION FOR MOLOKAI

HOW TO GET THERE. Molokai is served by 3 local airlines that offer frequent flights from Oahu and Maui. *Hawaiian Airlines* connects Honolulu to Molokai with several daily flights aboard Dash-7 aircraft. Smaller airlines such as *Air Molokai*'s twin-engine Cessna 402 aircraft and *Princeville Airways*' 18-passenger deHavilland Dash-6 Twin Otters run daily trips from Honolulu. Roundtrip prices from Oahu and Maui to Molokai start at $40. (Note: There are no evening operations at Molokai's Hoolehua Airport.)

The smaller airlines also fly regularly into Kalaupapa, the Hansen's Disease colony. Air Molokai has a $52 roundtrip fare from Honolulu but you must first have a land tour confirmation, since flight arrival times in the morning at Kalaupapa should be coordinated with authorized tours of the area that are conducted by Ike's Scenic Tours or Damien Molokai Tours. For more information on the land tour itself, contact Ike at 808–567–6437 or Box 26, Kalaupapa, Molokai, HI 96742; Damien Tours at 567–6171 or Box 1, Kalaupapa, Molokai, HI 96742.

ACCOMMODATIONS. Hotel price categories based on double occupancy are $80 and up, *Deluxe;* $60–$79, *Expensive;* $40–$60, *Moderate;* under $40, *Inexpensive.*

Kaluakoi Hotel and Golf Club. *Deluxe.* Box 1977, Maunaloa, Molokai, HI 96770 (552–2555). A convenient choice, with such amenities as 289 bungalow-style accommodations, shopping, restaurants, golf, and tennis, all located near a sandy beach at the Kaluakoi Resort. Rates vary according to room size and ocean, garden, or golf course views. Beachfront concession arranges canoe rides, Hobie Cat and moped rentals for guests.

Ke Nani Kai. *Expensive.* Box 126, Maunaloa, Molokai, HI 96770 (552–2761 or 800–367–7040). Condominiums at the Kaluakoi Resort complex. 120 fully equipped apartments. Swimming pool, whirlpool, and tennis courts.

The Molokai Shores. *Expensive.* Box 1037, Kaunakakai, Molokai, HI 96748 (553–5954 or 800–367–7042). Another oceanfront hotel with 102 fully equipped vacation apartments set on 4 acres of tropical gardens. Swimming pool and shop.

Paniolo Hale. *Expensive.* Box 146, Maunaloa, Molokai, HI 96770 (552–2731 or 800–367–2984). 77-unit condominium at the Kaluakoi Resort complex. Swimming pool, golf course, paddle tennis.

The Hotel Molokai. *Moderate.* Box 546, Kaunakakai, Molokai, HI 96748 (553–5347 or 800–367–5124). Oceanfront setting 2 miles east of Kaunakakai, features 55 cottage units, restaurant, swimming pool, shops, and also an abundance of friendly charm. Deluxe upper floor units or family rooms (family units accommodate up to 5 persons), standard and garden floor units.

The Wavecrest. *Moderate.* 155 Star Route, Kaunakakai, Molokai, HI 96748 (558–8101 or 800–367–2980). In east Molokai at Ualapue. 43 apartments in the 216-room beachfront resort are available for rental.

The Pau Hana Inn. *Inexpensive.* Box 860, Kaunakakai, Molokai, HI 96748 (553–5342 or 800–367–5124). An oceanfront hotel with 32 cottage units, dining room, swimming pool, and lots of friendliness. Prices vary according to view, number of people, and length of stay. For example, there are single standards in a building called the "Long House," deluxe kitchenette units, and comfortable duplex cottages.

RESTAURANTS. There are 2 fine restaurants at the Kaluakoi Hotel and Golf Club: **The Ohia Lodge** and the **Paniolo Broiler** (552–2555 for both), both moderate to expensive. For local-style food, drink, and "talk story" sessions, try **Jojo's** (552–2803) in Maunaloa town or eating spots in Kaunakakai, including the moderately priced oceanside restaurants at the Pau Hana Inn and Hotel Molokai. Breakfast fans rave about Hotel Molokai's banana French toast. A hearty breakfast is also served at Molokai's cozy **Kanemitsu Bakery** (553–5855), home of Hawaii's famous "Molokai Bread." (Kanemitsu closes on Tuesdays.) A variety of inexpensive ethnic dishes may be found at Kaunakakai's **Hop Inn** (553–5465), **Oviedo's** (553–5014), **Rabang's** (553–5878), and the **Mid-Nite Inn** (553–5302). The only eating spot in east Molokai is a snack shop at the **Neighborhood Store** (558–8933) in Pukoo.

HOW TO GET AROUND. Ground transfers by **Gray Line Molokai** or **Roberts Hawaii** from Molokai's Hoolehua airport to lodgings in town or at the Kaluakoi Resort range from $6 to $8. Reservations may be made by contacting Gray Line at 567–6177 or Box 253, Hoolehua, Molokai, HI 96729; Roberts at 552–2751 or Box 117, Maunaloa, Molokai, HI 96770.

Four firms—**Tropical Rent-A-Car, Budget Rent-A-Car, Dollar Rent-A-Car,** and **Avis Rent-A-Car**—offer U-drives at prices ranging from $25 daily for compacts to $35 for American models. Tropical Rent-A-Car (567–6118), Budget Rent-A-Car (567–6877), and Dollar Rent-A-Car (567–6156) have offices at Hoolehua Airport. The Molokai branch of Avis (local 567–6814, or toll free 800–331–1212) is located at the intersection of the airport road and the main highway. (Note: Most Molokai gas stations are closed on Sundays. Car rental rates vary with seasons, higher rates usually prevailing during December, January, and summer months.)

TOURS. In addition to specific Kalaupapa tours coordinated by Damien Molokai Tours or Ike's Scenic Tours (See "How to Get There" above), general tours of Molokai are operated by *Gray Line Molokai* and *Roberts Hawaii.* Both have air-conditioned **vans** and offer half- or full-day tours that include such points of interest as Kalaupapa lookout, Kaunakakai, and Halawa Valley. Prices range from $12 to $32, depending upon point of origin and length of tour. Call Gray Line at 567–6177, Roberts at 552–2751.

The Nature Conservancy of Hawaii offers tours of the rain forests and mountains of all the isles. Their visit to Molokai's Kamakou Preserve includes a walk through an ancient bog and a glimpse of some of Hawaii's endangered birds and plants. They also sponsor field trips which explore Moomomi Dunes on the north shore, site of important fossil and archaeological discoveries. Arrange in advance. Write 1116 Smith St., Suite 201, Honolulu, HI 96817, or call 808–537–4508.

A **bird's-eye view** of Molokai and its virtually inaccessible sea cliffs is the reward of the stouthearted who take to the skies with *Royal Helicopter Tours.* Rates start at $37.50 a person. The one-half hour North Coast tour costs $75, and the 1-hour circle island tour is $150. Contact them at 567–6733, or write to the firm at Molokai's Hoolehua Airport, 96729.

A popular way of seeing Kalaupapa is by the now-famous **Molokai Mule Ride,** atop the backs of sure-footed mules that traverse a 26-switchback trail from "topside" Molokai to the peninsula below where there's an educational tour of one of the most beautiful spots in Hawaii. Rare Adventures, Ltd. operates the $65 tour which includes guides, a van tour of the settlement, and nice picnic lunch. (Children under 16 not allowed.) For information write *Rare Adventures,* Box 200, Kualapuu, Molokai, HI 96757, or telephone 567–6088.

Camera safaris depart daily except Sunday from the Kaluakoi Resort for the Molokai Ranch Wildlife Park where nearly 500 African and Asian animals, including crown cranes and Barbary sheep, roam the preserve. Arrangements for the tour ($12 for adults and juniors; $6 for children under 12) may be made by contacting *Molokai Ranch Wildlife Safari,* Maunaloa, HI 96770, or by calling 552–2555.

The Molokai Wagon Ride ambles along the pretty southeast shore with stops at Iliiliopae Heiau, Hawaii's largest ancient place of worship; at a vast grove of palm, mango, and coconut trees; and at an exotic beach where traditional Hawaiian crafts are demonstrated. Rates are $25. For information write Larry Helm at Box 56, Hoolehua, HI 96729, or call 567–6773 or 558–8380.

SPORTS. Golf buffs may indulge at either of 2 spots—the quaint *Ironwood Hills Golf Course* with its 9 holes or at the championship 18-hole *Kaluakoi Golf Course.* If you're a guest at any Kaluakoi Resort accommodation, green fees are $34 with cart. Non-guests are charged $40 with cart. For more information call or write Ironwood Hills at 567–6121, Kualapuu, Molokai, HI 96757; the Kaluakoi Resort at 552–2739, Kepuhi Beach, HI 96770.

If **snorkeling, photographic expeditions,** or **sea cruises** are your bent, contact *Rodonis Sailing Charters.* Telephone 553–3311 or write the firm at Box 1037, Kaunakakai, Molokai, HI 96748. Half- and full-day charters can be booked on the "Adele II," a 35-ft. twin diesel cruiser, excellent for **sportsfishing.** Write Box 121, Kaunakakai, HI 96748 or call 558–8266 or 558–8342. For information about **windsurfing,** contact *Windsurfing Molokai* at 558–8253, Star Route 355A, Waialua, Molokai, HI 96748.

Kayaks provide thrills on the ocean for the adventuresome; kayaking, a relatively new addition to Molokai's sports scene, takes adventurers to the north coast of the island. (The interest in Hawaii kayaking was sparked by the book, "Paddling My Own Canoe," a woman's chronicle of her experiences while singlehandedly paddling along Molokai's remote, often dangerous, windward coastline.) During July and August, when seas are calmer but still unpredictable, experienced kayakers John and Kristie Gray offer weekly trips on inflatable kayaks which they guide on the ocean from Halawa Valley to Kalaupapa Peninsula. Prices start at $100 a day and include meals. For more information, write the *Grays* at *Pacific Outdoor Adventures,* Box 61609, Honolulu, HI 96822, or call 988–3913.

For an interior view of Molokai, supervised **horseback rides** are available through **Hawaiian Horsemanship Unlimited.** Write Box 94, Kualapuu, HI 96757 or call 552–0056.

CAMPING. There are two county parks on Molokai for camping: Alii No. 1 and Papohaku Beach (camping only in designated area, not permitted in park). $3 per adult, three-day limit. Write to the Department of Public Works, Kaunakakai, HI 96748 (553–3221). Tents are also permitted at the free (with permit) state mountain forest park at Palaau. Write Division of Parks, Land and Natural Resources, Box 153, Kaunakakai, HI 96746 (567–6083).

LANAI

The Warm and Rustic Pineapple Isle

By
THELMA T. CHANG

Describing Lanai, only a 20-minute flight from Honolulu, as "warm and rustic" is not a cliché. At this point in time, Lanai, with its population of 2,100, is just that, and more.

Lanai is also known as the "Pineapple Island," a place where the people know each other, "talk story," and share music after work, a place where many doors remain unlocked because trust is an unspoken assumption, a place where Mom and Pop stores—not gaudy souvenir stands—are a mainstay, a place where the term "rent a car" really means "rough it in a Jeep." The island's practical side may also be seen in its huge pineapple plantation—thousands of spiny acres of the green and gold fruit woven together by red dirt roads in the fertile Palawai Basin on the floor of an extinct volcanic crater. With few exceptions, most of Lanai's people are involved with pineapple just as their predecessors had been 60 years ago when the industry took hold and flourished.

Today Lanai stands on the brink of change. Pineapple planting and harvesting are back-bending chores—labor equations that add a question mark to the industry's long-term future in Hawaii. "Labor is cheap and abundant in foreign countries," may sound like an old song, but the reality of that time-worn phrase has slowly made its way to Lanai. However, Hawaii's trademark fruit continues to thrive; Lanai will probably remain the home of one of the world's largest pineapple plantations for many years.

Whatever the future may bring, Castle & Cooke, Lanai's major landowner since 1961 when it acquired the assets of Dole Corporation, is looking generally to diversification on the island, specifically resort development. Most of the company's real estate transactions are conducted through Oceanic Properties, a wholly owned subsidiary of Castle & Cooke.

As with slow-paced Molokai, the move has made some residents uneasy with the idea of perhaps losing a simple lifestyle based on mutual reciprocation and trust. They are concerned about crime, a rare occurrence on the island. Others are worried about dependency on outsiders. They desire both government and private sector support in developing a self-sufficient way of life, using such natural resources as wind, sun, and earth to harness the island's energy and potential for diversified crops. (Some residents complain about high electricity bills.) Still others see resort development near the island's Hulopoe Beach as the first step toward a loss of control of their own environment, including the use of Lanai's accessible swimming area and harbor. But there are also those who itch for more variety and opportunities. They, in time, leave the peaceful, friendly island for the "big cities," whether in Honolulu or on the Mainland.

Now, as in the past, Lanai has been the focus of different perceptions. For example, "Red Lanai" was how the ancient chants described the kidney-shaped island, referring to the soil that flew in the wind and tinted everything it touched a rusty hue.

Other people saw the island through a cloud of fear. For a long time Lanai remained uninhabited, early Polynesians judging the place to be more a home for ghosts than for living settlers. Still others viewed this third smallest island of the Hawaiian chain as a gentle hump, especially when seen from the more dominating volcanic mountains of Lanai's neighbors—Maui and Molokai.

On Lanai—just 18 miles long, 13 miles wide, and 140.4 square miles in land area—people acted on their perceptions. When it was believed that ghosts no longer prevailed on Lanai, Hawaiians from the Neighbor Islands began to migrate to the island, probably around the 1400s, and relied on the sea for their sustenance. They moved slowly inland, discovering that the fertile interior was excellent for the growing of taro, yams, and other crops. Before contact with the outside world and its new values and attitudes toward the environment, the people of Lanai lived in their harmonious state with the land.

In the late 1700s a ship's captain passed the island by, noting that Lanai looked "naked . . . thinly covered with shrivelled grass in a scorched state." But during the same era when Hawaii's King Kamehameha I was consolidating his control over most of the Hawaiian Islands, the monarch liked what he saw. During his reign the king kept a summer home at the southwestern coastal village of Kaunolu Bay, thus marking the beginning of the island's transition into modern history.

Dwight Baldwin and William Richards, Lanai's first known missionaries, arrived in 1835. By the mid-1800s other missionaries pursued their own vision of earthly utopia when a group of Hawaiian and American Mormons arrived on the island and established a City of Joseph on the fertile plains in central Lanai. But problems such as drought and insect infestations played havoc with the visionaries' dreams and the venture was all over within three years.

However, other people had ambitious plans for what appeared to some as a "blighted" island, devoid of the sugar and pineapple just beginning to thrive on Lanai's Neighbor Islands. In the early 1920s, Jim Dole's Hawaiian Pineapple Company purchased a major portion of the island from Harry and Frank Baldwin, the descendants of early missionaries, for $1.1 million, a tidy sum in that era. A model community sprouted with the development of Lanai City's plantation housing done in right-angle grids to house the original 150 immigrant laborers. Meanwhile, more than 15,000 acres of the island were turned over to pineapple production. Dole changed the face of Lanai.

Exploring Lanai

Your introduction to the island is through the flight itself, for there is a runway in the midst of what appears at first glance to be a carpet of thousands of pineapples. The fruits, crowned with sharp leaves, lace the sides of a good paved road that connects the five miles from the airport to Lanai City, where most of the island's people live.

"City" is a misnomer for Lanai's town. Here, among tiny shops, an old movie house that no longer operates, the post office and town's bulletin board, a funky hotel, Cook Island pine trees that resemble the Norfolk variety, and potted plants that sit in front of neat wooden houses, Lanai's genial people congregate after work and on weekends. Filipinos are about 65 percent of a population that also includes a variety of Asians, Hawaiians, Portuguese, Caucasians, and an "all of the above" mixture.

For the most part, they live a pleasant, rustic life 1,600 feet above sea level on a plateau below the slope of the 3,370-foot Lanaihale Mountain. Rather than jutting straight up and down in sheer cliff form, Lanaihale, which affords a magnificent view of Maui, Oahu, Kahoolawe, and Molokai, tapers gradually into the sea. Hence, its name "Lanai," or "the hump."

The Hotel Lanai, the island's only guest headquarters for now, is the town's "center." The modest 10-room lodge, nestled among pines and about a minute's walk from the town's square, is a gathering place for guests and local residents hungry for a homestyle meal, whether it is breakfast, lunch, or dinner. Near Lanai City is the construction site of Castle & Cooke's $17-million, 102-room, two-story hotel called the Lodge at Koele, sure to change the face of this tiny town.

The clear and cool atmosphere of Lanai City—the fragrance of pine and pineapples often wafting through the wind—go hand in hand with the stately pine trees that dot the landscape. Around 1910, naturalist George Munro, after whom Lanai's Munro Trail is named, successfully planted the pines that have since become an island landmark along the ridgeline. Besides adding beauty, the trees act as windbreakers around Lanai City and collect valuable moisture from passing clouds, increasing the island's limited supply of ground water. Thanks to Munro's penchant for sowing seeds from horseback, the green Christmas card look of the vicinity today makes it easy to imagine for a moment that you are in Colorado, not Hawaii, living John Denver songs.

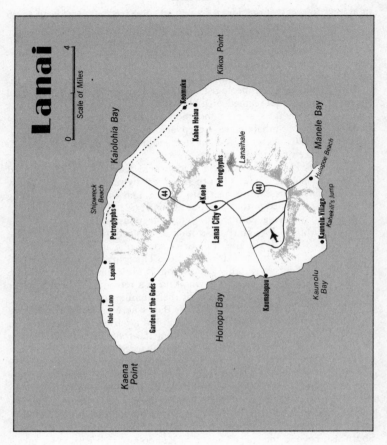

Along Paved Roads and Dusty Trails

Lanai has three paved primary roads—between 25 and 30 miles in all—that branch out from Lanai City to the working port of Kaumalapau Harbor, to Shipwreck Beach, and to accessible Hulopoe Beach. However, for the serious adventurer who revels in red dust, bramble bushes, and rugged hiking trails, forget air-conditioned cars and the other comforts of home. Dress sensibly and rent a sturdy jeep or other four-wheel drive vehicle that can traverse the rough terrain to historic sites, rock formations, and other isolated spots.

When you head southwest, you're on Lanai's "busiest" highway, which leads to Kaumalapau Harbor. The seven miles between Lanai City and the harbor is the same route that workers have taken for years, hauling millions of crated pineapples to the barges for shipment to Honolulu canneries, 60 nautical miles away.

Before taking off for pretty Kaunolu Bay (in fact, before heading anywhere off the beaten track on Lanai) it is advisable to ask hotel management or local residents for specific instructions, since there are few signs

or arrows to speak of outside of Lanai City. But basically you head south
for Kaunolu Bay, taking the main "pineapple" road off the highway that
skirts the pineapple fields.

The trip itself is an excursion into Hawaii's past: Kaunolu Bay, a favorite fishing retreat of King Kamehameha I; the Halulu Heiau; and the ru-
ined Hawaiian village of Kaunolu.

The location is an archeologist's dream and possesses the sentimental
charm of a place that teemed with life before it was abandoned in the late
1800s. There you'll see stone floors, house platforms, and petroglyphs of
sea birds in a once-inhabited cave excavated by Bishop Museum archeologists in the 1920s. As with all other such cultural sites in the Islands, care
should be taken not to disturb the area.

Close by is Kahekili's Jump, a place where Kamehameha is believed
to have watched his warriors test their bravery by running along a narrow
path, jumping more than 60 feet into the sea, and—the most hair-raising
of all—clearing a ledge that juts out about 15 feet from the cliff wall.

Modern-day diving enthusiasts enjoy the underwater version of the
sport near Manele Bay Harbor, around an easterly point from Hulopoe
Bay and its beach. It's a nine-mile drive south of Lanai City on Manele
Road to reach both bays of dazzling blue. The journey straight through
the pineapple fields eventually brings you to Hulopoe Beach, a favorite
recreation spot of local residents who find it a refreshing, tranquil place
to swim, picnic, and loll around with their families on a lazy day.

Change can already be seen at Manele Bay, where Lanai fishermen once
moored their family boats. Today, you'll find a variety of pleasure craft
in the bay, while onshore a new $95-million, 250-room hotel is in the midst
of construction and is expected to be completed during 1989.

For landlubbers the loveliest drive on Lanai is the one from Lanai City
and Koele through the tropical rain forest to Lanaihale. Here on a clear
day, from the top at 3,370 feet, all of the major Hawaiian Islands, with
the exception of Kauai and Niihau, are set like jewels in the sea. Directly
north, eight miles across Kalohi channel, is the long island of Molokai.
Oahu is northwest. Due east is the double-coned silhouette of Maui.
Southeast, beyond the rugged island of Kahoolawe that is used for target
practice by the military, lies the land mass of Hawaii—the Big Island, with
its volcanic cones of Mauna Loa and Mauna Kea peeking through the
clouds at nearly 14,000 feet.

Unless rains and other conditions have made the road virtually impossible to traverse, a four-wheel-drive vehicle may reach the Munro Trail from
Lanai City by heading north on Keomuku Road. Bear right on the "cemetery" road, where there should be a sign. Again you'll be rewarded by images of the past—the Luahiwa petroglyphs that were carved into hillsides
centuries ago. The Munro Trail continues past Hookio Gulch, to Koele,
then back to Lanai City.

Windward Lanai: Shipwreck Beach and the Garden of the Gods

Lanai's northeast shore is a delight for beachcombers, and you can
reach it by following Keomuku Road till the paved road ends. The dirt
trail to the left will take you to Shipwreck Beach, so named because the
strong trade winds between Maui and Molokai often became powerful
enough to drive wooden sailing ships and steamers up on Lanai's reefs.

The austere, deserted area looks like a Robinson Crusoe setting with its rusting World War II hulk offshore and an occasional find of driftwood or Japanese glass fishing floats.

The attractions of the coast also include the deserted village of Keomuku (it was abandoned in 1901 after the collapse of Maunalei Sugar Company), the remnants of old homes, picnic areas, and the ruins of Kahea Heiau. As with all other trails or rocky areas, be careful. On a sunny day (when it's raining, forget it) you can make the rough trek south to the former Hawaiian village of Naha on a jeep trail that passes beautiful Lopa Beach and continues for awhile along the eastern coast. Be prepared for a jolting ride. When you reach Naha you will come to the ridge road that climbs inland to join the Lanaihale Road.

Another fascinating jaunt on the island can be found seven miles from Lanai City—the geological curiosity known locally as "The Garden of the Gods." From town go north on Frazier Road till you hit a dirt trail which runs into a major pineapple road. Then turn left on a dirt road lined on both sides with ironwood trees. "Be warned that unless you know the area it's difficult to find so before you start out, ask a local resident who knows," says a Castle & Cooke official.

When you reach the windswept canyon, you'll sense an other-worldly, universal feeling in a setting that is strewn with boulders and disfigured lava formations. The rocks look as if they were capriciously dropped from the sky by a playful force. Take along a camera, for nowhere else on the Pineapple Island will you find such a spot as this.

Like the rest of Lanai, the "Garden of the Gods" gives you a feeling of exclusiveness as yet unencumbered by man-made noises, machinery, buildings, and complexity. Whether you're scuba-diving, traversing the jeep roads, studying Hawaii's past through the island's petroglyphs and *heiau,* or simply seeking relaxation, that overall atmosphere of spaciousness and simplicity is the source of Lanai's appeal.

PRACTICAL INFORMATION FOR LANAI

HOW TO GET THERE. Two airlines— *Hawaiian Airlines* and *Air Molokai*— serve the island of Lanai. Hawaiian Airlines has flights to and from Lanai from Honolulu daily except Saturday. *Air Molokai,* the smaller carrier, offers frequent flights to Lanai on a daily basis. Roundtrip fares from Honolulu start at $68.

ACCOMMODATIONS AND RESTAURANTS. The Hotel Lanai. Box A-119, Lanai, HI 96763 (565–7211 or 800–624–6689). Until construction is completed in 1989 on the new Manele Bay Hotel and the Lodge at Koele, the Hotel Lanai continues to be the island's single hotel, a pleasant and comfortable 10-room lodge built in the 1920s and refurbished in 1980. Rates range from $51 to $65, depending upon single, double, or triple occupancy. The charming dining room serves 3 meals a day, and you can relax with a book on the breezy front lanai.

Breakfast and lunch are also available at a few places down the hill from the hotel: **Dahang's Bakery** (565–6363), which sells Lanai Bread in addition to Molokai Bread; and **S & T Properties** (565–6537), which is opened at various hours (no set time).

For necessities and a dose of island friendliness, drop in at Lanai's 3 general stores: **Richard's Shopping Center** (565–6047), operated by the Tamashiro Family; **Pine Isle Market** (565–6488), owned by the Hondas; and **International Food and Clothing Center** (565–6433), run by the Dela Cruz Family.

HOW TO GET AROUND. There are **jeeps and sedans** for rent in Lanai City, but the 4-wheel-drive vehicle is recommended for the island's rough terrain. *Oshiro U-Drive and Taxi* (565–6952) can fix you up with a car for $25 to $28 a day, a pickup truck or station wagon for about $42 a day, and a 4-wheel-drive from $65 to $75 a day. *Lanai City Service* (565–6780) also offers similar vehicles at comparable prices. The firm also rents vans at $75 a day.

TOURS. *Ocean Activities Center* runs a tour boat to Lanai for an all-day excursion that includes lunch, van tour of the island, and snorkeling off Lanai's coast. $85 for adults, $50 for children. Call 800–367–8047, or write Ocean Activities Center, 3750 Wailea Alanui D–2, Wailea, Maui, HI 96753. *Lanai City Service* offers sightseeing tours in 14-passenger vans. Call 808–565–6780 or write Box N, Lanai City, HI 96763.

SPORTS. Visitors may **golf** at the 9-hole Cavendish course (some people describe it as "cute") at Lanai City. No carts or pro. Green fee, $5. There are 2 tennis courts at Lanai School.

Hunting season for axis deer is from March through May and licenses are required. State of Hawaii License deadlines may vary. Write to: Division of Forestry & Wildlife, State of Hawaii, 1151 Punchbowl St., Room 325, Honolulu, HI 96813 or call 548–8850.

For detailed information about **underwater diving** sites and Hawaiian **hiking trails** on Lanai, ask anyone at the hotel front desk.

For **snorkeling** there's a tour boat from Maui to Lanai (see "Tours" above).

CAMPING. There are six campsites on Lanai at Hulopoe Beach. $5 registration, $5 per person per night, seven-day limit. Write Koele Co., Box L, Lanai City, HI 96763 (565–6661).

KAUAI

Where Dreams Come True

By
MARTY WENTZEL

Marty Wentzel lives and writes in Hawaii where she has worked extensively in the travel and tourism fields. Her feature-length articles have appeared in many travel magazines and books, including Aloha Magazine, Discover Hawaii, Modern Bride *the* Sheraton Islands, *and the* Hawaii Hotel Network.

Imagine a place where miles and miles of pristine beaches stretch as far as the eye can see. Imagine great emerald cliffs whose razor-edged ridges march in wondrous repetition. Imagine cascading waterfalls, sleepy rivers and an extravagance of flora and fauna in a climate conducive to T-shirts and shorts. Imagine all this and you'll know what to expect on Kauai, the Garden Isle.

If you're looking for neon lights and life in the fast lane, don't go to Kauai. On the contrary! This gentle Pacific oasis is like a giant step backward to old Hawaii, where soft breezes breathe tales of the ancients and time passes in the ebb and flow of the tides. Kauai awaits its visitors with calm, unaffected beauty, oblivious to the glitter and glamor of its more cosmopolitan neighbor, Oahu. The pace is slow there, life is simple, and everywhere you look are picture-perfect images of a South Seas dream-come-true.

Kauai lives up to its nickname of the Garden Isle on a grand scale indeed. Your overwhelming first impression is one of green, every shade imaginable, from pastel limes to deep, dark jades. Kauai is comparable to a huge botanical garden which stimulates all the senses, from the smells of salty ocean air and the tastes of fresh fruits, to the magnificent sights of its god-like panoramas. Sparkling waterways spread generous nourishment to the tips of the island, sustaining this moist, lush paradise where Mother Nature reigns soft and supreme.

A visit to Kauai is almost 100 percent foolproof, for it offers a wealth of wondrous things to see and do. It's a great place to play, with untold opportunities for hiking, diving, hunting, swimming, boating, tennis, and much more, not to mention its world-famous golf courses. It boasts a buffet of four-star restaurants as well as charming family-style eateries with budget prices. Its accommodations run the gamut, from simple cabins in the woods to luxurious oceanside resorts featuring all the amenities. It's replete with Hawaiian history, facts and fantasies which live on in historic sites and buildings. But its universal appeal is an easy-going, laid-back pace of life luring all types of visitors, be they Hollywood stars or hermits, hopeless romantics or modern-day Captain Cooks. If you haven't learned the meaning of Hawaiian time yet, here's the place to do just that.

Kauai is a happy blend of superlatives, and it stands out from the rest of Hawaii in many ways. It was the first of the Islands to be formed, assuming its northernmost position millions of years ago. Along with Niihau, it is the only island which you can't see from any of the others. It is home to the world's wettest spot, Mt. Waialeale, which feeds Hawaii's only navigable rivers: Waimea, Makaweli, Hanalei, Wailua, and Hanapepe. The precious mokihana berry grows only on the Garden Isle, its anise scent permeating the lush mountain forests.

Myth has it that Kauai was the first home of Madame Pele, the highly revered volcano goddess. History books cite that Captain Cook made Kauai his first port of call when he blazed his historic trail to Hawaii.The mysterious *menehune* are said to have chosen Kauai over all the other islands as their home. The first successful sugar plantation rose up in little Koloa town, setting the pace for one of Hawaii's most enduring profit-makers. And Kauai's people are often called the friendliest to be found in the 50th state, a claim you'll be hard-pressed to dispute from the moment you're greeted at the airport until that final aloha.

Situated 95 miles northwest of Honolulu, Kauai makes for a quick and easy getaway from Oahu. Flights from Honolulu take you over such familiar Oahu landmarks as Pearl Harbor and Barbers Point plus the glorious Waianae Mountain Range. Drink your complimentary fruit punch quickly, for in just 20 minutes you'll find yourself landing in the midst of majestic mountains and mile after mile of sugar cane fields. You'll feel yourself beginning to unwind before you've even stepped off the plane.

Kauai is the fourth largest island in the Hawaiian chain, but it's only two-thirds as populated as second-ranked Maui. Its 40,000 inhabitants preside primarily in the 20 or so towns which line the shores. Much of its 350,000 acres are gloriously uninhabited, save for the invisible spirits of gods and goddesses from Hawaiian days gone by.

Kauai burst forth from a single, large volcano which formed the twin peaks of Kawaikini and Waialeale, great spires rising up in the middle of the island. Millions of years of mighty winds and waves molded this veritable Garden of Eden, a land ringed with age-old beaches whose sands have shifted silently through time. Centuries of tropical storms carved out the 15-mile stretch of sand-castle cliffs and verdurous valleys which are now a Kauai trademark: the Pali (cliffs) Coast on the northwest shore. To the northeast rises the Anahola Mountain Range and to the south the Hoary Heads reign.

All of this surrounds the great Alakai Swamp, an impenetrable area rich in rare plants and animals. Ten miles long and two miles wide, the Alakai Swamp serves as the fountainhead of Kauai's seven main rivers, those slow and steady craftsmen of the canyons and valleys visible today. Rising above it all is Mt. Waialeale, whose 5,243-foot summit (Kawaikini Peak) has earned the well-deserved reputation as the wettest place on earth. Waialeale receives an annual rainfall of 450 to 550 inches, which explains why the Hawaiians named it "rippling water." How wet is it? In October of 1981, the weight of the moisture was so substantial that it touched off a huge landslide. Tons and tons of mud were deposited into the Olokele Canyon in the biggest slippage Kauai has ever experienced.

Deep within the dense jungles of the Alakai Swamp reside hundreds of species of rare wildlife which enjoy the privacy of this overgrown interior. Ferns great and small line the soft valley walls, and the bright red *ohia* blossom shines out clearly against the olive backdrop. Endangered birds found nowhere else are occasionally seen and heard in these reaches, including the small *'o'o'a'a,* whose feathers were once used for the cloaks of kings. Here and elsewhere on Kauai grows a kaleidoscope of tropical flowers: Bright red poinsettias, multicolored bougainvillea, orange trumpet vines, night-blooming cereus, poinciana, maile, olapa, kukui, and jacaranda, to name just a few.

The north of the island tends to be rather rainy, creating a flourishing arboretum of flowering vines and sylvan woodlands. In sunny contrast, the rest of coastal Kauai receives little more than a dozen inches of rain, resulting in spectacular daily weather reports at the beachfront resorts. Spreading over it all are the dozens of rainbows appearing every day, adding multicolored mystery to this land where beauty knows no bounds.

With its wealth of natural blessings, this fairy-tale island has come to acquire centuries of fascinating folklore from the mists of time. The most popular of these stories concerns the *menehune,* a race of tiny yet industrious workers who lived on Kauai before the Polynesians. Much controversy surrounds these pygmy-sized people who stood only a couple of feet tall and whose claim to fame were the remarkable stone works found around the island. Few people saw them, for they preferred to work only at night. If they didn't finish their project by sunrise, they left it undone.

The menehune enjoyed their undertakings, asking as payment just one shrimp per person (their favorite food). Today the menehune are given credit for the many bridges, walls, and structures of which no one knows the origin. While many people laugh off these stories as simple myths, there are some Kauaians who actually claim to have menehune ancestors. Since the Tahitian word "manahune" means "lower class," were these industrious little creatures actually real-life Polynesian slaves? No one knows for sure. But until someone comes up with a better explanation for those prodigious creations visible around Kauai, the menehune have our vote.

From early on, Kauai has had its share of notable visitors. The first Polynesians arrived on Kauai around A.D. 750, setting up their communities on the serene banks of the Wailua River. This cool, protected landscape was conducive to the privacy which they sought for their sacred areas. Remnants of their villages are visible today, living reminders of a cherished part of Kauai's history.

Hawaii's contact with western civilization began with the arrival of Captain James Cook on January 18, 1778. He anchored his boats, the HMS *Resolution* and HMS *Discovery,* in the deep-water harbor off the southern shores of Waimea. As soon as he landed he was immediately well received. Although the chiefs had moved farther north to shady Wailua, Cook was still greeted in style by the islanders who lived in the grass huts by the sea. They took him on a tour of a nearby heiau, and they demonstrated their skills of making tapa, the soft Polynesian cloth fashioned from tree bark. They regaled him with gifts and entertainment, and they exchanged live pigs and fresh vegetables for his iron nails and trinkets. After five days, strong winds blew Captain Cook's ships away to the shores of neighboring Niihau, but already a new page had been turned on an important chapter for the island of Kauai.

Kauai is proud of its claim to fame as the only island not conquered by King Kamehameha. During his great unifying sweep in the 1790s, the king gathered a huge fleet to invade Kauai, at that time under the rule of King Kaumualii. But Kamehameha's forces weren't hearty enough to withstand Kauai's furious seas, and they gave up after two failed attempts. Eventually Kaumualii recognized Kamehameha's sovereignty and peacefully submitted the island to his reign in 1810. After that Hawaii was consolidated under a single leader and Kauai lost its previous political power. Yet Kaumualii handled the affair with a great deal of dignity, surrendering with diplomacy rather than war.

The first Congregational missionaries to come to Hawaii from Boston settled on Kauai, establishing their mission in the 1820s. From then on, several mission sites sprung up around the island, setting off a new look for the lifestyle of the native Hawaiians. Many of the missionaries' original structures remain today as testimony of their faith and endurance in this strange new land.

Kauai's pride and joy is its native son, Jonah Kuhio Kalanianaole, better known as Prince Kuhio. Born in Koloa near Poipu, this man went on to become the last member of Hawaiian royalty to wield political power. Hawaii loved Prince Kuhio so much that they elected him not only in 1902, but nine times thereafter. They even nicknamed him Prince Cupid! Prince Kuhio was Hawaii's first congressman, and he brought the concerns of all Hawaiians to the nation's capital, created more jobs, and established homestead land for them. No wonder, then, that we salute this beloved Kauaian each year on his birthday, March 26, an official state holiday.

Kauai's economic history is a sweet success story summed up primarily with one word: sugar. Hawaii's first commercial sugar plantation sprang up in Koloa in 1835. A grab-bag of ethnic groups came looking for new and promising lives in Kauai's many camp towns, which were situated along the shore for easy access to the ocean for exporting. Chinese, Japanese, Norwegians, Germans, Filipinos, Portuguese, Puerto Ricans, Koreans, Spanish . . . they arrived in hopeful droves, only to work in the hot, dusty cane fields under adverse conditions for minimal pay. For 50 years the industry boomed, but only a handful of these sugar mills remains on

Kauai today. The cultural diversity of Kauai's contemporary population directly reflects those early immigrant days on the sugar plantations.

In addition to sugar, the Garden Isle has become a veritable greenhouse for other economic endeavors as well. Gone are the pineapple fields and rice paddies which were attempted and abandoned, but today's farmers find success in cultivating macadamia nuts, taro, papayas, and guavas. Some commercial fishing takes place, but more prevalent is aquaculture, a method of raising fish which dates directly back to the days of the old Hawaiians. In ancient fashion, large rectangular pools are maintained in order to cultivate prawns as well as certain kinds of fish. Kilauea is Kauai's aquaculture center, attracting international attention as a leader in that industry.

Kauai's most recent economic boom has been in movie making, which draws as many people as any other attraction. Tourists aren't the only folks lured here with their cameras. Superstars and dashing directors find Kauai's lush lands and sandy shores ideal for their work. Its diversity of landscapes allows for a universe of set designs, from adventurous chase scenes through jungles to the simple life of a funky little town.

When Mitzi Gaynor sang and danced in *South Pacific,* she washed that man right out of her hair on Lumahai Beach. *Raiders of the Lost Ark* filmed chase scenes through Kauai's forests, and *The Thorn Birds* transformed the Garden Isle into the Australian outback. *King Kong* (in the 1976 remake) went ape on the remote Na Pali Coast, and Elvis Presley strutted his stuff on a beach in Wailua. Other remarkable reels which have featured Kauai include *Body Heat, 10, Fantasy Island,* and *Islands in the Stream.* But even the most panoramic screen and super-stereophonic sound can't do justice to the glory that is Kauai. It's clear that the best way to see Kauai is first-hand, with your own two eyes.

Exploring Kauai

One main road runs around the edge of Kauai, from Ke'e Beach in the north to Polihale Beach in the west. Either way, the road stops at the rugged Na Pali Coast, and when you get a look at this impenetrable mass of rock, you'll understand why no one ever bothered building an access road over it.

From Lihue, a trip in either direction adds up to about 40 miles of comfortable driving on well-maintained highways. As a result, it's easy to get around and hard to get lost on this circular isle. It takes approximately an hour and 10 minutes from Lihue to Haena, an hour and a half from Lihue to Kokee.

Although many folks explore the whole area in a hectic day, we recommend that you allow at least one day for each side of Kauai, because there are literally scores of lovely places to see and activities to enjoy. After all, you wouldn't want to miss a sleepy afternoon at Hanalei Bay Beach Park. Or a heart-thumping helicopter ride into Waimea Canyon. Or a leisurely cruise up the Wailua River to Fern Grotto. Or a night by the fireplace in the highlands of Kokee. Or a Na Pali zodiac boat ride. All these things take time!

There's no doubt that Kauai deserves all the devotion and exploration you can give it, and the rewards for your efforts will truly be great. No

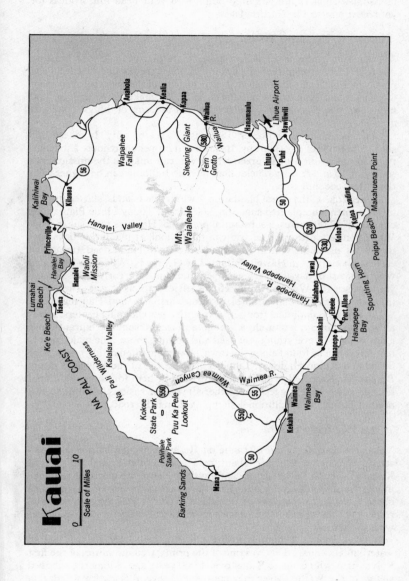

matter what your itinerary, you'll fall in love with Kauai's scenery and
its people. Chances are you'll go home with your head full of ideas for
your next trip to the Garden Isle.

Lihue, A Big Little Town

Your tour begins in Lihue, an appropriate place to get your bearings
due to its close proximity to the airport. Lihue is the commercial and business center of the Garden Isle as well as the seat of the county government
for Kauai and Niihau. Its population of 4,000 makes it Kauai's second
largest only to Kapaa, but it's definitely first in terms of things to see and
do.

Don't be mistaken, however. Lihue is NOT a big city. It reflects the
simpler lifestyle of days gone by. Its prim and proper courthouse and county buildings sit on a small green where you can imagine the missionaries
scurrying to and fro. By official mandate, no building can be higher than
the tallest coconut tree.

Lihue is one of the oldest plantation towns in the Islands, started in 1849
by three men who planted sugar on 2,000 acres. Today Lihue Plantations
consists of 17,000 acres, a substantial portion of Hawaii's total sugar crop.
While you're touring Lihue, you can take a look at plantation days past
by driving down Nawiliwili Road to Grove Farm Homestead, one of the
earliest plantations in Hawaii. Founded by George N. Wilcox in 1864, this
was the heart of day-to-day sugar operations until the early 1930s. Today
you can see the Wilcox Family Home left exactly as it was when lived
in, with an eclectic collection of furniture, artifacts, and Hawaiiana.

Lihue is an economical frontier town with a few shopping centers, several banks, a library, a church, a school, a museum, some restaurants, and
a few hotels . . . everything you need and nothing more. The major points
of interest can be found along the town's two main intersecting roads, Rice
Street and Kuhio Highway. Lihue is also the site of the Hawaii Visitors
Bureau for Kauai. You might want to stop in here for some additional
touring advice. We suggest you gather all your provisions in Lihue so you
needn't bother with additional shopping along the road.

The Heavenly North

As you head north out of Lihue on Highway 56, the landscape grows
steadily greener and more enchanting. The eastern and northern parts of
Kauai are chock full of history and myth. If there's an ounce of romance
in your soul, you'll understand why the chiefs and priests of old Hawaii
chose to move to this part of the island. Today's Hawaiians hold great
respect for the tales of their ancestors and treat their former residences
with the utmost regard.

It takes about 10 minutes to drive to Wailua, which means "sacred
water" in Hawaiian. This was one of the primary communities of the first
Polynesians who came to Kauai over 1,000 years ago. Along the subdued
waters of the Wailua River they constructed several *heiau* for worship in
the serenity of the surroundings.

Once you've reached Wailua, turn left onto Kuamoo Road (Highway
580), and drive along what once was called the King's Highway. Ancient
kings and queens were carried along this passage, since their feet were
thought too holy to touch the ground. On your immediate left look for
a Warrior Marker for Pohaku Ho'Ohanau. This gathering of stones is an

ancient heiau which has been restored by the Bishop Museum in conjunction with the Kauai Historical Society, and it is one of the most impressive and accessible of its kind on the island. Its centerpiece is a stone where people were sacrificed to the bloodthirsty god Ku.

In the midst of the heiau lies the Piko Stone, "piko" being the Hawaiian word for navel. Legend has it that the umbilical cord of a newborn infant was hidden in the cracks of this royal birthstone, for if it were stolen, the child would grow up to be a thief. If you follow the short path up the hill from this ancient site, you come to a tidy little Japanese cemetery and rustic chapel, where friends and family still gather to pay their respects with offerings and prayers.

Proceed along Highway 580 to a lookout at Opaekaa Falls, which translates into "rolling shrimp." This refers to the little prawns which once tossed and turned in the churning currents under the falls. Farther along the road you'll see a Warrior Marker on your left, pointing you to Kamokila, a splendid hilltop site. This former Hawaiian village on the banks of the river is now open for public perusal, with daily crafts demonstrations for your enjoyment.

The farther you drive up Highway 580, the more memorable are your views of the upper Wailua River. From the upper banks you can watch the little cruise boats as they work their way upstream. Their destination is Fern Grotto, a popular three-mile trip beginning at Wailua Marina and ending at an impressive lava tube surrounded by untold tropical splendor. If you have an hour and a half you should definitely hop on board one of these delightful cruises and visit that tropical fairyland. The entrance to the cool, secluded cave is framed by gigantic fishtail ferns, and an 80-foot waterfall plunges from the top of the grotto onto the rocks below. It's no wonder that countless loving couples have chosen Fern Grotto as the site of their wedding ceremony.

Head back to Highway 56, cross the road, and spend some time in Lydgate State Park, a coconut grove which harbors the City of Refuge. Hawaiian fugitives used to take cover in this beautiful oceanside haven to protect themselves from an otherwise nasty fate. A little farther up the road, stop at the little lagoon near the Coco Palms Hotel and see if you recognize it. Elvis Presley once sang and danced on this very beach in the vintage film, *Blue Hawaii.*

Drive about 10 minutes farther on Highway 56 until you reach the town of Waipouli, home of the Coconut Plantation Market Place. This conglomeration of boutiques and eateries has replaced what once was a royal retreat for the kings of old. The original groves of shady palms remain, however, to pamper today's visitors, be they paupers or princes.

As you proceed along Highway 56 between Waipouli and Kapaa, look to your left and see if you can spot the Sleeping Giant, a mountain ridge resembling a reclining monolith. They say this is the Giant Puni, friend of the menehune. The story goes that when the enemy snuck up on the snoozing Puni, they pelted him with rocks. He swallowed some of the rocks and ricocheted others off his belly, destroying the enemy's canoes. Since then, Puni has slept undisturbed, save for the occasional sounds of clicking cameras.

Plantation Towns

Next you come to the quaint little hamlet of Kapaa, a small plantation town with 19th-century wooden buildings and charming souvenir shops.

With 4,467 people, Kapaa is Kauai's most populated city, but you'd never know it by looking at its subdued streets and shops. Kapaa is known for its seven churches catering to parishioners whose faith ranges from Buddhist to Seventh-Day Adventist.

From Kapaa continue ahead through the equally charming area of Kealia, just two miles north. Kealia Valley and Stream offer some ideal spots for picnicking. While you're in Kealia, don't miss St. Catherine's Roman Catholic Church, a modern building with mural decorations by three of Hawaii's most outstanding artists: Jean Charlot, Juliette Mae Fraser, and Tseng Yu-ho. Beyond Kealia is Anahola, home of a delightful beach park where you just might plan your first in a continuing series of naps.

Be sure to spend some time in Kilauea, a plantation town known for its historic stone buildings. The octagonal St. Sylvester's Roman Catholic Church was constructed of native lava rock and wood, designed like a theater-in-the-round. Another little church made of lava rock is the nearby Christ Memorial Episcopal Church, dating from 1941. Its stained glass windows come from England and many of the stones in the graveyard outside come from an earlier Congregational parish on the same site. Sweet, juicy guavas are grown in Kilauea, and it's also the home of one of the world's largest prawn farms. The prawns are hatched in Hanapepe on the warmer south shore and later transported to Kilauea for growing.

When you reach the sign for the Kilauea Lighthouse, turn right off the highway. Soon you'll pass the quonset hut which once housed the generator plant for the now-defunct Kilauea Sugar Company, which closed down in the late 1960s after 71 years of operation. Today this is the site of a popular bakery, where a croissant and a cup of hot coffee really hit the spot.

The road takes you to Kilauea Lighthouse, a beacon for ships and planes en route to and from the Orient. Built in 1913, it once held the largest lighthouse lens of its kind anywhere in the world. When an automated light was installed in 1967, the old lighthouse became obsolete. Next to the lighthouse is the U.S. Fish and Wildlife Refuge, where eight species of endangered seabirds soar with abandon. If you look carefully seaward you might catch a glimpse of the rare Hawaiian green sea turtle and the Hawaiian monk seal.

Back on Highway 56, cross the Kalihiwai River, whose scenic overlook is worth a lengthy linger. Pull over, settle back, and enjoy the peaceful views of the vivid greens of the valley, the shimmering froth of the waterfalls, and the gentle swirls of the turquoise river flowing below. It's hard to believe that this is the sight of not one, but two tidal waves, one in 1946 (on April Fool's Day, no less) and another in 1957. There's no sign of that destructive disturbance now, for Mother Nature heals her Garden Isle in magical ways.

Fit for a Prince

Past Kalihiwai you find yourself winding through glorious pasturelands dotted with grazing cattle and galloping horses. Everywhere you are surrounded by majestic mountains and dazzling ocean views. This is Princeville country, source of much of Kauai's beef and home of the oldest ranch on Kauai. This vast homestead was established in 1853 by the British resident minister, Dr. Robert Wyllie. Wyllie, a man of considerable political power, served as an advisor to three different kings and hosted the royal family in 1860 at his expansive ranch estate. Wyllie named the place Princeville after the royal son, Prince Albert Edward Kauikeauoli, to whom the white aristocrat had become quite attached. Later the little prince died of an incurable illness, much to the dismay of the gentleman farmer.

Today's Princeville is Kauai's largest resort area. 1,000 acres of elegant hotels, condominiums, and shops surround the famous golf course which blends in beautifully with the landscape. Its 27 holes of ocean, woods, and lake play have hosted the Women's Kemper Open, the World Cup, and other prestigious sporting events. Even if you're not staying there, take a right turn at the Princeville sign, drive past the little guard house, and treat yourself to a tour of this luxurious community. You may just end up staying for lunch or dinner.

From Princeville to the end of the north shore road are a series of valleys and beaches of incomparable beauty, beginning on your immediate left with the Hanalei Valley Overlook. The glories of the Garden Isle spread out before you like a great big checkerboard of visual splendors. You can see the sleepy Hanalei River as it snakes its way to the sea in silver silence. Weatherworn mountains offer a serene backdrop, and during the rainy season tiny waterfalls drape them like jewels.

In the Hanalei Valley, Robert Wyllie attempted to establish a thriving coffee plantation in the 1850s. After his crops failed to make money, the Chinese planted rice here until the early 1900s. Today the floor of the Hanalei Valley is covered with taro far and wide—more than a half-mile of it! Over 50 percent of Hawaii's total taro crop is cultivated in this one spot. The lower 900 acres are a national wildlife refuge which is maintained by the U.S. Fish and Wildlife Service.

Let your eyes wander and in the distance you'll see a bridge crossing the Hanalei River. When you continue your drive downward along Highway 56, you'll cross that same bridge, built in 1912. This is the gateway to the three-block town of Hanalei. Hanalei Bay was one of Kauai's three major seaports. Now this enchanted little cove is famous for its winter surf and summer fishing.

Hanalei village is the site of the 1837 Waioli Mission, home for missionary teachers Lucy and Abner Wilcox. In front of the mission house is the New England-style Waioli Social Hall, dating from 1841. This fascinating building is a fine example of the Hawaiian architecture which influenced subsequent construction on Kauai. Also on the grounds is the Waioli Hui'ia Church built in 1912.

On to the End of the Road

Along Highway 56 are several one-way bridges built in the 1920s. If an approaching car is already on the bridge, hang back and wait until they have crossed over. Smile, wave, and take your time; that's the way they do it on Kauai's leisurely north shore. One of these bridges crosses Waioli Stream, which cuts through land owned in part by the Bishop Estate and partly by local Hawaiian families. In the meadow to your left you'll notice a grove of plum trees, which grow more and more abundantly as you head north.

Just down the road is one of the most photographed beaches in the world: Lumahai Beach. This precious cove of sand and sea was transformed into Nurses Beach in the movie *South Pacific,* epitomizing for the movie-going world a tropical paradise lovely beyond words. Pull over and park in one of the turnoffs on the right side of the road. Then walk down the small (and sometimes muddy) footpath leading through pandana trees to the beach. With its backdrop of steep cliffs and hala trees, its black lava rocks, and pure yellow sand, Lumahai Beach is even more beautiful than it was on the big screen.

Beyond Lumahai Beach you enter areas which were previously inhabited by tribes of *kahuna,* the upper class of men and women who were revered by the Hawaiians. Twin wooden bridges take you over the river in Wainiha where, according to legend, the hula was born.

Take a left after the second bridge and head back into the Wainiha Valley, where a tribe of menehune once thrived. This road takes you to the Wainiha Powerhouse, which provides Kauai with most of its water and hydroelectric power to light its homes and sustain its industry. From here you get outstanding views of the 4,000-foot-high Wainiha Pali, over whose cliffs mighty waterfalls steadily flow.

A marquee full of famous people have discovered the charms of Kauai's north shore, which offers them the peace and privacy they have long sought. From Wainiha to Ke'e Beach, the astounding beauty has lured such luminaries as Rich Little and Graham Nash to build their second (or third) homes. Here the mountains tumble down to the sea and the road is overcome by prolific vegetation. Bali Hai Peak looms before you, summing up the splendor of the South Seas with its silent strength. The predominant sounds are the calls of birds, the whisper of the winds, and the lapping of the waves. How can you go wrong?

Another group of people who were enchanted by the north shore area were the free-spirited hippies of the 1960s and early 1970s who created a community called Taylor Camp. Little shacks and rustic lean-tos comprised this mini-city where cares were few and artistic creativity was at a maximum. Unfortunately, Taylor Camp's residents paid little attention to the sanitary conditions of the park, and when their garbage began to pollute the surrounding forests and waters, the state evicted them (but only after a lengthy legal battle). Today Taylor Camp lives on only in memory, and nature has once again assumed its proper status as champion of the elements.

On the left side of your drive is Maniniholo Dry Cave, an eerie grotto dug by Maniniholo himself. This menehune chief thought that by digging back into the mountain he could catch the evil spirit which had stolen his fish. Later the ancient chiefs gathered to worship in this dark, dank cavern. Today you can walk back into the cave about 75 yards, but bring a flashlight if you're afraid of the dark. It's full of invisible powers from Hawaiian days gone by.

Past the dry cave are two wet caves called Waikapalae and Waikanaloa, both dug by Madame Pele, the volcano goddess. Once upon a time the waters were crystal clear, an inviting swimming hole for people and goldfish alike. Today the still green waters are unappealing to jump into, though some folks do it anyway. We suggest you stand on the rocks and enjoy the unusual geography and spiritual aura of these caves, yet another enigmatic piece in the Garden Island puzzle.

Highway 56 stops at Ke'e State Beach Park, where you can wile away the hours on the chaste sands and swim and snorkel in the serene sea swells. To your left the lofty Na Pali Coast extends to seeming infinity, a truly inspiring environment for a day at the beach.

From Ke'e Beach a path to your left leads to an open, grassy meadow with a stone altar. This is called Lohiau's Dance Pavilion, a sacred area dedicated to Laka, the hula goddess. On this very spot, Laka taught her students that ancient Hawaiian art of communicating through dance, and hula ceremonies were often presented here for the royalty of neighboring villages. Today's visitors are asked to treat the pavilion with care, for it is an area of great spiritual and historical meaning.

Kalalau

Ke'e Beach is the official end of the road, but you needn't stop your north shore explorations there. A variety of options awaits to help you uncover the wonders of the 15-mile stretch of Na Pali coastline. Deeply chiseled valleys and great green peaks invite exploration by air on one of the many helicopter tours available. By sea you can take a zodiac cruise past untouched beaches and wander through weather-carved sea caves with turtles and dolphins as your guides. Or you can explore this coast by land and hike the road least traveled by: the Kalalau Trail.

Many people call Kalalau Hawaii's premier hiking trail. This 11-mile zigzag up and down the grand ledges takes you as high as 3,000 feet above the ocean's crashing surf. Some parts of the path skirt steep cliffs which lead you precariously close to the edge, and it requires skill and stamina to foot it in one day. Most people break it up into a two-day hike, setting up camp at one of the stops along the way. Two miles in, Hanakapiai Beach makes for a delightful destination for a day hike or an overnight rest. You can also pitch a tent at the six-mile point in Hanakoa, a hanging valley where a rejuvenating pool awaits hot, tired travelers. Along the way, hikers encounter waterfalls and rushing streams, mountain goats and fresh fruit like guavas and mountain apples. The last part of the route is a repetition of ups and downs, breathtaking vistas, and breathless ascents, until at last you reach Kalalau, a mile-long stretch of sand and sea and sky.

Kalalau is Na Pali's largest valley, uninhabited save for the mountain goats whose cries you can hear in the canyons. Fruit and coffee trees, babbling brooks, and the remains of ancient houses recall the civilization which flourished here until the early 1900s. As soon as you arrive you'll sense a spirit of peace and quiet which nourishes the soul like nowhere else on earth.

One of the valley's most colorful residents was Koolau the Leper, whose adventurous story so fascinated author Jack London that he retold it in his book of Hawaiian tales, *The House of Pride*. In 1889 Koolau and his family fled to the valley in order to avoid deportation to Molokai. They hid between the ridges in the upper reaches of Kalalau, and when the deputy sheriff of Waimea came to get him, Koolau shot and killed him. Despite frequent attacks from the Hawaii National Guard, Koolau held firm, evading the militia who eventually gave him up as dead. Koolau and his family lived in the valley for another five years before leprosy accomplished what the bullets could not. Koolau and his son both died of the dread disease, and his wife buried them in the beautiful valley where she had shared his fugitive life.

Another Kalalau inhabitant of note was Dr. Bernard Wheatley, better known as the Hermit of Kalalau. In the early 1960s he renounced the material world and began looking for a simple life of truth and serenity. He found that personal sanctuary in Kalalau Valley. Wheatley spent a decade living in this primitive outpost, creating a life which was the epitome of self-sufficiency. He left his cave dwelling in the late 1970s, never to be heard of again. But the spirit of Bernard Wheatley lives on in the calm Kalalau Valley, a place which brings out a little bit of the hermit in all of us.

Heading South from Lihue

Your southward exploration of the Garden Isle takes you to a whole different kind of landscape. You might even think you've changed islands! It's warmer and drier in the south and west, and the overwhelming immediacy of mountains and sea which you encountered in the north gives way to more expansive stretches of sugar cane fields, open areas of uninterrupted beaches, and gaping valleys of immeasurable beauty.

From Lihue many people head straight for Poipu, but we recommend a side trip to Nawiliwili first. Just a mile south of the capital, Nawiliwili offers unmatched insights into the story of Kauai, both past and present. It is the island's major deep-water port and docking facility, and its main activities center around the simple wharves which line the shore. Often at the port you'll encounter cruise and container ships and U.S. Navy vessels. Willow trees embellish this sleepy harbor, whose major hotel, the Westin Kauai, opened in September of 1987 on the site of the former Kauai Surf. There are several charming waterside restaurants and lounges in which to relax, plus a nice public beach for some serious sun worshipping and swimming.

Nawiliwili holds the dubious honor of being the site of a gasoline storage tank which was hit by the Japanese Navy on December 31, 1941. Fortunately, this unexpected New Year's Eve present was a dud and didn't explode. This is also where you'll find the Nawiliwili Bulk Sugar Plant, the last word in Kauai's highly mechanized production of sugar. The raw sugar is transported by conveyor belt from the plant on the hill right into the holds of the freighters at the wharf, thus eliminating the expensive operation of shipping the sugar in bags. From Nawiliwili it is shipped directly to San Francisco for final processing.

Remember when Indiana Jones was chased through the jungles at the beginning of *Raiders of the Lost Ark?* He was really running amid the dense foliage of the Huleia River banks in Nawiliwili. What the movie didn't show you is the adjacent Menehune Fishpond, which is said to have been built in one night by you-know-who.

Nocturnal by nature and shy of human eyes, the menehune did this particular job for a princess and a prince with the stipulation that no mortal eye should see this great night's work. The prince and princess agreed, but they decided to peek anyway, and by the light of the moon they saw the menehune at work. Thousands of them stood in double rows along the river bank passing stones from Makaweli to the dam, a distance of 25 miles. By the same light of the moon, the menehune saw the royal couple and turned them to twin pillars of stone, which stand to this day on the mountainside above the river. Dawn broke before the job was done, and the menehune vanished into the forests of Kauai, leaving holes in the wall which were not completed until some enterprising Chinese plugged in the gaps in our own times.

Mullet are still cultivated in this ancient fishpond, whose remarkable four-by-five-foot-high walls rise up above the level of water in engineering perfection. A 900-foot-long wall has been built to cut off a bend in the stream. The road past the docks out of Nawiliwili takes you up to a sweeping panorama of this enchanted area, with the Hoary Head Mountains serving as an appropriately impressive backdrop. This area is called Niumalu, once the site of an ancient Hawaiian village.

From here, take Hulemalu Road north to Puhi Street, then continue to Highway 50 (Kaumualii Highway). Take a left and pass through the tiny plantation town of Puhi. Just past Puhi, keep your eyes open for Queen Victoria's profile, a mountain ridge to the left. Some folks claim they can see in this formation a resemblance to Queen Victoria, who is wearing a crown and facing east with one finger pointing toward the sky. The Hawaiians of old thought this profile was actually the goddess Hina, mother of Molokai. But other people claim that it is indeed Victoria who, using that raised finger to chastise her son Wilfred, is saying "Now Willy, Willy!"

On to Koloa

Just before the intersection of Highway 50 and 520, you'll find yourself in the natural pass between Mt. Waialeale on your right and the Hoary Head Range on your left. This is called the Koloa Gap. Dominating the Hoaries is Mount Haupu, on whose slopes grow the fragrant mokihana berries, unique to Kauai. The mokihana serves the island in lieu of an official flower. You often see them in leis mixed with the aromatic maile leaf.

A few miles out of Lihue on Highway 50, turn left and head south on Highway 520, also known as Maluhia ("serenity") Road. This is one of the prettiest stretches of road on Kauai, a naturally vaulted cathedral of towering eucalyptus trees. A few miles farther and you're in Koloa, which means "long cane." Don't blink or you might just miss this tiny hamlet! On the right is a stone smokestack, the only remains of Hawaii's first sugar mill. Built in 1835, it served as the center of Kauai's sugar industry. Koloa was also the mercantile and retail center for the whole south side of the island.

The main street of Koloa has undergone extensive restoration and is now a spiffy little stretch of modern boutiques and snack shops. They've restored Kauai's first hotel, the old medical dispensary, and the soda bottling plant, transforming them into settings for a potpourri of shops and services. There's even an antique popcorn wagon which serves hot dogs and snacks!

If you explore some of Koloa's back roads you'll find that the days of immigrants and missionaries have been preserved in such buildings as Kauai's oldest Catholic mission, St. Raphael's Church, off Highway 520. The old stone church was built in 1841 after the opposition of the Protestant missionaries was silenced by King Liholiho's Edict of Toleration. St. Raphael's is still in use today. Also preserved are the Koloa Church (1837) and Koloa Jodo Mission, a Buddhist temple (1834).

Continuing south, take Poipu Road until it intersects with Spouting Horn Road. This is Koloa Landing, once the third largest port of the Hawaiian Islands, after Honolulu and Lahaina, Maui. As many as 50 whaling vessels at once would anchor in this roadstead, replenishing their supplies with the help of the resident Hawaiians. The bustling community entertained the officers and crews of ships which docked here. Koloa Landing was also where newcoming immigrants were processed. Kauai's first public school was opened here, and Kauai's first doctor practiced in this busy burg.

Today Koloa Landing is not much more than a fork in the road. Turn left and head to Poipu's Kiahuna Gardens, the former estate of the late Mr. and Mrs. Hector Moir. Their home has been converted into a restaurant, and around the grounds are landscaped gardens with Hawaiian rocks, lava rock pools, orchids, African aloes, and blossoming plumeria trees. Its 4,000 varieties of plants have earned it a well-deserved spot in the book *Great Gardens of America*. The Hawaiians call this Pa'u A Laka (the Skirt of Laka), for this was one of the sites where the hula goddess Laka trained her students.

Sunny Poipu

Your next stop is Poipu, the south shore's main resort area and one of the largest lures on Kauai. In November of 1982 Poipu was hit hard by Hurricane Iwa, but since it was rebuilt it looks better than ever. With its sunny, dry weather, beautiful beaches and calm waters, Poipu is a surf bum's paradise. A string of sparkling condos and hotels lines the shore ready to serve the steady stream of shivering vacationers eager to find a place that's reliably warm. Poipu rarely lets them down.

If you feel like a walk, stroll along the Poipu Beach coast to Makahuena Point and beyond. There are petroglyphs on the sandstone ledges at the far end of the beach. Around the point is another beach, Mahaulepu, for those who want to be alone and gather driftwood. Winds and currents deposit flotsam and jetsam on this spot, and it is here that some of the ancient Hawaiians had their first contacts with metal as they picked up trinkets which floated over from Captain Cook's landing. Nearby Nukumoi Point is an excellent snorkeling spot. The road ends at a crater where Kauai's last volcanic eruption took place, now a quiet development for homes and condos.

Head back to the Koloa Landing fork, turn onto Lawai Road and follow it to Prince Kuhio Park, where our beloved congressman was born in 1871. At the end of this road is Spouting Horn, a rambunctious water spout in the shoreline rocks which acts like a geyser when the waves are forced through it. The noisy, moaning sound you hear is said to be caused by Lehu, the legendary lizard who was trapped long ago in the tube. Even when it isn't blowing its top, Spouting Horn offers great views of the southern coast. The rocks around the hole are slippery, so it's best to stay on the adjacent walkway. A note of caution: Beware of the barrage of souvenir sellers who line the path to the lookout. You can find much better values elsewhere.

Southern Hospitality

Highway 50 west takes you through a series of small, almost linear towns along the southern coast: Lawai, Kalaheo, and Hanapepe. In between each district the road passes acre upon acre of sugar cane fields, their tassels waving in the wind and shining in the sun.

Once the home of the Kauai Pineapple Company, Lawai still contains remnants of that cannery. This tiny plantation town is now best known for its botanical gardens and prolific fruit orchards. Lawai is the site of the Pacific Tropical Botanical Gardens, 186 acres dedicated to the research and propagation of its unusual living exhibits. Next to the gardens is the Allerton Estate, which was established by Queen Emma back in 1879. As Highway 50 ascends a hill, watch on the left for a small Buddhist shrine dedicated to the famous teacher Kobo Daishi. Eighty-eight small stones designate the sacred soil from Japan's 88 Holy Places of Daishi.

Kalaheo means "proud day," an appropriate moniker for this dignified little town which presides over rolling hills and valleys. An abundance of parks and gardens makes Kalaheo a pleasant spot for a shady picnic. Dominating the scene is a hilltop Eden called Kukuiolono Park, whose golf course is so splendid it often doubles as a site for outdoor weddings. The view from this perch above Kalaheo is one of Hawaii's finest. Another prolific attraction in this area is Olo Pua Gardens, once a plantation estate and now 12 acres of tropical trees and plants.

By all means your next stop should be the Hanapepe Valley and Canyon Lookout on Highway 50 between Kalaheo and Eleele. This lush divide was once the site of a populous Hawaiian settlement, and some of the taro terraces are still visible under the tropical overgrowth. This is where the last battle on Kauai was fought, a revolt against the Kamehameha dynasty in 1824 led by Humehume, the son of Kauai's King Kaumualii.

As you approach the Welcome sign to Hanapepe, turn right at the fork for a look at the old part of town. This fascinating hodgepodge of rickety wooden buildings and balconied Chinese shops is reminiscent of the 19th century. That's just what the director of *The Thorn Birds* had in mind when he transformed Hanapepe into the Australian outback for his film. The rest of Hanapepe is a quiet farming village which supplies Kauai with much of its produce.

Just past Hanapepe, turn left toward the ocean on Highway 543. Down this road is Salt Pond Beach Park, home of a group of the only salt ponds in the state of Hawaii. For almost 200 years saltmakers have meticulously maintained these mudlined drying beds in the same fashion as their Hawaiian forefathers, letting the sun evaporate the sea water to leave the salt. Also in this area is Port Allen Harbor, the shipping center for Kauai's west side and headquarters of the McBryde Sugar Company. Here you can see Kauai's first modern shopping center, which signaled a new era for the Garden Isle.

Just before you reach the Waimea River Bridge, turn left for a visit to the remains of the Old Russian Fort, Fort Elizabeth, built in 1816 by Anton Scheffer, an enterprising agent of the Imperial Russian government. King Kaumualii helped Scheffer construct this edifice out of traditional Kauai stonework. In the long run, Kaumualii chased him off Kauai and Russia finally disowned this shifty entrepreneur. Today only the ruins are left of this failed attempt at gaining Russian influence in the isles.

On the right side of the road by the police station is a turnoff to Menehune Ditch, signposted two and a half miles up the Waimea Valley. Once a great aqueduct which fed mountain water to the highlands, this structure was built before the arrival of the Hawaiians, or so say the archeologists. The flanged and fitted cut stone bricks are stacked two feet higher than the road and 200 feet long, and are assembled in such a way as indicates a knowledge of construction foreign to Hawaii. Menehune Ditch is inscribed with mysterious markings which can only be attributed to the menehune. Legend has it that when they completed this project, these industrious pygmies partied all night, making so much noise that it could be heard 100 miles away on Oahu.

Historic Waimea Town

Waimea is a town full of history. This is where Captain Cook first landed, although only a feeble little monument in the town center commemorates that landmark arrival. It was here that Kauai's King Kaumualii met with King Kamehameha and ceded Kauai to the unifying king. The first missionaries to Kauai made their settlements in Waimea, and the old Waimea Christian Hawaiian and Foreign Church was built here in 1846. Constructed out of huge timbers from the mountains eight miles away and limestone blocks from a nearby quarry, this labor of love took 12 years to construct and is still in use today.

The sandalwood trade flourished in Waimea as well, bringing money to the chiefs and foreign traders but misery and famine to the people who were drafted as slave labor to pillage the forests of these fragrant trees. As the sugar industry caught on, Waimea was turned into the bustling plantation town which you find today.

Modern-day Waimea keeps busy with its library, its banks, its school, and a handsome public swimming pool for which the entire community pitched in both funding and labor. Waimea is also the site of the oldest house on Kauai, the Gulick-Rowell house, where you can see one of Kauai's oldest and largest monkeypod trees.

From Waimea to the end of Highway 50 the road parallels a 15-mile long, luxurious stretch of deserted beaches. The best known of these is Barking Sands, which earned its amusing name from the growling sound created when people slid down its steep, 60-foot-high sand dune. The public is no longer allowed on this beach, which is where the Navy has its underwater test range for antisubmarine warfare training and firing. That's okay, though, because another spectacular beach awaits beyond Barking Sands: Polihale State Park.

Turn left at the Warrior Marker for one of the more unusual beach access roads you're likely to encounter—straight through sugar cane fields! A dusty, bumpy drive leads you to one of the island's most superb landscapes. Polihale is situated at the other end of the Pali Coast, where strong stands of cliffs flank miles of unspoiled beaches. The old Hawaiians held this area very dear, and people who now live in this part of the island claim frequent visitations by spirits of the past. One word of advice: If you plan to spend some time at Polihale, bring along a cooler and some picnic food. You'll be miles away from the nearest grocery store when your appetite alarm goes off.

Grand Canyon of the Pacific

There are two routes which lead up to Waimea Canyon. Twisty, turny Waimea Canyon Road, which runs directly out of Waimea town, can be dangerous in wet weather, while the better maintained Kokee Road (Highway 550) runs up from Kekaha, three miles past town. The early views from the former are far more spectacular, but either road will do, since they join forces a few miles up the hill. Before you begin your ascent, make sure you have enough gas, since the last station is located in Kekaha.

From the hot, coastal plain it gets cool very quickly as you head upland. You'll want to drive this road at a leisurely pace given its unexpected hairpin turns and the spectacular views. The ocean and Niihau can be seen behind you and Waimea Canyon spreads out to your right. Straight ahead is Puu Ka Pele ("the mountain of Pele"), whose 3,687-foot summit is often obscured behind a veil of mist.

Several turnoffs invite you to stop and gaze at Waimea Canyon, often referred to as the Grand Canyon of the Pacific. 3,500 feet deep, 2 miles wide, and 10 miles long, Waimea certainly isn't as vast as the real Grand Canyon, but it inspires a sense of awe and inspiration equivalent to the other wonders of the world.

Formed by an ancient crust fault, the canyon's beautiful layers of colors are a result of thousands of years of erosion. As the day proceeds, the play of light paints ever-changing images and auras across the landscape, tempting photographers and romantics alike to stand and gape in one spot for hours. Morning tones are the most subtle and the hardest to capture with a camera. The blues in the fresh early light suggest all the shades of iris; the greens are soft and varied, supplying a catalog of all the hues between yellow and blue; and the red is muted to a shade of dusty rose. In the long light of the late afternoon this red becomes a highly saturated, brilliant vermilion, almost as though the canyon were on fire. The blues, almost consumed by the red, glow with the low brilliance of indigo, and the mossy greens of morning burn with metallic glints of copper, bronze, and gold. Although any vantage point offers spectacular views, we recommend the Puu Ka Pele and Puu Hina Hina Lookouts for the most appealing panoramas.

Kokee and the Kalalau Lookout

If you can pull yourself away from the canyon, more magic awaits farther up the road. The sign welcoming you to Kokee State Park introduces you to the only populated place in all the uplands, Kokee. This 4,345-acre wilderness park is a fairyland of ferns and mosses which is almost too good to be true. Wild plum trees hang heavy with their purple fruit, and several types of ginger flower in abundance. Brilliant colors of endangered birds flicker above, and mountain cabins dot the hillsides as lazy wisps of smoke rise from their chimneys. Picnic and camping grounds and 45 miles of hiking trails invite you to stay for a while and partake fully in the wonders of nature.

At an elevation of 3,000 feet, the air in Kokee is chilly and crisp, and on a clear day the sky is bluer than you ever imagined blue could be. Kokee Lodge presents you with a charming inn setting for a cup of coffee and a home-cooked meal, and the Kokee Museum fills you in on the natural glories surrounding you. You'll know you're in Kokee when you hear the cockadoodle-do of the *moa*, the colorful, wild Hawaiian roosters which strut and crow around the grounds as if they owned the place.

Another distinguishing feature of Kokee is a NASA Tracking Station, where a room full of computers kept track of the Apollo 11 moon mission. This station flashed its laser beam all the way to the lunar surface, making historic contact with our astronauts.

From Kokee it's a four-mile drive through a dense tropical forest to the penultimate panorama: The Kalalau Lookout. There are two viewpoints worthy of lengthy meditation. At 4,120 feet you're on top of the world! The vast Kalalau Valley stretches out before you in a dazzling tapestry, and off in the distance a thread of shining sand separates the valley from the sea. Ridge after ridge, valley after valley, the scene spreads out before you. Trickling waterfalls tickle the clefts of the mountains, those strong sentinels keeping watch over this private place. Teeming rain forests fill the air with ever-fresh sights and smells and sounds. Wild goats scamper from ledge to ledge, their distant cries echoing across the sheer volcanic rock formations.

From the Puu Kila Lookout where the road ends, you can tread an easy trail along the rim of the valley for scores of different views of this heavenly scene. Take your time, for this is a spectacle beyond compare, one which will truly help you forget all your earthly cares. Here, as you ponder this majestic sweep to the sea, is perhaps the best place of all to get back in touch with nature. After all, that's what the Garden Isle is all about.

Niihau: Lost In Time

During your driving tour of Kauai you probably noticed Niihau, that mysterious island looming off the south coast. If you thought Kauai seemed like a step backward, its remote little neighbor is lost in time altogether, like a giant Rip van Winkle who refuses to wake up. Surrounded by sea mists, the island's hazy appearance embodies its detachment from the rest of the world. That's the way they like it on Niihau, appropriately dubbed the "Forbidden Isle."

Geographically speaking, Niihau lies just 17 miles from Kauai across the Kaulakahi Channel. In terms of lifestyle, however, it is millions of miles away from the rest of Hawaii, and the rest of the world, for that matter. We only know so much about this secluded community, for up until recently no uninvited guests were allowed to prowl around its premises. However, things changed in 1987. The Niihau Ranch instituted helicopter tours to the island, complete with stops at two remote beaches, away from the main town so as not to disturb its residents.

A single shield volcano formed Niihau, which eventually became the seventh largest island in the Hawaiian chain, superceding only Kahoolawe. At 6 by 18 miles in size, its 70 square miles are essentially flat, and the highest point reaches only 1,281 feet. Although there are no permanent streams on Niihau, it does have two lakes, Halulu and Halalii, the latter of which is the largest natural lake in all of Hawaii (182 acres).

Niihau has gone through much of history unattended, but the few disturbances on its shores have left indelible marks. In 1778 while Captain Cook was docked off Kauai, his boats were blown over to the beaches of Niihau. In order to freshen their supplies, Cook's men asked for salt and vegetables in exchange for their goats, pigs, and the seeds of several fruits and vegetables. This exchange introduced Niihau to its first Western plants and animals.

When Kamehameha gained control of Kauai in 1810, Niihau was part of the deal. But a more significant change of hands took place in 1864, when Mrs. Elizabeth Sinclair, a Scottish widow from New Zealand, purchased Niihau from King Kamehameha for $10,000. At the time, Mrs. Sinclair and her family were just passing through Hawaii on their way to California, but the crafty businesswoman knew a good deal when she saw one. As it turns out, Mrs. Sinclair was the great great grandmother of Bruce and Keith Robinson who, with their mother Helen, currently own this sequestered isle.

While on paper Niihau is politically a part of Kauai County, that's as far as their relationship goes. The Robinson family is responsible for establishing and maintaining the singular lifestyle found only on Niihau, the one place in the world where Hawaiian is spoken first and foremost. Even their dialects are different from the Hawaiian which is practiced elsewhere, and they have special words and accents which are foreign to all others. Everything is conducted in Hawaiian, although English is taught as a second language by the island's three grammar school teachers. This dedication to the native tongue is a prime example of what Niihau stands for: A preservation of the traditions and culture which comprise old Hawaii.

Niihau stands apart from the other islands in its simple, almost primitive way of life. They have no police force and no jails, no movie theaters, and no telephones. There is no harbor, and the boats which bring invited guests must anchor offshore. Their lack of paved roads is a direct throwback to days gone by, and they seem to get by without any community electricity or water systems. Since there is no hospital (or resident doctor or dentist, for that matter), pregnant women must go over to Kauai when their time is near. And if a Niihau native gets thirsty for some alcohol, he must take the shuttle boat to neighboring Kauai to sip a few. Try as it might to remain detached from the workings of the rest of Hawaii, Niihau did get involved in the 1959 vote on Hawaii's statehood as the only district to vote "no."

Short, wet winters and long, arid summers present an economic challenge to the Robinson family as they work to keep their tiny isle afloat. This enterprising clan owns and runs Robinson Ranch, where they raise cattle and sheep (the latter of which first came from New Zealand with Mrs. Sinclair herself). Niihau Sunset Brand Charcoal has become an equally rewarding endeavor, with half of its output shipped to the Mainland. The Robinsons are working hard to upgrade their charcoal production facilities with new, improved kilns. Beekeeping has also proved lucrative for Niihau, which has put out as much as 60,000 pounds per year of top-grade kiawe blossom honey. And the new helicopter tours have helped the financial outlook somewhat.

Niihau may be best known for its exquisite shell jewelry, tiny trademarks of the Forbidden Isle. Niihau shells aren't exclusive to Niihau, but more end up on its shores than anywhere else. For centuries women have patiently passed strings through these itty-bitty shells, some as small as one-fifth inch in diameter. Each day searchers sift through sands and sort out the blue, brown, burgundy, and speckled gems, with a good day bringing perhaps just a handful of suitable shells. It's no wonder that Niihau leis command thousands of dollars and priceless pride.

In a historic moment in December of 1985, this insular island extended an invitation to George Ariyoshi, the first governor to visit Niihau since William Quinn in 1961. Joining Ariyoshi was Jan TenBruggencate of the *Honolulu Advertiser,* the first reporter to step foot on the Forbidden Isle in 20-odd years. These honored guests found Niihau in the midst of an economic resurgence, and they marvelled at the intense pride and sincerity of its people.

But perhaps a more telling episode in Niihau's history occurred in December of 1941, when a Japanese pilot who was out of gas made a crash landing on Niihau. With him were his modern weapons of war and his brash, contemporary attitudes. True to form, the people of Niihau wanted nothing to do with him, and when he threatened their lives, one resident took the pilot's ammunition and flight papers. A brawl ensued, and the pilot shot the Hawaiian not once, but three times. By then the Hawaiian had had enough, and he picked up the pilot and hurled him against a stone wall. That settled *that.*

Since then, Niihau has been just fine on its own, thank you. Though its residents are free to leave the island to further their education, most of them eventually return to the lifestyle which they love, the tranquility of their ancestors. And so Niihau remains, far from the madding crowd, a tiny pearl of Hawaiiana in the Pacific.

PRACTICAL INFORMATION FOR KAUAI

HOW TO GET THERE. Lihue's new airport, which opened in 1987, offers impressive facilities for comfortable interisland travel. Two airlines offer service from Honolulu to Lihue. *Aloha Airlines* and *Hawaiian Airlines* each have 20 flights a day. The flight takes 25 minutes. *United Airlines* also flies directly into Lihue from both Los Angeles and San Francisco. *Princeville Airways* flies directly into Kauai's other airport near the Princeville Resort in Hanalei. Their DeHavilland jet prop twin otters make for an enjoyable way to see the north shore, for $41.95 one way. Passengers in the 18-seat aircraft have excellent visibility.

Lihue Airport's Visitor Information Center can answer most of your questions upon arrival. Bus transfer tariffs from the airport to Lihue cost about $4. It's $8 to Poipu hotels and $5 to the Wailua area. Most Princeville guests take the free shuttle from Princeville Airport.

ACCOMMODATIONS. Old-timers who mourn the loss of the old Kauai Surf should see its replacement, the multimillion-dollar Westin Kauai, which opened in Lihue in September of 1987. Other areas offering a large selection of vacation lodgings are Poipu, Wailua, Waipouli, Kapaa, and Hanalei, home of the luxurious Princeville Resort complex.

Hotel price categories are based on double occupancy: $121 and up, *Super Deluxe;* $91–$120, *Deluxe;* $61–$90, *Expensive;* $31–$60, *Moderate;* $30 and under, *Inexpensive.*

Lihue/Nawiliwili

Super Deluxe

The Westin Kauai. Kalapaki Beach, Lihue, HI 96766 (245–5050 or 800–228–3000). Fanciest hotel on Kauai. 850 rooms and suites, 3 restaurants, a 5-level disco, 210-ft.-wide pool, 40-acre lagoon, rare artworks.

Expensive

Kauai Hilton and Beach Villas. 4331 Kauai Beach Dr., Lihue, HI 96766 (245–1955 or 800–445–8667). 350 guest rooms, 150 beach villas with kitchens. Tennis, golf, 25-ft. waterfall-fed swimming pool, restaurants, lounges.

Inexpensive

Ahana Motel Apts. 3115 Akahi St., Lihue, HI 96766 (245–2206). 17 singles, doubles, suites, and kitchenettes. Convenient to Lihue attractions.

Hale Lihue. 2931 Kalena St., Lihue, HI 96766 (245–3151). 18 units including singles and doubles. Some air-conditioning, kitchenettes.

Ocean View. 3445 Wilcox Rd., Nawiliwili, HI 96766 (245–6345). 21 singles and doubles near the ocean. Color TV and refrigerators in lobby.

Tip Top Hotel. 3173 Akahi St., Lihue, HI 96766 (245–2333). A Lihue landmark. 34 air-conditioned units one mile from the airport.

Poipu/Koloa

Super Deluxe

Poipu Kapili. RR 1, Box 272, Koloa, HI 96756 (742–6449 or 800–367–8047). 60 posh vacation condos on the beach. Color TV, ceiling fans, pool, tennis.

Waiohai Resort. RR 1, Box 174, Koloa, HI 96756 (742–9511 or 800–227–4700). Top-ranked hotel. The 460 beachfront rooms have color TV, air-conditioning, refrigerators, lanais. Singles, doubles, suites. Three restaurants, 3 lounges, tennis, shops, 3 pools, hanging gardens.

Deluxe

Kiahuna Beachside. Box 369, Koloa, HI 96756 (742–7262 or 800–367–7040). 50 lovely condominiums by the ocean. Pool, tennis, golf, restaurant.

Kiahuna Plantation. RR 1, Box 73, Koloa, HI 96756 (742–6411 or 800–367–7052). A cluster of 333 plantation-style condos with a golf course, pool, tennis, restaurant, lounge.

Nihi Kai Villas. RR 1, Box 123, Koloa, HI 96756 (742–6458 or 800–367–2363). 70 1-, 2-, and 3-bedroom condos overlooking Brennecke's Beach. Pool, tennis.

Poipu Kai. RR 1, Box 173, Koloa, HI 96756 (742–6464 or 800–367–6046). A 110-acre condominium resort between Brennecke's Beach and Keoneloa Bay, with 76 1-, 2-, and 3-bedroom beachfront units. Kitchens, TV, 5 pools, tennis, restaurant.

Sheraton Kauai. Rt. 1, Box 303, Koloa, HI 96756 (742–1661 or 800–334–8484). A striking combination of Polynesian and modern architecture spread over 12 acres by the beach. 344 air-conditioned singles, doubles, and suites. Two pools, shops, restaurant.

Expensive

Kuhio Shores. RR 1, Box 70, Koloa, HI 96756 (742–6120 or 800–367–8022). 75 oceanview condos with 1 and 2 bedrooms.

Poipu Beach Hotel. RR 1, Box 174, Koloa, HI 96756 (742–1681 or 800–227–4700). 142 units set on a cove with a broad sandy beach. Pool, golf, tennis. Singles, doubles, suites, cottage.

Poipu Shores. RR 1, Box 95, Koloa, HI 96756 (742–6522 or 800–367–5686). 39 oceanfront 1-, 2-, and 3-bedroom condos. Pool, color TV.

Sunset Kahili. RR 1, Box 96, Koloa, HI 96756 (in Hawaii 742–1691 or 800–367–8047 ext. 212). On the water at Poipu. 35 1-, 2-, and 3-bedroom condos with color TV, pool.

Moderate

Garden Isle Cottages. RR 1, Box 355, Koloa, HI 96756 (742–6717). 13 cottages just across the road from the beach. One and 2 bedrooms, some kitchens.

Inexpensive

Kokee Lodge. Box 819, Waimea, HI 96796 (335–6061). Rustic cabins in Kauai's high country, Kokee State Park. Great place to rough it. Kitchens with dishes and silverware, bedding provided. Fireplaces. Firewood at small extra charge. Lodge nearby for home-cooked meals.

Wailua/Waipouli/Kapaa

Expensive

Coco Palms Resort. Box 631, Lihue, HI 96766 (822–4921 or 800–542–2626). Located at the mouth of the Wailua River in a 32-acre palm grove. A remarkable combination of activity and tranquility in a South Seas Island setting. Pools, tennis, shops, 5 restaurants, lounges, singles, doubles, suites, cottages, and the President's House, all with color TV, mostly air-conditioned.

Islander on the Beach. 484 Kuhio Hwy., Kapaa, HI 96746 (822–7587 or 800–367–7052). Part of Coconut Plantation with 200 oceanside hotel units. Singles and doubles. Pool, shops, color TV, air-conditioning.

Kaha Lani. 4460 Nehe Rd., Lihue, HI 96766 (822–9331 or 800–367–5124). A secluded, 74-unit condominium complex on the beach at Wailua. Pool, tennis, air-conditioning, color TV.

Kauai Beach Boy. 484 Kuhio Hwy., #100, Kapaa, HI 96746 (822–3441 or 800–227–4700). On mile-long Waipouli Beach and part of Coconut Plantation Resort. A 243-room hotel with beach and pool swimming plus tennis, golf, shuffleboard, a restaurant, lounge, shops, color TV, air-conditioning.

Lae Nani. 410 Papaloa Rd., Kapaa, HI 96746 (822–4938 or 800–367–6046). One-, 2-, and 3-bedroom condos on the beach at Wailua. Pool and tennis available.

Plantation Hale Resort. 484 Kuhio Hwy., Kapaa, HI 96746 (822–4941 or 800–367–6046). A 160-unit apartment hotel in a large coconut grove near Coconut Plantation Market Place. Close to Waipouli Beach. Pools, restaurant, color TV.

Pono Kai. 1250 Kuhio Hwy., Kapaa, HI 96746 (822–9831 or 800–367–5124). 100 condos on the beach in Kapaa. Pool, tennis, color TV.

Sheraton Coconut Beach Hotel. Box 830, Kapaa, HI 96746 (822–3455 or 800–334–8484). A $16-million showpiece on Waipouli Beach. 311 rooms plus shops, tennis, a pool, restaurant, lounge. Singles, doubles, suites.

Moderate

Kapaa Shores. 4–0900 Kuhio Hwy., Kapaa, HI 96746 (822–3055 or 800–367–7040). 81 beachfront condos with pool and tennis nearby.

Kauai Resort Hotel. 3–5920 Kuhio Hwy., Kapaa, HI 96746 (245–3931 or 800–367–5124). A gem of a hotel with 242 rooms set where the Wailua River meets the sea. Pool, shops, restaurant, lounge, color TV.

Kauai Sands. 420 Papaloa Rd., Kapaa, HI 96746 (822–4951 or 800–367–7000). A budget hotel on Waipouli Beach near the Wailua River. 200 studios and 2-bedroom apartments. Restaurant, pool, lounge, shops.

Princeville/Hanalei

Super Deluxe

Sheraton Princeville. Box 3069, Princeville, HI 96722 (826–9644 or 800–324–8484). Princeville's luxurious landmark with 300 hotel rooms in a natural cliffside location. Spectacular vistas of dreamy Hanalei Bay. Stylized replica of Hawaiian plantation life, with a library, game tables, afternoon tea, 3 restaurants, pool, lounge, shops, tennis, golf.

Expensive

Hale Moi. Box 1185, Hanalei, HI 96714 (826–9602 or 800–367–7042). 40 condos, studios and 1-bedroom units, with or without kitchen.

Hanalei Bay Resort. Box 220, Hanalei, HI 96714 (826–6522 or 800–367–7040). Perched on Princeville's dramatic bluffs. 176 rental units including studios, 1, 2, and 3 bedrooms. Two pools, tennis, golf, lounge, sauna, restaurant adjacent to the resort.

Hanalei Colony Resort. Box 206, Hanalei, HI 96714 (in Hawaii 826–6235 or 800–367–8047). For those who want to get away from it all, 48 posh beachside apartments with fine views of Haena's rugged shore. Pool, whirlpool, restaurant nearby.

Makai Club Cottages and Condominiums. Box 3040, Hanalei, HI 96722 (826–3820 or 800–367–7090). 40 1- and 2-bedroom condos and 17 cottages in Princeville.

Pali Ke Kua. Box 899, Hanalei, HI 96714 (826–9066 or 800–367–7042). 100 condos close to the Princeville bluff. Pool, restaurants.

Sandpiper Village. Box 460, Princeville, HI 96714 (826–9613 or 800–367–7040). 74 2- and 3-bedroom condos at Princeville. Pool, sauna, whirlpool.

Sealodge. 3615 Kingridge Dr., San Mateo, CA 94403 (415–573–0636). 86 oceanfront condominiums in Princeville. One and 2 bedrooms available. Pool, golf, tennis.

RESTAURANTS. From fast food to Continental cuisine, Kauai offers a veritable smorgasbord of dining establishments catering to all budgets. The best restaurants are generally found in the hotels. We call *Deluxe* $35 and up; *Expensive* $20–$34; *Moderate* $10–$19; and *Inexpensive* under $10. Prices are based on a 3-course meal for 1 person, excluding tax, tip, and drinks. Be sure to call ahead for reservations. Most of these restaurants honor the major credit cards.

Lihue

Casa Italiana. *Expensive.* 2989 Haleko Rd. (245–9586). Authentic Italian cuisine located in one of the few remaining plantation residences in Lihue. Big salad bar, homemade garlic and pepper breads, fresh pasta, espresso bar. Dinner served nightly 5:30–10:30 P.M.

JJ's Broiler. *Expensive.* 2971 Haleko Rd. (245–3841). Kauai's original steak house, located in a sugar plantation home built over 100 years ago. Slavonic steak is the specialty. Beef, lobster, and mahimahi are also good. Complete salad bar. Garden atmosphere. Dinner nightly 5–10 P.M.

Bull Shed. *Moderate.* Harbor Village Shopping Ctr. (245–4551). Fresh island seafood and poultry dishes plus famous midwestern beef entrees. Unique salad canoe. Great view of the ocean and Nawiliwili Harbor. Large wine list.

Dani's. *Moderate.* 4201 Rice St. (245–4991). A popular spot for breakfast, lunch, and dinner. Specializes in shrimp tempura and features Hawaiian, American, and Japanese dishes.

Eggbert's. *Moderate.* 4483 Rice St. (245–6325). Billed as Lihue's Family Specialty Restaurant. Breakfast, lunch, dinner, cocktail service from 7 A.M. Exotic island drinks.

Kukui Nut Tree Inn. *Moderate.* Kukui Grove Shopping Ctr. (245–7005). Wide selection of local-style cooking for breakfast, lunch, dinner. Famous for papaya seed dressing and top seafood. Kauai Kookies gift packs available. Bar service, too.

Burger King. *Inexpensive.* Kukui Grove Village Shopping Ctr. (245–5335). Juicy flame-broiled, all-beef burgers plus sandwiches, fries, and shakes served immediately.

Dairy Queen. *Inexpensive.* 4302 Rice St. (245–2141). Great ice cream delights plus an ideal stop for local plate lunches, sandwiches, burgers. Quick service.

Ho's Garden. *Inexpensive.* Lihue Pl., corner of Rice and Umi Sts. (245–5255). Chinese food features such favorites as roast duck, lemon chicken, beef broccoli with noodles, and special lunch and dinner plates. Take out available.

Lihue Cafe & Chop Sui. *Inexpensive.* 2978 Umi St. (245–6471). Family operated for over 50 years. Chinese and Japanese food for dinner daily except Sun. Take-out available.

Tip Top Cafe. *Inexpensive.* 3173 Akahi St. (245–2333). Simple, home-style setting for savory breakfasts, lunches, dinners daily. Popular local spot. Famous for its macadamia nut cookies.

South Shore

Plantation Gardens. *Deluxe.* Kiahuna Plantation, Poipu (742–1695). A former plantation home with a tropical garden setting. Fresh local and imported seafoods. Dinner only.

Tamarind Room. *Deluxe.* Waiohai Hotel, Poipu (742–9511). Elegant service and luxurious atmosphere, splendid food and an extensive wine list. Continental dining at its finest, with a different paté served nightly. Jackets for the men. Reservations. Dinner only.

Aquarium. *Expensive.* Nalo Rd., 3 blocks past Poipu Beach Park (742–9505). The South Shore's only Italian restaurant. Fresh pasta from San Francisco and homemade sauces. Steak and seafood also available, pizza to go. Dinner daily except Tues. Reservations suggested.

Beach House. *Expensive.* Spouting Horn Rd., Poipu (742–7575). Romantic dinners at the water's edge. Many window tables. Crab legs, lobster, prime rib.

Waiohai Terrace. *Expensive.* Waiohai Hotel, Poipu (742–9511). Home of a great Sunday champagne brunch 10 A.M.–2 P.M. Breakfast, lunch, dinner served daily. Big salad bar, baked onion soup, fresh catch of the day. Ocean views.

Brennecke's Beach Broiler. *Moderate.* Across from Poipu Beach Park (742–7588). A colorful crowd gathers here for kiawe-broiled food plus fresh clams, pasta, fruit, steaks, and burgers. Open daily for lunch and dinner.

Fez's Pizza. *Moderate.* Kawamoto Bldg., Koloa (742–9096). Deep-dish pizza plus full course dinners and sandwiches. Wide variety of domestic and imported beers. Lunch, dinner, take outs available.

Koloa Broiler. *Moderate.* Koloa (742–9122). South Kauai's oldest bar features terrific *mai tais* and friendly atmosphere. Broil-your-own steak and seafood. Lunch, dinner.

Koloa Fish & Chowder House. *Moderate.* Koloa (742–7377). Informal breakfast, lunches, dinners in a nostalgic, nautical setting. Kiawe-broiled fresh catch and shrimp scampi are best. Three types of chowders.

Brick Oven Pizza. *Inexpensive.* Hwy. 50, Kalaheo (332–8561). House specialty pizza made with white or whole wheat dough topped with tons of cheese, homemade sauce, and tasty toppings. Hot sandwiches, salads, beer, wine. Lunch, dinner, take outs, daily except Mon. Now also in Kukui Grove.

Green Garden. *Inexpensive.* Hwy. 50, Hanapepe (335–5422). A popular family restaurant since 1948. Home-grown orchids on every table. Large dining room. Varied breakfast, lunch, dinner menus. Daily specials. Outrageously good Lilikoi (passion fruit) chiffon pie. Closed Tues. nights.

Lawai Restaurant. *Inexpensive.* Kalaheo (332–9550). Open daily for breakfast, lunch, dinner. Specialties in Chinese, American, and Hawaiian food. Saimin and shave ice to go.

East Side

Coconut Palace. *Deluxe.* Coco Palms Resort, Wailua (822–4921). Dinner nightly highlighted by the 7:30 P.M. torch-lighting ceremony. Extensive exotic seafood entrees, distinguished appetizers, soups, and desserts. Reservations.

Seashell. *Expensive.* Coco Palms Resort, Wailua (822–4921). By the sea on Wailua Beach. Specialties include island prawns steamed in beer and a Boston-style clambake with all the trimmings. Good salad bar. Dinners.

Atami. *Moderate.* 4–910 Kuhio Hwy., Kapaa (822–1642). Sukiyaki, teriyaki, tempura-style shrimp, fish and vegetables, sushi, sashimi, and other Japanese fare. Lunch, dinner daily except Tues.

Rib 'N Tail. *Moderate.* Kapaa Shopping Ctr., Kapaa (822–9632). A tropical setting with a sparkling indoor waterfall. Steak, seafood, ribs, spaghetti, salad bar. Dinner and dancing nightly.

Wailua Marina. *Moderate.* Wailua Marina State Park, Wailua (822–4311). Home-style dining next to the river boats. American and Oriental dishes, cold snacks and sandwiches. Known for its fresh baked desserts. Lunch, dinner.

Farrell's. *Inexpensive.* Coconut Plantation, Kapaa (822–1911). Fountain fantasies and fun for the whole family. Sundaes are the specialty, but breakfast, lunch, and dinner are also served daily.

Kountry Kitchen. *Inexpensive.* 1485 Kuhio Hwy., Kapaa (822–3511). Oceanview dining in an old-time family restaurant. Big breakfasts, specialty lunch plates, good deals on dinners.

Waipouli Restaurant. *Inexpensive.* Waipouli Town Ctr., Kapaa (822–9311). Budget prices on international favorites: short ribs and shrimp, combination seafood plates, sweet-sour chicken, sukiyaki. Breakfast, lunch, dinner.

North Shore

Hale Kapa. *Deluxe.* Sheraton Princeville Hotel, Princeville (826–9644). Plantation decor and exquisite cuisine including European and ethnic foods. Reservations.

Nobles. *Deluxe.* Sheraton Princeville Hotel, Princeville (826–9644). Sheraton's signature restaurant with supreme elegance in dining. Attention to detail in menu as well as decor. Jackets for the men. Reservations.

Beamreach. *Expensive.* Pali Ke Kua, Princeville (826–9131). Opulent steak and seafood feasts in a beautiful environment. Excellent strawberry daiquiris. Open nightly for dinner. Reservations.

Cafe Hanalei. *Expensive.* Sheraton Princeville Hotel, Princeville (826–9644). Cozy elegance in an open-air cafe overlooking spectacular Hanalei Bay. Breakfast, lunch, dinner. Bounteous Fri. seafood buffet and Sun. brunch.

Charo's. *Expensive.* Colony Resort, Haena (826–6422). Romantic sunsets and beachfront dining. Fresh island fish and international specialties like Charo's Paella. Two miles from road's end. Lunch, dinner.

Dolphin. *Moderate.* Right past the 1-lane bridge on the river in Hanalei (826–6113). Featuring fresh fish, Alaskan king crab, steaks, casseroles, and a terrific Mud Pie. Tiki decor and tapa-covered tables. Dinner only.

Tahiti Nui. *Moderate.* Hanalei (826–6277). Lunch and dinner in a casual Tahitian setting. Family-style luau every Mon., Wed., and Fri. from 7 P.M. Fresh-caught seafood. Fresh homemade soups and desserts daily.

HOW TO GET AROUND. Since there is no public transportation on Kauai, it's easiest to get around by a **rental car** from Lihue Airport. The following companies have stands adjacent to the terminal or offer van shuttle service to their offices: *Alamo* (800–327–9633); *Avis* (800–331–1212); *Budget* (800–527–0707); *Dollar* (800–367–7006); *Hertz* (800–654–3131); *National* (800–328–4300); *Roberts Hawaii* (245–4008); *Thrifty* (245–7388); *Tropical* (800–367–5140); *United* (245–8894).

Transportation by **taxi** is also available, with *Akiko's* (822–3613) and *Tony's* (245–2774) both serving the airport. *North Shore Cab Co.* (826–6189) specializes in the Priceville area. A cab ride from Lihue to Princeville costs about $40.

For less expensive wheels try *Rent-A-Wreck,* 3156 Hoolako St., Lihue, HI 96766 (245–4755), or *Westside U-Drive,* Box 493, Kalaheo, HI 96741 (332–8644). A jeep is a great way to explore the island. If you're so inclined, try *Rent-A-Jeep,* 3137-A Kuhio Hwy., Lihue, HI 96766 (245–9622).

TOURIST INFORMATION SERVICES. The Kauai *Hawaii Visitors Bureau* is located in the Lihue Plaza Bldg., Suite 207, 3016 Umi St., Lihue, HI 96766 (245–3971). They offer a wide range of brochures, maps, and guides to the various attractions of the Garden Isle, with knowledgeable information specialists on hand to answer your questions. *Island Adventure,* Box 3370, Lihue, HI 96766 (245–9662 or 800–331–8044) helps you book tours, water sports, camping, and kayak excursions.

SEASONAL EVENTS. Every day is special on the Garden Isle, but if you visit during the following events, be sure to check out these annual happenings. Some dates vary slightly from year to year, so for precise information pick up the Hawaii Special Events Calendar from the Hawaii Visitors Bureau.

February. Mid-month brings the *Captain Cook Festival,* which includes a big party with food, drinks, entertainment, canoe races, a 7.4-mile run and reenactment of Captain Cook's landing, all in Waimea. In late February or early March the *LPGA Women's Kemper Open Golf Tournament* takes place at the stunning Princeville course. This includes the *Helene Curtis Pro-Am.*

March. *Kuhio Day,* March 26, is a state holiday celebrating the birth of Prince Kuhio, Hawaii's first delegate to Congress. Since Prince Kuhio was born on the Garden Isle, a week of pageantry, parades, canoe races, and a royal ball are the featured events on Kauai. *The Carole Kai Bed*

Race is a nonsensical event full of fun, held annually as a fundraiser in Lihue.

May. May Day is Lei Day in Hawaii! On the first of the month, the *Kauai Museum* sponsors an annual lei-making contest. In Princeville it's *May Day by the Bay,* with crafts and ethnic food booths.

June. *Kamehameha Day,* June 11, honors Hawaii's great unifier with a pageant, outrigger canoe races, a street party, arts and crafts. The weekend before, the island of Kauai celebrates the holiday in grand style at the Lihue and Kukui Grove Shopping Centers.

July. *The Fourth of July* is celebrated for 2 days in Kekaha, with a carnival, parade, contests, and more. A *Summer Hoolaulea* (party) is held at the Kauai Museum, highlighted by a festival of hula, arts and crafts.

August. Early August brings the *Po'oku Hanalei Stampede,* an annual statewide rodeo at Po'oku Stables, Hanalei.

September. Labor Day Weekend heralds the *Kauai County Fair* with exhibits of flowers and produce, 4H livestock and entertainment at the Kauai Memorial Convention Hall, Lihue. *Aloha Week,* at the end of the month, is a major celebration with much dancing in the streets and lots of friendly competition among the ethnic groups.

October. The first weekend of the month is a vigorous one with the *Kauai Loves You Triathlon,* an APT World Championship Super Series Event comprised of a 1.5-mile swim, 54-mile bike ride, and 12.4-mile run beginning and ending in Hanalei.

November. *The Kauai Museum Holiday Festival* is a Christmas event featuring handcrafted items and baked goods. It takes place in late November (or early December).

December. *The Kauai Jr. Miss Presentation* is held the first week of the month in the Kauai War Memorial Convention Hall, Lihue.

TOURS. By land, sea, and air, a tour of Kauai can take you places you might not otherwise be able to reach. Tours may be booked at hotel desks or directly through the following organizations.

Robert's Hawaii, Box 3389, Lihue, HI 96766 (245–9109), offers an 8-hour **guided tour** of the Wailua River to Waimea Canyon. The cost is $326 in a chartered chauffeured limo and $28.85 per person by bus. *Gray Line,* Lihue Airport, Lihue, HI 96766 (800–367–2420), has a Waimea Canyon/Wailua River trip for $22 plus $7 for the river boat. *Kauai Mountain Tours,* Box 3069, Lihue, HI 96766 (245–7224), takes folks on 7-hour off-road tours of the Na Pali-Kona Forest Reserve in 8-passenger station wagons. The cost, with picnic lunch, is $70. *See All Hawaii Tours,* 677 Ala Moana Blvd., Suite 907, Honolulu, HI 96813 (800–367–5134), has Kauai-in-a-day tours for $115, with a 5:45 A.M. pickup in Waikiki, back by 6:30 P.M. This includes the Wailua River Boat Trip.

If you want to fly high, *Papillon Helicopters,* Box 339, Hanalei, HI 96714 (800–367–7095), takes you on exclusive tours of the entire island for $115. A sunset fantasy trip in Waimea Canyon and along the Na Pali Coast costs $160, and into Waialeale Crater for a waterfall stop, costs $225 (breakfast and lunch included; 5 hours). Other chopper companies include *Bruce Needham Helicopters,* Box 156, Hanapepe, HI 96716 (335–5009). *Kauai Helicopters,* 3225 Akahi St., Lihue, HI 96766 (245–7403). *Kenai Helicopters,* Box 3270, Lihue, HI 96766 (800–662–2133). *Menehune Helicopter Tours,* 3222 Kuhio Hwy., Suite 2, Lihue, HI 96766 (245–7705). *Ohana Helicopters,* 3222 Kuhio Hwy., Suite 4, Lihue, HI 96766

(800–222–6989). *South Seas Helicopters,* Box 1445, Lihue, HI 96766 (800–367–2914). *Will Squyres Helicopter Tours,* Box 1770, Lihue, HI 96766 (245–8881). *Island Helicopters* flies its 4-passenger Bell Jet Rangers on a grand tour for $111. Write Box 3101, Lihue, HI 96766 (245–2588). *Princeville Airways* offers flightseeing tours of Kauai from Princeville Airport by 18-seat Twin Otter. The cost for 30–60-min. tours ranges from $50–$90. Tel. 800–323–3345.

Get splashy on a **sea tour** with Clancy Greff, whose *Captain Zodiac Raft Expeditions,* Box 456, Hanalei, HI 96714 (826–9371), takes you along the thrilling Na Pali Coast. His tours are thwarted only by winter's heavy surf conditions. It's $90 all day, $55 half day. You can also cruise the coast with *Na Pali-Kauai Boat Charters,* Box 3224, Princeville, HI 96722 (826–7254 or 800–367–8047, ext. 155). Their offerings include seasonal whale-watching tours, south shore expeditions, and a day-long snorkeling trip for $85. The boat trip up the Wailua River to Fern Grotto takes 1½ hours and costs $8. Write *Smith's Motor Boat Service,* 174 Wailua Rd., Kapaa, HI 96746 (822–4111). They'll also set you up with a Fern Grotto wedding package for $250 with all the trimmings. Other boat tours include *Lady Ann Cruises,* Box 3422, Lihue, HI 96766 (245–8538) and *Waialeale Boat Tours,* Wailua Marina, Kapaa, HI 96746 (822–4908).

PARKS AND GARDENS. In addition to the glorious wonders of nature which the gods so generously bestowed upon Kauai, there are several public parks and gardens to help you discover the joys of the Garden Isle.

Kiahuna Gardens. Poipu Rd., Poipu, HI (742–6411). Rare cactus and succulents abound in this fascinating landscape which features one of the largest selections of African aloe plants. The daily 10 A.M. tour includes a visit to the miniHawaiian garden with demonstrations of how herbs and plants were used by the early Hawaiians. Open daily 9 A.M.–6 P.M. Free.

Kukuiolono Park, which means "lights of the god Lono," stretches 9 acres at the crest of a hill above Kalaheo. Formerly the private estate of Walter McBryde, pioneer founder of the McBryde Sugar Plantation, the park is a favorite picnic spot for local residents, and its hilltop golf course offers such splendid views that it's hard to keep your mind on the ball. The Japanese garden is a miniature miracle. Free.

Olu Pua Botanical Gardens, Hawaiian for "floral serenity," is aptly named. A plantation manager's estate when it was built in 1932, the 12-acre gardens feature all kinds of tropical trees and plants. The gardens are a half mile up a private road off Hwy. 50. Look for the Warrior Marker. Open 8:30 A.M.–5 P.M. $6 adults, $2 children under 12, $4 senior citizens. Telephone 332–8182.

Pacific Tropical Botanical Garden. Box 340, Lawai, HI 96765 (332–8131 or 332–8901). This is the only national privately supported tropical botanical garden chartered by Congress. The 186-acre site is also an area of research, education, and living collections. The 100-acre Allerton Estate flanks the gardens, begun in 1879 by Queen Emma. Tours daily by reservations only.

Smith's Tropical Paradise (822–4654). Adjacent to the Wailua Marina are 30 acres of lagoons, jungle paths, tropical plants, peacocks, re-created thatched Polynesian dwellings, a luau pavilion, and a stage for live shows. Trams depart every hour for tours. $5 adults, $2 children under 11.

BEACHES. As the oldest island in the chain, Kauai has had plenty of time to develop extraordinarily beautiful beaches. Some of them are easily accessible while others can be reached only by boat or foot.

Anahola Beach Park on the east shore offers calm waters for safe swimming and snorkeling. With the Makalena Mountains as a backdrop, this quietly curving strand is popular with picnickers. Restrooms, showers.

Anini Beach, near Princeville on the north shore, is safe year 'round for swimming, snorkeling, and windsurfing. Restrooms, showers.

Brennecke's Beach in Poipu is well known as a summertime bodysurfing and bodyboarding haven, but winter waves keep the smart folks on the sidelines.

Haena Beach lies near the end of the road on the north shore. This is a pleasant spot for sunning, swimming, and near-shore scuba-diving. Restroom, showers.

Hanakapiai Beach. A 2-mile hike in from Ke'e Beach leads you to this crescent bay of unspoiled beauty. Rip tides and winter waves can be extremely unpredictable here, and caution is stressed.

Hanalei Beach Park. This north shore beach is also seasonally dangerous, but during calm months it offers great swimming. Great photo opportunities. Restrooms, showers.

Kalapaki Beach, located in Nawiliwili, offers safe small-wave swimming, surfing, bodyboarding, and windsurfing.

Ke'e Beach awaits at the end of the north shore road just past Haena Beach Park, and offers fine swimming, snorkeling, and near-shore scuba-diving when the conditions are calm. Restrooms, showers.

Kekaha Beach Park on the south shore is a long, luxurious strip of sand recalling the beaches of California. Great for dune buggy action!

Lumahai Beach, made famous in *South Pacific,* awaits on the north shore near Hanalei Bay. A small trail down from the road takes you to this protected area.

Lydate Beach Park in Wailua is chock full of Hawaiian history. This family park area features safe swimming year-round. Restrooms, showers.

Poipu Beach Park near Brennecke's Beach draws bodysurfers and bodyboarders plus swimmers, snorkelers, and scuba divers. You can even take out a catamaran here. Restrooms, showers.

Polihale Beach Park awaits at the end of the south shore road. Turn left at the Warrior Marker and drive through a series of cane roads to this cliff-flanked expanse with wide open spaces. Swim here only when the surf is small. Restrooms, showers.

Salt Pond Beach Park in Hanapepe lies adjacent to the old Hawaiian salt ponds still in use today. Off Hwy. 50. Safe swimming, showers, restrooms, pavilion.

Shipwreck Beach past Brennecke's Beach is named after a sampan which sank there. A short walk down a dirt road takes you to this favorite weekend spot for swimmers and fishermen.

Wailua Beach offers convenient swimming, surfing, and bodyboarding on the east shore. It is, however, seasonally dangerous.

SPORTS. Active vacationers can't miss on Kauai, where the great outof-doors is great indeed. Whether you're a serious sportsman or just looking for some fun in the sun, the following list should have something to suit everybody.

Cruises/Sailing. *Blue Water Sailing* (822–0525) offers trips off the beautiful south shore aboard a 42-foot Pearson Ketch rigged yacht. They also offer whale watching and sportfishing. *Na Pali-Kauai Boat Charters,* Box 3224, Princeville, HI 96722 (826–7254 or 800–367–8047, ext. 155), features day-long snorkeling trips along the Na Pali coast for $85, and half-day for $55–$65. *Lady Ann Cruises* (Box 3422, Lihue, HI 96766, 245–8538 or 800–367–8047, ext. 446) features Na Pali Coast tours, weather permitting, from a 2½-hour whale watch for $35 to a 4½-hour snorkel with lunch for $75. *Captain Andy's Sailing Adventures,* (Box 1291, Koloa, HI 96756, 822–7833), lets you navigate the south shore on a Hawaiian catamaran, with great views of dolphins, turtles, and flying fish.

Fishing. Rainbow trout season opens on the first Sat. of August and remains open for 16 days. After that, fishing is permitted only on weekends and holidays through the end of September. Other fish, such as bluegill, can be caught daily all year. A freshwater fishing license is required and can be obtained from the Dept. of Land and Natural Resources, Box 1671, Lihue, HI 96766 (245–4433). A 30-day license for visitors is $3.75.

If you're up for some inland freshwater bass fishing, call *Bass Guides of Kauai,* Box 3525, Lihue, HI 96766 (822–1405). For a half-day trip it costs $90 for 1 person, $125 for 2 (2-person maximum).

Boat charters and guide service for **deep-sea fishing** are available from *Na Pali-Kauai Boat Charters,* Box 3224, Princeville, HI 96722 (826–7254 or 800–367–8047, ext. 155). They take anglers out on exclusive and shared trips from $55 to $75 per person. *Sea Breeze Sportfishing Charters,* Box 594, Kilauea, HI 96754 (828–1285), offers further fun for coastal fishing on a custom-built 26-ft. twin diesel. It holds up to 6 people and leaves at 7 A.M. out of the north shore at a cost of $70 per person (shared). *Sportfishing Kauai,* Box 1185, Koloa, HI 96756 (742–7013), takes its 29-ft. Bertram on trips for 4, 6, or 8 hours, with prices ranging from $85 to $600 (shared or exclusive).

Golf. Those in the know claim that Kauai has Hawaii's best golf courses, and undoubtedly some of the prettiest locations for a day on the greens. *The Kiahuna Golf Club* (RR 1, Box 78, Koloa, HI 96756, 742–9595), a resort course designed by Robert Trent Jones, Jr., is open to the public for play on 18 holes for $50. Pro shop, rentals, restaurant, bar. *Kukuiolono Park and Golf Course* (Kalaheo, HI 96741, 332–9151) features glorious hilltop views. There's even a Japanese *torii* to shoot around; $5 daily. Nine holes, pro shop, rentals, snack shop. Ranked among America's 100 greatest courses is the *Princeville Makai Golf Course* (Box 3040, Princeville, HI 96722, 826–3580), designed by Robert Trent Jones, Jr; $27-$34 guests, $44-$50 nonguests. *Wailua Municipal Golf Course* (4396 Rice St., Lihue, HI 96766, 245–8092), is a fine county course by the Wailua River and the beach. Its 18 holes have hosted several national tournaments. Pro shop, driving range, restaurant; $10 weekdays, $11 weekends.

Hiking. *Kokee State Park* boasts 45 miles of great hiking trails of varying difficulty, all glorious and worth the walk. The *Iliau Nature Loop* is an easy stroll and the *Kukui Trail* challenges the hearty hiker to trek right down the side of the Waimea Canyon. All hikers should register at the park headquarters, which offers trail maps and information. *The Kalalau Trail* begins at the end of Hwy. 56 in Haena. The entire 11-mile hike to Kalalau Beach is a true test of endurance, and most hikers prefer the easy 2-mile trek into Hanakapiai Beach and back. For your own safety, no matter where you hike, bring a friend, carry sufficient water, stay on the trail, and avoid hiking when it's wet and slippery.

Horseback Riding. *High Gates Ranch* (6280 Olohena Rd., Kapaa, HI 96746, 922–3182) takes you on escorted mountain trail rides including a 4-hour swim tour for $55. Standard rates are $18 per hour for adults and $9 per hour for children. *Po'oku Stables* (Box 888, Hanalei, HI 96714, 826–6777) serves the Princeville area with guided horseback tours. Rides into the valley are $17, beach rides $35, and 3-hour waterfall picnic rides with lunch cost $55.

Hunting. Kauai's 4 hunting areas are Wailua, Puu Ka Pele, Kekaha, and Kalepa. Game birds include Japanese quail, barred dove, lace-necked dove, partridge, black Francolin, California quail, and pheasants. The season runs from November through mid-January, but check with Lihue's Division of Conservation Enforcement, 3060 Eiwa St., Lihue, HI 96766 (245–4444).

Mammal hunting seasons vary. Check at the Lihue office for current information. You can hunt blacktail deer along the ridges of Kokee's western slopes in October only, with weekend limits. Those applying must draw numbers. Nonresident licenses are $15; feral goats and pigs are open to non-resident hunters.

Snorkeling/Diving. *Aquatics Kauai* (733 Kuhio Hwy., Kapaa, HI 96746, 822–9213) offers a half-day snorkeling trip for $45, half-day scuba instruction for $65, night dives for $60, plus advanced courses for certified divers. *Fathom Five Divers* (Box 907, Koloa, HI, 96756; 742–6991) is a professional dive shop with personalized scuba instruction and daily trips. Certification course runs $300–$400, while a beginning dive with gear is $60. *Ocean Odyssey* (Box 807, Kapaa, HI 96746, 822–9680), offers snorkel and dive tours from $25 (introductory) to $275 (PADI certification classes). *Sea Sage* (4-1378 Kuhio Hwy., Kapaa, HI 96746, 822–3841) takes you on a 2-tank boat dive with gear for $75.

Tennis. There are 20 public lighted courts and more than 70 private ones at the hotels, with 9 at *Coco Palms,* 22 at *Princeville,* and 24 at *Kiahuna Plantation,* the *Waiohai,* and other sites in Poipu. Resort courts may cost up to $10 per hour per person, though many are free to guests.

CAMPING. From oceanside beaches to the tops of mountains, Kauai has a variety of parks for pitching your tent. Plan your outings ahead of time in order to get a permit. Permits are free and can be obtained by sending specific dates, campsites, and copies of each camper's identification. Write the Dept. of Land and Natural Resources, State Parks Division, Box 1671, Lihue, HI 96766 or call 254–4444. Popular campsites include *Kokee State Park, Polihale Beach Park,* and *Hanalei Beach Park.*

Kahili Mountain Park, Box 298, Koloa, HI 96756, is an all-weather cabin development for rough-luxury camping. It even has a Japanese hot bath. Rates start at $16.50 for a double cabinette with community shower and bath. Private bath in a cabin double runs $30. A 2-bedroom deluxe runs $50. They appeal to the non-hotel set, with no noise after 11 P.M. Entrance is off Hwy. 50, a short distance beyond the intersection of Hwy. 520 to Koloa.

HISTORIC SITES AND BUILDINGS. Captain Cook's Landing and Monument, located in the center of Waimea, pays tribute to that famous British explorer who first touched Hawaiian soil in January 1778.

Kilauea Lighthouse, 6 miles south of Hanalei off Kuhio Hwy., is the State of Hawaii's northernmost point. The adjacent seabird sanctuary is open for guided nature walks from noon to 4 P.M. Sun. through Fri. Here you can see the red-footed booby and Leyson albatross.

Lihue Lutheran Church, near the Lihue Sugar Mill, served a population which was largely German. Hawaii's oldest Lutheran Church, it was built in 1883 in classic New England style. Look for the Warrior Marker on Hwy. 50 south.

Old Koloa Town, intersection of Poipu and Koloa Rds., was Kauai's first successful sugar plantation. The recently restored town has seen a century and a half of Hawaiian history. Free walking tours are offered twice a week offering a look at this gracious plantation heritage (742–9773).

Old Russian Fort, near Waimea town line off Hwy. 50, was built in 1817 when Russian Anton Scheffer convinced Kauai's King Kaumaulii that they could conquer the islands together. The king helped Scheffer build a fort on the banks of the Waimea River out of traditional Kauai stonework. You can tour the remains of the star-shaped compound daily for free.

Prince Kuhio Birthplace Monument, Prince Kuhio Park, Lawai Rd., Poipu, salutes one of Hawaii's best-loved statesmen and a long-time delegate to Congress.

MUSEUMS. Grove Farm Homestead (245–3202), located off Nawiliwili Rd. in Lihue, is an 80-acre "living museum" centering around the Wilcox plantation, preserved as it was when it was lived in. Founded in 1864, this is one of the earliest plantations in Hawaii. Tours are available.

Kauai Museum, 4228 Rice St., Lihue, HI (245–6931), is a perfect introduction to the Garden Isle. Its permanent exhibit is "The Story of Kauai," and there are also art and ethnic heritage displays of Hawaiiana and works by local artists. Books and souvenirs for sale. Open Mon.–Fri., 9:30 A.M.–4:30 P.M. Admission is $3.

Kilohana, Hwy. 50, 2 miles west of Lihue, is a 35-acre attraction centered around the historic Wilcox house. Agricultural exhibits, local arts and crafts, and cultural events take place in and around the 15,000-square-foot plantation estate built in the 1830s. Picnic areas, carriage rides, a courtyard restaurant and unique shops. Open from 9 A.M. daily (245–5608).

Kokee Museum (335–6061) is adjacent to the Kokee Lodge, Waimea Canyon Rd. in Kokee State Park. It offers a good display of the flora and fauna of Waimea Canyon, geographic descriptions of the area, old Hawaiian artifacts, and a variety of souvenirs. You'll also find rubbings of petroglyphs found on Kauai.

Waioli Mission House (245–3202), just off Hwy. 56 in Hanalei, is a mission station founded in 1837 by an American missionary and his wife. Next to it are the Waioli Social Hall (1841) and Waioli Hui'ia Church (1912). Free, half-hour guided tours are available throughout the year, although donations are accepted.

SHOPPING. Kauai has only a handful of shopping centers, but they seem to do the trick on this easy-going island. **Kukui Grove** on Hwy. 50 south is Kauai's largest shopping center. You can pick up the bulk of your vacation supplies at the Star Market, Woolworths, and Longs Drugs located there. In Lihue proper is **Rice Shopping Ctr.,** with a supermarket and shops offering fashions, health food, and bargain souvenirs. Nawiliwili has **Harbor Village Shopping Ctr.,** and the Gem Dept. Store in **Lihue Shopping Ctr.** is quite handy for last-minute needs.

Coconut Plantation's Market Place covers 8 acres in Waipouli with over 70 shops situated around a colorful waterworks. They have 2 cinemas, restaurants, snack bars, and even a free hula show. Smaller shopping centers include **Hee Fat Market Place** in Kapaa, home of Ben Franklin Variety Store, Big Save Supermarket, and assorted boutiques and eateries. Adjacent to the entrance to the **Princeville Resort,** a small shopping center offers a supermarket, hardware store, pizza place, steak house, and gift shops.

Hanalei's **Ching Young Village,** patterned after the Japanese Village Plaza Shopping Center in Little Tokyo, is the first retail center owned and operated by native Hawaiians. Its tiny Hawaiian Museum is worth browsing while you're there.

NIGHTLIFE. Evening entertainment is extremely limited on quiet Kauai. A handful of hotels present Polynesian-style music at sunset and a few restaurants offer mellow tunes for dancing during cocktail hour.

Kauai, Captured Fantasy. The Westin Kauai's resident show stars a talented ensemble of 10 island singers and dancers. It takes place in the Royal Boathouse, an oceanside club serving a 5-course dinner. Presented at 8:15 P.M. daily except Mon. $49 includes a cocktail, dinner, and the show (245–5050).

Park Place. Boasting Kauai's largest dance floor, this hot disco plays top 40s music in a garden setting. On Wed., happy hour lasts until midnight. Thurs. is Ladies Night. Harbor Village Shopping Ctr. (245–5775).

Index

Academy of Arts, 139–140
Aiea, 90
Air travel
  baggage regulations, 5
  to Hawaiian Islands, 2–3, 95, 167,
    259
  interisland, 3, 167, 198, 226, 236,
    259
  Kauai tours, 266–267
  one-day tour of islands, 4–5
  volcano tours, 177
Airport buses, 116, 167, 207
Ala Moana, 72, 107–108, 130
Alakai Swamp, 240
Albert, Prince, 41
Alcoholic beverages
  brewery of saki, 63
  laws on, 10
  wine on Maui, 194, 209
  winery, 194, 209
All Islands Makahiki, 122
Aloha (the word), 35–36
Aloha Stadium, 14, 123, 134
Aloha Tower, 45, 70, 141
Aloha Week, 2, 122, 176
American Continental restaurants,
  110–111
Amusement park, 128
Aqualunging, 131
Aquarium and marine park, 125–127
Archaeology, 39–40, 159–160
Art galleries, 143–144, 156, 214–215
Astronauts, 65
Astronomical observatories, 166
Austro-Hungarian restaurant, 111
Automobiles
  licenses for, 4
  rental. *See* Rental cars

Bank hours, 10
Baseball, 14, 134
Basketball, 14, 120, 123, 134
Beaches, 11, 47–54. *See also each
    island*
  black-sand, 52, 159, 180
Bed and breakfast, 7–8, 109
Bicycles, 133, 209
  renting, 118, 177
"Big Five" companies, 43
Big Island, as nickname for the
    island of Hawaii, 153

Bishop Estate, 62
Bishop Museum, 137–138, 245
Black Point, 62
Bligh, Captain William, 161
Blow Hole, 80–81
Boat cruises. *See* Cruises
"Boat Day," 46, 76–77
Bodysurfing, 11, 49, 52, 54, 84, 130,
    179, 268
Bonsai, 176
Boxing, 14, 134
Brigham Young University, 86, 127
British restaurants, 111
British visitors, 5–6
Buddhism, 78, 85, 89, 121, 122, 208,
    251, 253
  festival day of, 2, 122
Burns, Robert, 118
Buses (Honolulu), 116
Business hours, 10

Calendars of events, 2, 118–123,
    175–176, 207–208, 265, 266
Camping, 134–135, 183, 213–214,
    228–229, 237, 270
Canadians, proof of place of birth
    required from, 5
Canoes, 11–12, 120, 121, 122, 131,
    133, 138, 157, 160, 221
Capitol Building (Honolulu), 73
Captain Cook (city), 169
Carthaginian II (ship), 43, 189, 214
Castle & Cooke (Dole Company),
    26, 54, 65–66, 88, 95, 231
Castle Park Hawaii, 128
Caves, 93, 166, 196, 248, 249
Cherry Blossom festival, 2, 119
Children, beaches for, 49, 179–180,
    268
Chinese, 32, 44, 119, 121, 214–215
  churches of, 79–80
Chinese restaurants, 111, 115, 263,
    264
Chinese wares, 147–148
Christmas, 123, 176, 266
Climate, 1–2, 24–25, 48
  Kauai rainfall, 240
Clothing, 5
Cockfighting, 14
Coconut groves, 221, 245
Coffee, 161, 176, 184, 247

Condominiums, 8, 27–28
Cook, Captain James, 22, 38–39, 161, 175, 252
  death of, 141, 161, 183
  Kauai landing of, 38, 239, 241, 254, 256, 265, 270
Cost of trip, 6–7
Crime. *See* Security
Cruises
  around Oahu, 124
  to Hawaiian Islands, 3–4
  from Kauai, 267, 269
  from Molokai, 228
  sunset dinner, 152, 209

Damien, Father, 218, 222, 223
Dance, 30, 120, 142
Diamond.Head, 62, 67
Discos, 150, 185
Dogs, quarantine of, 5
Dole. *See* Castle & Cooke
Drama, 122, 142–143
Drinking houses, 115
Drinking laws, 10
Dune buggies, 268

East Indian restaurants, 112
Easter Island, 138
East-West Center, 60–61, 123
Emma, Queen, 41, 73, 76, 253
  Summer Palace of, 140

Falls, 64, 85–86, 124–128, 154, 177, 184, 197, 224–225, 245
Fashion and fabrics, 146–147
Fast food, 115
Fern Grotto, 245
Filipino restaurant, 112
Filipinos, 32, 72, 120
.Films, 31, 122, 142. *See also* Movie making
Fish market, 184
Fish ponds, 210, 218, 223, 242, 250–251
Fishing
  deep-sea, 12, 133, 176, 181, 212, 269
  freshwater, 12, 269
Fishing villages
  last working, 161
  reconstructed, 40
Food, 34–35
  Hawaiian, 8–10
Food stores, 149–150
Football, 14, 15, 118, 123, 134
Fort Shafter, 44, 90
Fort Street Mall, 70
Foster Botanic Garden, 128–129
French restaurants, 112, 115, 173
From Here to Eternity (novel), 44, 89
Fuller, Buckminster, 57

Garden Isle, as nickname for Kauai, 239
"Garden of the Gods," 235
Gardens. *See under each island*
German restaurant, 112
Glass-bottom boats, 84, 177, 209
Gliding, 133
Golf, 13, 15
  Hawaii (island), 15, 81, 93, 119, 132, 134, 181–182
  Kauai, 247, 253, 265, 269
  Lanai, 236
  Maui, 191, 212
  Molokai, 228
  Oahu, 13, 15, 93, 119, 132
Grand Canyon of the Pacific, 254–255
Greek restaurant, 112

Halawa Valley, 224–225
Haleakala, 14, 28–29, 194–195, 198, 205, 209–210, 212
Haleiwa, 87, 116
Hamakua Coast, 165, 168
Hana, 194, 195–196, 198, 202
Hanalei, 53, 247, 261–262, 265, 268
Hanapepe, 253, 264
Handicapped travelers, tips for, 16
Hansen's Disease (leprosy), 218, 222
Hawaii (island), 26, 153–185
  beaches of, 51–52, 163, 178–180
  camping on, 183
  churches on, 158, 159, 160, 162, 163, 184
  exploring, 154–166
  golf on, 13, 15
  historical sites on, 40–41, 183–184
  hotels on, 167–172
  Kona coast of, 160–161, 170–171, 173–174, 181
  map of, 155
  parks and gardens of, 157, 162, 163, 165–166, 177–178, 193
  restaurants on, 173–174
  sports on, 175–176, 181–183
  tours of, 176–177
  transportation on, 174–175
  volcanoes of, 13, 29–30, 153–154, 156–158, 165–166, 168–169, 174, 177
"Hawaii 5-0" TV series, 91
Hawaii State Legislature, annual opening of, 2, 118
Hawaii Visitors Bureau, 1
Hawaiian cuisine, 8–9
Hawaiian Islands
  ethnic groups in, 32–33, 43, 56
  geology of, 23
  history of, 22, 37–46, 64–65, 240–241. *See also various rulers;* Menehune; Vietnam War; World War II

map of, vii–viii
motto of, 39
number and size of islands of, 26
statehood for, 45, 121
Hawaiian language, 17–20
on Niihau, 257
Hawaiian restaurants, 112, 262
Hawaiian woodcarving, 149
Hawaiians, ethnic
ancient sports of, 87
culture of, 30–32, 35–36, 42–43
holidays of, 2, 10, 118–122
medicine of, 90
museum collections on, 137–138,
140, 183–184, 189, 214
music of, 119, 120
number of, 32
religion of, 40, 92, 93, 137, 162,
186, 224, 248. *See under* Heiaus
Sacred Birthstones of, 89. *See
also* Human sacrifice
Hawi, 163, 172
Heiaus
Hawaii (island), 40, 159, 160, 161,
162, 163, 164, 178, 180, 184,
210, 224
Kauai, 244–245
Lanai, 234
Maui, 188–189, 190, 210
Molokai, 218, 224
Oahu, 87, 90, 137
Health food, 115
Helicopter tours, 124, 177, 209,
227–228, 266–267
Hickam Air Force Base, 65
Hiking, 14, 132–133, 157, 183, 212,
236, 249–250, 269–270
in Volcanoes National Park,
157–158
Hilo, 158, 167–168, 174, 176
Holidays, 2, 10
Honokaa, 164–165
Honolulu, 57–80. *See also* Oahu;
Waikiki
art galleries in, 143–144
Chinatown in, 34–35, 44, 71–72,
121, 123
dance in, 30, 120, 142
exploring, 57–80
hotels of, 95–108
houses and estates in, 62–63
library of, 76
maps of, 58–59, 68–69, 74–75
Marathon of, 2, 14, 123
museums of, 137–141
music in, 30–31, 77, 119–122, 142,
150–152
public transportation in, 116–117
restaurants in, 109–115
shopping in, 144–150
spectator sports of, 14–15
sunset dinner cruises from, 152

theater in, 122, 142–143
tours of, 123–124
yacht harbor of, 67
zoo of, 62, 121, 125
Honolulu Hale (City Hall), 76
Horse racing, 175
Horseback riding, 14, 28, 133–134,
182, 195, 209, 228, 270
Hotels, 1, 7–8, 27–28. *See also each
island*
Hualalai, 153
Hula, 31–32, 120, 121, 249
Hulihee Palace, 162, 183
Human sacrifice, 40, 42, 65, 158,
210
Hunting, 13, 122, 133, 165–166, 182,
212, 236, 270

Iao Valley, 189, 210
Ice skating, 134
Import and export restrictions, 5
Indian imports, 148
Indonesian restaurants, 112
Iolani Barracks, 73
Iolani Palace, 41, 72, 73, 138–139
Irish restaurant, 112
Italian restaurants, 113, 262, 263

Japanese, 32, 44
festivals of, 119, 120, 121
temples and churches of, 44, 61,
78–79, 85, 89, 253
theater and dance of, 2, 31, 121
Japanese flower arranging, 175–176
Japanese restaurants, 113, 174, 206,
262–265
Japanese wares, 147–148
Jewelry, 149
Jogging. *See* Running and jogging

Kaahumanu, Queen, 136, 163
Kaanapali, 190–191, 200, 205
Kaena Point, 93–94
Kahakuloa, 191
Kahana, 85, 115
Kahikilani, Prince, 87
Kahoolawe, 26, 197
Kahului, 187–189, 204, 206
Kahunas, 218, 248
Kailua, 40, 84, 115
Kailua-Kona, 160, 162–163,
170–171, 173–174, 176, 185
Kaiser, Henry J., 56–57
Ka Lae, 160
Kalakaua, David, King, 31–32, 41,
64, 138–139, 162, 176
Kalalau Valley and Trail, 249–250
Kalaheo, 253, 264
Kalaupapa, 218, 222
Kaluakoi, 219
Kamakou, 223

Kamehameha Day, 2, 10, 120, 176, 207, 266
Kamehameha I, the Great, King, 39, 40, 41–42, 137, 162, 231, 234
  birthplace and youth of, 40, 158, 164
  conquest of Hawaiian Islands by, 40, 64–65, 66, 218, 223, 241, 254
  death and remains of, 41–42, 63–64
  statues of, 76, 164, 176
Kamehameha II, King, 41
Kamehameha III, King, 39, 41, 139, 214
Kamehameha IV, King (Alexander Liholiho), 41, 63, 74
Kamehameha V, King, 41, 121, 221
Kamehameha Schools, 65
Kamokila, 245
Kamuela, 164, 171
Kapaa, 245–246, 261, 264
Kapaau, 164
Kapalua, 200, 205
Kapiolani, Queen, 64
Kapu system, 42, 163
Kauai, 238–272
  beaches of, 52–53, 246, 247–248, 249, 252, 253, 254, 268
  camping on, 270
  churches on, 246, 247, 251, 254, 271
  exploring, 242–258
  historic sites and buildings on, 254, 270–271
  hotels on, 259–262
  map of, 243
  museums on, 271–272
  nightlife on, 272
  parks and gardens of, 240, 245, 249–250, 252, 253, 254, 255, 267
  restaurants on, 262–265
  shopping on, 271–272
  sports on, 268–270
  tours of, 266–267
  transportation on, 265
Kaunakakai, 221, 226–227
Kaunolu Bay, 234
Kawaiahao Church, 136–137
Kawaikini, 239, 240
Kayaks, 228
Keauhou, 162, 169, 174, 179, 185
Keomuku, 235
Kihei, 191–192, 201, 202, 203, 204
Kilauea (Hawaii Island), 30, 154, 156–157
Kilauea (Kauai), 246
King's Village, 67
Kipahulu, 196–197
Kites, 133
Kodak Hula Show, 67

Kohala and Kohala coast, 12, 154, 163, 171–172, 173–174
Kokee, 30, 255, 271
Koko Head and Crater, 80–81, 91, 129
Kolekole Pass and Stone, 88, 92
Koloa, 251–252, 260, 263, 271
Koolau Range, 81, 91
"Korean" bars, 115
Korean restaurants, 113
Koreans, 32, 44, 79–80, 120
Kosher restaurant, 113
Kuhio Day (and Prince Kuhio), 2, 10, 119, 241, 265, 271
Kukaniloko, 89
Kula, 193

La Perouse Bay, 193
Lahaina, 42–43, 44, 187, 189–190, 200, 201, 202, 203, 204–205, 206
Laie, 86, 127–128, 130
Lanai, 26, 230–237
  beaches of, 54, 233, 234
  camping on, 237
  exploring, 232–235
  hotel of, 233, 236
  hunting on, 13
  map of, 232
  restaurants on, 236
  sports on, 236–237
  tours of, 236
  transportation on, 236
Land reform, 33
Lanikai, 84
Lawai, 252–253
Leis, 120, 176, 216, 266
Leprosy. *See* Hansen's Disease
Library, 76
Lighthouses, 67, 81, 94, 159, 246, 271
Liholiho, Alexander. *See* Kamehameha IV, King
Lihue, 244, 259, 262–263, 271
Liliuokalani, Queen, 41, 73, 138–139, 178
Limousine services, 117, 175, 207
Lindbergh, Charles A., 197
Luaus, 8–9

Maalaea, 191–192, 204
Macadamia nuts, 164–165, 185
Makaha, 93, 108, 116, 130
Makawao, 193
Makena, 51, 192
Manoa Valley, 60–62, 128
Maui, 26, 27, 186–216
  beaches of, 50–51, 190, 191–192, 210–211
  camping on, 213–214
  churches and temples on, 189, 190, 193, 196, 197, 214
  exploring, 187–297

historical sites on, 42, 214–215
hotels on, 198–205
Japanese temples on, 44
map of, 188
Marine Art Expo on, 32
parks and gardens on, 189, 192, 193, 194–195, 196, 209–210
restaurants on, 205–206
sports on, 11, 207–208, 211–213
tours of, 208–209
transportation on, 206–207
Mauna Kea, 13, 29–30, 153, 154, 165, 166, 173
Mauna Loa, 29–30, 153, 154, 157, 165–166
Maunaloa (Molokai), 219, 221, 226
Menehune, 239, 240, 248, 250, 253–254
Mexican restaurants, 113–114
Mid-Pacific Institute, 61
Milolii, 160–161
Miss Chinatown, 121
Miss Hawaii, 120
Miss Kauai, 266
Miss Maui, 207
Mission Houses, 136, 271
Missionaries, 42–43, 136, 162–163, 176, 184, 190, 197, 222, 231, 241, 247
  museums of, 136, 190, 214, 271
Moanalua Valley, 66
Moby-Dick (novel), 126, 189
Mokihana berry, 239
Mokuhooniki Island, 224
Molokai, 26, 217–229
  beaches of, 53–54, 219, 224
  churches on, 221, 222, 223
  exploring, 219–225
  hotels on, 226, 227
  hunting on, 13
  map of, 220
  parks and gardens on, 222–223
  restaurants on, 227
  sports on, 14, 29, 228
  tours on, 227–228
  transportation on, 227
Molokai bread, 221, 227, 236
Monanalua Golf Course, 13, 66
Moped rentals, 117–118, 175
Mormons, 86, 127–128, 231
Motels, 7
Movie making, 53, 242, 248, 250, 253, 268
Mule ride, 228
Munro Trail, 233, 234
Museums
  aerospace, 141
  art, 73, 76, 139–140
  bottle, 141
  geology, 184
  Hawaiian culture, 137–138, 140, 183–184, 189, 214

Kauai, 271
maritime, 141, 214
military and naval, 140–141
of missionaries, 136–137, 190, 214, 271
natural history, 86, 137–138, 271
Pacific whaling, 126–127
Parker Ranch, 184
plantation. *See* Sugar plantations and mills
Polynesian cultural, 127–128
printing, 190, 214
prison, 214
railway, 141
sailing ship, 141
sugar, 189, 214
whaling, 190, 214
Music, 30–31, 77, 119–122, 142, 208. *See also* Nightlife

Napili, 202, 206
Na Pali Coast, 242, 249, 269
Naha stone, 158
Narcissus Festival, 2, 118
Nawiliwili, 250–251, 259, 268
Neal Blaisdell Center, 77, 151
Neighbor Islands, 27
Nightlife, 150–152, 185, 215–216, 272
Niihau, 26, 256–258
Nuuanu Pali and Valley, 63–64, 91

Oahu, 27, 55–152. *See also* Honolulu; Waikiki
  aquarium and marine park of, 125–127
  beaches of, 48–52, 84, 86–87, 93, 129–131
  camping on, 134–135
  churches and temples on, 44, 56, 61, 63–64, 71, 78–80, 85, 89
  exploring, 80–96
  historic sites of, 41–42, 67, 70, 72–78, 85, 135–137
  hotels of, outside of Honolulu, 108–109
  map of, 82–83
  parks and gardens of, 62, 67, 76, 84, 85, 86–87, 92, 121, 125–129
  restaurants on, outside of Honolulu, 115–116
  shopping on, 72, 144–150
  sports on, 10–15, 29, 93, 131–134
  tours of, 123–124
  transportation on, 116–118
  visual arts of, 32, 60
Oheo Gulch, 197, 211
Old Russian Fort, 253, 271
Opera, 119, 142
Orchids, 2, 122, 154, 158, 176, 177
Oriental ware and gifts, 147–149

Outer Islands, as older name for Neighbor Islands, 27
Outrigger canoes. *See* Canoes

Package tours, 4–5
Paia, 206
Painting. *See* Visual arts
Para-sailing, 29, 131
Parker Ranch, 154, 164, 176, 184
Parks. *See under each island*
Pearl City, 116
Pearl Harbor, 44, 135–136
  tours to, 123, 124, 135
Pedicabs, 118
Petroglyphs, 163, 177, 179, 234, 252, 271
Pets, quarantine of, 5
Phallic Rock, 223
Photographers, hints for, 15–16
Photographic collection, 138
Pidgin English, 20
Piko Stone, 245
Pineapple, 65–66, 87–88, 218, 230–231, 252
Planetarium, 138
Plants, restrictions on, 5
Poipu, 52, 252, 260, 263
Polo, 119
Polynesian Cultural Center, 127–128
Princeville, 246–247, 261–262, 264–265
Prison, 19th-century, 214
Pronunciation of Hawaiian names, 17
Protea, 193
Puka shells, 93
Puna, 159
Punahou School, 61, 119
Punchbowl, 63, 77, 120
Puu Ualakaa park, 125–126
Puuhonua O Honaunau, 40, 154, 161, 178
Puukohola Heiau, 40
Puu-o-Mahuka, 87

Queen's Medical Center, 73, 76

Rabbit Island, 81
Railroad, 190–191
Railroad locomotive, restored, 214
Ranches, 193–194, 196, 246–247.
  See also Parker Ranch
Rental cars, 117, 175, 206–207, 227, 236, 265
Restaurants, 8–10. *See also under each island*
Rivers, Hawaii's only navigable, 239
Rodeos, 14, 175, 176, 208, 266
Royal Hawaiian Band, 45, 73
Royal Mausoleum, 41, 63–64, 122
Rugby, 122

Running and jogging, 14, 28, 62, 123, 132
  marathons, 2, 14, 123, 175, 176, 207
Russian fort, 253, 271

Sacred Birthstones, 89
Sacred Falls, 85–86
Saddle Road, 165–166
Sailing. *See* Yachts
Saltbeds, 253, 268
Salvation Army, 61
Schofield Barracks, 44, 88, 89
Scuba diving, 50, 52, 54, 177, 212–213, 270
Sculpture. *See* Visual arts
Sea Life Park, 126–127
Seafood restaurants, 114, 173, 205, 206, 262–265
Seasonal events. *See* Calendars of events
Security, 16, 71, 93, 130, 131, 135
Senior-citizen discounts, 16
Seven Pools, 197, 211, 212
Shipwreck Beach, 234–235
Shintoism, 78–79
Shopping, 144–150, 185, 187, 215, 271–272
Skiing, 14, 166, 175, 182
Skindiving, 12–13, 130, 131
Sleeping Giant, 245
Snorkeling, 50–54, 179–180, 191, 209, 228, 237, 252, 270
South Pacific (movie), 52, 242, 268
South Point (Hawaii island), 159–160, 184
Spanish restaurant, 114
Sports, 10–15
  spectator, 14–15, 118, 121, 134
State fairs, 120, 121
Stevenson, Robert Louis, 49, 61
Sugar plantations and mills, 43–44
  Hawaii (island), 159, 184
  Kauai, 239, 241–242, 244, 246, 251, 253
  Maui, 190, 214
  Oahu, 88, 89, 90, 92
Sumo, 134
Sunburn, 48
Surfing, 48–52, 84, 86–87, 93, 120, 122, 123, 131, 180
Swimming. *See* Beaches
Symphony orchestra, 30–31, 119, 142

Taoist shrine, 71
Taro, 85, 165, 184, 247, 253
Taxis, 116, 117, 167, 175, 207, 265
Telephones, 16–17
Temples, 44, 71, 78–79, 85, 208, 214–215, 251
  Mormon, 86

Tennis, 13, 132, 176, 182–183, 192, 212, 236, 270
Thai restaurants, 114
Theater, 122, 142–143
Thorn Birds, The (novel), 242, 253
Time zone, 10
Tourist information, 1, 118, 175, 207, 265
Tripler Army Hospital, 90
Twain, Mark, 30, 160
Typee (novel), 127

Ukelele festival, 121
Ulupalakua Ranch, 193–194
United States Air Force, 44, 65, 166, 195
United States Army, 44, 88–89, 90, 165, 224
museum of, 140–141
United States Coast Guard, 67
United States Marine Corps, 44, 53, 84, 165
United States Navy, 26, 44, 92, 93, 135–136, 250, 254
museums of, 141
University of Hawaii, 14, 60, 84, 122, 166
Upside-Down Falls, 64

Vegetarian restaurants, 115
Veterans' cemetery, 63, 77–78, 119
Vietnam War, 65, 77, 140–141
Vietnamese restaurant, 114
Visual arts, 32–60, 73, 76–77, 86, 184, 246. *See also* Art galleries; Museums—art
painted church on Hawaii island, 162, 184
Volcanoes, active and extinct, 23
Hawaii (island), 13, 29–30, 153–154, 156–158, 165–166, 168–169, 174, 177
Kauai, 239–240
Maui, 186, 194–195
Oahu, 67, 80–81

Wahaiwa reservoir, 12
Wahiawa, 88
Waiakea reservoir, 12
Waialeale, 239, 240

Waianae Mountains, 91–92
Waikiki, 27, 45–46, 60, 62
aquarium of, 125
beach of, 10, 49, 118, 129, 131
golf of, 15
hotels of, 57, 95–107
map of hotels of, 96–97
nightlife in, 150–152
restaurants in, 109–115
walking in, 66–67
Waikoloa, 14
Wailea, 50, 192, 201, 206
Wailua, 12, 244, 261, 264, 268
Wailuku, 189, 202, 203
Waimanalo, 81
Waimea (Hawaii island), 164
Waimea (Kauai), 254–255, 260, 265
Waimea (Oahu), 87, 128, 130–131
Wainiha, 248
Waiohinu, 160
Waipio Valley, 165, 184
Waipouli, 261
Water sports, 10–13, 29, 47–54. *See also* Beaches; Yachts; *specific water sports*
Weightlifting, 14
Wesak Day, 2, 119
Whale watching, 191, 209, 269
Whalers, 42–43, 190, 251
Wheeler Air Force Base, 89
Wildlife park, 219, 228
Wildlife preserves, 210, 223, 240, 246, 247
Windmills, experimental, 86
Windsurfing, 50, 121, 131, 183, 207, 212, 228, 268
Wine house, 114
Winery, 194, 209
Woodcarving, 149
World War II, 44, 53, 65, 77, 88–90, 140–141, 224, 250, 257–258

Yachts, 12, 67, 119–122, 133, 209, 269
Young, John, 41, 64
Youth hostels, 8, 109

Zoos, 62, 121, 125, 178, 188, 210, 219, 228

Fodor's Travel Guides

U.S. Guides

Alaska
American Cities
The American South
Arizona
Atlantic City & the
  New Jersey Shore
Boston
California
Cape Cod
Carolinas & the
  Georgia Coast
Chesapeake
Chicago
Colorado
Dallas & Fort Worth
Disney World & the
  Orlando Area

The Far West
Florida
Greater Miami,
  Fort Lauderdale,
  Palm Beach
Hawaii
Hawaii (Great Travel
  Values)
Houston & Galveston
I-10: California to
  Florida
I-55: Chicago to New
  Orleans
I-75: Michigan to
  Florida
I-80: San Francisco to
  New York

I-95: Maine to Miami
Las Vegas
Los Angeles, Orange
  County, Palm Springs
Maui
New England
New Mexico
New Orleans
New Orleans (Pocket
  Guide)
New York City
New York City (Pocket
  Guide)
New York State
Pacific North Coast
Philadelphia
Puerto Rico (Fun in)

Rockies
San Diego
San Francisco
San Francisco (Pocket
  Guide)
Texas
United States of
  America
Virgin Islands
  (U.S. & British)
Virginia
Waikiki
Washington, DC
Williamsburg,
  Jamestown &
  Yorktown

Foreign Guides

Acapulco
Amsterdam
Australia, New Zealand
  & the South Pacific
Austria
The Bahamas
The Bahamas (Pocket
  Guide)
Barbados (Fun in)
Beijing, Guangzhou &
  Shanghai
Belgium & Luxembourg
Bermuda
Brazil
Britain (Great Travel
  Values)
Canada
Canada (Great Travel
  Values)
Canada's Maritime
  Provinces
Cancún, Cozumel,
  Mérida, The
  Yucatán
Caribbean
Caribbean (Great
  Travel Values)

Central America
Copenhagen,
  Stockholm, Oslo,
  Helsinki, Reykjavik
Eastern Europe
Egypt
Europe
Europe (Budget)
Florence & Venice
France
France (Great Travel
  Values)
Germany
Germany (Great Travel
  Values)
Great Britain
Greece
Holland
Hong Kong & Macau
Hungary
India
Ireland
Israel
Italy
Italy (Great Travel
  Values)
Jamaica (Fun in)

Japan
Japan (Great Travel
  Values)
Jordan & the Holy Land
Kenya
Korea
Lisbon
Loire Valley
London
London (Pocket Guide)
London (Great Travel
  Values)
Madrid
Mexico
Mexico (Great Travel
  Values)
Mexico City & Acapulco
Mexico's Baja & Puerto
  Vallarta, Mazatlán,
  Manzanillo, Copper
  Canyon
Montreal
Munich
New Zealand
North Africa
Paris
Paris (Pocket Guide)

People's Republic of
  China
Portugal
Province of Quebec
Rio de Janeiro
The Riviera (Fun on)
Rome
St. Martin/St. Maarten
Scandinavia
Scotland
Singapore
South America
South Pacific
Southeast Asia
Soviet Union
Spain
Spain (Great Travel
  Values)
Sweden
Switzerland
Sydney
Tokyo
Toronto
Turkey
Vienna
Yugoslavia

Special-Interest Guides

Bed & Breakfast
  Guide: North America
1936...On the
  Continent

Royalty Watching
Selected Hotels of
  Europe

Selected Resorts
  and Hotels of the U.S.
Ski Resorts of North
  America

Views to Dine by
  around the World